INSTITUTIONS OF

Institutions of Law

An Essay in Legal Theory

NEIL MacCORMICK

OXFORD

UNIVERSITY PRESS

OXFORD
UNIVERSITY PRESS

Great Clarendon Street, Oxford OX2 6DP

Oxford University Press is a department of the University of Oxford.
It furthers the University's objective of excellence in research, scholarship,
and education by publishing worldwide in

Oxford New York

Auckland Cape Town Dar es Salaam Hong Kong Karachi
Kuala Lumpur Madrid Melbourne Mexico City Nairobi
New Delhi Shanghai Taipei Toronto

With offices in

Argentina Austria Brazil Chile Czech Republic France Greece
Guatemala Hungary Italy Japan Poland Portugal Singapore
South Korea Switzerland Thailand Turkey Ukraine Vietnam

Oxford is a registered trade mark of Oxford University Press
in the UK and in certain other countries

Published in the United States
by Oxford University Press Inc., New York

© Neil MacCormick, 2007

The moral rights of the author have been asserted
Database right Oxford University Press (maker)

Crown copyright material is reproduced under Class Licence
Number C01P0000148 with the permission of OPSI
and the Queen's Printer for Scotland

First published 2007
First published in paperback 2008

All rights reserved. No part of this publication may be reproduced,
stored in a retrieval system, or transmitted, in any form or by any means,
without the prior permission in writing of Oxford University Press,
or as expressly permitted by law, or under terms agreed with the appropriate
reprographics rights organization. Enquiries concerning reproduction
outside the scope of the above should be sent to the Rights Department,
Oxford University Press, at the address above

You must not circulate this book in any other binding or cover
and you must impose the same condition on any acquirer

British Library Cataloguing in Publication Data

Data available

Library of Congress Cataloging in Publication Data

MacCormick, Neil.
  Institutions of law: an essay in legal theory / Neil MacCormick.
    p. cm.
Includes bibliographical references and index.
  ISBN-13: 978–0–19–826791–1 (hardback: alk. paper) 1. Legal positivism.
I. Title.
K331.M34 2007
340'.112–dc22

                                            2006033081

Typeset by Newgen Imaging Systems (P) Ltd., Chennai, India
Printed in Great Britain
on acid-free paper by
Biddles Ltd., King's Lynn, Norfolk

ISBN 978–0–19–826791–1 (Hbk)   978–0–19–953543–9 (Pbk)

1 3 5 7 9 10 8 6 4 2

Preface

This book sets out my version of the institutional theory of law. This theory has been taking shape since my 1973 inaugural lecture, 'Law as Institutional Fact'. Many of the ideas in it have been put forward in more tentative or preliminary form in other papers and books, and in lectures over the past thirty-five years. The theory has evolved beyond the legal positivist tenets to which I subscribed in 1973. In response to the debates of these decades, my position has changed to one of post-positivism. Law as institutional normative order is, of course, dependent on human customs and on authoritative decisions, and is in this sense a 'posited' or 'positive' phenomenon. As such it is conceptually distinct from morality, according to any moral theory in which the autonomous moral agent plays a central role in determining moral obligations. This distinctiveness however does not entail that there are no moral limits to what it is conceptually reasonable to acknowledge as 'law' in the sense of 'institutional normative order'. There are such limits. Extremes of injustice are incompatible with law.

Two great thinkers dominated legal theory in the twentieth century, Hans Kelsen and H L A Hart. Their work, more than that of any other near-contemporaries, established for me the model of what a legal theorist must try to do. But neither, for all his genius, fully succeeded in the attempt. Kelsen's *Pure Theory of Law* and Hart's *The Concept of Law* have come under telling criticism. Their place in history is unchallengeable, but for the present and for the future fresh work remains to be done.

That work still needs to address the issues of general jurisprudence using an approach grounded in philosophical analysis. One who seeks to follow these great thinkers must, however, attend to things at which they neither could, nor would have been inclined to, look closely. A rounded philosophical view of the character of law and legal systems must take well into account the huge recent flowering in sociology of law and other social-scientific studies of law and legal institutions. Such studies do not answer philosophical questions—but they certainly help in framing them.

If this book succeeds in the task I set for myself in writing it, it will substantially enhance its readers' understanding of law. I hope to achieve this for students, for lawyers both in practice and in academia, and for philosophers and social scientists concerned about law as a fundamental element in human social existence. I have written this book in Scotland, and am mindful of the inspiration to be drawn from the great writers of our Enlightenment. Like their work, this ought to be accessible and interesting also to the thoughtful citizen, of any profession or none, for whom the place of law in human life is a matter of interest and concern.

My task so described is a daunting one. Such a bold self-promotion will expose me to deserved derision if the work 'falls dead-born from the press'. However that may be, and whatever faults remain here to be found, there would have been many more but for great help from colleagues. I give heartfelt thanks to Garrett Barden for a penetrating but friendly-critical reading of the whole text in a near-final draft, and to Sundram Soosay, a superb research associate whose insightful suggestions brought about countless improvements. Without the backing and assistance of Flora MacCormick, I would never have finished the job at all. Parts of the draft were read by Emilios Christodoulidis, Wojciech Sadurski, Victor Tadros, Gillian Black, and Zenon Bankowski, and John Cairns, Hector MacQueen, and Burkhard Schäfer helped me with many references. Early in the project, William Twining read chapters 1 and 2 prior to their publication in an earlier form. During 2005, I was Freehills Visitor at the University of New South Wales, where Martin Krygier, Kevin Walton, and Dean Leon Trakman and colleagues were helpfully critical of chapters 1 and 2 at a seminar presentation. I am also very grateful to the Freehills law partnership of Sydney NSW for its support of my visit, and the opportunity to air some ideas about intellectual property to a staff seminar. A lecture to the Australian Legal Philosophy Students Association organized by Max del Mar in Brisbane gave an opportunity to put chapter 4 into at least preliminary form. As Pedrick Lecturer in Arizona State University, hosted by Jim Weinstein, Jim Nickel, and Dean Patricia White, I received great help from the members of a faculty seminar in putting chapter 16 into improved shape. In the early development of various parts of the text, I incurred particular debts to Joe Thomson, T B Smith, Nils Jareborg, Zenon Bankowski, Joseph Raz, Robert Alexy, Heike Jung, Jes Bjarup, and Stuart Midgley. Several visits to the Law School of the University of Texas at Austin, but especially one during 1998, gave opportunities to work out important points, and to learn much from Bill Powers, Sandy Levinson, Brian Leiter and others. My colleagues and students over many years have been sources of inspiration too numerous to name, but not forgotten as creditors of my obligation of gratitude. I have tried to ensure that my footnotes to the main text acknowledge intellectual debts wherever I remain conscious of these.

This is the third volume to appear in the quartet on *Law, State, and Practical Reason* but it ought to be considered as thematically the first, given its foundational character for the others. The whole project has received outstandingly generous support from the Leverhulme Trust, which granted me a personal research professorship in 1997–99, and permitted me to continue it from 2004 after a period of absence as a Member of the European Parliament. I cannot sufficiently express my appreciation of the Trustees' support, but hope the work I have produced will be seen as worthy of it. The final volume in the series, on practical reasoning in morality and law, is currently commencing preparation.

Edinburgh   Neil MacCormick
July 2006

Acknowledgements

Some chapters in this book contain more or less substantially rewritten elements from work published earlier, and are published in the present form with the consent of previous publishers, which consent I gratefully acknowledge.

Chapters 1 and 2 replicate with minor amendments 'Norms, Institutions, and Institutional Facts' Law and Philosophy 17, 1–45 (1998) (Kluwer Academic Publishers); they are published here with kind permission of Springer Science and Business Media.

Chapter 4, section 2 appeared in preliminary form as 'Does Law Really Matter?' (2005) Australian Legal Philosophy Students Association, Annual Publication 5–23.

An earlier version of chapter 5 appeared under the name 'Persons as Institutional Facts' in O Weinberger and W Krawietz (eds), *Reine Rechtslehre im Spiegel Ihrer Fortsetzer und Kritiker* (Vienna and New York: Springer-Verlag, 1988) 371–393; with kind permission of Springer Science and Business Media.

An earlier version of chapter 6 appeared under the name 'Wrongs and Duties' in M Friedman, L May, K Parsons, and J Stiff (eds), *Rights and Reason: Essays in honor of Carl Wellman* (Dordrecht: Kluwer Academic Publishers, 2000) 139–155; with kind permission of Springer Science and Business Media.

An earlier version of chapter 9 appeared under the name 'Powers and Power-Conferring Norms' in Stanley Paulson (ed), *Normativity and Norms: Critical Perspectives on Kelsenian Themes* (Oxford: Oxford University Press, 1999), chapter 26.

All of chapters 5 to 9 in an earlier form constituted the entry 'General Legal Concepts' in T B Smith and R Black (eds), *The Laws of Scotland: Stair Memorial Encyclopaedia* (Edinburgh: Law Society of Scotland/Butterworths, vol 11, 1990) paragraphs 1001–1200.

Parts of chapters 6, 12, and 13 originate from 'Taking Responsibility Seriously' Edinburgh Law Review 10 (2005) 168–175, with kind permission of the Trustees.

Parts of chapters 8 and 13 originate from 'On the Very Idea of Intellectual Property: An Essay according to the Institutionalist Theory of Law' Intellectual Property Quarterly (2002) 228–239.

Chapter 14, in an earlier version, appeared as 'The Relative Heteronomy of Law' in European Journal of Philosophy 3 (1995) 69–85; with thanks to Blackwell Publishing.

Contents—Summary

Contents—Detailed

PART 2. PERSONS, ACTS, AND RELATIONS

Table of Cases

Introduction

Institutions of Law is a statement of the institutional theory of law. This theory aims to develop a better understanding of law than other current legal theories offer. It starts from a definition of law, namely this: *Law is institutional normative order*. This is not an exercise in conventional semantics that attempts to capture the conventional sense of the term 'law' as used by competent English speakers. It is what might be called an 'explanatory definition', for to explain the elements of the definition is to explain significant aspects of what all competent speakers already recognize as law. (That is, recognize as 'law' in one important sense of the term. There are other senses of the term which this definition leaves out, but these will be noted in due course.)

In explaining the elements of the definition, it is first necessary to explain 'norms', and then to follow that by explaining 'normative order'. Finally, by discussing the institutionalization of normative order, one reaches a grasp of the whole defining phrase 'institutional normative order'. At the outset, in discussing norms, the primary perspective adopted is that of the norm-user, not of the norm-giver. It is one of the fundamental aspects of our nature that we human beings are norm-users, for this is built in to that most quintessential human quality, our ability to speak to each other and communicate by writing and otherwise—to engage in linguistic communication in all its forms. Languages have a structure—grammar, syntax and semantics—that depends on highly complex norms that were never consciously made by anybody. Their complexity is so challenging that grammarians and linguistics experts still struggle to express (or rationally reconstruct) clearly and comprehensively the norms implicit in each of the very large number of extant languages in the world.

A much simpler example of norms that most of us use every day and unreflectively is provided by the example of the practice of queuing, which is the subject matter of chapter 1. One kind of orderliness that we sometimes discern in human behaviour occurs when people follow common norms of conduct. We line up to wait for the bus, and when it arrives we get on in order without pushing or shoving (sometimes!). Where there is order or orderliness of this kind, I call it 'normative order'.

It can happen that orderliness of this kind depends on some kind of pre-arrangement. For example, the main railway station in Edinburgh has a system for advance booking of rail tickets that requires intending purchasers to take a numbered ticket from a ticket-dispenser. Then the purchaser waits in the waiting area—or, when the line is long, goes out for a coffee, and returns later to wait near the counter. Numbers are electronically displayed in sequence, and when one's own number is called, one goes to the currently vacant counter-stand and makes one's booking.

This involves 'institutionalization' of the queuing practice in this particular context (as is discussed more fully in chapter 2). For we do not only have norm-users, but also norm-givers, who regulate how the numbered roll is to be dispensed, and how staff are to treat purchasers in that light. There are also norm-implementers, the counter clerks and the duty manager who see to it that the rules are implemented as designed and in an orderly way. This explains how 'normative order' can take the special form of 'institutional normative order'. 'Rules' is a useful specialist term by which to refer to norms thus given and applied by persons in some kind of authority.

Taken in a grander way, the constitutional structure of the modern state in its wide variety of manifestations can be understood as an especially complex example of 'institutionalization' in this sense. Chapter 3 explores this theme in some detail, discussing the character of states and of constitutions, and related matters such as the separation of powers. But the very institutionalization of rules and their application gives rise both to wide scope for argument about interpretation and to scope for scepticism about the extent to which the official rules truly account for how people conduct themselves in real life. The issue of the potential 'gap' between law as enacted and law as acted out is the theme of chapter 4.

The exploration of the explanatory definition 'law is institutional normative order' occupies part 1 of the book. Law taken in this sense is obviously a centrally important feature of states as such and, in particular, of constitutionalist states or 'law-states'. The law of the state is for many people, particularly for most legal professionals and law-students, the law that matters most to them. But it is not the only kind of law. International sporting organizations, confederations like the European Union, treaty-based inter-state entities like the Council of Europe, or NATO, and many others, exhibit institutional normative order in their own way too. So do churches and various kinds of religious and charitable organizations. So does the international community as such, certainly since at least the establishment of the Permanent Court of International Justice (whose Statute was adopted by the General Assembly of the League of Nations in 1920) and all the more so since the foundation of the United Nations, the adoption of the UN Charter, and the establishment of the International Court of Justice.

'Law' is also, of course, often used in a wider sense, to include also non-institutionalized forms of order, such as 'the moral law' or 'customary law', and even cases of order that is not normative, as in the 'laws of motion' or 'laws of thermodynamics'. I intend no imperialism against these other kinds of law or usages of the term 'law', which most people can negotiate quite happily in their ordinary discourse and conversation. Also, however, I make no apology for giving priority to expounding a theory about law in its state and state-like contexts. This has been, quite properly, the principal focus of my attention in the thirty-five years

I have spent as Regius Professor of Public Law and the Law of Nature and Nations in the University of Edinburgh.

In part 2 of the book, attention turns to the kinds of relationships that law constitutes and regulates. Law is, in a very old phrase, about 'persons, things and actions'. So what does law constitute as a person, and how does it enable us to interpret the quality of 'personateness' in the legal setting? How does law regulate action and activity through concepts like 'wrong' ('offence', 'crime', 'tort', 'delict', etc) and 'duty'? To what sorts of relations between persons—'obligations', 'rights', 'liberties', 'powers', 'immunities', for example—does it give rise, and how does it regulate persons and things—rights of use, rights of ownership, and all the other such rights—in a word, 'property'?

There has been a lot of recent and current writing about rights and related concepts, but surprisingly little that seeks to integrate this with a sustained theoretical account of the law that gives rise to them. The legal context ought not, however, to be taken for granted. It is a specific virtue of part 2 that it properly contextualizes rights as relations or positions arising within institutional normative order, and appreciated by an interpretation of specific situations read against general rules and principles.

Not merely should legal relationships be contextualized within a theoretically satisfactory elucidation of the character of law, but that elucidation must include consideration of law in its context within the state and civil society, to each of which it is essential as a constitutive element. This is the task of part 3. Moving on from the somewhat abstract consideration of legal power that concludes the previous part, chapter 10 discusses powers in public law, and the distinctive character of public as against private power, leading into a discussion of the interface between public law and politics. The distinction between politics and public law is an important one to maintain, but not in ways that ignore or underestimate their crucial mutual interaction. This has much to do with sustaining the character of a state as a law-state. ('Law-state' is here used to refer to a state-under-law, or a constitutionalist state, in which the exercise of power is subjected to effective constitutional constraints and the rule of law obtains; it is equivalent to the German term '*Rechtsstaat*'.[1])

A critical problem since the emergence of states in their modern form has been guarding against excess of, and abuse of, public power while also ensuring the adequacy of the governing authorities' powers to the proper tasks of governance. Constitutionally entrenched rights have been one basis for a solution to this problem and, since 1945, this has been increasingly backed-up through

---

[1] See also N MacCormick, *Questioning Sovereignty: Law, State and Nation in the European Commonwealth* (Oxford: Oxford University Press, 1999) 9–11.

international guarantees of 'fundamental' or 'human' rights, and indeed their institutionalization in various forms. This is the topic of chapter 11.

States can be, though they have not always been, theatres for the development of 'civil society', in which relations of civility subsist between strangers who extend to each other a kind of impersonal trust. Individuals within civil society, even when they are strangers to each other, do not view each other as presumptive threats to their safety or to the security of their property. Sadly, that presumption can be displaced, sometimes all too readily. But the law, and in particular a fairly administered body of criminal law within a satisfactory criminal justice system, is one essential underpinning of civility, or social peace, in this sense. Chapter 12 reviews the role of criminal law in this light. Chapter 13 looks finally at the interface of law and economy, focused on the rules and institutions of private law. This again presupposes a high degree of civility in civil society, within which institutions of private property, contract and all the ancillary elements of a market economy can flourish.

Finally, part 4 deals with certain fundamental conceptual issues concerning law and morality, and concerning method in legal theory. Much discussion of 'law and morality' assumes a rather unexamined form of moral realism or an equally unexamined moral relativism. What cannot be stressed too strongly is that any question about the conceptual or other linkages between law and morality (or, if you wish, between 'state law' and 'the moral law') is as much an issue about the true character of morality as one about the true character of law. One vision of the moral life and of moral obligation stresses its essentially non-institutional character. Moral agents are autonomous, self-governing individuals whose moral commitments derive from their own discursive appreciation of the requirements of a life well and decently lived alongside other autonomous moral agents in a human community. To one who holds this view, there are no moral authorities and no institutionalized moral rules or relations. In that case, since state law according to the present theory is defined in terms of its institutionalized character, there is a deep conceptual distinction between them. Both concern normative order, but one concerns the normative order upheld by autonomous individuals, the other the institutionalized order sustained by states and their authorities. Chapter 14 expounds this view.

Chapter 15 acknowledges, however, that establishing this distinction does not close the question whether law has to have any essential moral element in it. The answer suggested is that some minimum of justice is essential. There is nothing in the character of institutional normative order that requires us to acknowledge as law practices or rules or ordinances that any reasonably statable moral position acceptable to any autonomous agent would characterize as serious violations of basic demands of justice. Some minimum requirement of the avoidance of grave injustice can properly be accepted as setting a limit to the validity of laws. In the contemporary world, such limits have indeed to some extent been institutionalized through the human rights instruments discussed in chapter 11. This conclusion requires acknowledgement that the institutional theory of law in its present form, though originally developed within that strand of thought known as 'legal positivism', is not now a 'positivist' theory. Whether or not any one chooses to class it as belonging within the tradition of 'natural law', it is certainly post-positivistic.

Such, in outline, is the kind of philosophical account of law offered in this book. It faces up to the fact that law is an enormous and complex subject. In the contemporary world, under globalization and in the face of other epochal changes, it grows ever more complex. No one can hope to be an expert in more than a few small parts of it. Yet no part is fully intelligible without a grasp of its place in the larger whole of which it is a part. That is why one needs some grand overview that explains the fundamental elements and the way they hang together. A work like the present, contributing to what is sometimes called 'general jurisprudence', aims at such an overview.

Explanation of this kind involves an analytical approach to the subject matter. Analysis assumes that large complex wholes are made up of simpler elements, and that explaining the elements and how they interact is necessary to understanding the complex whole. Analysis alone, however, is insufficient. Synthesis is a necessary complement to analysis. The parts are fully comprehensible only as elements of the whole, and the wholeness of the whole therefore bears on the character of its elements. One who seeks to explain something analytically may start by identifying elements and relations between them, but success in this task depends on already having worked through to a view of the whole, and used that to re-assess the character of the parts. There is a never-finally-complete interaction between reviewing the whole as made up of its elements and the elements as deriving their character from the whole.

In the case of a subject like law, how should the tasks of analysis and synthesis be approached? We are dealing with elements of human consciousness and human interaction—for, as noted, we are dealing with norms and the normative, and considering these initially from a user's perspective. The subject studied does not primarily concern or consist of physical or biological processes, but belongs to the sphere of meaningful human action and interaction. This entails that we need to consider the subject matter in the light of its humanly meaningful character. To understand that which is meaningful requires interpreting it, hence an analytical approach of the kind proposed here is also an 'interpretative' or 'hermeneutic' one. The aim is to account for what makes it meaningful, and for how its meanings are constructed. The standpoint adopted for doing this is that of an informed observer.

Law involves both front-line activities of law-making, judging, advocacy, counselling, drafting and doing, and second-line activities of observing these activities from within the practice taken as a whole. The actor of the second line, the student or scholar of law, concerned with jurisprudential or doctrinal exposition of it, has a certain detachment by contrast with front-line actors. On the other hand, this second-line actor has also a relatively high degree of engagement by contrast with purely external observers. These latter (for example) take the whole corpus of legal activity, including the output of legal scholars and legal theorists, as a subject matter for study from the standpoint of sociological or anthropological inquiry or of economics or political science.

The present work concerns itself with the branch of human study that aims at the elucidation and exposition of the basis of normative order through a rationally structured account of the 'system' set out as a body of norms of human conduct. This is sometimes called 'legal science', sometimes 'jurisprudence', sometimes 'academic law', sometimes 'legal scholarship'. One of the aims of this book is to achieve a satisfactory philosophical account of the presuppositions that lie behind such studies. What do we have to suppose to be true if the pretension of legal scholarship to some kind of scientific status is to hold good? This is a matter of trying to establish the conditions that make possible claims of legal science to constitute a genuine and significant body of knowledge, worthy of pursuit in institutions of higher learning and research like our great universities. Alternatively, one may look at this from the point of view of the student, who may reasonably demand to know what order and structure there is to be found in the jumble of materials that she confronts as 'law'.

Either way, the viewpoint from which we approach the present task is that of an observer-from-within rather than of an activist. This contrasts with other jurisprudential approaches which suggest, for example, the standpoint of '*Iudex*', a representative judge in the highest domestic tribunal, as that from which to obtain a particularly rich vision and understanding of law.[2] By contrast with such, the present work unapologetically adopts a professorial standpoint. There is no reason to doubt that the systematization of law, to the extent that it has come to pass, has been primarily an achievement of legal science rather than of legal practice. This is not to deny that persons occupying the position of Ross's '*Iudex*', or others in other forms of legal practice, have been extremely prominent in developing a rational and 'scientific' study of law. Nor should one deny that judicial expositions and interpretations of legal doctrine have a particularly authoritative role in developing legal doctrine in contemporary polities living under law.

Nevertheless, the role of expositor is a distinct role from that of a judge. In the minimal sense, the judge's task is to decide controversies brought before the court in accordance with the law, by applying the law in accordance with what is represented as its appropriate interpretation. Only such ventures into legal exposition

[2] H Ross, *Law as a Social Institution* (Oxford: Hart Publishing, 2001). Ross warns of the necessity to declare the point of view from which one approaches legal theory, and he stresses the social and relational aspects of state law in contemporary society, in particular the connection between socio-economic power relations and legal relationships.

as are required for that task belong to the judge as such. In many legal traditions, judges have also played a distinguished part as legal scholars and authors of influential doctrinal writing, the more influential indeed to the extent that their judicial experience and eminence stood behind their expository work.

Whether an interpretative-analytical study of the present kind is of any value is a debatable question. Rather than enter into this debate here, however, it seems wiser first to present an account of the law according to the institutional theory and let readers judge for themselves whether they find it illuminating for whatever purposes they bring to the reading of it. In the concluding chapter, rather than here at the outset, there is a discussion of the assumptions concerning juristic method and theory of knowledge that are presupposed in attempts to construct legal understanding along the present lines. The greatest test of any method of inquiry is, however, the quality of the results achieved. Abstract discussion of methodology has its own importance, but only in relation to methods which generate interesting and significant findings. Whether such are to be found here is for the reader to judge.

PART 1

NORM, INSTITUTION, AND ORDER

1

On Normative Order

1.1 Introduction

Law is institutional normative order, and the law of the contemporary state is one form of law. There are others, such as international law, the law of emerging new politico-legal forms such as the European Union, canon law, shari'a law, the laws of sporting organizations and of the games they regulate, and doubtless many others. All have in common the aspiration to order (in the sense of 'orderliness', not that of 'command'). An elaborate set of patterns for human conduct is taken to be 'binding' on all persons within the ordered domain, and order prevails among the persons addressed to the extent that they succeed in matching their conduct to the stipulated patterns. The possibility of orderliness arising out of conformity to such patterns depends, obviously, on the set of patterns amounting to a rationally intelligible totality. Therefore there is a postulated systematic quality about the supposed conduct-patterns or 'norms' that underlie the aspiration to order.

1.2 On Institutional Facts

The world of human beings is one that includes not only sheer physical facts and realities, but also institutional facts. By way of preliminary definition, these are facts that depend on the interpretation of things, events, and pieces of behaviour by reference to some normative framework. I hold in my hand a piece of brightly coloured plastic with curious marks on it. This is a credit card. I wear on my wrist a disc attached to a strap with a clear surface on one side behind which are visible marks evenly distributed around the perimeter of a white surface. This is a watch. I have in my pocket metallic disks with the effigy of a human face on one side. The disks are different in size and colour and in the markings they bear. They are coins, and I use them for buying newspapers and other such things.

   We deal here with social realities that are 'institutional' through and through. This can be verified by reference to the working definition above, and by reflecting on what other information we need apart from physical facts in order to perceive the plastic as credit card, the wrist-object as a watch, the metal pieces as currency coins. In each case, there is presupposed a formidable body of legal or other rules, concerning consumer credit, standards of time-measurement, or the definition of money and legal tender in the context of contracts and debts. Without these, the physical object would lack or lose its current meaning. Interpretation of the things and their use in the light of the relevant rules is what makes such physical objects have the meaning they have. This goes some way towards establishing a preliminary idea of 'institutional facts' as omnipresent and inherent elements of social reality. It is an idea that has had a powerful impact ever since it first came to life in the work of Elizabeth Anscombe and John Searle, the latter of whom in particular has made extensive contributions to elucidating underlying concepts over many years.[1]

For those concerned with law in the sense of the law of a contemporary state, 'municipal positive law', the idea of institutional facts links up easily with the idea that an important element in such law is formed by 'institutions' such as contract, property, marriage, trust, foundation (*Stiftung*), and the like. It also connects with the idea that law is 'institutional' in the sense of being administered through 'institutions' such as courts, legislatures, public prosecution agencies, police forces, and the like. Reflection on these ideas casts light on many questions that have preoccupied legal thinkers over the centuries. Highly important legal-theoretical accounts of the institutional character of law are found in the work of such contemporaries as Ota Weinberger[2] (with whom I have collaborated in attempting an introductory essay by way of an 'institutional theory of law'[3]), Dick Ruiter, Joxerramon Bengoetxea, Eerik Lagerspetz, and Massimo La Torre.[4]

Another legal usage of the term 'institution' deserves mention here, if only to administer a caveat about its relevance to most of what follows. This usage derives from the classical Latin word signifying a textbook, namely, '*institutio*'. This term

---

[1] G E M Anscombe, 'On Brute Facts' Analysis 18 (1958) 69–72; J R Searle, *Speech Acts* (Cambridge: Cambridge University Press, 1969); Searle's work continues through *Expression and Meaning: Studies in the Theory of Speech Acts* (Cambridge: Cambridge University Press, 1979); with D Vanderveken, *Foundations of Illocutionary Logic* (Cambridge: Cambridge University Press, 1985), and *The Construction of Social Reality* (Harmondsworth: Allen Lane, 1995).

[2] See, in particular, O Weinberger, *Law, Institution, and Legal Politics: Fundamental Problems of Legal and Social Philosophy* (Dordrecht: Kluwer Academic Publishers, 1991).

[3] N MacCormick and O Weinberger, *Grundlagen des Institutionalistischen Rechtspositivismus* (Schriften zur Rechtstheorie, Heft 113) (Berlin: Duncker und Humblot, 1985); *An Institutional Theory of Law* (Dordrecht: D Reidel, 1986); *Il Diritto Come Istituzione* (trans M La Torre) (Milan: Dott A Giuffré, 1990); *Pour une theorie institutionnelle du droit* (trans O Not and P Coppens) (Brussels: Story Scientia LGDG, 1992).

[4] D W P Ruiter, *Institutional Legal Facts* (Dordrecht: Kluwer Academic Publishers, 1993); *Legal Institutions* (Dordrecht: Kluwer Academic Publishers, 2001); J Bengoetxea, *The Legal Reasoning of the European Court of Justice* (Oxford: Clarendon Press, 1993); E Lagerspetz, *The Opposite Mirrors* (Dordrecht: Kluwer Academic Publishers, 1995); M La Torre, *Norme, Istituzioni, Valore: per una teoria istituzionalistica del diritto* (Rome: Laterza, 1999); B Tamanaha, *A General Jurisprudence of Law and Society* (Oxford: Oxford University Press, 2001) at 136–146 suggests that the institutionalized character of law is a commonplace among most contemporary positivists. This may be so, but developing the insight has been a different matter.

occurs in the title of two of the most famous legal textbooks in history, the *Institutions* (or, sometimes, '*Institutes*') respectively of Gaius and of Justinian.[5] These two books, the former primarily through its influence on the form and content of the latter, exercised over many centuries a powerful grip on the juristic imagination. They spawned imitations in the way of 'Institutions' of national law produced by systematizing expositors of legal doctrine, especially in the seventeenth and eighteenth centuries when the emergence of the modern state led to the formulation of systematic accounts of the law in this or that country.[6]

The 'textbook' sense of 'institution' is clearly quite different from the other senses indicated above (except, of course, to the extent that educational practices and the norms they involve may be what give rise to textbook traditions[7] in legal education and practice, as in other disciplines). But, by a quirk of fate, it happened in some systems that particularly distinguished writers from the early modern period came to be regarded as especially authoritative, and their writings came to be considered a subordinate 'source of law' alongside statute law and judicial precedent, though weaker in authority. Thus the idea of an 'institutional writer' has come to belong among the institutions of law in a stronger sense than that attested by the mere use and popularity (or lack of it) of textbooks in the curricula and teaching practice of law schools.[8]

In seeking to clarify our understanding of law according to the explanatory definition offered by the institutional theory, it is desirable to clarify three notions: that of the 'normative', that of 'order', and that of 'institutionality'. Law belongs to the genus 'normative order', and is within that genus the particular species 'institutional normative order'.[9] To clarify this, let us consider the illustrative

---

[5] J B Moyle (ed), *Imperatoris Iustiniani Institutiones: Libri Quattuor* (Oxford: Clarendon Press, 5th edn, 1912); P Birks and G McLeod (trans, with introduction), *Justinian's Institutes* (London: Duckworth, 1987); F de Zulueta (trans, with commentary), *The Institutes of Gaius* (Oxford: Clarendon Press, vol I, 1945; vol II, 1953).

[6] K Luig, 'The Institutes of National Law' Juridical Review (NS) (1972) 193–226; J Cairns, 'The Moveable Text of Mackenzie: Bibliographical Problems for the Scottish Concept of Institutional Writing' in J W Cairns and O F Robinson (eds), *Critical Studies in Ancient Law, Comparative Law and Legal History* (Oxford: Hart Publishing, 2001) 235–248.

[7] For two views of the 'textbook tradition' in legal education, see W Twining, 'Is Your Textbook Really Necessary?' Journal of the Society of Public Teachers of Law (NS) 11 (1970) 81–89; T B Smith, 'Authors and Authority' Journal of the Society of Public Teachers of Law (NS) 12 (1972–3) 3–21; Twining, 'Treatises and textbooks: A Reply to T B Smith' Journal of the Society of Public Teachers of Law (NS) 12 (1972–3) 267–274.

[8] R White and I Willock, *The Legal System of Scotland* (London & Edinburgh: LexisNexis/Reed Elsevier, 3rd edn, 2003) 135–138; cf G W Paton, (ed D P Derham), *A Text Book of Jurisprudence* (Oxford: Clarendon Press, 3rd edn, 1964) 228–234.

[9] On 'institutional normative order' as expounded for two other contexts, see N MacCormick, *Questioning Sovereignty: Law, State, and Nation in the European Commonwealth* (Oxford: Clarendon Press, 1999) ch 1; *Rhetoric and the Rule of Law* (Oxford: Oxford University Press, 2005) ch 1. By contrast, Hart considered attempts at definition *per genus et differentiam* as unhelpful in legal theory. H L A Hart, *Essays in Jurisprudence and Philosophy* (Oxford: Clarendon Press, 1983) at 21–48 ('Definition and Theory in Jurisprudence') especially at 21–23, and see also 'Introduction' at 4–6.

example of a 'queue' or a 'line' such as people sometimes form at some such point of service or of opportunity as a bus-stop, or a coffee stall, or a ferry terminal. It is a mundane and everyday example, and gains from this a certain useful familiarity for the purpose of such a discussion.

1.3 The Normative

Standing in line, or 'forming a queue', whether at a supermarket checkout or at a bus-stop, or when approaching a hold-up or bottleneck in a busy road, or in countless other settings and situations, occurs very frequently in the everyday experience of contemporary human beings. Sometimes, it occurs quite spontaneously and without any official intervention or direction, sometimes in a more organized and directed way. The practice of 'queuing', or 'standing in line', is surely a matter of common experience. To the extent that people 'take their turn' in a queue or line, there is an orderly movement through the checkout, or on to a tramcar or bus, to the limit of places available on board, and then on to the next tram or bus that calls at the stop; or there is an orderly procession of vehicles through some traffic bottleneck. Weaker or less forceful individuals are not forced out or 'jumped over' till nobody else is left trying to get through. From nearly everybody's point of view a kind of fairness and efficiency prevails. This need not work perfectly in order to work satisfactorily. There may always be somebody with brass neck enough to jump the queue, or to speed up the fast lane to the very last point before edging into the slow lane through the bottleneck, effectively by challenging other drivers to put up with a pretty severe bump to their car (at least) or tolerate misconduct.

Most people acknowledge that it is sometimes all right to go to the head of the line without waiting your turn. (You have a medical emergency at home and have dashed out to the supermarket for urgent supplies; you are desperate to get to college in time to sit your exam; you are a doctor hurrying to a seriously ill patient.) This is different from the unwarranted self-preference of individuals who always or often try to cut in or queue-jump with flimsy or no justification, though perhaps there are few persons indeed who are completely immune from occasional lapses into unwarranted self-preference in this way. There can indeed, as experience testifies, be a successful practice, even a kind of socio-moral institution, of queuing or waiting in line, despite an absence of perfect conformity to the practice. But there is also some minimum threshold of compliance below which the practice would be unsustainable. It would be literally impossible to be the only person that 'takes her turn' because 'turns' require a mutually co-ordinated practice of two or more. When a substantial majority of potential competitors for a certain opportunity fails to acknowledge turn-taking, it amounts to pointless self-abnegation if one or a few act as though most others were ready to take their turn.

Turn-taking or queuing is then normative. For where there is a queue for something you want, you ought to take your turn in it, and people who do take their turn do so because in their opinion that is what one ought to do—that is, ought to do in the given context. Such an action-guiding 'ought' alerts us to the presence of some kind of norm, and to the normative character of the opinions that people hold in such a setting. Interestingly enough, such a normative practice and such a normative opinion can exist and be quite viable even in the absence of any single canonically formulated or formulable rule that everybody could cite as the rule about queuing. People know how to queue, and can tell cases of queue-jumping, and protest about them, even if they have never articulated exactly what their governing norm is. That does not mean we cannot reflect on how to make explicit an implicit norm of conduct apt to the situation or the type-case. Maybe the following would be a reasonable attempt:

In cases where people seek a service or opportunity that cannot be supplied to everybody simultaneously, each ought to take their place in line after any one who arrived earlier at the point of service or place of opportunity, and each is entitled to go ahead of any who arrived later, and entitled to expect others to observe this, and to respond critically or even obstructively towards people who jump the line.

It is at least open to discussion whether or not this is a good general statement that satisfactorily captures in an abstract way the normative idea of turn-taking, and that could be reformulated in a more concrete way relating to a specific service or opportunity. But the viability of the practice is obviously not dependent on the accuracy of this or any other particular attempt to put in explicit terms an implicit norm of conduct for queuing.

Even if you and I had a careful discussion and worked at my formulation and refined it so that we had a rule-statement that seemed exactly right to us two, nothing guarantees that this would seem equally right to a third person, or a fourth, let alone everybody in this queue or that one or in all the lines anyone ever stood in. This reveals an important truth: queuing is a socially located and essentially interpersonal activity that is oriented to a common normative opinion. But the common opinion does not presuppose any single common pre-articulation of the norm at the heart of the normative opinion. Wherever there is a queue, everybody involved has a similar aim of obtaining a certain service or opportunity and recognizes that others are seeking the same thing at the same time. If people do form a queue, this helps them achieve their several overlapping aims in mutual civility rather than through open conflict. And there has to be mutual understanding of this and hence some common or overlapping normative opinion.

Queuing is therefore, like many grander and farther-reaching parts of our individual and collective life, one among what we could call, after the style of Ronald Dworkin, an 'interpretive' practice, and the concept 'queue' seems to fall in the class of what he calls 'interpretive concepts'.[10] It is characteristic of such a setting that community of practice cannot be imputed to a priori identity of understanding or of articulation or explicit conceptualization. But there can be adequate community of practice to engender a measure of orderliness. This very orderliness seems explicable by reference to an implicit queuing norm whose articulate understanding would be a matter of interpretative debate among those who acknowledge the practice as an essentially shared or common one and try to 'play fair' within it, adequately satisfying each others' mutual expectations.

1.4 Normative Order

Queuing or standing in line also furnishes an example of 'order' in its presently material sense. People's positioning in a queue is ordered, not random. The 'order' here is not only an actual and predictable pattern that could be studied 'externally' and reported statistically.[11] It is a 'normative order' because, or to the extent that, one can account for it by reference to the fact that actors are guiding what they do by reference to an opinion concerning what they and others ought to do. We can account for the externally observable order in a case of this kind by imputing it to actions of individuals who have a certain mutual awareness, together with mutual or reciprocal expectations. The result is a kind of common action by mutually aware participants. Each one acts on the understanding (or the assumption, not necessarily particularly articulate) that each of the others is oriented towards more or less the same opinion concerning what everyone ought to do. This opinion about what people ought to do, dependent on what Eerik Lagerspetz has characterized as 'mutual beliefs'[12], amounts to an implicit norm that can be made explicit in the way suggested above.

Any such account of things is, however, subject to the caveat that it is a potentially contestable interpretation of the governing idea. There is a shared or common sense of 'the right thing to do', but this does not at all depend on there being one single officially formulated rule that each person can recite or learn by rote. For indeed the practice is an interpretative one, in which each party 'reads' the

---

[10] R Dworkin, *Law's Empire* (Cambridge, Ma: Harvard University Press, 1986) 45–86, especially 46–53. On etymological grounds I prefer the term 'interpretative' to Dworkin's 'interpretive', and I use the former throughout the present work, except where the context is that of trying to describe or apply Dworkin's conception of the 'interpretive'.

[11] This idea of 'external' observation of conduct derives from H L A Hart's *Concept of Law* (Oxford: Clarendon Press, 2nd edn, 1994) 55–60, extensively discussed in N MacCormick, *Legal Reasoning and Legal Theory* (Oxford: Clarendon Press, 1978, revised edn, 1994) 275–292; for further discussion, see ch 4 below.

[12] E Lagerspetz, *The Opposite Mirrors* (Dordrecht: Kluwer Academic Publishers, 1996) 30–50; D W P Ruiter, *Legal Institutions* (Dordrecht: Kluwer Academic Publishers, 2001) at 22–23 suggests a possible correction to the Lagerspetz version of mutual beliefs on the ground of its attempting to reduce collective intentionality to an aggregation of states of individual minds.

situation as s/he thinks others are reading it, and forms an opinion with regard to the opinion he/she thinks others hold, though this is not necessarily any kind of reflective deliberation about others' opinions.

Assuming, then, that a practice of queuing is viable in a given context despite the absence of any explicit agreement on its meaning or its governing norm(s), it seems reasonable to suggest that there must be some quite deep community of underlying ideas, or some common guiding idea, that makes the practice intelligible. In the contemporary world, there is a practice of turn-taking. Perhaps this has its deep foundations in a contemporary egalitarianism. This supports the idea that the provision of a service or opportunity that has to be taken up one-at-a-time should be done on the basis of a sequence that is universalistic rather than discriminatory on the ground of special personal or social characteristics. The very arbitrariness of making priority depend on temporal order of arrival at the point of service or of opportunity is usually satisfactory from this point of view. In more hierarchical societies or social contexts, priority according to rank will perhaps prevail, with 'first come, first served' applying only among peers within a hierarchy. Even in our relatively egalitarian times there are more than a few observable situations in which hierarchical orders of precedence still have some bite, or even a taken-for-granted rightness.[13]

Certainly, queuing is a generic practice with many variants, not a single invariant thing. A supermarket line in Texas is not exactly like a railway ticket line in Italy, or a motorway bottleneck in England, or a queue for taxis at Toronto airport, or a queue to buy stamps in a Swedish post office, or a queue for lunch in a colloquium in the Netherlands. We all try to pick up local nuance as we move around, and attempts to make explicit an implicit norm would be considerably complicated by the need to relativize the articulation to the kind of queue and the relevant cultural context.

We can surely be confident that the so-called 'first come, first served principle' has many differences of nuance, and of detail, or has exceptions ('children first', 'children after adults', 'special consideration for very old people', 'special consideration for disabled war veterans', for example) in different places, different cultural

---

[13] It is worth remarking, with acknowledgement of indebtedness to W Twining, that the requirement to wait in line is often an imposed one, for example when adults in authority, such as schoolteachers, direct children in their charge to line up for some treatment or service of some kind or even, indeed, to await a punishment. It may well be that as individuals we first internalize norms about queuing in such hierarchical situations where the equality of those standing in line is only an equality of equal subjection. Queuing under authority belongs at a later point in the present order of presentation, early in ch 2. The order of presentation here serves an analytical purpose, and should not be taken to be an account of the way anyone or everyone initially acquires a sense of, or a disposition towards, the practice of queuing as a normative practice. It is a general truth that heteronomy precedes autonomy, and views or practices that we come to endorse autonomously usually emerge through processes of socialization (cf ch 14 below). However people may have come to a sense of rightness about taking their turn, it seems that many are willing to act on it without intervention by any supervising authority, so long as others seem ready to do so as well, in a situation of ostensibly satisfied mutual beliefs.

milieux, different kinds of services or opportunities, different providers of services, and so on. Different people trying to articulate a more concrete version of the underlying idea for a particular setting would come up with different formulations, all quite reasonable. For the suppositions made here are that there need not be any single normative formulation that attracts universal agreement, and there is no special reason to suppose that among a range of reasonable interpretations just one has to be the right one. The reason why there does not have to be a single right one is that for a practice like this to work satisfactorily, there only has to be overlapping consensus, or broad commonality of attitude, among the participants. Conceptually exact answers to empirically vague questions can be illuminating, helpful, reasonable, and can have any of a number of such virtues; but not that of being uniquely right.[14]

Using reflections about the queue as a basis for generalization, we may suggest with reasonable confidence that there is a possibility of orderliness in human affairs some of the time in some places about some matters. There is order wherever people conduct themselves in relation to others on the basis of an opinion concerning the right thing to do which they suppose to be a mutual opinion, provided that there turns out to be sufficient community (not perfect identity) of opinions held and acted on. I act as I think it right to do, subject to thinking you also think it right and act reciprocally on your opinion, and so on. We have mutual beliefs that are normative in content, and enough people act on these beliefs for it to be the case that mutual beliefs are normally satisfied, and that detected cases of nonconformity are treated as wrong on the same account. Normally, overt reactions of people to conduct they treat as wrong are in some measure disagreeable to those at whom they are directed, and this may indeed involve quite considerable severity of reaction even if not involving any formal sanction. There does not have to be explicit articulation of a rule or set of rules that constitutes the practice in question, since mutual interpretations of mutual normative beliefs will suffice. But this will be intelligible only to the extent that we think we can refer it to some underlying guiding idea that is both normative and value-laden in character.

To conclude: there can be normative order without explicitly formulated norms. This happens wherever implicit norms are in fact largely observed and respected, without any other element of supervision, direction or enforcement than that constituted by a pressure of common (not necessarily either universal or identically expressed) normative opinion among those who interact with each other. An example is provided by the case of those who have arrived around the same time at the same point of opportunity or service, and have formed a queue and accepted service in order as right and proper.

[14] T Seung, *Intuition and Construction: The Foundation of Normative Theory* (New Haven, Conn: Yale University Press, 1993) 33–37. Cf B Bix, *Law, Language, and Legal Determinacy* (Oxford: Oxford University Press, 1993) 63–67.

1.5 On Conventions: Informal Practices

Reflection on common experience makes it obvious that queuing can, and does quite often, happen in a wholly informal and unregulated way, without intervention of any kind of person or agency that holds authority over those who queue up and regulates or manages the queue in some way. To be sure, this is in some measure culturally relative. It is commonly said that English people ('English' indeed as distinct from 'British') have a special genius for queuing. It was also the case that shortages made queuing an endemic feature of life for ordinary people in the circumstances of the former Soviet bloc—there was a recurrent joke in Poland about a person going down the street, observing the end of a queue and joining it. Asked by the next arrival what the queue was for, the former confessed to not knowing, but to having joined the line on the assumption that whatever the queue was for, it would be for some scarce necessity or desired luxury. The opportunity to get such a thing (whatever it was) should not lightly be foregone, he remarked.

However it may be as to these points of cultural relativity, it seems reasonable to conclude that normative order can exist in some cultural and social settings on the basis simply of mutual belief and inexplicit norms with overlapping mutual understanding and interpretation of the kind described here. The name that will here be given to such practices is 'informal normative practices', and the kind of order they constitute 'informal normative order'. The constitutional lawyers' idea of a 'convention' ought to be reviewed in this light, alongside reflection on other kinds and contexts of conduct that is conventional rather than authoritatively regulated.[15] Customs that are considered normative, whether in international law and relations or in other settings include conventions in the present sense, and may indeed comprise only conventions.[16] For it is precisely those implicit norms' orientation to which is constitutive of informal normative order that we most naturally call 'conventional' or 'conventions'. Although in many important cases, scholars and practical persons devote interpretative efforts to make a satisfactory and clear explicit statement of an implicit norm, each such attempt, so far as it is merely interpretative, is intrinsically contestable. To the extent that a formulation is subject to ascribed authority as a precedent or an institutionally authoritative

---

[15] Cf G Marshall, *Constitutional Conventions: the Rules and Forms of Political Accountability* (Oxford: Clarendon Press, 1984). It is worth remarking that constitutional conventions, though themselves implicit norms and informal ones in the sense of lacking any single authoritative formulation, nevertheless regulate the conduct of officers and agencies of state which for the most part are defined in a highly formalized and institutionalized way. Citing Sir K Wheare, Marshall refers to conventions as 'binding rules' (p 7), but in a context (pp 7–13) in which it is clear that these are norms that lack any single authoritative formulation, hence do not count as 'rules' in the terminology used here. More generally, see D Lewis, *Convention: a Philosophical Study* (Oxford: Basil Blackwell, 1986).

[16] See Ruiter, *Legal Institutions* 122–127 for an outstandingly clear account of the character of custom in international and municipal law.

formulation, the act of formulating the implicit norm has a transforming effect. For the formulation uttered becomes, in this very act of formulation, some kind of an authoritative rule or maxim. Apart from the mentioned cases of constitutional conventions, and customary law (international or municipal), a large part of our ideas about etiquette and good manners, and many other important elements of social usage, as well as the grammatical and semantic norms of natural languages, are conventions in this sense.

This is a sense that has to be carefully distinguished from the usage of 'convention' as meaning a solemnly formulated agreement or treaty among states such as the Geneva Conventions on refugees or prisoners of war and other such weighty sources of 'conventional' (as distinct from 'customary') international law. It is an unfortunate feature of linguistic evolution that we have in English two legal uses of the terms 'convention' and 'conventional'. These are sharply at odds, even mutually contradictory—the point about the informally conventional elements of constitutional law is that they are essentially customary, while 'conventional international law' is the part that depends on multilateral treaties solemnly adopted, and is thus to be cleanly distinguished from the customary part of international law.

1.6 Conclusion

It is important to understand the idea of the normative—the idea is of our having ways to differentiate right from wrong in what we do, of having common or overlapping conceptions of what one ought to do in various recurring situations. People's responses to such conceptions of right and wrong can match each other in a reciprocal way even in quite informal settings, so that there is a kind of order in their behaviour. To focus on that, and to grasp it, is to grasp the basic idea of normative order. Already, we discover a fundamental assumption about human nature. Human beings are norm-users, whose interactions with each other depend on mutually recognizable patterns that can be articulated in terms of right versus wrong conduct, or of what one ought to do in a certain setting. Understanding this use of norms precedes understanding any possibility of deliberately creating relevant norms that are to become patterns for behaviour.

Yet deliberate creation of norms also occurs. Norm-usage can acquire a more formal character, indeed, can become 'institutionalized'. To understand this is to understand the transition into institutional normative order, and thus law.

2

On Institutional Order

2.1 Introduction

Convention is not all. Queuing itself is not always a matter of purely informal normative order grounded in the social conventions of ordinary everyday life. It is often organized under authority of one kind or another. At airports, there are lines at check-in, different lines for economy, business class and first class passengers. There is a line again at the boarding gate, sometimes sub-regulated in terms of passengers' seat-row numbers, sometimes not. Supermarkets and passport offices, post offices, and state liquor monopoly stores in countries where these exist, supply numbered tickets on paper rolls, and one's place in line is determined by the numerical order of one's ticket. Banks and railway stations have roped-off lines that feed the front person to the next available ticket sales point or teller's counter. Outside stations and airports, there are taxi-marshals who organize and police taxi-queues, both to secure a taxi quickly and fairly for each passenger in turn and to ensure speedy throughput of taxis at the bottleneck that typically forms at the pick-up point at busy times. Sometimes (especially welcome in cold places) the taxi-line incorporates use of a numerical ticket roll, so that passengers can safely wait their turn in warmth indoors rather than brave sub-arctic temperatures on the sidewalk. In schools, teachers require their pupils to line up for personal lessons or in the school lunch queue, and insist on orderly behaviour by their charges. In the tough US penitentiary of movie fiction and, no doubt, of grim reality dangerous prisoners are kept in orderly lines for meal-service under the wary eye of armed guards.

These commonplace instances all remind us that there are many contexts in which the practice of queuing comes under the authority of some kind of manager or governor, some person in authority. To receive the service on offer, one is required to follow the norms laid down by the service-provider, and the immediate service-provider is usually acting under some superior authority within the relevant organization. The norms to which lined-up persons have to be orienting themselves are not merely conventional or implicit, not reliant simply (or at all, perhaps) on mutual beliefs and expectations. They are norms explicitly laid down by those in charge of providing the service on offer.

2.2 Beyond Informality

In an informal normative practice of queuing, it can itself be a relatively vague issue to be sure when a line has formed, who is in it, in what exact order, and subject to what legitimacy of holding a place for an absentee, for example one who has gone to the lavatory. But when the practice is transposed into an official or commercial setting, somebody can be given the task of deciding these things, and a system, such as the numbered ticket-roll, can be set up to render precise what in the informal setting is vague. The official or employee in charge usually has or assumes authority to determine how to settle disputed or unclear or unforeseen problems in the arrangements that come to light in their day-to-day running. All the more is this so in a situation in which some form of standing authority or power is held by one person (or a group) over others, and where this power is used to direct the subject-group to line up for meals, or for a work-rota, or whatever. Schoolteachers or other adults in relation to schoolchildren, or prison guards in relation to prisoners, or officers and NCOs in the armed forces in relation to their subordinates, or managers in relation to other members of staff in workplaces, are all rather obvious instances of this. It is important to acknowledge that such situations exist, and that they show how attitudes to queuing may be far removed from those of mutual voluntary co-operation, though perhaps never quite excluding every trace of this. To consider such cases of managed lines is to consider the possibility of a transition from a purely informal practice to a more formal or formalized one. It is no longer then a matter of negotiating different interpretations of vague conventions, but it is a matter for decision, when some doubt arises about priority in a queue. In the case of queues with numerical rolls of tickets, there is an obvious possible difficulty about persons who are absent or inattentive when their number is called or displayed. If number fifty is called, and nobody shows up after a brief pause, fifty-one is called, and then, if nobody shows up, fifty-two—and so on. But what happens if, when fifty-four is called the holder of ticket number fifty appears and asks for service? Does the counter attendant accept that fifty is the lowest number present, and serve the holder before serving number fifty-five or some later number? Or is the correct answer to be that 'fifty' is now an expired ticket, and the holder must rejoin the queue at the end, taking the next number available on the paper roll? In such a situation, there is nothing for it but that a decision be made, and the decision-maker of first instance is the attendant at the counter. But the problem is a potentially recurring one, and inconsistency between different attendants at different times could be bad for customer relations. So, quite likely, the store proprietor or store manager makes a general rule and issues it expressly in writing or orally to all counter staff. It may even prove advisable to set up a notice by the ticket-roll explaining what the rule is, to avoid confusion or any sense of unfairness on the customers' part.

Wherever there is decision-making authority, there is in principle the possibility of making explicit decisions about priority in given cases. Where problems are recurrent and consistency of treatment is for some reason important, decisions can be taken explicitly or implicitly in such a way as to lay down general rules aimed at dealing with such recurrent problems. Unlike informal norms or conventions, explicitly made rules have an expressly promulgated text. Interpretation of norms in the form of explicit rules necessarily involves attending to the very words used by the rule-maker, and reflecting on the underlying point of the words only where the words seem unclear or where what seems their obvious meaning leads to what seem weird results in practice. By contrast, informal norms emerge from practices based on mutual expectations and beliefs, and any attempt to formulate in express terms the implicit norm depends on interpreting the practice and its point. Here, interpretation precedes formulation. But in the case of rules explicitly issued, interpretation succeeds formulation.

One common and understandable usage applies the term 'rule' particularly to the case of the formally enunciated norm issued by somebody in some position of decision-making authority. To say 'there is a rule about that' in a practical context of potential interpersonal dispute or conflict is to invite the challenge to produce the text of the rule and show who issued it, and with what authority to do so. Where there is a rule in this sense of the term, there is a fixed text, the one issued by a person having some kind of authority to do so. This implies the existence of a two- (or more than two-) tier normative practice. In terms of our running example, the queue, there is both a practice of queuing, and a practice of authorizing some individuals to manage lines of people waiting for whatever service or opportunity is in issue. Queuing remains a normative practice, statable in terms of norms about what ought to be done, what is the right thing to do, who has the right to be served next, and so forth. In addition, however, there is a normative practice of authorizing a supervisory person to monitor the queue, to ensure that each person who gets into the line in the appropriate way gets served in the right order, and that no one breaks the order by jumping ahead or suffers a loss of entitlement by being jumped over. Equally normative will be the necessary process of decision-making about forfeiture of turns if a person fails to appear when appropriately called, and so on. There are now, we may say, deciding-about-queuing norms, as well as the queuing norms themselves.

In this structured, more-than-one-tier, setting there is authority to issue statements of first-tier queuing norms. What the supervisor says determines what is the operative priority-rule when a problem comes up about who is properly to be deemed at the head of the queue now, and so on. And the management can to a considerable degree clarify matters by making ever more exact provision about how the arrangement is to work, if it turns out that there are difficulties of interpretation that are (for example) causing annoyance among customers, who might take their business elsewhere.

The defining characteristic of this kind of normative order is the possibility it opens to avoid exclusive reliance on somewhat vague implicit norms. Problems of a kind apparently endemic in informal orders can be avoided by resorting to issuance of expressly articulated norms, making explicit what is to be done or decided in expressly foreseen circumstances, the very effect of the explicitness being to diminish vagueness. Imagine this example:

> If a person's number is called and the bearer of the ticket with that number does not come forward, the supervisor should make two further calls in a clear, loud voice, and make a quick visual check of the waiting area to check if there are any apparently deaf people or physically handicapped people struggling to get into position; if there is still no show, the next number in serial order should be called, and so on.

If matters have come to this point of clarity, it seems easy to imagine the need for a new ruling by somebody, if only the supervisor, on how to handle the case if a person turns up after the call, having missed her or his call, the first time. Do they get placed back in the line, now at the front of it because in possession of the lowest number now current; or is their prior entitlement now cancelled, leaving them to either abandon the attempt or take a new numbered ticket from the ticket dispenser, and start again at the back of the line? In the latter case, is the supervisor to have any discretion to waive the strict rule in cases of special hardship?

A problem of this kind is bound to arise once there is clear provision about what counts as a failure to show up (missing three calls), for there is now a dilemma about how to treat the 'no show' who eventually appears from the lavatory, or from a reverie, or from the coffee shop, or from wherever. There can only be: either pure discretion on the supervisor's part, with no fixed rule, or a 'new head of the queue' rule or a 'back to the end again' rule, with or without discretion on the supervisor's part in special hardship cases. (Niklas Luhmann points out that every attempt to reduce complexity by articulating an explicit provision of this sort is apt to generate a new complexity as dilemmas appear in relation to the new provision, calling for some new explicit provision, and so on.[1])

2.3 Expressly Articulated Norms—'Rules'

We have arrived at the idea of a rule, that is, an explicitly articulated norm (no longer a purely implicit one). The case here is one in which the explicit articulation is made by a person who has a position of authority. This can be either authority to decide how to apply first-tier norms, both implicit and explicit, or authority to lay down explicit norms that clarify or vary what was previously

---

[1] N Luhmann, *A Sociological Theory of Law* (trans E King, ed M Albrow) (London: Routledge and Kegan Paul, 1985) 193–199.

implicit and therefore also vague. For a certain bounded sphere of activity, special authority attaches to a particular articulation of a norm concerning the activity, or part of it. The articulation in question has two essential elements: the first specifies a kind of situation that may arise, and the second lays down what has to be done, or to come about, or to be deemed the case, whenever that situation arises. Let us call the specified situation the 'operative facts' or '*OF*', and let us call what has to be done, or to come about, or to be deemed the case in that situation, the 'normative consequence', '*NC*'. The kind of explicitly articulated norm we are considering thus has this general form:

Whenever *OF*, then *NC*

One common usage of the term 'rule' is with reference to explicitly articulated norms that exhibit, or that can be recast in, this form. A further essential feature is that some kind of authority attaches to the process by which and/or the agency by which the explicit articulation was made. The word 'rule' has many usages and nuances of usage, but I believe it is most typically used to denote a norm with the characteristics of structure and origin identified here. Stipulatively, for the purposes of the institutional theory of law I am putting forward here, I restrict the unqualified use of the term 'rule' to such norms.

Since we are considering the queue as a running example, we might consider possible rules that could be envisaged for formally managed queues. If issued by an appropriate authority, these would be examples of valid rules:

- Whenever a transaction is concluded, the counter-clerk should check which is the next number in the series awaiting call, and call for the holder of that number.

- Whenever a ticket-holder fails to come forward after three calls, and after a check for deaf or physically handicapped people has been sufficiently carried out, the ticket is [to be deemed] cancelled, and the next number should be called.

- Whenever a ticket has been cancelled, the holder may take a fresh ticket from the dispenser; but may only be called for service when the number of the fresh ticket comes up in due order.

Is the idea of an 'implicit rule' of any value here, or should we restrict the term 'rule' only to such explicit formulations? It seems important to allow for a category of 'implicit rules'. One aspect of authority in the situation we are discussing is simply authority to direct and regulate the queue, guided by relevant rules as one interprets and applies them. Often this will be done by simple decision, such as: 'It's not your turn, you'll have to wait'. But where an explanation is attached to such a decision, this may amount to a kind of partly explicit ruling on a point of doubt in interpreting the rules. For example: 'I am sorry, since you weren't here when your number was called, you will have to get a new ticket and go to the back of the queue now, please'. Here, even if no such rule has hitherto been articulated, the giving of the reason entails reaching an implicit decision that whenever a person's number has been called unsuccessfully, the ticket is cancelled. We shall use the term 'implicit rule' to refer to the norm that can be derived from a ruling of this kind. (The implicit rule is so derivable, as will be seen, to the extent that we hold such rulings to be universalizable. The classic instance of implicit rules of this kind is in a doctrine of precedent, where the elusive 'ratio decidendi' of a case is the implicit rule laid down by the court whose decision in a particular case constitutes a precedent that is applicable generally.[2] This does depend on the institutional relations among judges and courts, and on an attitude to constancy of decision across different occasions in time as well as on the bare idea of universalizability.)

2.4 The Practical Force of Rules: 'Exclusion' or 'Entrenchment'?

This seems straightforward enough, but there remains a problem about rules that we need to confront. What is their practical force? Some people have a notion that if you have articulated a rule in the 'Whenever *OF*, then *NC*' form, you must either give it absolute and invariant application, or be convicted of mere pretence and hypocrisy. Some people think you can take a much more flexible approach and still have a genuine enough rule. On any view, the link between operative facts and normative consequence is indeed a normative one, guiding judgment and action in the way we have noted. But it seems that there can be disagreement about the practical force that attaches to this normative nexus. This should not be interpreted as a conceptual disagreement in which somebody is correct and somebody else is in error. The truth is that this is itself a practical question: what force ought to attach to rules? Let me suggest a schema for appreciating this, involving one of three possibilities.

Rules can have variable practical force, for they can be treated as being rules of absolute application, as being rules of strict application, or as being rules of discretionary application.

- A rule is of **absolute application** if it is to be understood and applied on the footing that each and every occasion of the occurrence of *OF* must be attended unfailingly by *NC*, and *NC* may not be put into effect except when either *OF* obtains or some other rule independently providing for *NC* is satisfied by virtue of the ascertained presence of its operative facts. Typical examples of rules of absolute application are those of the rules of essentially mathematical and closed-ended games like chess.[3]

---

[2] For extended discussion of these points in the framework of the present institutional theory, see N MacCormick, *Rhetoric and the Rule of Law* (Oxford: Oxford University Press, 2005) chs 5 and 8.

[3] Cf F Atria, *On Law and Legal Reasoning* (Oxford: Hart Publishing, 2002) at 15, 25–26, 45–47, making a similar point in different terminology; in its earlier form as a PhD dissertation, this work had a decided influence on the present text.

- A rule is of **strict application** if it is to be understood and applied on the footing that circumstances bearing on the values secured by it may occasionally arise such that there will be very considerable derogation from those values if on a particular occasion *NC* is invoked just because of the presence of *OF*. By its spirit, the rule should not be applied, but by its letter it should. The person charged with applying the rule and managing the activity within which the rule has application is given some degree of guided discretion to make exceptions, or to override the rule, in special, or very special, cases.

- A rule is of **discretionary application** if the decision-maker is expected to consider every case in the light of all factors that appear relevant given the values and goals of the relevant activity or enterprise, and to decide in accordance with the clear balance of factors, but when all things are equal, or when the balance of factors is rather fine and difficult to judge, the decision-maker is expected to use the rule as a fall-back way of deciding the case.

It will be seen that rules of absolute application are at one end of a spectrum with rules of discretionary application at the opposite end of it. In between, rules of strict application represent a variable quantity to the extent that there can be different degrees of strictness.[4]

What then determines to which class, or where on the spectrum, a particular rule or set of rules belongs? Since it has been stipulated that explicitly formulated rules all have the same canonical form, the difference we seek is not to be found in the content of rules themselves. Where then? The answer is obvious—it depends not on the content of the first-tier rules about a practice, but on second-tier norms laying down the terms of authorization or empowerment of the decision-maker. *'Here are the rules you have to apply; you are to treat them as being of absolute application/of strict application/of discretionary application.'*

Where rules are of strict application, that leaves the decision-maker a bounded discretion in special cases, and here, as a fortiori in the case of rules that are of discretionary application, there ought to be some effort made to secure that the decision-maker has an adequate understanding of the factors or kinds of consideration that are appropriate to guiding the exercise of discretion.

Where rules are either of absolute application or of strict application, they will belong to the category called by Joseph Raz 'exclusionary reasons' or (in more recent work) 'protected reasons'.[5] Even more aptly, Frederick Schauer has used the closely similar concept of 'entrenched generalizations'.[6] What 'entrenches' a rule

---

[4] F Schauer makes a somewhat similar point in *Playing by the Rules: a Philosophical Examination of Rule-based Decision-Making in Law and Life* (Oxford: Clarendon Press, 1991), in his chapter 6 on 'the force of rules', but the present account, though profiting from his proposal, differs somewhat from it.

[5] See J Raz, *Practical Reason and Norms* (Princeton, NJ: Princeton University Press, 1990) 193–199.   [6] F Schauer, *Playing by the Rules* (Oxford: Clarendon Press, 1991) 38–52.

in the relevant sense, according to the present thesis, is the terms of authorization of the decision-maker. What renders it exclusionary is the absolute or strict character of the application demanded by terms of authorization. If a rule is of absolute application, the only issue that arises for the person bound to apply it in this way is whether *OF* obtains or not. Other factors that might ordinarily have a bearing on whether *NC* is appropriate to the present case, all things considered, are not to be considered by this decision-maker in respect of the decision she or he must make. For all things are not to be considered, not by this decision-maker, not in relation to this decision-making task, anyway. If a rule is of strict application, it remains all-important to decide whether or not *OF* obtains. All things are still not to be considered in a completely open-ended way. But there are certain factors that must also be considered if they are present, and they have to be evaluated with some care to see whether a special or very special case exists, justifying implementation of *NC* though *OF* is not fully satisfied, or non-implementation, or qualified or incomplete implementation, of *NC* even though *OF* is fully satisfied. A rule of discretionary application is not itself exclusionary or entrenched, but it is a tie-breaker where the other relevant factors fail to give clear or conclusive guidance. So it would be by no means correct to say that rules of discretionary force count for nothing or are merely a pretence or façade.[7]

2.5 Discretion: Values and Principles

Nevertheless, it will be well to say a little about discretion, and the idea that there can be a 'guided' discretion. Discretion involves an appeal to a person's judgment in a way that merely applying a rule provided its operative facts are satisfied does not.[8] If in a situation of decision, I wonder what is the wisest or the fairest or the most reasonable or the most efficient thing to do, there may be many aspects of the situation to be taken into account. If I am the taxi-marshal, and if my view of the job is, or my instructions are, that I have to run the taxi-queue as efficiently as possible, I shall focus on whatever tends to maximize the speed with which taxis identify hires, get them loaded, and get away, leaving space at the pick-up point for the next cab to come in. That would lead me to judge that there should be no very great delay after my calling a number to await the ticket-holder. Moreover, to avoid confusion and prevent inattentiveness on the part of those waiting for a taxi, it would seem best from this point of view to treat a number as cancelled once it has been called and there is a no-show. This could also be considered more fair to those who do wait attentively, than if I allow somebody to show up later than the calling of the number, when I am now ten or twenty farther into the series.

---

[7] In England, though there are many precedents governing the award of equitable remedies, the remedies themselves remain discretionary. This is a relevant instance.

[8] Cf R Dworkin, *Taking Rights Seriously* (London: Duckworth, 1977) 31–32, 68–71.

What is more, the circumstances militate against my entering into elaborate discussions with people who feel aggrieved by my decisions. So in this case considerations of fairness take second place to considerations of efficiency.

If it is not efficiency but fairness a decision-maker has mainly to consider, different factors predominate in properly weighing up what to do. Then one has to ponder the interests and expectations of all those affected, and consider the impact over time of one rather than another way of handling a problem. If charged with deciding 'reasonably', the balancing task one would face becomes even more complicated, since here one has to consider the relative demands of efficiency and fairness, and perhaps other salient values, and apply common sense to working out a satisfactory course of action.

Since it is good to be fair, good to be wise, good to be efficient, good to be reasonable, we can recognize these concepts as naming 'values'. They are different values, and thus a judgment grounded primarily in one is different from a judgment grounded primarily in another. Being values, they permit of satisfaction to a greater or lesser degree; hence situations can be better or worse, not simply right or wrong judged in terms of a certain value. This aspect of such concepts is sometimes captured by referring to them as 'standards', for in applying any one of them, a decision-maker is envisaged as having to be sure that it is satisfied at least up to a certain point, or to an adequate standard.

Unlike rules, whose operative facts delineate specific circumstances of application, values are pervasive. It is not just good to be fair in administering a queue, it is good to be fair in almost all circumstances of life, and likewise with efficiency, wisdom ('prudence'), reasonableness and rationality, kindness and humanity, and so on. The list of pervasive values is quite a long one, though some have claimed that all can be brought within a few broad headings.[9] Around each we are able to cluster some normative generalizations whose observance helps to secure the value in question. 'One ought to hear both sides of a story in any case of dispute', 'one ought not to upset a person's reasonable expectations', 'one ought to consider the impact of a decision on the well-being of everyone with a legitimate interest in the matter', are examples relevant to fairness. Since they are, like the values in question, pervasive, we do not normally find it helpful to structure them in accordance with the formula '*Whenever OF, then NC*'. These are norms that bear on decision-making in almost any circumstance, so there is no point in singling out particular circumstances of application. They are what we commonly call 'principles', or indeed 'general principles'. Principles can be excluded from consideration

---

[9] See J Bentham, *An Introduction to the Principles of Morals and Legislation* (eds J H Burns and H L A Hart) (London: Athlone Press 1970) ch 1, for a discussion of 'happiness' as the single basic value of human experience, understood in terms of a surplus of pleasure over pain. J Finnis, in *Natural Law and Natural Rights* (Oxford: Clarendon Press, 1980) suggests that there are seven basic goods, namely, life, knowledge, aesthetic experience, friendship, play, religion, and practical reasonableness, and that these are not reducible to each other, not substitutable, and not mere instances of a single *summum bonum*.

by a decision-maker who is charged with applying rules of absolute application, or limited in effect to a greater or lesser degree in the case of rules of strict application, but we do not on that account trouble to qualify our principles with some such formula as '*Except where this principle is excluded, one ought to . . .*'. That simply goes without saying. But when we say, cautiously, '*As a matter of principle, the right thing to do here is probably thus and so . . .*' we draw attention to the possibility that there may be some rule that will exclude the answer derived from general principles alone.

2.6 Standards in Rules

It is possible that explicitly formulated rules themselves incorporate standards in their operative facts or in their normative consequences. This is indeed very common in many domains of law, especially private and commercial law, and in non-criminal branches of public law. The Uniform Commercial Code in the USA (like the Sale and Supply of Goods Act 1994 in the UK) is replete with illustrations of this; here is an example:

(1) Where any tender or delivery by the seller is rejected because non-conforming and the time for performance has not yet expired, the seller may *seasonably* notify the buyer of his intention to cure and may then within the contract time make a conforming delivery.

(2) Where the buyer rejects a non-conforming tender which the seller has *reasonable* grounds to believe would be *acceptable* with or without money allowance the seller may if he *seasonably* notifies the buyer have a further *reasonable* time to substitute a conforming tender. (Italics added throughout).

Here, a decision-maker, including a business executive deciding what to do, or a lawyer deciding what to advise, or a court deciding on a litigated dispute over a sale in relation to which the other operative facts appear to be satisfied, has to evaluate the situation—seasonable or not? Reasonable or not? This involves judgment of a bounded kind, for what is in issue is only the seasonable or the reasonable in a quite specific context of a sale of goods by description or by sample, where there are probably known usages of trade in a given market.

The advantage of articulating rules with such built-in standards is that the rule in question can then be treated as a rule of strict or even of absolute application without the risk of decisions that depart vastly from those that would be satisfactory to a person of informed common sense. Of course, this requires that those who exercise discretion be themselves persons of good discretion and judgment. To the extent that they are, a compromise is struck between the merits of clarity and predictability engendered by the strict or absolute use of rules to regulate a situation, and the merits of flexibility and common sense that emerge where one can pass a free judgment in terms of relevant principles unhampered by the exclusionary effect of such rules.

From the point of view of the present attempt to provide an analytical framework for the following discussion, we need not enter further into the question of the advantages and disadvantages of different approaches to rule-formulation and the use of standards, and the quantum of discretion that it may be wise to allow a decision-maker to have in one context or another. Suffice it to note that when rules are articulated so as to incorporate standards, their operative facts include what we may call 'operative values' as well.[10]

2.7 Institution and Order

In any event, it is of great importance to attend to the difference between informal or conventional norms on the one hand, and on the other hand the explicit or implicit rules that may be introduced and established, or developed and recognized, by persons holding some position of authority. In this regard, avoidance of an infinite regress requires us to suppose that, ultimately, some authority-conferring norms must be conventional rather than institutional. How far a kind of quasi-convention can be sustained, even temporarily, by force and fear, or even by terror, is an open question. In the case of the queue, we can remind ourselves that many instances of forming a line and taking one's turn arise in quite informal settings, without taxi-marshals or post office managers administering them in terms of some established system, from which comes the decision-making authority of marshal or manager. Queues frequently form as a matter of informal normative order. This has an interesting bearing on the kind of information we derive from observation. I do not just see a dozen people standing in a certain spatial interrelationship, say on the verge of a narrow lake, although I do indeed see that. I see what I infer is a queue of people waiting for a boat to ferry them to the other side. My factual information is infused with a normative understanding. I assume that they are doing something which each of them understands as norm-governed in a reciprocal way, even though the norm may be wholly implicit and taken-for-granted. To whatever extent some form of force or coercion is present, our understanding may focus more on an interpretation of the participants' interpretation of threats and behaviour necessary for threat avoidance, between those exercising force and those experiencing this as coercive toward themselves.

According to institutionalist usage (at any rate, the usage proposed here), we may say that the existence of a queue is a matter of 'institutional fact', not simply one of 'brute fact'. Our judgment of the state of the world is not simply in terms of pure physical facts and relationships, but in terms of an understanding of such facts and relationships as humanly meaningful because imputable to shared human norms of conduct. This indeed depends on an observer's beliefs about

---

[10] See also N MacCormick, *Rhetoric and the Rule of Law* at 73–75, and ch 9 passim.

people's interpretation of the situation in the light of what they understand to be a common social norm, even if their conceptions and interpretations are overlapping and inexact rather than shared in explicit common terms such as those that institutionalization makes possible. We know why this is so. Humans are norm-users. Regard for norms leads people into patterns of behaviour. Our own human interests make us ready to look out for patterns of the kind that connect to the expectations and judgments of our fellow humans rather than other kinds, when we are engaging in ordinary practical life rather than abstract scientific inquiry about it. We do not merely observe, but join in—for example, if ourselves hoping to cross the lake.

Recurrent instances of ordered practice imputable to the same or generically similar norms bear names, such as 'standing in line', or 'queuing', or again, 'promising', or 'leading a congregation in prayer', or 'running a race' (as distinct from simply 'running'), or 'ballroom dancing', or 'giving a lecture', or . . . the list is endless. According to a common usage, which will be adopted here, these can all be deemed 'institutions', just as judgments about instance of them are judgments of institutional fact. Of course, they may be very informal institutions indeed, just as normative practices may be wholly informal and dependent on convention rather than any articulated rule.

But order can become formalized. We might even say that it can be institutionalized. We have already seen how this can happen, as when there is a taxi-marshal as well as a taxi-queue, or a manager who administers the queuing arrangements in the post office. The existence of the second tier of the practice leads to or is accompanied by an increasingly explicit articulation of the first tier. There are explicit rules, not mere conventions. The position held by marshal or manager is almost certainly itself an expressly created job, perhaps with a formal job description set up within an organization with a quite elaborate structure of interrelated roles or jobs and with officers or employees appointed to carry them out. In such a context there is clearly what we may call 'institutional normative order', not merely informal normative order, with informal institutions.

A consequential feature of the formalized institution is worth mentioning. Where the formation of a line or queue is not simply a largely spontaneous response by particular people to a problem of co-ordination, but is organized in the context of the airport taxis or the post office or the railway ticket counter or the supermarket checkout, avoiding the queue or jumping it becomes very much harder, almost impossible. For those in charge of the service are most likely simply to refuse service to someone who has not waited his or her turn according to the rules that have been established. Let us imagine a person who conceives his or her status (albeit not recognized by the service-providers) to be so exalted that ordinary folks should give way to them. Even such a one, who refuses to recognize the legitimacy or fairness or even the existence of the queuing rule in relation to himself or herself, is faced with a disagreeable fact. He or she cannot get the service sought except by acting in accordance with that very rule. That is to say, he or she cannot do so unless prepared to take some kind of forceful action that goes the length of a breach of the peace, or even theft, or assault, or, in an extreme, murder. Many who might cheerfully enough jump queues draw the line at engaging in such relatively serious wrongdoing, hence they are constrained even by rules they would otherwise set at naught. In this way, institutional facts become hard realities, facts that constrain us, not merely norms that guide our autonomous judgment.

2.8 Institutions of Positive Law: Preliminary Remarks

The constraining quality of the queue as an organized social institution is replicated even more clearly in the even more formalized case of institutions that belong within the framework of municipal positive law, state law. In the case of the railway ticket-counter, the queue organized by the local manager is, of course, a queue for railway tickets. Behind this lies the law of some state. Buying a railway ticket is entering into a contract of carriage, governed not only by the general law of contract but by a considerable volume of detailed regulations special to carriage of persons by rail. One can say the same in relation to carriage by air or by sea, and the same again of the contract for travel insurance acquired by the prudent person before embarking on a journey attended by greater or different risks from those affecting ordinary everyday life.

So far as concerns the normativity of state law, all this falls in the realm of the 'ought'. You ought to acquire a ticket to gain the right to a seat in the train or on the plane. If you are a rightful ticket-holder, the railway or airline company has a duty to, and thus has to, carry you in accordance with all the conditions of carriage to which you and it have agreed in the contract concluded with purchase of the ticket. The company must also, according to the law of the state, conform with all the other regulatory obligations governing the relevant mode of carriage. Penalties may be levied upon proof of breach of such regulations.

On the other hand, it is to all intents and purposes totally impossible to effect entry on to a regular service flight run by a commercial airline unless you have a ticket, and have checked in, and gone through the whole institutional ritual so familiar to contemporary travellers. Rail travel differs only in degree. Indeed, travel on many railway lines in many countries is now controlled by turnstiles that will open only on insertion of a valid ticket. It is physically impossible (or at least difficult) to gain access to the service without satisfying the rules of the institution. Normative forms turn out to be impenetrable practical constraints, except for the violent hijacker or the cunning and desperate stowaway.

Property likewise is deeply dependent on norms, indeed on highly detailed, formally articulated rules, often of seemingly labyrinthine complexity. Having rights of property in some physical object, or over some (normatively demarcated) piece of land entails being protected by rules that require others to leave you unimpeded in possession and use of the thing or the plot of land (fully discussed in chapter 8 below). It presupposes that you acquired the rights in normatively regulated ways, by gift, purchase, or first or adverse possession. All this is ordinarily overshadowed by the plain social fact of physical control over the thing or land and access to it, by the sense of psychological security and easy familiarity, by the unreflective acceptance by others, at any rate others who also have some things to call their own, that this is yours and you have the say about what goes on here, how this car or computer is used and by whom.

Our perception of the space around us is of land parcelled into plots with houses or shops or factories or farm fields and hill pastures, interspersed with public parks, open highways, and so forth. On the land are things that belong to people. Well-to-do people own stocks and shares and other intangible assets, and these actually presuppose the whole normative fabric of laws governing government debts and the structure of and rules concerning shares in private corporations. Ordinarily, however, we contemplate simply these abstract entities (represented often through pieces of specially printed paper) just as so many other 'things' that may be owned. Next year's not-yet-sown crop of oats can 'change hands' as readily as a bag of oatmeal from last year's now harvested one. Rights to 'futures' are as real 'institutional things' as bags of oats are physical ones—the right of property in the bag of oatmeal being in legal truth no more tangible or less institutional than the right over the future crops, or over stock options, or any other such bizarre imaginary entity over which fortunes may be won or lost. The fortune that is won or lost consists of money. And money is simply a medium of exchange that exists through the faith humans have in the norms, mostly indeed explicit legal rules of state law, governing the exchange process and the character of legal tender and the right to mint coins or to print and issue bank notes. Most recently, with the arrival of a Europe-wide currency, the euro, we see a relevant body of law that is supra-statal in character.

2.9 Institutional Agencies

To conclude this chapter, a few words are required on institutional agencies and their role in the institutionalization of order. We have seen the possibility of a two-or-more tier practice, for example in relation to the instance of the queue. In a manner which is not at all surprising to lawyers, we discover that there are two distinguishable elements in this: the element of rule-formulation and the element of rule-administration. The former is fairly obvious and straightforward. The latter is itself divisible into two or three further elements. One concerns deciding on how to apply the rules in cases of dispute, the other concerns maintaining appropriate facilities, such as turnstiles or numbered ticket-rolls. It can also include seeing to enforcement of decisions, and generally acting to ensure conformity to good practice. There is no reason, of course, to suppose that different people always have to be made responsible, or to take responsibility, for these various elements. It is, however, possible for the functions to be divided among different persons or staffs, so that there would be rule-makers, decision-makers, administrators of facilities, and enforcement agencies.

Under the law of a modern constitutional state, it need scarcely be said, the functions of legislation, adjudication, execution and administration and law-enforcement are parcelled out to substantially differentiated agencies, though not always without some overlap among them. The avoidance of undue overlap is enjoined by the principle of separation of powers, a principle which many justly consider to be essential to the maintenance of free government rather than despotic power. Of course, one must add that not all instances of institutional normative order, that is, of law, have respected or even acknowledged the principle of separation of powers. Ancient empires and city states, mediaeval feudal monarchies and modern enlightened despotisms, as well as (more questionably) socialist states and one-party régimes have had law of their own kind without separation of powers in anything like the forms it now assumes in contemporary constitutional states.

The principal focus of the present work is on law as it manifests itself in a *Rechtsstaat*, or 'law-state' to which I have been referring hitherto as the 'modern constitutional state'.[11] The point here is to note that there are distinct public institutions—'institution-agencies' let us call them—charged with legislative functions, with adjudicative functions, with executive-administrative functions, and with law-enforcement functions. Crucial to the coherent unity of the state to which these institutions belong is their effective co-ordination and balanced interaction in performing their functions. This co-ordination and balance is itself a feature of the normative order of the state, and the body of law with which we engage in comprehending this high-level element of institutional normative order is, of course, constitutional law. The next chapter will consider this.

Meanwhile, let it simply be noted that in the established parlance of lawyers 'institutions' are remarkably various in kind. Legislatures, courts, cabinets and government departments, police forces and other enforcement agencies are one kind of institution—we may call them institution-agencies, for their point and function is to act in various characteristic ways. Companies or corporations enjoying juristic personality by virtue of being incorporated under appropriate statute law are also institutional agencies. Contracts, trusts, property, marriage and the family and other like institutions are not themselves agencies but arrangements that result from acts of persons and/or agencies. Here, they will be referred to, when there is any risk of ambiguity, as 'institution-arrangements'.[12] There are also

---

[11] On the concept of the law-state or constitutional state, see MacCormick, *Questioning Sovereignty* ch 2; the issue is fully taken up in ch 3 below.

[12] N MacCormick, 'Institutions, Arrangements, and Practical Information' Ratio Juris 1 (1988) 73–82.

'institution-things', in the form of various forms of 'incorporeal thing', that is, invisible, non-tangible objects existing by virtue of legal provisions, such as stocks and shares in companies, copyrights, patents and other 'intellectual property rights', of which more will be said in later chapters.

In the case of all three types, that is, institution-agencies, institution-arrangements, and institution-things, a particular structure of governing rules can be discerned. The first set, here called 'institutive rules', determines by what acts and procedures one can set up an agency (for example, rules that set up a new legislative body, or about incorporation of a company), or an arrangement (for example, rules on formation of contracts) or a thing (for example, rules on claiming a patent). The second set determines what are the normative consequences of its existence—a parliament may enact laws and do other legally significant things, a contract regulates what the parties must do to keep it, and a patent grounds claims to exclusivity in the processes it specifies. The third set has to do with terminating or winding up the agency, arrangement, or thing. This triadic presentation of 'institutive, consequential, and terminative rules'[13] corresponds to an expository strategy commonly used by legal commentators, to some extent reflected in the practical usages of lawyers and courts. In each case, it is necessary also to have some grasp of the main point of the institution in question. Legislatures are for making or reforming laws. Contracts are ways of making agreements binding among people. Trusts are ways of dedicating property to particular uses or for the benefit of particular persons or public goods. Patents are ways of securing exclusive rights to exploit inventions, with a view to encouraging inventiveness and facilitating the recovery of research and development costs, and so on. We may say that an explanation of any institution requires an account of the relevant rules set out in the light of its point. This idea that things have a point can be compared with the Aristotelian idea that entities of many kinds have to be accounted for in terms of their 'final cause'.[14] That a seed develops into a plant which in turn if fertilized produces more seeds is important in the understanding of (vegetable) seeds. All the more in the case of social institutions, we can explain them only if we know to what end they are supposed to function. Contracts are for undertaking obligations, football clubs for organizing football teams and football games and so on. This does not mean that they cannot be used—quite legitimately used in many cases—for all the varieties of human purposes to which arrangements of such a kind can be adapted. But it is the institution that normally

---

[13] This way of representing institutions was first put forward in my 'Law as Institutional Fact', an inaugural lecture presented in Edinburgh University in 1973—see Law Quarterly Review 70 (1974) 102–129; also N MacCormick and O Weinberger, *An Institutional Theory of Law: New Approaches to Legal Positivism* (Dordrecht: D Reidel, 1986) ch 2.

[14] Compare Aristotle, *A Treatise on Government* (trans W Ellis) (London: J M Dent, 1912) 1252b–1253a: 'For what every being is in its most perfect state, that certainly is the nature of that being, whether it be a man, a horse, or a house: besides, whatsoever produces the final cause and the end which we desire, must be best; but a government complete in itself is that final cause and what is best'.

functions towards a given broadly-stated end—its 'final cause'—that is so adapted. This point is taken up in greater detail in chapter 16 of the present book. It is sufficient here to remark that John Searle's contrast between 'constitutive' and 'regulative' rules of institutions, even in the form in which it has been further elaborated by Dick Ruiter, seems to me less satisfactory than the triadic presentation suggested here, when this is supplemented by reference to an institution's final cause or principal point.[15]

---

[15] A full argument for this view is given in N MacCormick, 'Norms, Institutions and Institutional Facts' Law and Philosophy 17 (1998) 1–45 at 36–44. Searle (*Speech Acts*, 34–51) argues for the existence of 'constitutive rules' that can all be cast in the form 'x counts as y in circumstances c'. This seems unhelpfully over-broad, for almost anything can count as almost anything else in apt circumstances. A bottle can count as a weapon in a pub brawl without any of these concepts having to be considered as a social institution, or a legal institution, or a cultural one either. On the other hand, it is true that a glass vessel with a narrow neck used for storing liquids counts as a bottle. This may indeed tell me something about the noun 'bottle' or even the concept 'bottle' within the English language. If there is anything we should call an institutional element here, this would relate to the sense in which nouns or concepts might be characterized as institutions within languages; but this would not give helpful information about institutions in the wider practical sense with which the institutional theory of law is concerned. For an elaborated statement of the contrary view by D Ruiter, see his *Legal Institutions*, ch 4.

3

Law and the Constitutional State

3.1 Introduction

The last chapter ended in reflection on the way in which specialized agencies can come into being with authority under higher-level rules to carry out the essential tasks of government. These are tasks of making law and keeping the executive under scrutiny, tasks of executive government concerned with the pursuit of public policy in implementation of the law or otherwise within a legal framework, and tasks of adjudication aimed at upholding the law, both in disputes between private persons and in matters involving private persons and public authorities. The distinction between legislature, executive, and judiciary is, as was noted, a feature of the modern constitutional state. Upholding the principle of separation of these powers is the particular hallmark of this kind of polity. Democratic forms of election to public office as a member of the legislature or as the chief or a member of the executive government, though not (with a few exceptions) to judicial office, have come to be a feature of these states also. This has been more a consequence than a cause of establishing a successful separation of powers within a 'balanced constitution'.[1]

The present chapter commences with a discussion of states, proceeds to a consideration of constitutions as legal frameworks for states, then reflects on the institutions of public law set up by or under constitutions. There follow some preliminary remarks on 'Civil Society and the State' that look forward to part 3, followed by a brief interim conclusion on 'Law as Institutional Normative Order'.

3.2 States

All states, whether or not conforming to the pattern of a constitutional state to be discussed here, have four essential characteristics. First, they are *territorial*, that is, they lay claim to and exercise, to at least a significant degree, effective control over a specific territory, in a way that involves when necessary the use of coercive force

---

[1] Cf R C van Caenegem, *An Historical Introduction to Western Constitutional Law* (Cambridge: Cambridge University Press, 1995) 19–20.

against external and internal threats. Secondly, they claim *legitimacy*: that is, their governing authorities claim that in exercising such effective control they do so as of right and are properly recognized as being rightfully in authority over the territory. Thirdly, they claim *independence*, that is, their governing authorities claim that the people of the state are entitled to a form of government free from external interference by other states. The fourth, closely related, feature is that these claims are acknowledged by other states. For in international law, a state is a territory with a *recognized and effective government*, and states are entitled to respect under the principle of mutual non-interference. (Nowadays there is growing recognition of an exception to non-interference in the case of a duty of humanitarian intervention where a state's governing authorities are grossly violating fundamental human rights,[2] a topic to which we shall return in a later chapter.)

Government requires the maintenance of some kind of order, and to the extent that order is secured by reference to a body of rules that addresses the population and that the enforcement agencies take seriously, there is a legal element in government. It is under these same rules that non-official use of force to pursue claims and take action against alleged wrongdoing is prohibited. This is essential to the state's claim to a monopoly of legitimate force, though that claim is usually also backed up by some ideological claims of a democratic or a nationalistic or republican or religious kind. Seen in this way, states are conceptually identified primarily in territorial and political terms.[3] Also, however, they have a basis in international law as this emerged in the period after the Peace of Westphalia of 1648, and came to be expressed by theorists of international law starting with De Vattel in 1758.[4] (In a slightly anachronistic way, it has become common to describe states in the form they had acquired by the twentieth century as 'Westphalian' states.)

In what circumstances can a state have differentiated and mutually balancing powers of government? The answer that follows from the discussion in chapters 1 and 2 is that they can do so by having appropriate practices of a kind that can be summed-up in terms of norms, rules, and principles of conduct. If it is acknowledged that everyone in the state ought to accept and act in accordance with statutes enacted by a certain parliament, and if it is acknowledged that the parliament's membership is established by a certain recognized and itself regulated process of election, this means that institutionalized law-making exists. If it is acknowledged that executive power is exercised by or in the name of a head of state, subject to the answerability of executive ministers to the parliament, and

---

[2] Geoffrey Robertson, *Crimes against Humanity in International Criminal Law: The Struggle for Global Justice* (London: Allen Lane, 1999).

[3] Cf MacCormick, *Questioning Sovereignty* 17–18.

[4] E de Vattel, *The Law of Nations or Principles of the Law of Nature Applied to the Conduct and Affairs of Nations and Sovereigns* (ed J Chitty) (Philadelphia Pa: T & J W Johnson & Co, 1883); cf P Allott, *The Health of Nations: Society and Law Beyond the State* (Cambridge: Cambridge University Press, 2002) 41–45.

that their exercise of power in ways affecting the rights of other persons must be in accordance with some rule of law, then executive government is thus institutional- ized. If it is acknowledged that the ultimate authority in the interpretation of the rules enacted by the legislature, including those that regulate executive activity, is exercised by a corps of judges organized in a system of courts, then judicial power is institutionalized. 'If it is acknowledged,' I have said. 'Acknowledged by whom?' is obviously the next question. The answer must be rather like that which applies in the case of queuing. It has to be acknowledged by enough people for the practice to be a viable one. In a state, it must be remembered, coercive force is organized. Practices whose legitimacy is not acknowledged by those who command the state's forces are unlikely to be effective. In respect of practices that those same forces support as legitimate, the dissent of other sections of the community may not be sufficient to make the practices unviable.

All this must seem quite banal, and also must seem to conceal far more than it reveals. In any real parliament, the body of electoral law determining its composi- tion and the proper practice of elections and the organization of political parties is enormous and elaborate. So are the procedural rules concerning the conduct of business in the parliament, and how it must proceed when enacting binding rules—'statutes' or 'laws'—of the state. The same goes for the voluminous body of public law concerning the organization of the executive government and subordin- ate public authorities, including possibly also regional and local authorities. Similarly voluminous are statutes establishing and regulating courts of justice and arraying them into criminal or civil, possibly also commercial, administrative or taxation jurisdictions, with at least one, and more often two, levels of appeal courts. There is often also a final constitutional court that interprets the law of the constitution that sustains the whole set-up. In addition to all that, all courts have elaborate sets of rules of court regulating their procedure.

Moreover, in some states it is openly acknowledged that decisions by the courts, particularly the higher courts in the hierarchy of appeals, constitute precedents that other courts are bound to follow except in exceptional circumstances, hence forming rules for the conduct of persons in general, not only the courts. In other states, precedents are considered to have authority only for the particular case, though also having a kind of exemplary value in guiding interpretation of the law in future similar cases. Whether formally recognized or not, precedent can thus be a source of rules and principles and of approaches to interpretation that add up to a body of 'case law' running parallel to the laws laid down in enacted statutes.[5] The various states that belong to the common law tradition have inherited from pre- modern times a body of law originally grounded in custom but nowadays having its most authoritative source in judicial precedents of the higher courts, including

---

[5] For an account of different national legal systems' approaches to precedent, and differences about the formal recognition of precedent as a 'source of law', see D N MacCormick and R S Summers (eds) *Interpreting Precedents: A Comparative Study* (Aldershot: Dartmouth, 1997).

precedents of courts from long-past eras of law. A further authoritative source, as noted earlier, is found in 'institutional' writings by jurists of earlier ages. Anyway, all such law is now subject to amendment by decision of the contemporary legislature.[6]

The huge bulk of this specialist public law governing the conduct of the several branches of government is itself highly institutionalized. How then can chapter 2's simple-minded account of a transition from informal queuing to formalized queuing have anything to say by way of an explanation of this? The vital point to observe by way of answer is that nothing comes out of nothing. Constitutional law and all the specialized elements of public law are surely normative, surely set standards about how officials and others ought to—indeed, must—conduct themselves. What, however, makes them normative, what gives them their 'ought-quality' on which we can base the key distinction of what is right from what is wrong? My suggestion throughout this work has in effect been that the key to normativity lies in what H L A Hart called the 'internal aspect' of conduct.[7] For this, there have to be standards that participants in practices implicitly or explicitly refer to in forming reciprocal expectations of conduct and in acting accordingly.

The human capacity—the quintessentially human capacity—for interactive co-ordination[8] in this 'ought-based' way is what lies behind every kind of more formal rule-making and rule-application. For the point about legislated rules is that the legislature makes them on the assumption that they ought to be obeyed and ought to be enforced (and the better enforced the likelier obeyed). The point about formal adjudication lies in the assumption that the addressees of the judgment ought to accept and implement it, and other enforcement agencies ought to see to this if either party proves recalcitrant. The point of an executive decision to allocate certain sums in the state's budget for the armed forces and certain others to the health services is that these sums ought then (if approved in a Finance Act, no doubt) to be spent as authorized, no more and no less. The 'ought' that issues from these decision-making processes has to have entered it from the beginning. Where does it come from? The answer lies in informal, non-institutionalized conventions seated in the customs and usages of the citizens of the state, including particularly those from time to time called to serve in public offices. In saying that, one should also bear in mind, in relation to those states which are to a greater or lesser extent democratic, that turning out to vote in

---

[6] Cf N Luhmann, *Law as a Social System* (trans K A Ziegert) (Oxford: Oxford University Press, 2004) 363–4 on the emergence of democracy and the development of legislation.

[7] H L A Hart, *The Concept of Law* (eds P Bulloch and J Raz) (Oxford: Clarendon Press, 2nd edn with Postscript, 1994) 56–57, 88–90, 102–104. There are some difficulties about this, with which I try to deal in ch 4 below.

[8] On the idea of co-ordination problems, and possibilities of solution, see D Lewis, *Convention: a Philosophical Study* (Oxford: Basil Blackwell, 1986) 5–51; cf G Postema, 'Co-ordination and Convention at the Foundations of Law' Journal of Legal Studies 11 (1982) 165–189.

elections is properly considered to be the exercise of a fundamental public function. So even in the massively institutionalized order of a constitutional state there lies behind the powers of each of its great institutions a convention or custom[9] whereby it ought to be respected in carrying out its functions as these are constitutionally conferred. To the extent that such a norm is not observed, normativity is also missing, though a crude practical effectiveness in the exercise of sheer physical power may remain.

Conventions and shared usage have another vital role to play in the sustenance of a constitutional order involving a separation of powers. Checks and balances among the different branches of government are often said to be essential to the successful constitutional self-government of a state, particularly with a view to sustaining the conditions of a free government, in contrast to some form of tyranny or despotism.[10] The point is that each branch of government should be checked and controlled by another, or should contain internal checking practices, or both.[11] The executive must pursue vigorous policies in relation to the economy and the social conditions of the state and must see to the maintenance of effective internal and external security, through law-enforcement agencies internally and military forces (including intelligence services) externally. But the more vigorous the executive, the greater the risk of over-extension or abuse of power to the detriment of the citizens or some sub-set of them. So it is important that the executive be politically accountable in some way to the legislature, and the principle of legality of government action—the 'Rule of Law'—requires also that there be statutory authority for acts of the executive that impinge on citizens and other private persons. So the legislature controls the framework within which the executive can act. At least, it does so provided the courts have adequate power and independence to ensure the legality of governmental action when this is challenged by appropriate forms of action before the courts (appropriate forms of action thus have to be provided through the statutes and rules of the relevant court). The courts in turn must be sensitive not to usurp the province of the legislature in deciding the content of the law and the direction of law reform from time to time. But they must at the same time also police the boundaries of the legislature's province by ensuring that it does not override constitutional restrictions on it, or act beyond the authority conferred on the legislature where such a grant of authority is in issue.

Checks and balances of this kind are variously interpreted in various contemporary states with different constitutional traditions that have developed within

---

[9] On custom, see J Bjarup, 'Social Action: the Foundation of Customary Law' in P Ørebech, F Bosselman, J Bjarup et al, *The Role of Customary Law in Sustainable Development* (Cambridge: Cambridge University Press, 2005) 89–157, especially at 135–151.

[10] van Caenegem, *Historical Introduction*, 168, 185.

[11] M J C Vile, *Constitutionalism and the Separation of Powers* (Oxford: Clarendon Press, 1967); G Marshall, *Constitutional Theory* (Oxford: Clarendon Press, 1971).

essentially the same broad family of constitutionalist thought.[12] All face the risk of deadlock. Each of the principal constitutional organs can block or render impotent actions of another. A dynamic balance can degenerate into stasis and immobility, provoking the kind of constitutional crisis that has so often been broken only by the 'strong man' who suspends the constitution and assumes personal rule with the backing at least of the military. No amount of formal rule-making can resolve the issue of balance to sustain an effective dynamic working system— if only because, in conditions of crisis, the issue is likely to concern or include the very question as to who has authority to make the rule that authoritatively breaks the deadlock. Since formal rule-making can never completely secure balance and reciprocity in practice, the alternative to 'strong man' interventions lies in constitutional conventions—as discussed already in chapter 2. These are essential to the balance-sustaining function, and themselves depend on a shared or overlapping 'internal point of view' among those exercising roles determined by the constitution in the three great branches of the state.

This draws attention to a fact on which David Hume remarked to telling effect.[13] If, he said, constitutions are a kind of social contract agreed upon by all affected and brought into force by popular will, you would expect states to be most soundly established nearest the time of their adoption of a new constitution. In the case of monarchical government, the introduction of a new royal house, as in Great Britain in the early eighteenth century, would be a parallel case. History, however, shows that the newness of a constitution or a royal house is far from tending to secure its stability. Constitutions grow more stable the longer they acquire an overlay, or underpinning, of custom, usage and convention. The same goes for the sense of legitimacy of a monarchy. The step from an ideally structured state to a working constitutional order is one that takes time and (subject to certain exceptions) acquires an increasing sense of legitimacy with the passage of time.

In saying this, however, I may be thought to be making the error of generalizing from one case that happens to be familiar to me. The United Kingdom constitution (so far as there is such a thing) is fundamentally a matter of custom and convention, supplemented by various more or less solemn statutes and treaties and by judicial precedents. Moreover, its version of the separation of powers is a rather precarious one,[14] since the central constitutional doctrine of the legal

---

[12] van Caenegem, *Historical Introduction* 150–174; P Craig, *Public Law and Democracy in the United Kingdom and the United States of America* (Oxford: Clarendon Press, 1990) 16–21, 56–58, 113–116, 159–160.

[13] See D Hume, 'Of the Original Contract', in *Essays Moral, Political and Literary* (Oxford: Oxford University Press, 1963) 452–473.

[14] It is even possible to assert that Montesquieu completely misunderstood and misinterpreted the constitutional system of Great Britain ('England', he called it) in discerning a 'separation of powers' there at all. See L Claus, 'Montesquieu's Mistakes and the True Meaning of Separation' Oxford Journal of Legal Studies 25 (2005) 419–452—but for a different view see van Caenegem, *Historical Introduction* 123–124.

sovereignty of the monarch in Parliament implies that the legislature has the last word about everything. In the circumstances of strongly organized political parties, with pre-eminence attaching to the Prime Minister as leader of the largest party in Parliament, the theoretical absoluteness of the legislature can come dangerously close to a near-absolute position for the executive. Certainly, the functioning of the state is more flexible and fluid, and the balance between elements more volatile, than under the more normal contemporary form of state, based on a 'written' or, as I shall call it, a 'formal' constitution.[15]

3.3 Constitutions

It might be said, not at all unreasonably, that the story of this chapter so far has been too roundabout. The obvious thing about states is that, in addition to the four characteristics I mentioned, they all have constitutions. If you ask how powers and functions of government are divided among different agencies, and how checks and controls are then maintained between and within different branches of government, there is an obvious answer. It is that you do this by adopting a constitution that makes appropriate provisions, and then by observing in good faith the constitution you have adopted. Who, then, are you? Here we confront a long-recognized paradox. Whoever assumes the constituent power to constitute a state has to presuppose that they are already members of the state they constitute.[16] Indeed, it is the specific distinguishing mark of new republics from old kingdoms that republics are constituted by the sovereign will of their citizens, or of the nation. (Feudal kingdoms emerged from wars or conquests, and only gradually did kings come to accept that they too were bound by the law and custom of the realm they ruled). In the republic, however, neither citizens nor nation exist until the constitution brings them into being as such, or confers that character upon them.[17]

One way out of this bind is to say, with Hans Kelsen, that the authority of the founders of a constitution simply has to be presupposed—no positive, laid-down rule could confer upon constitution-makers the authority to do so.[18] Everyone just has to act as if they had such authority—at least, they have to do so in the event that the constitution they made comes to be efficacious as the normative basis for state activity, that in virtue of which acts are right or wrong, valid or invalid. Given a constitutional order that is by-and-large efficacious, it makes

---

[15] An account of the distinction between 'formal' and 'functional' constitutions is given in N MacCormick, *Who's Afraid of a European Constitution?* (Exeter: Imprint Academic, 2005) 39–46.

[16] Cf H Lindahl, 'Sovereignty and Representation in the European Union' in N Walker (ed), *Sovereignty in Transition* (Oxford: Hart Publishing, 2004) 87–114 at 90–107.

[17] Cf A Tomkins, *Our Republican Constitution* (Oxford: Hart Publishing, 2005).

[18] H Kelsen, *The Pure Theory of Law* (trans M Knight) (Berkeley and Los Angeles: University of California Press, 1967) 193–219.

sense to treat the constitution as that which ought to be respected. That is, it makes sense to act on the footing that state coercion ought to be exercised only in accordance with the provisions laid down by the constitutional founders, and that all other forms of coercion ought to be repressed as legally wrongful. Thus, from a theorist's point of view, each state constitution is backed by a presupposed 'basic norm' or *Grundnorm*, in all those states in which there is an effective normative order based on a constitution.

Two points need to be made. First, this presupposes that we know what a constitution is. This knowledge is necessarily based on an understanding of the already discussed functions of allocating powers and establishing checks and balances among them. That is, it is from an appreciation of the functioning of a territorial legal order with judiciary, executive and legislature in some kind of working interrelationship that we can explain what goes into a constitution. Secondly, the existence of a constitution is not primarily a matter of the adoption, by whatever procedure, of a formal document that purports to distribute powers of government in the way we have discussed. It is, again, an issue of functionality, to do with the response of political actors over time to the norms formulated in the text of the constitution. These either are or are not taken seriously as governing norms of conduct. To some variable degree, but at least in the great majority of relevant situations, conduct must be oriented towards these norms by actors, and understood by reference to the same norms by those acted upon. Only those that are in this sense taken seriously do really exist as working constitutions.

In the typical case of a modern state like France or Portugal or Poland or Japan, or a modern federation like Germany or the USA or Canada or Australia or Switzerland, the constitution has both formal and functional aspects. Formally one can point to a text that was first drafted by some convention or committee then adopted as the constitution of the state or federation named in it by the citizens whose citizenship is confirmed in it. The date of its adoption and the dates of any subsequent amendments that have brought the text to its present form can be specified, indeed are usually stated in the text itself in its currently authoritative printed version. Functionally, it either is, at least to a reasonable extent, or it is not even to a reasonable extent, a genuinely observed source of the genuinely observed norms followed by those carrying out official public roles specified in or under it (including roles of the armed forces of the state).[19] Only someone who seeks to understand conduct normatively in the way discussed at such length in the first two chapters of the present work can tell whether or not the formal constitution is also functional in the life of the state, its officials and its citizens. Only if the formal constitution is functional to a reasonable degree can it be acknowledged as a genuine constitution, rather than a failed constitution or a mere sham.

By no means all states or federations that have adopted democratic constitutions as a basis for free government under the rule of law have succeeded in being

[19] Again, see MacCormick, *Who's Afraid of a European Constitution?* 39–46.

what they tried to become by adopting the constitution. Dictators (military, or civilian with support of the military) and oligarchies can seize the commanding roles within a state and subvert the institutional balance that its constitution pretends to establish. They can even continue with the show of parliamentary elections and the pretence of an independent judiciary, while in truth the organization and execution of governmental powers is centralized, autocratic, discretionary and (quite possibly) corrupt. Even in cases that fall short of this kind of collapse of constitutional government, there can be fairly widespread cynicism and corruption. Only in some cases does the formal constitution really shape or constrain most of the activities of the state at official level, thereby securing a stable rule of law for citizens and indeed all persons subject to the state's jurisdiction by residence or otherwise. There, we may say, there is a coincidence of formal and functional constitution.

By this analysis, conversely, it is possible to have a functional constitution, even without the adoption of any formal documentary or written constitution. There are at least two contemporary illustrations of this, in the United Kingdom—which is a state—and the European Union—which is not a state, but a confederation or 'commonwealth' of states.[20] Historically, studies of the constitutional order of the United Kingdom (at the time commonly called 'England') in contrast with other contemporary kingdoms, gave clues to the structure of a functioning constitutional state. None of these studies was more influential, for all its inaccuracies,[21] than that of Montesquieu.[22] Together with various essays in political theory about the 'social contract' by thinkers such as John Locke,[23] David Hume,[24] and Jean-Jacques Rousseau,[25] and about constitutions themselves by such as Tom Paine,[26] these studies contributed greatly to the ideas of those who drew up the new constitutions of the late eighteenth century. That of the USA has proved remarkably durable, through a civil war and more than two dozen amendments. That of revolutionary France has had more discontinuities, yet the current constitution of the Fifth Republic recognizably owes a great deal to its eighteenth century origins, overlaid by experiences of the nineteenth and twentieth centuries. Other contemporary republics have learned from and adapted the kind of model

[20] Cf N MacCormick, *Questioning Sovereignty: Law, State and Nation in the European Commonwealth* (Oxford: Oxford University Press, 1999) 137–156.

[21] Or alleged inaccuracies, as per L Claus, 'Montesquieu's Mistakes and the True Meaning of Separation' Oxford Journal of Legal Studies 25 (2005) 419–452.

[22] Montesquieu (Charles de Secondat, Baron de Montesquieu), *The Spirit of the Laws* (trans and ed A M Cohler, B C Miller, H S Stone) (Cambridge: Cambridge University Press, 1989).

[23] John Locke, *The Second Treatise of Civil Government* (ed J Gough) (Oxford: Basil Blackwell, 3rd edn, 1966).

[24] As cited above, n 13.

[25] J-J Rousseau, *The Social Contract* in Rousseau, *Collected Writings* (ed R D Masters and C Kelly), vol 4 (trans J R Bush, R D Masters, and C Kelly) (Hanover, NH: University of New England Press, 1994).

[26] T Paine, *The Rights of Man* (with introduction by E Foner, notes by H Collins) (New York/London: Penguin, 1985).

yielded by the USA and France and others in that line of descent. There are still also contemporary constitutional monarchies, existing in a remarkable number of countries, most of them apparently rather stable. There, monarchy functions under constitutions that were in different ways drawn up by trying to make formally explicit what had emerged by a more evolutionary process in the United Kingdom or other old monarchies like those of Sweden, Denmark or the Netherlands. The UK has in its own turn amended and adjusted its (never fully formalized) constitutional arrangements in the light of prevailing political ideas and pragmatic necessities. It is a continuing case of a functional constitution that has achieved no formal expression through a deliberate act of holistic constitution-making.[27]

Meanwhile, in the European Union, there has been a series of treaties that established and then extended the European Communities, equipping them with organs such as the Commission, Council of Ministers, and Court of Justice. This was the legal basis of the Community that became encapsulated in the European Union by the Treaty of Maastricht of 1992. The whole complex of treaties has been considered by the Court of Justice to amount to a 'constitutional charter' of the European Community and now Union.[28] The Court in this line of decisions held that the treaties necessarily conferred on itself the final power of interpretation of their own provisions. Under the interpretation favoured by the Court, and over the long run accepted, with whatever reservations, by the member states of the Union, the treaties and the laws made under them ('Regulations', 'Directives', 'Framework Decisions') constitute a new legal order of its own kind.[29] This legal order has direct effect to create rights and obligations for citizens and corporations as well as for the states themselves. Its laws have primacy over the laws of the member states within the areas of competence transferred to the organs of the Community or Union by the states in the treaties (as interpreted by the Court). There is a self-referential quality about all this—the treaties as interpreted by the Court gave the authority for the Court to interpret the treaties as a new legal order distinct both from international law and the laws of the member states. Self-reference of this kind is typical of independent constitutional orders. Indeed, another case of self-reference is found in the adoption by citizens of the constitution that creates or confirms their status as citizens.[30]

---

[27] van Caenegem, *Historical Introduction* gives a clear account of the development of most of the states mentioned in this and the preceding paragraph (196–200, UK; 200–217, France; 217–229, Germany; 230–241, Belgium and the Netherlands). Cf E Wicks, *The Evolution of a Constitution: Eight Key Moments in British Constitutional History* (Oxford: Hart Publishing, 2006).

[28] Case 294/83 *Parti Ecologiste 'Les Verts'* v *European Parliament* [1986] ECR 1339; *Opinion 1/91 (Draft Opinion on the EEA)* [1991] ECR I 6079; J H H Weiler, *The Constitution of Europe* (Cambridge: Cambridge University Press, 1999) 12–26.

[29] S Douglas-Scott, *Constitutional Law of the European Union* (Harlow: Longman, 2002) 516–520; J Shaw, 'Europe's Constitutional Future' Public Law (2005) 132–151.

[30] On self-referentiality, see G Teubner, *Law as an Autopoietic System* (trans A Bankowska and R Adler, ed Z Bankowski) (Oxford: Blackwell, 1993) 19–24.

During 2002 and 2003, a Convention established by the European Council under its Declaration of Laeken took wide consultations and undertook intensive studies, then drafted a 'Treaty Establishing a Constitution for Europe'. This was further amended during an Intergovernmental Conference meeting intermittently in 2003 and 2004, and the Heads of State and Government adopted a final version of the Treaty, signing it on 29 October 2004. To come into effect, it required ratification by all member states, including the ten new states which acceded to the Union on 1 May 2004. By referendum decisions of quite substantial majorities in France in May 2005 and the Netherlands in June of the same year, the process of ratifying the Treaty and thus adopting the Constitution was derailed for the time being, perhaps forever. There had been an opportunity to substitute a formal constitution for the existing functional constitution contained within the treaties, but there was no sufficient surge of enthusiasm to turn this possibility into an actual achievement, and meantime the old functional constitution continues in operation.[31]

To conclude this section: the institutionalization of legal order in a state or other polity depends on the evolution or adoption of a constitution that establishes the essential agencies of government and assigns powers to them. These institution-agencies have to be understood in terms of the defining functions they fulfil, as well as by reference to how persons come to hold office in them, how they must conduct themselves in fulfilling their functions, and how they may demit office. All constitutions have to be understood functionally, but usually also have a formal and definitive text adopted by some constituent act. The formal constitution has also to be a functional—and functioning—constitution if a state is to acquire or sustain the character of a law-state, in which the rule of law is realized to some substantial extent in the conduct of its governance. A customary or conventional basic norm is the necessary normative foundation of the whole structure.

3.4 Institutions of Public Law

The institutional analysis developed so far ought now to be summarized. In relation to constitutional law, and more broadly to public law in general, we find functions assigned to institutional agencies. Institutive rules set these up as legal entities ('There shall be a Scottish Parliament' says, for example, the opening subsection of the opening section of the Scotland Act 1998, and many other related rules say how exactly it is to be composed and to function). Such entities

---

[31] For a personal account of these events and an evaluation of the upshot, see MacCormick, *Who's Afraid of a European Constitution?*; more objectively, compare P Norman, *The Accidental Constitution: the Story of the European Constitutional Convention* (Brussels: EuroComment, 2003) and A Lamassoure, *Histoire secrète de la constitution européenne* (Paris, Editions Albin Michel SA for Fondation Robert Schuman, 2004).

are then given ('consequential') powers and duties, with express or implied limits. These rules presuppose the legal existence of the entity in question, since they are in the form of sentences in which the name of the entity is their grammatical subject. ('The Scottish Parliament may make laws, to be known as Acts of the Scottish Parliament', for example—Scotland Act s 28(1)). Entities of this kind can carry out their functions—exercise powers and perform duties—only if they have human beings as their members or agents. Further institutive rules lay down the conditions for becoming, or being appointed, or (in the running example of a parliament) elected to the position of a relevant member. Such members have consequential rights and powers, and those that are exercised in a collective manner take effect as exercises of the powers that belong to the constitutional entity itself. Terminative rules also exist concerning when and how members demit membership, or the entity itself may be disbanded.

This patterned way of representing the structured character of constitutional or sub-constitutional rules relating to entities and agencies that exercise public functions can be replicated in a quite general way. All have a commencement, a duration in time and a possible termination. All have members who take up membership or office on particular conditions, exercise it effectually to the extent that they observe the consequential rules of their office, and eventually, if only by death, lose or demit office. It is by reflecting on the functions or point (or final cause) of different kinds of agency that one can appreciate the range and extent of activities a state performs or causes to be performed in the public domain. Certain characteristic ones are necessary and omnipresent.

Legislatures are one example. It is a particular, indeed defining, feature of institutional order that it contains in itself the possibility of making norms of conduct explicit, by giving to specific texts produced by relevant agencies obligatory force and effect. In content such texts contain sentences that are linguistically appropriate to express requirements concerning conduct, or empowerments, or limitations on these by way of exemptions or exceptions, or by way of disempowerment. Sometimes, they contain other normative material (eg, concerning rights) that is related to requirements and empowerments in ways to be considered later. What it means to say that they can be understood as making norms explicit can be clarified by reference back to the introductory discussion of the queue. There, it was noted that what may in some circumstances be attributable to implicit and inexact practice-norms, expressed in mutual expectations about who ought to go forward for service next, can become in other circumstances a practice subject to authoritatively issued rules. Constitution texts, where there is a formal constitution, have this very property that they make what might otherwise be a somewhat vaguely understood convention into a hard-and-fast rule.

Supreme and subordinate legislative authorities—parliaments and the like—with their legislative, that is, rule-making, power are an essential element in institutional normative order. Their defining function is their ability to make general rules of universal and uniform application throughout the state's territory, governing all persons therein, or to make them for some definite sub-set that is in its entirety regulated universally and uniformly. Legislatures as such are not necessarily disempowered from also making specific or individualized norms, though the principles of constitutionalist governance are in many states interpreted as precluding this. Everywhere, their main business is general rule-making, whatever other more particularistic activity there may be powers to carry out.

It typically belongs to the executive branch of government and to administrative or localized agencies to take decisions having a more particular or temporary or short-term effect. Such decisions can also constitute norms, but they may be individual norms, or norms applying to small sets of addressees. They can, for example in licensing and related domains, be in the form of exceptional or individually addressed permissions or licences. Thus there may be general rules of law that prohibit driving motor vehicles on public highways except in the case of persons holding valid drivers' permits or licences, who are driving validly licensed vehicles. Or it may be prohibited to develop land outside its normal established use except when planning permission has been validly granted by a relevant public authority. In such cases there must be an agency or agencies with power to grant a valid licence or planning permission. The effect of this is to bring the grantee of the licence or the permission within the exception to the general prohibition in question. Permissions that exempt from some general prohibition have significant normative effect. They are also apt to be of some, perhaps considerable, economic value.

The whole idea of 'binding rules' (and of effective exemptions) demands further consideration. What does it mean for a rule-text such as that contained in the section of an Act of Parliament to be a 'binding rule'? Whom does it bind, and how? One part of the answer was already given in the discussion of the idea of a 'basic norm'. If it is obligatory to respect the constitution, this entails its being obligatory to conduct oneself in accordance with norms that are in turn valid in accordance with the constitution. Hence it is obligatory to respect rules, decisions, and orders or permissions that are made by properly established agencies, and thus by persons properly instituted in office as members or officials of such agencies. (This is normally challengeable by some means, to the extent that acts infringing constitutional limitations, including those guaranteed in a charter of rights, may be set aside as null and of no effect.) Whom does this obligatory character bind? The answer from a point of view internal to the legal order is: everyone who is within the territory constitutionally belonging to the state, except for specifically exempted classes, such as those having diplomatic immunity, and everybody whom the state constitution identifies as owing allegiance to it.

Does it follow that all those for whom this is obligatory must acknowledge it to be so, or must feel committed or bound, or give some high priority in their moral reasoning to fulfilling a duty of respect to the constitution and the laws made under it? Clearly not; no empirical claim of that kind follows at all, and the evidence of ordinary experience suggests that no real states ever achieve full-hearted commitment to a law-abiding life from the totality, or perhaps even a majority, of those who are obligated according to the law and the constitution. No assumption about empirical attitudes can or should be built into an attempt to grasp the concepts involved here.[32]

Different considerations apply, however, to persons holding office within, or membership of, state agencies. Oaths or affirmations of loyalty to law and constitution (perhaps personified as committing one to fidelity to the person of the head of state, as occurs in some monarchies) are commonly required of those holding office, and the higher the office, the more solemnly so. These are, on close consideration, not merely formal solemnities. They express something logically implicit in holding offices of the kind in contemplation. These agencies, and these offices in them, have existence only as legal-institutional facts. There is no position to hold except if the law declares it so, and if this law is made effectual. There would a pragmatic self-contradiction in formally accepting office while expressly declaring a refusal to uphold the law, or to uphold it save on a selective basis.[33] It would be like uttering the sentence 'I refuse to speak English' intending this as a refusal ever to speak English (for one breaks the resolve not to speak English in the very act of uttering it in English). In this sense, there is a logical commitment to a 'basic norm', that the constitution and the law made under it must be obeyed, in the act of taking or exercising public office.

This, however, does not entail that every office-holder actually does fulfil this fundamental duty of office. Hypocrisy and corruption are always possible, and it is an open question how much concealed malpractice a constitutional state can survive, assuming (as one must) that some jobbery and malpractice is always likely to be present. But as malpractice it does have to be *concealed* and cannot by any means be openly avowed. Thus a duty of fidelity, though not a guarantee of its being respected, is a necessary accompaniment of public office. The possibility of sustaining a functional constitution that is truly compatible with the formal constitution is conditional on very substantial fulfilment of the duty of fidelity by the great majority of office-holders for the greatest part of the time. Where this obtains, we could consider the state as possessing a 'constitution in the plenary sense'.[34] This is one crucially important condition of a constitution's being, as Kelsen put it, by and large efficacious.[35] Hart's thesis that the 'fundamental rule of recognition' had to be accepted 'from the internal point of view' by the officials of a legal system is similar in effect.[36] But his concept of a 'rule of recognition' is

[32] On the risks of unfounded empirical assumptions, see B Tamanaha, *A General Jurisprudence of Law and Society* (Oxford: Oxford University Press, 2001) 58–65.
[33] An exception exists in the case of elected politicians in parliaments and the like who seek election on the basis of support for campaigns of selective civil disobedience, and get elected on this basis.
[34] The idea that wherever functional and formal constitutions largely coincide one can discern a 'constitution in the plenary sense' is proposed in N MacCormick, 'On the Very Idea of a European Constitution: Jurisprudential Reflections from the European Parliament' Juridisk Tidskrift (2001–2) 529–541.   [35] Kelsen, *The Pure Theory of Law* 211–214.
[36] Hart, *Concept of Law* 148.

different from the concept of a 'basic norm' developed here, as an inheritance from Kelsen's line of thought. Hart's idea belongs at a different place in the overall account (see pp 56–57 below).

There is another aspect of the effectiveness of a constitution and of laws. This concerns enforcement rather than obligation as such. The institution of legislation makes possible the formal structuring of public institution-agencies and the conditions of holding office within them. It also makes it possible to formulate as explicit rules the norms of conduct that impose requirements upon both officials and persons acting outside any official capacity. A fundamental place among the law's requirements is held, as we saw already, by the rules about what conduct is wrongful and in this sense prohibited. These subdivide in the modern state into the two classical types of the criminally wrongful, and thus punishable, and the civilly wrongful, and thus subject to civil remedies such as awards of damages.

If the state is to be a theatre of relative civil peace, and if its law is to be a law of peace promising protection to citizens and other residents, it is necessary that most people most of the time refrain from what the law stigmatizes as wrongdoing. It is also, therefore, necessary that the state sustain effective law-enforcement agencies. In relation to punishable crimes, this requires the existence of police forces and prosecution services, courts of criminal jurisdiction, and agencies (prison service, etc) charged with implementing sentences passed by courts upon those convicted after prosecution. In the case of civilly wrongful conduct, effective civil courts must exist, with procedures enabling those who claim to have suffered wrongs to have their claim properly heard in courts that are also open to hear any defence offered by the alleged wrongdoer. There must be effective means of enforcing civil remedies awarded by courts in such cases, through associated public agencies.

To the extent that such institutions exist and function effectively, all persons have reason to take seriously the requirements the law imposes. They have reason to do so whether or not they are personally inclined to endorse the law's requirements as morally desirable or morally obligatory, and whether or not willing to pursue personal preferences where these diverge from what the law requires. There are powerful reasons for conformity, and these can have a daunting reality even for someone who, on good grounds, dissents for fundamental reasons from the state's rules requiring certain conduct. This could be the case in relation to rules upholding apartheid, or requiring denunciation of Jews, or discrimination against ethnic or religious minorities, to take examples that have recent or current grim reality. Evil rules may be enforced rules, and those who perceive the evil, even or especially those who openly resist it, are fully and painfully exposed to the risk or the actuality of enforcement action. The peace of the institutional state and its institutional law is not in every case the peace of justice.

Law-enforcement is not perfectly carried out anywhere, but in every viable state there is necessarily some serious and sustained official effort to enforce most legal requirements against most offenders and against people who have sustained adverse civil judgments but have not observed them. The more there are such serious efforts at enforcement, the more reason citizens and residents have to be law-abiding, both on grounds of prudence and on grounds of reciprocity, for all have reason to suppose that no-one's self-disciplined respect for legal rules simply creates space for others to take unfair advantage. It is not of the essence of law to be a coercive system, as many commentators have claimed.[37] But it is a defining character of states that they are territorial and coercive associations, claiming a monopoly of the legitimate use of coercion within their territories. (Strictly they can sustain this claim to a *legitimate* monopoly only provided they succeed in upholding certain basic human rights, and do not themselves engage in violations of rights or crimes against humanity. Unfortunately those with the least genuine legitimacy are the least likely to admit this, and thus to admit they should forfeit the monopoly they purport to exercise, often with extreme violence.) Hence it is a necessary aspect of state-law that it is coercively enforced through the use, when necessary, of physical means to compel compliance. State law is a coercive as well as an institutional form of normative order.

This has in turn profound implications for the idea of 'institutional normative order' in the theatre of the state. State agencies and the officials that represent or constitute them do not exist only in a shadowy domain of normative reality available to the contemplation of the mind. They are an omnipresent aspect of contemporary societal reality, exercising both coercive and thus also, in a more diffuse way, enormously persuasive impacts on the choices people make. This is how they bear upon human social reality throughout its whole texture. Normative powers are not themselves the same thing as physical power or economic power or the power of social prestige.[38] But empowerment by the law of the state contributes incalculably to all these and other forms of power. Whether this means that law and state are essentially 'violent' institutions is questionable. The argument[39] that constitutions originate in revolutions and at any rate are founded on the threat of violence since there is always a gap between the announcement of a constitution and its acceptance by the populace seems far-fetched. Even what has commenced violently may over time come to function in a mainly peaceable way, though

---

[37] See most recently G Lamond, 'The Coerciveness of Law' Oxford Journal of Legal Studies 20 (2000) 39–62, and 'Coercion and the Nature of Law' Legal Theory 7 (2001) 35–57. Lamond takes issue with my thesis in 'Coercion and Law', ch 12 in N MacCormick *Legal Right and Social Democracy* (Oxford: Clarendon Press, 1982) that legal coercion intervenes at the point of enforcing civil remedies or criminal punishments, but that the existence of provisions for civil remedies and criminal penalties is not itself a form of coercion. He does not, however, engage in any convincing explanation for his rejection of the narrower conception of coercion for which I argue there. He also, in my submission, fails to note that it is the state which is a coercive association, hence state law that is coercive either on his broader or my narrower conception of coercion. Coercion in either sense is a feature of state law, not of all law as such.   [38] Ch 9 below.

[39] J Derrida, 'The Force of Law' in *Deconstruction and the Possibility of Justice* (ed D Cornell et al) (New York: Routledge, 1992) 19 at 36; cf M Davies *Delimiting the Law: 'Postmodernism' and the Politics of Law* (London: Pluto, 1992) 77 and I Ward, *Kantianism, Postmodernism and Critical Legal Thought* (Dordrecht: Kluwer, 1997) 75. Cf Tamanaha, *General Jurisprudence* 65–71.

not without the threat of coercive force against law-breakers. The thesis that all functioning constitutions depend on custom and convention suggests that there is a tendency to diminish violence over time, not that it can ever be eliminated, given the human condition.

Adjudication has already entered the account of institutional normative order. Not only are there institutional agencies (perhaps too grey a term to capture the grandeur and solemnity of a democratic parliament for ordinary purposes, but justified for present theoretical ones) that can and do enact rules of law. Not only are there heads of state and of government, with cabinets of ministers arrayed around them and all manner of ministries and specialized agencies arrayed around the ministers, and local and regional authorities that replicate in defined localities some of the features of the central state. There are also courts and judges, and clusters of surrounding officers of court and other officials. For many approaches to legal theory these are the quintessentially legal institutions, though not all have been as articulate about the reasons for taking what Hamish Ross has called a 'Iudexian' approach as he has been.[40] His argument is that the standpoint of a judge in a highest-level state court is the one that can enable us to discern most clearly the most prominent features of the legal landscape.

We have already seen one critically important reason for tying the idea of law very closely to the idea of a court, at any rate in the context of a discussion of state-law. The enforceability of requirements imposed by legal rules, and other aspects of the recognition of effects of validly exercised legal powers, ties the quality of 'law-ness' to the process of enforcement. The essential function (final cause) or point of courts and the judges who staff them is the hearing and determining of issues for trial under law whenever a binding decision is required on a case competently brought to court. Courts have different types of jurisdiction, for example as between criminal and civil jurisdictions, specialized tribunals in public law or family law or labour disputes, constitutional courts or councils, *Conseils d'Etat* dealing with administrative law in a manner which lies outside the sphere of the judiciary strictly so-called. But it is certainly the case that all law that is regularly enforced law is enforced through some court or court-like agency. So, if it is a defining feature of state law that it is a coercively enforced institutional normative order, then the possession of an institutionalized system of courts and other tribunals is a part of that defining feature.

Moreover, it is important to remember that the concept or term 'law' and its cognates are in day-to-day use within such an order. Usage in this setting generates a specific sense of the term 'law' according to which rules that purport to be legal

---

[40] H Ross, *Law as a Social Institution* (Oxford: Hart Publishing, 2001). Others who implicitly share the view made explicit by Ross include H L A Hart, R Dworkin, and more or less the whole of the 'American Realist' and 'Critical Legal Studies' movement in its North American form. It is perhaps a particular feature of legal theorizing in common law countries to be so strongly judge-centred.

rules count as genuine and valid rules of law belonging to the relevant order only so far as they are recognized and applied by courts and tribunals. If there is some rule purporting to have an appropriate pedigree within some law-making institution, but this is a rule that no tribunal exercising any relevant jurisdiction is considered, or considers itself, duty-bound to apply, can this really be called a rule *of law* within that legal system? Or is it something else? A convention or a guideline or an extra-judicial standard, or, at best, some sort of 'soft law'?

We have at last entered fully into the terrain of Hart's celebrated 'rule of recognition'. Hart's legal theory places at the apex of any legal system the 'ultimate rule of recognition' which contains a ranked set of 'criteria of validity' of law. This rule if it exists at all exists as a complex social fact concerning the mutual acknowledgement of shared and reciprocal attitudes among the superior officials of a legal system. These superior officials must each regard themselves and others as obligated to observe and apply all, and only, the rules that satisfy a specific set of criteria of validity.[41] Clearly, this is normative. The criteria say what ought to be accepted as law, not what is in fact. So an Act of Parliament (for example) is already law even before any Court has been called upon to apply it. For all judges have to acknowledge that whatever parliament enacts is valid as law, and ought to be applied as such.

This theory, not surprisingly, seems to give a good account of the workings of a quite highly centralized state with a tradition of ultimately entrusting all litigation and all criminal causes to a single set of 'common law' courts, the highest of which is technically also one of the houses of the legislature. This is the case in the United Kingdom. There is a single élite corps of judges whose judicial decisions under the doctrine of binding precedent themselves generate a kind of law ('case law'). They have developed a doctrine of the sovereignty of the (monarch in) parliament. Thus all enacted rules validly passed by parliament have to be acknowledged as binding law whatever their content, and whatever else otherwise counts as law has to be considered repealed in the face of a later inconsistent Act of Parliament. In fact, this simplified vision never applied uniformly to the whole United Kingdom, and since the development of the European Union, and with the adoption of the principles of the direct effect and supremacy of European Community Law within the United Kingdom, it has to be severely qualified.[42] As has been pointed out by others, criteria of recognition—and rules of recognition—are court-relative. In federal systems, different courts have different criteria, according to whether they are state or federal courts. In many states, there is a difference between public law tribunals and private law tribunals, and in quasi-federal states there can be other localized differences.[43] So the elegant simplicity of Hart's 'rule

---

[41] Hart, *Concept of Law* 100–109.

[42] For a full account of these and related matters in the spirit of the institutional theory of law, see N MacCormick, *Questioning Sovereignty* (Oxford: Clarendon Press, 1999), especially ch 5.

[43] K Greenawalt, 'Hart's Rule of Recognition and the United States' Ratio Juris 1 (1988) 40–57; cf M Bayles, *Hart's Legal Philosophy* (Dordrecht: Kluwer, 1992) 77–83.

of recognition' theory disqualifies it as a satisfactory general account of law in all constitutional states. If there is a single ultimate rule of every institutional normative order that is the law of a state, it cannot be a rule of recognition. Courts and tribunals of all sorts must indeed have criteria of recognition that identify what rules their members are duty-bound to apply as law in the discharge of their specific constitutional functions, and there must be some overall coherence among various court hierarchies within a single state. But achieving that coherence is a task for the constitution and for constitutional law (or even for constitutional politics). If anything could be regarded as a single and unitary ultimate rule for a state's legal system as such, it would have to be the rule that the constitution as a whole must be respected. This brings us back to a new variant on Kelsen's *Grundnorm*, not a version of Hart's rule of recognition.

As acknowledged above, it is indeed the case that the character of state-law as enforced law is crucially affected by the fact that enforcement in individual cases has to be mediated through the judgments of courts and tribunals. This entails that the law as it is enforced is necessarily the law as the courts interpret it, their orders and decisions being necessary steps towards its being enforced. The courts inevitably have a power of interpretation, and thus a power to further determine the law's meaning as it passes from general constitutional norms that empower legislative acts, through legislative acts that institute general rules of law, to judicial decisions. Their interpretative decisions give such norms and enacted rules concrete meaning for specific cases, whether or not any doctrine of respect for precedents, or practice of respecting them, in turn clothes these decisions of the courts with a kind of law-making effect for future cases.

'What is the law?' can be a general question of legal theory, or it can be a practical question posed inside a state's legal order concerning the requirements that apply to some person in a concrete situation. In the latter sense, there is little value in an answer that fails to attend carefully to the conclusions about validity of rules, and the interpretations of valid rules and relevant precedents, that the judges have handed down or are likely to hand down. This would be important, for example, in the case of a professional legal adviser advising a client. That the law, for these practical purposes, is what the courts and judges say it is, is a trivial truth. This does not however apply in the same way to the general theoretical question. Judges have no particular standing as legal theorists, despite their necessary authority as practical jurists.[44]

The theory of institutional normative order enables us to survey legal orders in all their manifestations and to note, for example, differences from system to system in the rules and practices concerning recognition of binding precedents. This in turn makes it possible to see what specially privileged status attaches to a judge's

---

[44] R Dworkin takes a sharply different view on this, holding that the question 'What is law?' is always a practical question, indeed always the same practical question, no matter who asks or answers it. Discussion of this point is deferred till ch 16—see n 8 and accompanying text there.

'law-saying' on particular practical questions within that judge's defined jurisdiction (law-saying competence) in some particular system. The theory thus stands above and apart from particular law-sayings of a jurisdiction-bound kind in offering a view of the general character of the normative orders in which binding jurisdictions are found.

3.5 Civil Society and the State: Introduction

Constitutions and sub-constitutional public law are not alone sufficient to constitute or facilitate the existence of civil society within and alongside the state. Civil society is that state of affairs in which persons can interact reciprocally with each other as at least formally equal beings, however different individuals may be in character, beliefs, origins, and resources. Civil society is the context of voluntary associations and of economic activity among free persons. The activity envisaged includes orientation both to non-commercial ends (religion, philanthropy, political speculation and mobilization, environmentalism and the like) and to commercial or economic ones. Civil society requires the secure existence of an effectively guaranteed body of law. This means that the constitutional obligations of courts must include the obligation to uphold and apply an adequate body of private law, including commercial law, and criminal law. These are bodies of law that sustain the framework for civil society, and they exist alongside explicit constitutional law and those other subordinate parts of public law that regulate agencies of state. Such a body of law amounts to a set of articulated and express rules (supplemented or not by precedents and the partly implicit rules of case-law) concerning persons, things (property rights and succession rights), obligations among private persons, and forms of action whereby to enforce private obligations and vindicate private rights. There must also be a corpus of rules defining the forms of criminal wrongdoing, and generally prohibiting wilful commission of crimes, with authorization of public officers to instigate appropriate judicial intervention and trial in the event of alleged breaches of criminal law. In commercial law must be handled the specialities of corporate personality and the rights and obligations arising thereunder, as well as employment rights and powers. Powers and obligations involved in commercial transactions must be defined, and connected again to provisions for regulated litigation before the courts, or before arbitrators with powers partly defined by general commercial law, partly by private commercial agreements.

To the extent that the courts and other official agencies do actually respect and uphold these bodies of law, as well as, and in the spirit of, the constitution, state law acquires that institutional reality of which we have spoken. The particular institutions of private and commercial law that were mentioned earlier acquire the actuality that effectively constrains action by imposing requirements on it. This constraining actuality is a practically unavoidable counterpart to their normativity

as rules that have formal validity and thus enforceability within the whole constitutional system. This does not presuppose either that all persons affected have fair
or equal opportunities of participation in civil society or in the advantages it
makes available to some at least of its members. Nor does it imply that all persons
who are institutionally bound by the law are either fully aware of it, or consider
themselves bound in conscience by it, or endorse it as a scheme of interpersonal
justice. But it seems to be a practical necessity that some should, and a high
probability that those who find the burdens imposed by law to be at least compen-
sated by the benefits it confers will, accept the law as binding on moral as well as
prudential grounds. Such individuals and groups can be considered as autonomously
endorsing the law and freely acknowledging the binding character of the legal
norms involved. Persons in that position typically find their mutual expectations,
and their other-directed normative expectations, reinforced by official action. For
such persons, the security provided by regular, even if not invariable, official
enforcement of law confers a further sense of legitimacy on the norms endorsed
and the expectations and judgments founded on the norms.

It is true indeed that without effective political power, and effective political
co-ordination among power-holders, a state cannot be kept in existence. It is likewise true that a constitution and a constitutional state cannot exist without power
that upholds the norms both of the constitution itself and of the whole legal
system that the constitution validates as binding law for officials and citizens alike.
Yet popular legitimacy is a powerful source of political power. Human beings are
led by opinion more than by force, and the opinion that power is being exercised
under law is a notable inducement to accept as legitimately in authority those who
do in fact exercise effective political power over the state's claimed territory. So law
can contribute to power perhaps almost as much as power contributes to law,
wherever people subscribe to an ideology that proclaims the value of rational
government under law.[45] For then even the most cynical and deviously motivated
public official has a strong motivation to act out the public observances of
commitment to law, however little these may truly express an inward motivation
of the private will.

3.6 Conclusion: Law as Institutional Normative Order

The constitution and sub-constitutional law of any state amount to a huge quantity of normative material. Yet we are now in a position to see how the institutions
they establish create the basis for the formalization and articulation of these very
rules and many other rules for the conduct of human life and affairs for citizens

---

[45] M Loughlin, 'Ten Tenets of Sovereignty', in N Walker (ed), *Sovereignty in Transition* 55–86,
at 75–76, incorrectly ascribes to me a denial of the views expressed in this and the preceding
paragraph.

and members of civil society. The normative quality of the whole depends on a conventional norm according to which all persons holding public office ought to observe and uphold the constitution and the laws validly made under it. Observance of this conventional or customary basic norm is essential to the existence of a constitutional state in which the rule of law can thrive—that is, a 'law-state' or *Rechtsstaat*. By virtue of this, a vast array of rules and principles are in force within the territory of the state, and these determine the legal position of all persons within the jurisdiction of that state, and the legal relations that obtain between all the persons, in ways that may or not be of conscious concern to them from time to time. The same goes, *mutatis mutandis*, for polities within the state, such as England, Wales, Scotland and Northern Ireland within the United Kingdom, or the Länder within Germany, or autonomous regions within Spain, and for confederal polities or commonwealths that bring together many states on a basis of shared and divided sovereignty, as in the European Union.

4

A Problem: Rules or Habits?

4.1 Introduction

The account of norms, rules and principles given so far in this book suggests that norms are most fundamentally to be viewed from the perspective of norm-users rather than that of norm-givers. In this, it draws considerably on the work of H L A Hart, particularly in relation to what he called the 'internal aspect' of rules and rule-governed conduct.[1] What Hart argued was that, when rules are in operation, not merely can we see externally observable regularities in people's behaviour, we can also look from the inside, as it were, and see that there is a reason for the regularities. For example, we do not only see people standing in a row; we also infer that each has taken her or his place in a queue for some service. Hart said this depended on a 'critical reflective attitude' of participants in the pattern of behaviour, who take this pattern to be a standard for judging their own and others' conduct. Another example is that of behaviour at traffic lights.[2] You stand at an intersection and watch what is going on. As a statistician you might produce observations according to which 99.9% of vehicles stop as they approach the intersection when the light is red, while one or two fail to do so. According to Hart, this could justify the conclusion, 'People in this city have a habit of stopping at traffic lights'. As everyone knows, however, that is not the whole truth. Red traffic lights are not only a sign from which we can infer or predict the likely stopping of vehicles. Looked at from the drivers' point of view, a red light is a signal to them to stop. Most drivers act on the signal, and do stop when the lights change to, or are at, red. Seeing it in this way, one realizes that people have a set of 'critical reflective' views about driving cars, including such an attitude to the pattern expressed by: 'stop when the light is red'.

---

[1] H L A Hart, *The Concept of Law* (Oxford: Clarendon Press, 2nd edn, 1994); cf N MacCormick, *H L A Hart* (London: Edward Arnold, 1981). For valuable criticism of Hart's version of the internal/external distinction, including criticism of the use to which Joseph Raz and I have put this, see B Z Tamanaha, *Realistic Socio-Legal Theory* (Oxford: Clarendon Press, 1997) 180–181. Throughout the present work, I have tried to avoid the errors identified by Tamanaha.

[2] Hart, *The Concept of Law* 87–8.

This is a good clear illustration of Hart's point. But how convincing is it? What if someone were to object in such terms as these:

> That sounds clear enough, but as a matter of fact, I do just have a habit of stopping at the traffic lights. I never think about it. I just see a traffic light at red and I stop. There's no mediation through critical reflective attitudes or any of that kind of stuff, it's just 'there's a red light and you stop without thinking', and that seems to me to be what everyone does.

The beginning of an answer would be to point out that when you are learning to drive you are taught, indeed when you are learning to be a pedestrian you are taught, that cars *have to* stop when the lights are red. Also, you mustn't walk across the road until they're red, and perhaps until the green man signal appears. What you have to learn is a rule about the right way to drive and a similar one about sensible safety precautions for pedestrians. And certainly, when somebody does jump the lights, or is slow to take off when they change, or engages in jaywalking, there is a blaring of horns from all around. Other road users give vent to a sharply critical response, even if not a particularly 'reflective' one. So far, so good—but this does not really show the claimed contrast between rule and habit.

4.2 Habit and Rule Reconsidered

Here, it is important to pick up a point by Martin Krygier,[3] namely that, while it is true and important that rules and rule-governed behaviour have what Hart called this 'internal aspect', so do habits. In *The Concept of Law*, Hart was insistent that 'habit' is a kind of external observer's concept, as in the example of one who makes statistical reports on the stopping behaviour of cars or their drivers.[4] This belongs to the conception of 'habit' that Hart ascribed to John Austin.[5] Under this conception, we are simply interested in detecting regular patterns in what happens, and we can construct statistical reports, thus discovering what people habitually do, and that does not involve anything other than a purely 'external' view of what is going on. That John Austin's theory of law is cast in terms of such an external view is central to Hart's critique of it. While Austin defines 'sovereigns' in terms of subjects' habit of obedience to them, and defines laws as sovereigns' commands, Hart insists that what has to be in operation is more than a mere habit of obedience (statistical regularity of obedient behaviour). Behind it all must lie

---

[3] M Krygier, '*The Concept of Law* and Social Theory' (1982) 2 Oxford Journal of Legal Studies 2 (1982) 155–80 especially at 170–171: 'as we know, many people are quite attached to their habits'—but habits are not the kind of thing you 'obey', as Krygier pointedly observes.

[4] *The Concept of Law* 55–60.

[5] J Austin, *The Province of Jurisprudence Determined* (ed W E Rumble) (Cambridge: Cambridge University Press, 1995) chs 1 and 2. R Moles suggests, rather convincingly, that Hart misrepresents Austin's conception of a habit. See R N Moles, *Definition and Rule in Legal Theory: a reassessment of H L A Hart and the positivist tradition* (Oxford: Basil Blackwell, 1987).

a rule that gives some kind of authority to the one who gives the orders and is obeyed.

Krygier makes the counter-point that such a characterization of habits is not actually right. Habits belong in the same domain of discourse as rules. Each can be used to account for what we do, though of course the accounts they give differ— but they differ from inside the 'internal point of view'. People can become very attached to their habits, and can act on the basis of their comfortable habits without thinking they are following any kind of a rule, just as they can be very committed to acting in accordance with rules that they hold dear. People can get annoyed when their habits are disrupted, just as they get annoyed when the rules are flouted. It is annoying when the road you normally take to work has to be blocked for repairs or to dig up gas-pipes or whatever. This disrupts your habit and (in perhaps only a small way) upsets or irritates you. Similarly, if the newsagent has run out of copies of your normal daily paper. People have all sorts of habits, and are comfortable with them. Rules matter to us, but habits matter to us also, and one's habits can be a reason for doing things as much as rules can. So there are many important points to be made about the internal point of view, but just treating it as a mark of a difference between rules and habits isn't quite the right way to take this forward.

This can be connected also to grander philosophical themes. Consider Aristotle's[6] contention that the mark of the really good person is that she or he acts well out of habit rather than out of reflection. To put this more colloquially, if you want to find a really good person, somebody whose presence you really value, you don't want one of those people that are always wrestling with their duty—people who wrestle with their duty often don't do it. You want the people who unreflectively do the right thing. Aristotle discusses how this comes about, and concludes that over time people can *learn* the habits of virtue. To begin with, you're taught, you're pressurized by your peers and parents and teachers and the like. (An example drawn from the present book could be that they insist that you stand in line and take your turn and learn about not always pushing to the front.) Later, perhaps you think through the moral reasons that apply in the given situation, and decide what it is right to do in this case. Consciously, even effortfully, you shape your conduct accordingly. After a time, however, if you do keep making the effort, it gets easier. You come to acquire the habit of doing the right thing without much thought or effort. Aristotle's point is that the really good people are the habitually good, not the thoughtful and reflectively good. They have done their thinking and reflecting, and they have done it to good effect, so that good behaviour is now 'second nature'.

By contrast, Kant would contend that the only wholly good thing is a good will, which is to say, the will shaping itself in accordance with duty for the sake of

---

[6] Aristotle, *Nicomachean Ethics* (many edns) Book II, ch 1.

duty.[7] Perhaps one can make something of an argument that Kant would approve of somebody who had acquired a settled habit of doing their duty, and regard this settled habit as an instance of the good will.[8] Even so, there remains a real contrast between the stress on active self-regulation by the autonomous decision-maker, and the Aristotelian picture of the person who acts habitually in (for example) the way the categorical imperative commands. The latter does so out of a standing disposition rather than moment-by-moment critical reflective consideration of situations of choice, with conscious acts of will-formation involved in making one's choices. We are left entertaining the question whether 'habit' is in this way of ethical and potentially jurisprudential interest and indeed value.

Let us reflect again on Austin's *Province of Jurisprudence Determined* and his thesis about the sovereign and the habit of obedience. This is well known, and has been convincingly refuted by thinkers as diverse as James Bryce[9] and H L A Hart.[10] Less well known is Austin's *Plea for the Constitution*,[11] in which he advances the arch-conservative view he held in his later years about constitutional reform in the United Kingdom. There is an interesting sideline there on 'habits'. Austin does not simply say that, as a matter of definition, we have law where there is a sovereign and the sovereign is the person or body to whom the people are in the habit of obedience. He says that it is a good thing when people have a habit of following law. The only safe way to have law is where people unreflectively and habitually accept the orders issued by their superiors. There is a strong echo of David Hume[12] in this reflection of Austin's. If you are interested in constitutional stability, if you are interested in what makes legal systems work well, don't seek a critical reflective population; seek an habitually and unreflectively law-abiding population.

That is one element in Austin's argument against talk of any further constitutional reform beyond the enfranchisement of the (upper) middle classes that had been achieved in the UK by the Reform Act of 1832. Talk of reform, he thought, was apt to make people reflect on the rationale for the order of government as it currently is, and could lead to the masses misunderstanding that rationale. Ordinary working people would be stimulated into having thoughts above their

---

[7] J Ladd (trans), *Kant: The Metaphysical Elements of Justice* (Indianapolis, Ind: Bobbs-Merrill, 1965) 10–14.

[8] But see, for example, O O'Neill, *Towards Justice and Virtue* (Cambridge: Cambridge University Press, 1996) ch 7.

[9] J Bryce, *Studies in History and Jurisprudence* (Oxford: Clarendon Press, 1901), vol II at 537–541.   [10] Hart, *The Concept of Law* 50–78.

[11] J Austin, *A Plea for the Constitution* (London, 1859) discussed by W L Morison, *John Austin* (London: Edward Arnold, 1982) 122–125 responding to Eira Ruben, 'John Austin's Political Pamphlets 1824–1859', in E Attwooll (ed), *Perspectives in Jurisprudence* (Glasgow: Glasgow University Press, 1977) especially at 20–21.

[12] See, eg, Hume, *Essays*, at 37: 'Habit soon consolidates what other principles of human nature had imperfectly founded; and men once accustomed to obedience, never think of departing from that path, in which they and their ancestors have constantly trod . . .'.

station in life, and might be led into courses of action that are damaging to the general utility, and thus to their own prospects of happiness. They would want to change things that in their own true interest ought not to be changed.

So there's another point: it seems not just to be the case that the dividing line between rules and habits is less significant than Hart suggested. The point is that there may even be something to be said for habits as more valuable than rules. You could put this in a more pleasingly Aristotelian way, or in a disagreeably reactionary Austinian way. You could find similar arguments in F A Hayek.[13] All in all, you might begin to think there is more to be said about habits and their place in constitutional, legal and political thought than the orthodox jurisprudence of the past half-century has allowed.

Sundram Soosay makes this very argument, and connects it to contemporary work in the cognitive sciences and psychology.[14] He argues that we should take much, or most, of what analytical jurists have written about law-as-a-system-of-rules with a substantial pinch of salt, especially the bits which purport to be or to pass as sociological observations, or that presuppose inexplicit and unproven psychological theses. This is a serious point. For example, in one passage in *The Concept of Law* Hart says that Kelsen must be wrong in his claim that the primary form of law is a sanction-stipulating norm. To give an example of what Kelsen meant, take the case of theft. Kelsen says that the primary form of a law against theft says that if a person steals, they ought to be convicted, and on conviction they ought to be sentenced to a term of prison not exceeding a certain maximum. This exhibits the real character of law as a specific social technique, said Kelsen, and the so-called 'duty not to steal' is merely derivative. It is a secondary inference from law in its primary form, and likewise all powers conferred by law can be understood as more or less elaborate conditions concerning the lawful imposition of sanctions.

Hart's objection to all this is trenchant: ' . . . power conferring rules are thought of, spoken of, and used in social life differently from rules which impose duties, and they are valued for different reasons'.[15] Yet this in turn is a very rash claim when you think of it. There has been some controversy in the light of Nicola Lacey's biography of Hart concerning how far he did take much interest, or should have taken a greater interest, in the descriptive sociology to which he makes reference in the preface to *The Concept of Law*.[16] But much of what he says about attitudes to rules amounts to empirical assertions not backed by empirical

---

[13] F A Hayek, *Law, Legislation and Liberty: A New Statement of the Liberal Principles of Justice and Political Economy* (London: Routledge & Kegan Paul, 1982) at Vol I (*Rules and Order*), ch 5, where he argues that unreflective customary law that has evolved through precedents is usually preferable to statute law.

[14] See S Soosay, 'Is the Law an Affair of Rules?' in Australian Legal Philosophy Students Association, *2005 Annual Publication* (Brisbane, 2005; <http://www.alpsa.net/r-annual.htm>) 24–40. Cf Soosay, *Skills, Habits and Expertise in the Life of the Law* (Edinburgh: Edinburgh University PhD Thesis, 2005). [15] *The Concept of Law* 41.

[16] See N Lacey, *A Life of H L A Hart: The Nightmare and the Noble Dream* (Oxford: Oxford University Press, 2004) 228–233, 336–337.

evidence. Soosay contends that, whatever was the case in 1961, there are now available extensive resources of modern psychology and, in particular, of cognitive science. What the cognitive scientists have shown is that the human mind, the human brain, is capable of adjusting itself to all sorts of behavioural and other problems, precisely by way of routinizing, that is, forming habits.

We might consider something which is an effortfully-acquired skill to begin with. Learning to drive a car would be a case in point. In relation to such activities, it has been shown that the brain develops cognitive pathways that eliminate the effort and enable the learner gradually to cope with problem cases in what becomes a routine way. This process depresses from consciousness what was initially a matter of consciously following rules or other patterns. In the context of driving, let us return to the example of a red traffic light. When you are a learner driver, dealing with traffic signals is an emotionally fraught experience. You are still having to think consciously about de-clutching and changing down, then applying the brake and putting the gears into neutral at the same time as watching other cars and pedestrians and keeping a lookout for traffic signals and their colour-changes. When you first approach a controlled intersection, even though you understand the meanings of the different colours and their combinations, you undergo a frightening experience, for you are having to do so many things at the same time, and to do them correctly. You must act correctly both in a technical sense to achieve proper control of your car and correctly in the legal sense, so as not to jump the lights or sail through them in blithe unawareness of what is going on around you. That's all pretty hard stuff and, while learning, we have all watched with envy our more accomplished contemporaries who can really drive and who are not reduced to near panic by the sudden appearance of a traffic signal switching from amber to red.

Yet most who have undergone this experience emerge as competent and (more or less) law-abiding drivers themselves. Cognitive scientists have offered an explanation of how this comes about. Crudely put, they tell us that brains habituate themselves to new skills by working out a routine. That starts with being taught the technical requirements and the rules, and then getting to the point where you have mastered the technical skills and have completely internalized the rules. By this stage, they are no longer a part of the content of your conscious mind, which is thereby freed for less routine matters like planning a route to your destination and figuring out how to handle the business you will do there, or whatever. Final acquisition of the skill marks the point at which the rules, which are sort of props, disappear from sight. It's a bit like Wittgenstein's ladder that you climb up and then throw away. That's the sort of picture you should have. Rules may be tools for learning skills, but the skills once learnt transcend the rules.

Quite apart from the technical evidence, this seems very convincing to ordinary common sense when we are thinking about physical skills like driving a car or playing golf (learning how to swing a golf club and all that sort of thing). Does it also apply to law, or other domains of what is obviously in some way normative? I take a piece of coloured plastic out of my wallet. We all know that this object functions as a way of getting credit while shopping. It works in this way because of the law of contract and because of a huge standard-form contract that everyone signs but probably no more than a tiny minority of card-users ever reads. This sets the terms of the contract between the card-user and the credit company, or the bank, along with further conditions imposed by current consumer credit legislation.

There seem to be many relevant legal norms here. In their light, this is not simply a piece of coloured plastic but a credit card which enables its user to purchase goods on credit provided that in due course the debt so incurred is paid, along with any interest that has accrued. They are norms of which most credit card-users are largely or entirely ignorant. But those users certainly have well-established and relevant habits. On the basis of the cognitive psychologists' studies that I mentioned before, the Soosay account demands to know what is it that makes people like me keep saying, 'Yes, but it's the rules that make sense of the credit card'? What makes me so sure that these are the necessary infrastructure, the necessary scaffolding around credit card purchases? The fact is that people use cards without thinking about the rules. That's how the credit industry works, because people don't hang themselves up on the rules. They just know how to use their card, they have a PIN number, they have a broad idea of what their debts are, how they are piling up, and how they are going to repay them. Some people get into a terrible mess with them, but the system works because most people can handle debt, not because they are thinking about rules. It works because they are not thinking about them, but have acquired routines that enable them to handle this financial-cum-legal facility without excessive thought.

What makes the modern credit economy work, it could be argued, is the absence of thought about rules, not the presence of thought about rules. So if we are interested in *The Concept of Law* in the light of its author's claim to be engaging in descriptive sociology as well as philosophical analysis, there is a bit of a difficulty here. It is not just that ordinary life actually works without much regard to the vast array of rules that regulate credit cards and their use. The fact is that the way the human being or the human brain functions requires the putting aside of these things, the learning of the skills, and then the forgetting of the scaffolding. What is most interesting about rules is the way they are *not* thought of, spoken about, or consciously used at all in social life when it is working smoothly.

Taking together the points gathered from Krygier, Aristotle, Austin and Soosay, there is clearly a case for the re-evaluation of 'habits' in life and in law. Habits are the outward evidence of our brains' adaptation to repetitive features of the environment we dwell in. That we are able most of the time to rely on them without suffering nasty surprises is what makes ordinary life possible, and frees us to apply thoughtful intelligence where it is needed, to actually or potentially surprising or problematic incidents and situations. Niklas Luhmann's sociology of law makes

a similar point about the need for 'redundancy' and the reduction of surprise
which systems like that of the law achieve.[17]

It might be said that any explicit formulation of a rule that is supposed to capture
the point of some habitual settled practice is bound to be somewhat artificial.
Actually, a simple example is to be found in my attempt to formulate a norm
about queuing. It seemed plausible to say that many people follow the practice of
lining up for services without ever formulating any explicit rule about it, and that
once one tries to formulate a rule about it, there is no great likelihood that any
formulation will seem right to all or more than a few participants. Pierre Bourdieu
makes the point that anthropologists from one culture who undertake field studies of another culture and try to describe it in terms of its implicit rules inevitably
mis-describe it just because the participants do not themselves formulate explicit
rules.[18] Typically, rules only get formulated in real life once a practice is beginning
to break down or be questioned.

We might add, though, that institutionalization is clearly a context in which
explicit rule-formulation takes place, for reasons of the kind discussed in relation
to the example of the supermarket queue at the delicatessen counter, or in relation
to airport security. All the more so is the context of the contemporary constitutional state a theatre of overwhelming outputs of formulated rules. These are formulated by the legislature, formulated by the executive or by local authorities
using delegated powers, formulated by railway companies, formulated as standard
terms of consumer contracts, formulated in EC Regulations and Directives, and
so on and so on. It is not conceivable that any lay citizen—or indeed any lawyer—
should have detailed awareness of any more than a tiny fraction—or any at all—of
this colossal bundle of rule-texts. What then becomes of the 'internal point
of view'? How can a discussion of informal normative practices like queuing
contribute anything at all to an understanding of the point and uses of these
largely unknown texts? What can they contribute to human social existence?

4.3 Habits about Rules

One answer to this is to refer back to the thesis advanced in chapter 3 that underlying any viable constitutional order there has to be a practice or convention that
could be formulated in terms of a rule that the constitution and laws binding
under it ought to be observed. We saw that there is good reason to hold that no
one purporting to hold and exercise public office under a constitution could
coherently make an open denial of allegiance to such a rule once formulated,

---

[17] N Luhmann, *Law as a Social System* (trans K A Ziegert) (Oxford: Oxford University Press,
2004) 60–62.
[18] See P Bourdieu, *Outline of a Theory of Practice* (trans R Nice) (Cambridge: Cambridge
University Press, 1977) 2.

however corruptly they might be willing to behave in secret. A working constitutional order obviously depends on the active allegiance of most office-holders, and on an effort to sustain mutual checks and balances in a coherent way. Institutionalized legal orders depend on habits about rules, that is, on habitual reference in some contexts to special sorts of text like those in the statute book and those in the law reports.

This involves the maintenance of a standing practical attitude towards institutionally established rule-texts (statutes, precedents, or whatever) when these are cited and brought to attention as relevant to some context. Lawyers engaged in litigation or in prosecuting crime have to draw to the attention of a court the provisions of statutes, precedents and the like that they consider relevant for the case they have to make. Public officials, according to their area of responsibility, have to keep themselves informed of the materials that govern their powers and duties in the area in question, and should notify citizens of relevant requirements when necessary. Lawyers in private practice have to maintain a substantial expertise about the bodies of established law that bear upon their clients' business or relate to their complaints or possible litigation. And so on. The habit or practical disposition of personnel engaged in legal work must include a disposition to give respect to and seek respect for any relevant provisions found in the texts of valid statutes and binding precedents, read in the light of the principles and values to which they give expression. (Perhaps in some cases this will be more a matter of finding a way round them, acknowledging that they do exist and could be a kind of trap.)

Such statutes and precedents, validated by the constitution, apply according to their terms to many, many people—citizens and permanent or temporary residents—who are largely or even completely ignorant of the legal rules they contain, certainly at the level of detail. To the extent that rules embody reasonable and popularly supportable principles, the rules in their application may be expected not to occasion excessive surprise or resentment. But that would be a long way short of any kind of active engagement in a 'critical reflective attitude' about every legal rule all the time.

Brian Tamanaha has documented one case of a contemporary constitutionalist state —Micronesia, in particular the island of Yap—where there is, in exactly the way I have suggested above, a working constitution and a viable and effective state apparatus. Yet here the 'citizens' of the state carry on with family and business life and almost all their affairs on the basis of a normative order wholly different from that of the state—one expressive of immemorial custom. They interact with the state officials and accept their rulings and decisions to the extent that this happens to be practically necessary. But apart from that, state-law does not touch their consciousness at all.[19] To what extent apparently more 'normal' states—eg, the

---

[19] B Z Tamanaha, *A General Jurisprudence of Law and Society* (Oxford: Oxford University Press, 2001) 145–146, drawing on B Z Tamanaha, *Understanding Law in Micronesia: an Interpretive*

UK—really differ in this respect from Yap is an open empirical question. Common sense suggests that countries like the UK or France probably differ somewhat, for example in not having a single entire customary code running in parallel with their 'official' law. The habits of many people in many sections of society probably do chime reasonably well with the norms of the official law, but there may be many sections of society in which this is far from how things are. This, however, is at best a matter of mere armchair observation, not supported by any sort of methodologically respectable empirical study. Tamanaha rightly suggests that work on such topics would be highly significant and informative, and he has sketched some possible approaches to conducting such research.[20]

4.4 Mind the Gap!

On the London Underground, some station platforms are aligned rather far back from the rail carriages when these are stopped in the station. 'Mind the Gap!' says a disembodied voice over the station public address system as trains come into these stations and draw to a halt, exposing dismounting passengers to the risk of a nasty fall between train and platform. A similar warning should be applied to works of doctrinal scholarship in law, including works of institutionalist jurisprudence, for reasons now explored. The very fact of institutionalization of legislative power means that the results of exercise of that power may be statutory texts that are very imperfectly, if at all, observed as working norms from any norm-user's point of view. Conventional norms cannot diverge much from what people actually do, because their existence is determined by what people actually do. Institutionalized norms can so diverge, even if the basis of their institutionalization does depend on a common habit of respect for the constitution, and even if the latter habit is quite widespread.

Potentially, or indeed actually, there are two kinds of gap that we should bear in mind.[21] First, judges and lawyers and other court officials are likely to have their own routines and habits and ways of carrying out their official or professional work. Even if these start out from the kind of rule-learning that car-driving lessons involve, the formal rules will come to be modified and overlaid with other considerations and habits in the overall folk-ways of working legal life in any real setting.

Approach to Transplanted Law (Leiden: Brill Publishers, 1993); cf A Watson, *Legal Transplants: An Approach to Comparative Law* (Athens, Ga: University of Georgia Press, 2nd edn, 1993).

[20] Tamanaha, *General Jurisprudence* 131–155.

[21] For an already classical account, see D Nelken, 'The "Gap Problem" in the Sociology of Law: A Theoretical Review' Windsor Yearbook of Access to Justice 1 (1981) 35–61, concluding about the way in which '[a relevant] investigation may include a concern over the way in which politicians, officials and others come to make certain claims on behalf of the law, the factors which affect their achievement and the extent to which such a "gap" is perceived by others in society' (60). Tamanaha, *General Jurisprudence* 131–132 brings the story up-to-date.

Moreover, at least some legal practitioners will surely regard (and think themselves right to regard) the official rules as obstacles set in the way of their clients' pursuit of business. So they will tend to 'respect' these rule-texts only by finding ways of circumventing them without actual breaches taking place or being obvious—they do not approach them as norms that indicate patterns of behaviour that they think desirable in themselves. The great 'American Realist' Karl Llewellyn drew attention to this kind of thing long ago.[22] Since then, there has been a great deal of interesting work in the sociology of law and the sociology of the legal profession, as well as in criminology, that explores and gives evidence for these and other possibilities of 'gaps' between enacted law and practised law, even within the law-work of officials and professionals.[23] Moreover, there is a fair amount of cultural variability between different national cultures and among different sub-cultures within states that apparently influences the general approach, perhaps not to the idea that laws ought in some sense to be respected, but certainly to the question of what counts as due respect.[24] Successful lawyers in private practice of the law do not ignore the law—of course not. But their success in practice derives from a great deal more practical knowledge, know-how, and wisdom than could be gleaned from however voluminous a grasp of the whole body of statute law, whether or not supplemented with voracious reading of cases and precedents.

The second sense of the 'gap' is the one particularly flagged-up by Tamanaha, the 'efficacy gap', as one might call it.[25] However legal professionals and legal officials negotiate their way around the law, it is very much an open question how much of the official law is any part of the working consciousness of laypersons. It is also questionable to what extent their sense of what is right and proper depends on, and how far it diverges from, what the official law enjoins either in the sense of abstract texts or in the mediated form filtered through professional and official practice. A philosophical jurist engaged in an interpretive-analytical inquiry concerning institutions of law has to acknowledge that such gaps are inevitable, while conceding that the inquiry in hand contributes nothing to our comprehension of the extent of either sort of gap in any particular case.

Why go on then? There are two answers to this. First, it has to be noted that there is a large conceptual framework which is available to people to appeal to, and to which they do frequently appeal. People know they have rights and occasionally they assert them. People know there are things that are crimes, and usually seek to avoid committing them, at least when detection is at all likely. They know what

---

[22] K N Llewellyn, 'The Normative, the Legal and the Law-Jobs' Yale Law Journal 49 (1940) 1355–1400 and *The Bramble Bush* (New York: Oceana, 1951); see also W Twining, *Karl Llewellyn and the American Realist Movement* (London: Weidenfeld and Nicolson, 1973) 170–203.

[23] See citations in Nelken and Tamanaha, n 21 above.

[24] Cf D Nelken, 'Changing Legal Cultures' in M B Likosky (ed), *Transnational Legal Processes* (London: Butterworths, 2002) 41–58.

[25] Tamanaha, *General Jurisprudence* 131 (advising against any too strong assimilation of the 'gap' in this sense and the other sense considered here).

belongs to them and wish others to respect their belongings. If challenged by a police officer they may indignantly say that what they have been doing is quite within their rights. The language of right and wrong, of rights and duties, of property and theft, is part of ordinary everyday currency as any reading of daily newspapers or popular novels, or any viewing of television soap-operas makes totally obvious. Of course, people get exercised about these things only episodically—they are not rights-monsters always brooding about their rights. But, quite often, their rights and others' wrongs matter to them quite acutely. So how do they know about these rights and wrongs? What is there to know? Must we read these concepts through the interpretative framework of 'institutional normative order' as this has been explained so far? The answer to that question is in the affirmative, and it is an answer expounded extensively in part 2 of this book, starting in the next chapter.

The second answer to the question of why to go on with the institutional account notwithstanding the admitted 'gap' problems depends on certain other highly salient features of life in contemporary conditions. There are states, and they do exercise territorial governmental power, even while increasingly acknowledging international standards of acceptable conduct that are binding on the state authorities. There are new phenomena in the way of organized state-unions such as the European Union that challenge traditional political and legal categories, and lead one to drop dark remarks about their 'sui generic' character, on the basis that they seem to be organizations 'of their own kind', not neatly assignable to any existing category.[26] There are transnational corporations and there is an ever more globalized economy, yet even these transnationals have to have some home base in some state and to acknowledge legal conditions for recognition of corporate activity wherever they engage in trade.

Even when we talk about society, we are very often apt to prefix it with a state or national label—'British society . . . ', 'French society . . . ', 'Ghanaian society . . . ', 'Malaysian society . . . ', and so on. State and society are not identical concepts, but they are overlapping contexts of human existence and activity. Another interesting prefix we may add to 'society' is 'civil'—'civil society'. The significance of this is that there seem to be many and intimate connections between law, state, and civil society. The special point about civil society, as the name suggests, is the civility that can obtain among persons who are relative strangers to each other—or even complete strangers.[27] Civility is the opposite of

---

[26] N MacCormick, *Who's afraid of a European Constitution?* (Exeter: Imprint Academic, 2005); also 'The European Constitutional Process: A Theoretical View' *Anales de la Cátedra Francisco Suárez* 39 (2005) 299–319.

[27] There is more to civility than a mere absence of violence and extensiveness of trust, though these are indeed essential to it. See P Selznick, *The Moral Commonwealth* (Berkeley/Los Angeles/London: University of California Press, 1992) 387–427: 'Civility governs diversity, protects autonomy, and upholds toleration' (at 387); M Krygier, *Civil Passions* (Melbourne, Victoria: Black Inc, 2005)

the state of actual or potential war of all against all that Thomas Hobbes typified as being the 'state of nature' which humans would have to endure where the state had broken down.[28] (We should remember that Hobbes himself lived through a bitter and violent civil war, so knew by direct acquaintance what he was talking about.) Civility is a condition in which people may go unarmed about their business, having no special reason to fear violence from those they happen to meet. They also have some reason to suppose that threats to upset this state of affairs will be countered by police action organized through the state on behalf of civil society.

Where a condition of civil society obtains, a discourse of politics is possible. People can try to resolve differences by arguments, debates and votes, not with drawn swords. Also, they can enter into dealings with strangers and take part in all sorts of trade and exchange, relying on some state or union for a tolerably stable currency as a medium of exchange, and for a court system that will if necessary enforce broken contracts. Not merely does civility make politics possible, it makes possible a free economy, rather than one maintained by some form of managerial coercion. Where the state, and the interactions of many states, are characterized by civility, politics and economics become possible. But such civility depends, it seems, on some measure of respect for the rule of law internally to states and among them. It is then possible to comprehend that each of law, politics, and the economy is a subsystem of a greater social system that comprehends them all, and to which each makes a decisive contribution that is not reducible to that of any other. Moreover, each is a condition for the flourishing of the other—no law without politics, no politics without law, no thriving economy without both of the others, neither of which can flourish absent a thriving economy. In such a context, the Kelsenian slogan that, considered as such, 'legal norms may have any content'[29] cannot be seriously countenanced. Surely there are many variables in what can be enacted as law or adopted as a binding precedent. Surely there is no moral code inscribed in the human heart or anywhere else that we can simply read off into the texts of our codes and statutes. But to detach criminal law, public law and private law from the functions they fulfil in securing civility, structuring political life, and facilitating the economy is inconceivable. At least some readers of this book will consider themselves to be persons who inhabit a society characterized by a substantial degree of civility, in a state with a political order that is quite stable despite

163–176 discusses the 'Uses of Civility' in terms similar to those suggested here, but also explaining the broader ramifications of the idea: 'Civil societies maximise the chances of having non-predatory relationships among strangers' (at 173).

[28] T Hobbes, *Leviathan* in Sir W Molesworth (ed), *The Collected English Works of Thomas Hobbes* (London: Routledge/Thoemmes, 1997).

[29] H Kelsen, *General Theory of Law and State* (trans A Wedberg) (New York, NY: Russell & Russell, 1961) 113.

vigorous mutual opposition of parties, and in circumstances of a reasonably well-functioning economy. Such readers should consider whether their lived experience is not the best evidence they could have that law is at work to some reasonable extent in the state they live in. On reflecting about law in society, we have indeed to 'Mind the Gap!', but we cannot suppose it to be a total rupture. Further exploration of the interfaces between law, state, and civil society will be the business of part 3 of this book.

PART 2

PERSONS, ACTS, AND RELATIONS

The scholarly and doctrinal representation of legal materials proceeds by way of a kind of 'rational reconstruction' of them.[1] This makes it desirable to consider the kind of conceptual framework through which materials of this kind are represented. There is a whole vocabulary of 'rights, duties, privileges, powers, and immunities' (to name but a few) which is in use. It is also a part of ordinary discourse about law, when people discuss their legal position among themselves or with professionals, when some matter of relevant concern has come to attention. Use of these terms, and of the concepts for which they stand, does not depend on false (or any) empirical assumptions about the attitudes of people in society. Its point can be revealed through a conceptual analysis of the kinds of materials that an institutional normative order contains.

The basis of this analysis is that normative order purports to regulate the conduct and affairs of persons, both among themselves and in relation to their use of things. Such regulation establishes particular kinds of relationships—normative relationships—between persons. To the extent that the order is realized in social practice, these relationships can be of active concern to persons who find themselves in them. An instance of such a relationship would be if A has a duty to teach B a piano lesson, and B has a right to be taught this lesson by A. The piano's availability for use will depend on who owns it and what licence has been given by its owner—a third party, let us suppose—for its use in the piano lesson. So there are relevant relations between A and B and between them and the third party piano-owner. These include various relationships in respect of the thing, the piano.

There are various kinds of attributes that may be identified in dealing with this material. Some concern normative positions, others concern normative relations. There are simple normative positions, like that of being a person with certain capacities for action in the law. Human beings or groups of human beings and perhaps other kinds of entity can have this attribute. To ascribe it to them is to

---

[1] N MacCormick, *Rhetoric and the Rule of Law* (Oxford: Oxford University Press, 2005) 28–29.

interpret the biological living entity as a person in the legal sense. Personhood in law is thus a matter of institutional fact. So is being a person with a certain right against another person, for here we interpret one aspect of the relationship between these two in terms of legal norms. It is not, of course, necessary to engage in such interpretation, but it is always a possibility and it is often of strong interest to actual people to find out, and assert, their rights, or to acknowledge their mutual duties and act on them. Some normative attributes, such as having a right against another, are intrinsically relational.[2] They are not simple attributes like that of being a person, for relational attributes are attributes such that one person's having one such attribute entails that someone else exists with a matching but different attribute. If somebody is a husband, it follows that he is a male person who stands in a certain relationship with another, female, person who has the attribute of being a wife, indeed *his* wife just as he is *her* husband. The setting in which these relational attributes can be ascribed to individuals is, of course, the relationship of marriage. Being relational in this way is a very common feature of most normative attributes (consider employer/employee, buyer/seller, letter/hirer, and so on).

Here we shall proceed to an analysis of these, starting with the most basic legal entity of all, the person—or, if you wish, the most basic normative attribute known to law, that of being a person. Thereafter we shall consider wrongs and duties (chapter 6), then rights both passive and active (chapter 7) and rights in relation to things (ownership of property, and other real rights—chapter 8), and finally (chapter 9) an account will be given of power and immunity.

---

[2] I owe this insight entirely to Dr M Stepanians, who developed it in his *Habilitationsschrift* successfully presented to the University of the Saarland in 2005. See M Stepanians, *Rights as Relational Properties—In Defense of Right/Duty-Correlativity* (Habilitation thesis, University of the Saarland, 2005) at p 41. Stepanians in turn has developed the idea on the basis of his reading of D M Armstrong, *Universals: an Opinionated Introduction* (Boulder, Colorado: Westview Press, 1989) 65ff. Here, however, I speak of 'relational attributes' rather than using Stepanians' terminology of 'relational properties', to avoid inevitable confusion when we come to discussing property relations in the legal sense.

5

On Persons

5.1 Introduction

Even in the twenty-first century, one can still say rather as Gaius said twenty centuries ago, that all law concerns persons, things and actions.[1] Law imposes requirements on persons about their conduct. It does so also with a view to protecting persons from the misconduct of others. It regulates persons in their access to things that they need for survival, health and comfort. It provides systems of exchange whereby people can get from each other things that they need. When arrangements break down, or when harm is done or things unwarrantedly taken, sanctioning action may be taken either at the instance of public authorities or at the instance of private persons, leading possibly to criminal penalties or to enforceable civil remedies. An understanding of law and how it works therefore calls for reflection on the idea of a person, and on the kinds of relations among persons that come about within the kind of normative order that law, in particular state law, constitutes. We also need to reflect on relations between persons and things. The obvious starting point, however, is persons. What are they? After answering that question, the chapter proceeds to consider the various capacities of persons, both passive ones and active ones, and concludes with a discussion of status.

5.2 What is a Person?

There can be no normative order without persons, for what is ordered is the conduct of persons and the treatment they are to receive. Institutional normative order itself institutionalizes the concept of the person.[2] Indeed, Article 6 of the Universal Declaration of Human Rights ordains that: 'Everyone has the right to recognition everywhere as a person before the law'. Being a person is additional to being a human being, albeit everyone who is human has a right to this additional recognition.

---

[1] Gaius, *Institutiones (The Institutes of Gaius*, ed and trans F de Zulueta) (Oxford: Clarendon Press, 1946–1953) I.1.

[2] Cf D W P Ruiter, *Legal Institutions* (Dordrecht, Kluwer, 2001) 102–106.

Fundamental to the existence of a person are capability to have interests and to suffer harm, and capability for rational and intentional action. These are grounds for recognizing entities as persons, but not legal criteria of personateness, for each legal system lays down its own criteria settling who or what counts as a person. Being a person has both active and passive aspects. The active aspect of personateness is reflected in the normative character of law. State law establishes rules and principles according to which certain acts and omissions are wrong and their converse obligatory. So those who make or enunciate such rules and principles necessarily contemplate the existence of conscious rational beings who can by their own will make their intentional actions conform to them, or indeed violate them. That there are active persons is presupposed in every act of stating or enacting a rule of conduct. The passive aspect predominates when we consider what rules and requirements about conduct it is reasonable to lay down as laws. It is reasonable that these should aim, at least in part, to protect the interests of persons from being detrimentally affected by what others do or fail to do. Laws are for the regulation of persons in their active aspect, with a view, at least in part, to protecting persons in their passive aspects, that is, to protecting them from harms (invasions of interests) and perhaps with a view also to positively advancing interests of theirs. Some persons, it will be noted, receive passive protection even though they are not, or not yet, recognized as being persons able to act in law.

Both active and passive aspects of the grounds of personateness imply the continuity of persons in time, and some degree of actual or imputed consciousness of this.[3] For intentionality in action entails an agent's anticipating in thought an action to be performed at some later moment by that same agent; and rational intentionality entails the capability to take decisions with a view to their coherence in an overall plan of life. And, on the other hand, the interests of rational beings are not confined to present and momentary states of gratification but include more significantly whatever is conducive to the overall well-being of the person through time. It follows that there has to be some criterion of personal identity through time, and some way of determining the temporal duration of any person's existence as such. All of which may be thought no more than an obscure way of saying that human beings are born, live and die, and in some sense remain the same person from birth to death.

---

[3] J Locke, *An Essay Concerning Human Understanding* (edited with an introduction, critical apparatus and glossary by P H Nidditch) (Oxford: Clarendon Press, 1975). Book II, ch xxvii, s 9: 'To find out wherein personal identity consists, we must consider what *person* stands for; which, I think, is a thinking intelligent being, that has reason and reflection, and can consider itself as itself, the same thinking thing, in different times and places . . . '. Concern with the problem of continuity in personality has remained prominent in more recent philosophical discussion: see D Parfit, *Reasons and Persons* (Oxford: Oxford University Press, 1984) ch 11, s 80 and citations therein. Whether psychic continuity and self-consciousness can be considered essential to legal personality is plainly a doubtful point if the distinction between natural and juristic persons is taken according to its common understanding—but that understanding is somewhat under attack in this chapter.

Obscurity, however, belongs more to these processes as affected by modern medical technology than to our way of speaking about them. Both for moral and for legal purposes, the question of the moment of commencement of the personate existence of a human being is a difficult and disputed one. Consider the following questions: in what if any circumstances may a human foetus be aborted, or created and sustained outside a uterus and there used for purposes other than implantation in the womb of an intending and otherwise infertile mother?[4] What, if any, duties of care are owed toward or in respect of the unborn or (in case of putative 'wrongful life' claims) unconceived foetus?[5] What, if any, rights can exist in favour of or vest in the child at birth in view of pre-natal events affecting it detrimentally or beneficially?[6] What, if any, rights do parents or others have in respect of injuries inflicted on a foetus in utero, or in respect of congenital defects against which genetic counselling or screening failed to produce due warning?[7] What, if any, rights accrue under 'surrogate parenthood' agreements?[8]

These and other like questions all reflect a profound uncertainty as to how exactly, and with what consequences, the commencement of personality ought to be dated in the case of human beings as 'natural persons'. There is ancient (but still sound and relevant) doctrine in the civilian systems summed up in the brocard, '*nasciturus pro iam nato habetur quamdiu agitur de eius commodo*'. This means that 'one who is about to be born is to be treated as if already born whenever that is to her or his advantage'. Thus, for example, in succession law, a child in utero at the time of the father's death receives the same share of a legacy 'to each of my children' as the other siblings, though the right to the share only vests in a child that is born alive, and vests only at birth.[9] One could argue that, according to the spirit of that maxim, and taking account of the way it has been applied in many legal systems, a sensible approach to dealing with the commencement of life would be as follows.

---

[4] M Warnock (ed), *A Question of Life: the Warnock report on human fertilisation and embryology* (Oxford: Blackwell, 1985; see also Cmnd 9314, 1984), 29–35. Cf J K Mason and G Laurie, *Mason & McCall Smith's Law and Medical Ethics* (with a chapter by M Aziz) (Oxford: Oxford University Press, 7th edn, 2005) 98–103, 142–167.

[5] Cf Scottish Law Commission, *Liability for Antenatal Injury* (Scot Law Com No 30: Cmnd 5371 (1973)); also *Report of the Royal Commission on Civil Liability for Personal Injury* (Cmnd 7054-I (1978) paras 1414–1453, 1478–1486. On the unsustainability in English law of claims based on 'wrongful life', see *McKay* v *Essex Area Health Authority* [1982] QB 1166.

[6] Scottish Law Commission, *Liability for Antenatal Injury* (n 5 above); T B Smith, *A Short Commentary on the Law of Scotland* (Edinburgh: W Green & Son, 1962) 245–246; *Elliot* v *Joicey* 1935 SC (HL) 57 at 70.

[7] Cf *Soutar* v *Mulhern* 1907 SC 723; D M Walker, *The Law of Delict in Scotland* (Edinburgh: W Green & Son, 2nd edn, 1981) 716–717.

[8] Warnock, *Question of Life* 42–47; J K Mason and G Laurie, *Mason & McCall Smith's Law and Medical Ethics* 105–118; cf *A* v *C* [1985] FLR 445 (CA) and *Re C* [1985] FLR 846. It would seem unjust if a natural mother fulfilled her part under a surrogacy agreement and consented to adoption by the surrogate parents but was then denied any payment, or required to restore any payment previously made. Yet public policy seems to preclude treating any element in such an agreement as a valid and enforceable contract.

[9] See also C Wellman, *Medical Law and Moral Rights* (Dordrecht: Springer, 2005) at 70–73 on the 'born alive rule' in Anglo-American law.

Acts affecting a woman during pregnancy, or perhaps even before it, can be harmful to her and harmful to the foetus in ways that adversely affect the child once born, assuming it has survived these harms. The issue that then arises is whether the child after birth should have any right to compensation (or some other remedy) for this harm, supposing that the person causing the harm did so in a way that might in principle be characterized as legally wrongful. The right to a remedy[10] for such harm would be conditional on live birth, and would vest in the born child, not even notionally in the foetus before birth. But the remedy is for a harm that was done to the now born child while it was in utero. In many legal systems, the basis of liability for harm caused by negligent conduct is that there must have been both a duty to take reasonable care to avoid doing foreseeable harms and a breach of that duty. For such systems, the only reasonable analysis in the case of ante-natal harm is that the breach of duty took place when the harm was done, but that no right to a remedy for this comes into existence until (if ever) the child is born alive. To grant the remedy implies granting that a duty may be owed to a *nasciturus*, though without practical consequences in favour of the *nasciturus* till he/she is born.

This indeed seems to make good sense. When drug companies market drugs for prescription to pregnant women, for example, to help control nausea during pregnancy, the risk they ought to have in mind and guard against is precisely that they may harm the foetus as well as the woman. Some accounts of this type of case suggest that the duty comes into existence and is enforceable only at the date of birth. These are unpersuasive. They suggest that the law is to be read as imposing a duty at a time at which it cannot possibly guide the action it is supposed to guide. For the relevant guidance is to take care towards women during pregnancy to avoid the risk that drugs developed for administration during pregnancy may damage the developing child in the womb. To express the sense of this body of law in an intelligible way, one should insist that the duty is imposed with reference to the action-guidance it gives, and is a duty owed both to mother and to foetus. The remedial rights or obligations of reparation that can vest in or arise in favour of human beings at, and not before, birth, can indeed relate to harms and injuries previously inflicted. This implies that duties may be owed both to and towards the foetus or '*nasciturus*' and that breaches of such duty ought to be actionable on condition of live birth, but only on that condition. This may be taken as implying that rights of a purely passive kind are vested in the foetus, and can be wrongfully invaded; hence some minimal form of personality exists from the moment of conception.[11]

---

[10] In private law, a person who suffers wrongful harm, or whose rights are otherwise violated or invaded, normally has what is sometimes called a 'remedial right' or 'secondary right', that is, a right that the wrongdoer make some compensation or take other action to desist from the violation. Such rights are typically judicially enforceable with a view to making good so far as possible the violation of the 'primary right'. This is further discussed in ch 7 below.

[11] For a sharply opposed view, see Wellman, *Medical Law and Moral Rights* 80–85; Wellman's general theory of rights involves what may be considered a conflation of primary and secondary rights

What does not follow is that the same rights need hold in favour of the foetus against all parties to the same extent, in particular against the putative mother. Thus it is neither illogical nor conceptually absurd to insist on the rights of the foetus as against third parties while permitting (under certain conditions) the procurement of an abortion at the instance of the putative mother.[12] Whether this solution is morally right or morally wrong is a matter of acute contemporary controversy. A part of this controversy surrounds the issue whether it can be right to demand prevention of harm to a being which may in some circumstances be lawfully deprived of life. But there seems to me no reason why not, if one acknowledges that the conditional right to procure an abortion belongs only to the woman, and is not a matter of pure choice. This is at least a coherent approach. The only coherent alternatives available are that which says human life starts at conception, and from that date all the normal human rights to life and protection from harm vest in the *nasciturus* morally and ought to be recognized legally; or that which states that human life starts at birth, and only from that date do all the normal human rights to life and protection from harm vest in the neonate morally as they ought also to be recognized legally. The suggested middle way seems preferable to either of these two views.

Likewise, as to the continuing identity of persons through time, transplant surgery gives rise to conceptual problems whose solutions still lie at the level of science fiction and philosophical speculation.[13] But supposing a brain transplant were to occur in the case of wasting bodily disease of one party and some acute brain damage of another. Would the resulting entity be Campbell, whose body survives with Cameron's brain in it, or Cameron, whose brain survives in Campbell's body? What if Cameron had been female and Campbell male? Can human identity survive change in sex? (And what about the continuing identity of trans-sexuals who undergo sex-change operations anyway? If such a person has been married, is the marriage nullified ipso jure, or must it be dissolved?[14] If there

together to establish what he calls 'dominion'. If that move is unsuccessful, the conclusions reached above seem unshakeable. For discussion of this and other issues surrounding the 'control' theory of rights, see ch 7 below.

   12 *Vo* v *France* ECHR No 53924/00, ss 41, 62–64, 70, 84. A woman's pregnancy was terminated through wrongful negligence, but the Grand Chamber of the European Court of Human Rights (judgment of 8 July 2004) held that the right to life conferred by Art 2 of the Human Rights Convention did not give rise to any remedy in favour of the foetus in such a case. This, however, does not shed light on the question about any right to a remedy for non-fatal injuries suffered by a foetus that is subsequently born alive but impaired. See also *Paton* v *British Pregnancy Advisory Council Trustees* [1979] QB 276 and *C* v *S* [1988] QB 135; in England, a foetus may not be made a Ward of Court: *Re F (in utero)* [1988], which is quite consistent with the line taken here about the restriction in time concerning the vesting of remedial rights.

   13 See Parfit, *Reasons and Persons* Part III, especially chs 10 and 11.

   14 Cf *Corbett* v *Corbett* [1971] P 83, declaring null according to English law a 'marriage' between two persons both of whom had been male at birth, but one of whom had undergone a sex-change operation. Perhaps in similar circumstances a 'civil partnership' under recent legislation in favour of same-sex couples would be possible, in those legal systems that recognize such partnerships.

are children of the marriage, when do they acquire rights of succession to their
'father'?) If, as seems best, one treats psychic continuity as necessary (though
perhaps of itself not sufficient) to the continuing identity of a person, this will
solve or help in principle to solve some of the puzzles arising in such cases. But it
will generate further puzzles. For if there can be 'split personality' cases such as
those fictionally explored in James Hogg's *Justified Sinner*[15] or R L Stevenson's
Jekyll and Hyde,[16] it may appear to follow that one physical body can be the locus
of (or 'belong to') two distinct persons. What is then the lawful, to say nothing of
the just, result when one of the persons commits crimes which lead to lawful
conviction and imprisonment whereupon the other petitions for liberation of 'his'
(or 'her') body from jail?

The instance of organ transplantation has already implicitly introduced the
topic of ascertaining the occurrence of death. It appears well-established in principle,
and now also by judicial precedent, that the correct method of ascertainment of
death is through the concept of 'brain stem death'.[17] It follows that once a person
has suffered brain stem death, no subsequent operation causing organic damage
or such other event as the termination of heart-beat or of lung-ventilation will
constitute a legally relevant killing for any purpose. If this view is sound, it necessarily implies that, whatever else is true in our above hypothetical case of
Campbell and Cameron, Campbell is in that case dead and cannot be deemed
revived by the insertion of Cameron's brain. Indeed, if the resultant person were
not a continuing Cameron, there would seem to be no other solution than that
Cameron has been killed, or even murdered. Yet if the argument is not sound, all
those who engage in transplant surgery using deceased persons' organs are guilty
of, or accessories to, some form of unlawful homicide.

None of these questions need be pursued here to a final conclusion. Airing such
questions, however, shows that, although it is a mere truism that all human beings
are conceived, then born, then live for some space of time at the end of which they
die, it is not a merely trivial truth that questions as to the commencement,
endurance and termination of personality have to be answered by law. These have
to be answers expressible in terms of some reasonable principles. Ideally, they
should be stated in the form of legal rules for the avoidance of doubt and difficulty
in areas such as those considered above. In this respect there is a perfect analogy
with other bearers of legal personality which are not individual human beings—
bodies corporate, and whatever other objects or beings may be admitted to the
class of 'juristic persons'.

[15] J Hogg, *Confessions of a Justified Sinner* (London: David Campbell Publishers, 1992).
[16] R L Stevenson, *The Strange Case of Dr Jekyll and Mr Hyde, and other tales* (edited, with an introduction and notes by Roger Luckhurst) (Oxford: Oxford University Press, 2006).
[17] *Finlayson* v *H M Advocate* [1979] JC 33. J K Mason, *Human Life and Medical Practice*
(Edinburgh: Edinburgh University Press, 1988) 42–55; now see J K Mason and G Laurie, *Mason &
McCall Smith's Law and Medical Ethics* 465–474.

Already, in switching to talk of juristic persons one seems to be giving countenance to the idea that the legal personateness of human beings, or so-called 'natural persons', is a kind of natural fact, whilst that of other entities exists only in contemplation of law. This idea came under withering criticism from Hans Kelsen. He rightly pointed out that legal systems exclude some human beings from the category of persons, or admit them only to reduced forms of it. To treat people as persons in law is as much conditional on legal provisions as it is to treat corporations (or whatever) as persons in law. There is a good point here. It is indeed true that the personality of human beings *in law* is neither less nor more 'juristic' than that of any other entity that the law recognizes.[18] Nevertheless, the reasons for recognizing human persons differ from those for recognizing corporations and the like, so it makes sense to retain some distinction of terminology such as that between what are in juristic terms 'natural persons' and what are in those terms 'artificial' or 'juristic' persons.

To generalize: we may say of every type of legal person that legal rules and principles must exist to make some provision concerning the commencement of a person of any given type, concerning the duration and identity through time of any and every such person, and as to the final termination of the person, whether by natural or civil death, voluntary or involuntary liquidation, winding-up or whatever. Moreover, of any person or class of person recognized as such by law, it must be possible to specify in general terms what kind(s) of protection the law affords to it/him/her/them while in existence. It must also be possible to specify what kinds of acts it can be recognized as performing and being responsible for. It is common to classify these matters under the term 'capacity', and to distinguish in the light of what has just been said between 'passive capacity' and 'active capacity'. Different persons or kinds of person enjoy or can exercise different capacities, under appropriate conditions, limitations or qualifications.

Introduction of the question of passive and active capacities of persons brings one back to the originally proposed ground for the recognition of personality.[19] That is a 'capability to have interests and to suffer harm and capability for rational and intentional action'. It is now opportune to consider a possible objection to this proposal. The possible objection is that only individual humans satisfy this criterion, since only they have a real capability either to act or to suffer. Hence every other 'person' would be one by mere fiction and by special creation or concession of law.[20] Such an objection is false, for it turns upon a false view of acting

---

[18] H Kelsen, *The Pure Theory of Law* (trans M Knight) (Berkeley and Los Angeles: University of California Press, 1967) 168–192.

[19] It is worth repeating that this is the ground upon which it is proper and reasonable to recognize an entity as a person, but it is not itself a criterion of personateness. Criteria of this kind are determined as a matter of positive law within legal systems, and in this respect some criteria are more reasonable than others.

[20] On 'fiction' theories versus 'realist' theories, see G W Paton, *A Textbook of Jurisprudence* (edited by G W Paton and D P Derham) (Oxford: Clarendon Press, 4th edn, 1972) 407–419.

and being acted upon. The key fact to note is that human beings are in their very nature collaborative and social beings and that there are some acts which can only be joint acts of collaborating individuals, like procreating a child or winning a game of football or playing Beethoven's *Fifth Symphony*. Likewise, there are some harms and misfortunes which are necessarily corporate. These include the loss suffered by a family through the death of one of its members, or defeat of a team in a game of football, or of a country in a war. Compare the case of being interrupted or shouted down while playing Beethoven's *Fifth* or performing the play *Hamlet*. These examples are not, or not primarily, legal examples or ones necessarily involving any application of the law, but they draw attention to real social facts that the law has by some means to take into account. Acting corporately, or group-wise, is entirely natural to human beings, although indeed it is dependent on human convention, contrivance and organization. Convention, contrivance, and organization are also natural to human beings.

This is the kind of reality which has always been recognized in, for example, the Scots lawyers' acceptance of firms as having a reality over and above the partners of the moment, and hence of firms of partners as enjoying at least quasi-personality. Only to be regretted in this instance is the rather absurd fact that in most of the points on which this sensible recognition of social reality might have been pushed home to real legal advantage, the law has held back from achieving this.[21] The fact of the matter surely is that the law's *non-personification* of certain types of social collectivity is far more a matter of fiction than its conferment of personality is in the case of others. The fiction is not that the Royal Bank of Scotland has corporate identity, but that the National Union of Bank Employees lacks it. Indeed, clubs, trade unions and other unincorporated associations often have (as F W Maitland noted[22]) much more reality than some such legally incorporated bodies as the one-man company in the celebrated case of *Salomon* v *Salomon and Co Ltd*.[23] In the common law systems, there are various devices by way of manipulation of the law of trusts, of agency, and of contract, whereby to accommodate the social realities of unrecognized corporateness. The artificiality of these devices seems rather more obvious than the supposed artificiality of legal corporate personality.

This is not, however, to deny that resort to the fiction of non-incorporation may be grounded in consciously contemplated reasons of legislative policy, as in the case of British trade unions. Had they not been put in this position it would

---

[21] P Hemphill, 'The Personality of Partnerships in Scotland' 1984 Juridical Review 208.

[22] F W Maitland, 'Moral Personality and Legal Personality' in Maitland, *Selected Essays* (edited by H D Hazeltine, G Lapsley and P H Winfield) (Cambridge: Cambridge University Press, 1936) ch 5. Compare Maitland's 'Introduction' (at xviii- xliv) to his translation of O Gierke, *Political Theories of the Middle Ages* (Cambridge: Cambridge University Press, 1900).

[23] *Salomon* v *Salomon and Co. Ltd.* [1897] AC 22. Mr Salomon formed a company with six other members of his family. He was the majority shareholder; the others held one nominal share each. The company subsequently ran into trading difficulties and was eventually wound up. The issue was whether the company was a person quite distinct from its substantial owner, Mr Salomon. The House of Lords held that it was, and that Mr Salomon was not answerable for its debts.

have been impossible for Parliament to have protected the funds subscribed by working people from being liable to seizure as damages for harms done by strike action. At the relevant time, the majority in Parliament was of the opinion that judicial development of the civil law concerning wrongful collective action was unfairly biased in favour of the employers' interests. Judicial circumvention of such a policy[24] is understandable in terms of the social realities, but in context it amounted to a circumvention of the balance the legislature had tried to strike.

To acknowledge that some human actions are essentially corporate ones is not *eo ipso* to identify which ones are. Certainly, in the realms of corporate personality it is always essential to determine which human acts, decisions and intentions are imputable[25] to which corporate entities, and under what description and with what resultant variation in corporate rights and liabilities. Even apart from law, it is necessarily the case that the imputability of acts to groups and associations depends upon conventions and rules, for only organized groups can act or suffer as such, not merely as collections of socially acting or suffering humans. The organization of groups and associations is organization through and under conventions and rules which among other things determine what interests are corporate interests and what acts of what people in what circumstances count as acts of the corporate group or association. What the law does is to establish a relatively clear framework of rules determining these matters in the case of those groups whose corporate identity is recognized as legal incorporation involving the conferment of *juristic* personality on the group. This has an effect similar to that whereby personality is accorded in juristic terms to some human beings in all legal systems, and to all human beings in those systems which exclude chattel slavery and with it the reification (and, by the same token, de-humanization) of human beings.

In short, legal corporate personality is a device for recognizing the unitary and purposive character of various kinds of group activity among human beings. By this device, certain acts or events are recognized in law as bringing into existence a group that has its own personateness distinct from that of any individual human beings who are in law its members, servants or agents.[26] The consequence is that certain acts, decisions and intentions can be imputed to the group as its acts, decisions or intentions. Further, certain states of affairs can be deemed legally relevant interests of the corporation. Certain human beings appropriately identified may act as agents or servants of the corporation so long as it exists. Such existence

---

[24] Consider *Taff Vale Railway Co v Amalgamated Society of Railway Servants* [1901] AC 426, and see J A G Griffith, *The Politics of the Judiciary* (London: Fontana Press, 5th edn, 1997) 63–98.

[25] On imputation or 'attribution', see Kelsen *Pure Theory* 76–83 and 188–191, and compare the similar concept of 'attribution' developed by J C Gray in *The Nature and Sources of the Law* (edited from the author's notes by Roland Gray) (Birmingham, Ala: Legal Classics Library, 2nd edn, 1985) ch 2. Cf H L A Hart 'Definition and Theory in Jurisprudence' in H L A Hart, *Essays in Jurisprudence and Philosophy* (Oxford: Clarendon Press, 1983) at 43–47; see also Law Quarterly Review 70 (1954) at 54–56.

[26] Cf P Cane, *Responsibility in Law and Morality* (Oxford: Hart Publishing, 2002) 145–147.

is not, however, perpetual, for the law also prescribes that on the occurrence of certain acts or events the existence of the corporation as a person comes to an end for legal purposes. As with other persons, the law regulates in general and in particular the legal capacities to be enjoyed by corporate persons. It is time, therefore, to consider the topic of 'capacity', considering both passive and active elements in this.

5.3 The Capacities of Persons: Passive Capacity

5.3.1 Pure Passive Capacity

Passive capacity is properly identified as an entity's capability in law to be the beneficiary of some legal provision or provisions, in the sense that these provisions are interpreted as aiming at protecting such an entity from some harm or at advancing some interest or another of that entity. This depends upon our interpretation of the justifying ground for some law or another. For example, if the law whereby assault is a punishable crime is justified at least partly on the ground that it tends to protect human beings from the threat of or the actuality of physical violence to their bodies, then a presumed aim is to protect humans, or some humans, from this harm. If the sole true justification, however, were that these laws protect the public peace to the advantage of interests of state, then the presumed aim is not the protection of humans, though the means to the true aim of advancing the state's interest in peace is also advantageous to humans. By contrast, one can be confident that the law prohibiting demolition of historic buildings has as its presumed aim advancing the cultural interests of humans, not the physical integrity of buildings (this latter being merely a means to the justifying end of the law). The case of laws against cruelty to animals is in this respect a disputable case, for on some views it is justified primarily as protecting the human interest in humane conduct, on others it is justified primarily as protecting animals from suffering gratuitously inflicted.

In these cases of purely passive protectedness it is, of course, a matter of interpretation and of judgment to determine what is the beneficiary of the law and what the mere means to some ulterior presumed good. Furthermore, there may be cases in which the legal provisions in question are primarily criminal or quasi-criminal in character, so that the power and discretion over the law's enforcement processes vests in public prosecutors. Here, it may appear to be a purely abstract and academic exercise to ascertain who has the capacity of being, and is, the beneficiary of some legal provision or provisions.

Yet where the provisions in question are statutory in character, the question can arise whether or not commission of the statutory offence can also constitute a 'breach of statutory duty'.[27] In that case, any injury, damage or loss sustained as

----

[27] See 6.4, below.

a sufficiently foreseeable or 'proximate' consequence of the breach gives rise to a remedial right in favour of the injured party. For the purposes of resolving this question it is all-important to have a view whether or not committing the statutory offence does or can in principle involve *wronging, inflicting a wrong upon*, some other being. That in turn requires that the entity in question have the capacity for suffering legal wrongs. It must also be, in the given case, a member of the class whose actual protection by the law is among the justifying aims of the law in question. A relevant instance is given by our earlier discussion of the question whether acts that culpably harm a foetus can be wrongs in the sense of breaches of a duty owed to it.

5.3.2 Passive Transactional Capacity

Nor are these the only ways in which capacity to be the beneficiary of the law can be manifested. When it comes to private law, one may be able to be the beneficiary of a promise albeit incapable of making a binding promise oneself, or even of accepting the terms of a conditional offer. One may be capable of becoming an owner of property by gift, even if incapable of managing it. One may be capable of sustaining legally relevant injury by breach of some legal duty, and of acquiring thereupon some remedial right albeit incapable of exercising that right. One may be capable of being the beneficiary of a guardian's or a trustee's duties as such, even though one is incapable of enforcing 'in one's own right' any breaches of duty.

These illustrations draw attention to a second type of situation in which a person may, albeit wholly passively, take part in the law's drama. For here we are considering various types of legal transactions. It is a feature of such transactions that not only must the active part in them be taken by some person with appropriate capacity to act in that way, but it must also be the case that the person to whom the performance is directed is endowed with sufficient capacity for the transaction to take its intended effect. The same would apply to transactions the intended effect of which is to effect the imposition of some legal burden on the other party. A burden such as a legal duty can be imposed only on a being that is capable of being a duty-bearer. Capacity to take the benefit or the burden created through a certain transaction we shall call 'passive transactional capacity'. This is the capacity to be acted upon with legal effect through some form of legal transaction or act-in-the-law, whether the effect be beneficial or detrimental. (Those who doubt its significance may wish to reflect on the fact that a gift of property on trust for the benefit of a baby is valid, whereas one for the benefit of a pet dog is not.)

The moment one moves into the arena of civil wrongs (torts or delicts) *to* persons with consequential obligations of reparation, or contracts or other voluntary obligations undertaken *in favour of* other persons, one necessarily further envisages a transition from passive into active capacity. The same goes in respect of the enjoyment of rights in relation to things, discussed in chapter 8 below.

The legal ability to enforce, secure, uphold or vindicate—or waive or abandon—one's rights involves a capacity to perform 'juristic acts' or 'acts-in-the-law', that is, to carry out legal transactions. If a person lacks such capacity, that person's purely passive rights outside the criminal law will surely tend to be neglected or even flouted for want of someone available and able to assert these rights with legal effect. It is exactly to this end that various devices of representation have been evolved or developed by law. These ensure that some person having active capacity in law is made responsible to act for the interest of the person endowed with purely passive capacity. In such cases the will of the representative (tutor, guardian, trustee or agent or whatever) is sometimes attributed to or imputed to the party represented; in other cases it simply takes effect for the benefit of the person under incapacity. However, before proceeding to consider active capacity, we must note that passive capacity is fully conceivable as inhering in some being or entity wholly lacking in any active capacity. Possession in some measure of some range of passive capacity should be considered the minimum element of legal personateness. Where some state of affairs is conceived of sufficient value to merit some legal protection for its own sake, it may even be the case that conferment of some minimal personate status even on inanimate objects can be considered a useful device. Thus it has even been suggested that environmental protection laws could be made much more effective if legal standing were to be conferred upon trees and the like.[28] No doubt this was a somewhat extravagant proposal, and half jocular in intent, but it is a useful reminder of the potential scope of legal personality; and of the fact that although legal capacities are ordinarily correlated with natural human or at least animal capabilities, this does not have to be so always.

The present theses about the minimal elements of personality are controversial. For example, some Scottish authorities, eg, the institutional writer John Erskine of Carnock[29] as quite recently approved by the Court of Session, deny that there is legal personality in the absence of any active capacity or of capacity to hold property. This is the situation of very young children in Scots law. Similarly, G J Bell characterized the situation of 'pupils' (very young children) as 'in contemplation of law, a state of absolute incapacity'.[30] Such views of purely passive capacity as

[28] C Stone, 'Should Trees have Standing: towards Legal Rights for Natural Objects' Southern California Law Review 59 (1985) 1–37. If we did recognize trees like the giant Douglas firs of California as having some minimal legal standing, it would be easier, says Stone, to devise effective protection for these priceless parts of the natural environment.

[29] J Erskine, *An Institute of the Law of Scotland* (ed James Badenach Nicolson, reprinted with introduction by W W McBryde) (Edinburgh: Butterworths and Law Society of Scotland, 8th edn, 1989) I.7.14.

[30] G J Bell, *Principles of the Law of Scotland* (revised and enlarged by William Guthrie; reprinted with introduction by William M Gordon) (Edinburgh: Butterworths and Law Society of Scotland, 10th edn, 1989), s 2067. Bell's dictum and that of Erskine were affirmed in *Finnie v Finnie* [1984] SLT 439, Lord Cameron saying: 'A pupil is incapable of acting on his own, nor has he the capacity to consent. "[H]e has no person in the legal sense of the word . . . " (Erskine, *Institute*, I.7.14) . . . in our law a pupil is without personality: in effect this personality [*sic*] is subsumed in that of his tutor or tutrix.' But compare now Age of Legal Capacity (Scotland) Act 1991. By this statute (s 1), children under the

insufficient to constitute legal personality may seem to be fortified by discussion of the possibility that trees 'should . . . have standing'. It is submitted, however, that a better view is one which acknowledges personality as extending over the capacity to suffer—to be legally wronged—as well as over the capacity to do; that is, over active capacity in its various forms. Moreover, as we shall see, active capacity presupposes, in some cases, a passive capacity in some persons (or all persons) to be affected by the exercise of powers, whether beneficially or onerously.

5.4 The Capacities of Persons: Active Capacity in General

It is here envisaged that there are two forms or aspects of active legal capacity. The first, which will be called 'capacity-responsibility',[31] is the capacity to act and be held responsible for what one does, or for what one brings about by acting. We are dealing with that sense of 'action' in which under law it is possible to impute responsibility for results and consequences of acting to the being or entity whose bodily or mental activity is to be treated as the cause of the result or consequence under consideration. Such capacity for action normally entails also being able to incur liability for one's actions or their consequences, whether this be liability to punishment or penalty or liability to claims for civil reparation or other remedies. The second, which will be called 'transactional capacity' is the capacity to carry out legal transactions ('juristic acts', 'acts-in-the-law') with valid legal effect.[32] Such capacity for transactions relates generally to transactions of a certain type, as in the case of contractual capacity, or capacity to vote in public elections, or to be a director of a company, or to grant a valid discharge for payments due, and so on.

For both forms of active capacity, what the law stipulates is some standing feature or features of persons in virtue of which they are treated in law as able to act and normally also to be held liable for actions,[33] or to transact and to have one's transactions of various sorts considered as valid. To put it the other way round: the (active) legal capacities a person has are the conditions in law of his or her being able to act with full legal effect either in the way of committing some wrongful act or exercising some liberty of action, or in the way of effecting some

---

age of sixteen are made to be incapable of entering legal transactions, though with certain exceptions. Active and passive transactional capacity are thus largely excluded. But note also s 2 (3): 'Nothing in this Act shall . . . (e) prevent any person under the age of 16 years from receiving or holding any right, title or interest'. Hence passive capacity is legally recognized.

[31] See H L A Hart, *Punishment and Responsibility* (Oxford: Clarendon Press, 1968) 265; but Hart's account is superseded now by P Cane, *Responsibility in Law and Morality* (Oxford: Hart Publishing, 2002) 29–30, 35–36, 143–145, 150–151. 'The relevant capacity is the capacity to be guided by rules'.

[32] It is, surely, capacity of this kind that is the only one in issue in the texts considered at n 25 above.

[33] Being held liable is a matter of passive transactional capacity; being recognized as able to act in a way that violates the law and thus incurs liability is a matter of active capacity.

legal transaction. These capacities are by law made dependent on enduring (though not necessarily permanent) features of a person. These may be legally determined but non-institutional features of the person, such as age, sex, or mental competence, or legally determined and institutional features such as citizenship, legitimacy, matrimonial status, or solvency, which are actually conferred by law. Where capacity-determining features are non-institutional, and in that sense 'natural', the ascription or non-ascription of capacities by the law is commonly justified as grounded in (and thus simply replicating) natural abilities and disabilities of persons of the given class. For example, the incapacities formerly affecting women and still affecting young children and those of unsound mind were represented as justified by the natural disabilities consequent on femininity, infancy, and insanity. The same kind of argument has been used in cases of racial qualifications and disqualifications. For present purposes it is assumed that such arguments are as well-founded in the case of nonage and insanity as they are outrageous and ill-founded in the case of sex and race; but even this is disputed by some writers.[34] In the case of institutional incapacitating features such as bankruptcy and imprisonment, it is a part of the point of the institutions in question that they result in certain incapacities.

Any conception of law that envisages it as in any way guiding or regulating the conduct of conscious and rational agents by means of their awareness of the law's requirements has to have at least an implicit concept of active capacity.[35] For this postulates some actual or possible awareness of the subjects of the law or of particular laws that their conduct is subject to this or that legal provision. Hence the law must contain, at least implicitly, some reference to the qualities of persons which bring them within the scope of given legal provisions. Some of these qualities will belong to the class of enduring features of the person, others to more transient roles, activities or circumstances (such as being an employer, driving a car, or labouring under error or the influence of drink or drugs, or being a victim of fraud or duress). Qualities of the former sort are, as we have seen, those which are determinants of legal capacity and legal incapacity. In this light, it should be noted that what have here been identified as the two forms or aspects of active capacity match the two modes in which law is considered by leading jurists to regulate or guide conduct. These are, on the one hand, the mode of imposing categorical requirements on conduct[36] (making acts or omissions wrong or their converse obligatory) and, on the other, that of empowering persons to effect legal results by legal transactions. Relevant legal transactions are ones that conform with determinate legal conditions of a kind that will be

[34] R Farson, *Birthrights* (Harmondsworth: Penguin Books, 1978) denies the justification of restrictions on children's capacities; but for a more balanced view see R Adler, *Taking Juvenile Justice Seriously* (Edinburgh: Scottish Academic Press, 1985) ch 3.

[35] See again Cane, *Responsibility in Law and Morality* 35.

[36] Sometimes called 'duty-imposing rules', eg, by H L A Hart (*The Concept of Law* 78–79), but see 6.4, below for a discussion of the concept of duty.

explored in the discussion of legal powers in chapter 9. Meanwhile, in the following two sections further consideration will be given to capacity-responsibility and transactional capacity.

5.5 Capacity Responsibility

It may appear that this is in essence a more passive than active capacity, since it involves the question whether or not one can be subjected to criminal or civil liability to sanctions for one's acts. But, as we shall see subsequently (7.3, below), capacity responsibility also entails a capacity to have and to exercise active rights. And although capacity-for-liability is indeed a form of passive transactional capacity, what is important here is the distinction which exists between capacity to be held liable and capacity to do that to which liability attaches. In the case of children under some such legally stipulated age as seven years, and in the case of persons deemed insane according to law, an ability to form a criminal intent is considered to be absent.[37] Such persons therefore lack the capacity to commit crimes, and accordingly cannot be liable to be held legally guilty of crimes, whether or not the public safety or the law justifies in that case other measures of constraint in cases of involvement in seriously harmful behaviour.[38] It is also a perennial topic of controversy whether corporations are capable of forming a criminal intent and hence whether they are capable of committing any crime or offence whose definition includes a mental element.[39]

The proper answer to this question is, of course, that the imputation of wrongful intent to bodies corporate may stand on somewhat different ground than in the case of natural persons. Nevertheless it is eminently as justifiable in this case, since intentions are definable as the results of deliberation terminating in decision, and hence whoever takes the company's decisions necessarily thereby forms the company's intentions. So it is possible to regard a corporation as *capax doli*, that is, legally capable of criminal wrongdoing in its own person, as distinct from having mere answerability vicariously for the wrongs of others. In many systems, however, the law has groped only slowly and uncertainly to a clear and principled resolution of this matter.[40]

As the case of vicarious liability in the civil law shows, it is possible to detach the obligation of reparation for harms wrongfully inflicted from the breach of duty or other wrongdoing upon which it is consequential. In those cases of employment, agency and the like, in which vicarious liability is imposed on such grounds as that a wrong was committed by an employee in the course of employment, one party's

[37] N Walker, *Crime and Insanity in England Vol 1, Historical perspective* (Edinburgh: Edinburgh University Press, 1968) 84–124.
[38] Walker, *Crime and Insanity, Vol 2, New Solutions and New Problems* (Edinburgh: Edinburgh University Press, 1973) 18–156.   [39] Cane, *Responsibility in Law and Morality* 157–164.
[40] Cane, loc cit.

breach of duty or of obligation or other wrongful act causing harm legally results not merely in that party's incurring an obligation to make good the damage done but also in the employer's jointly and severally incurring an obligation of the same tenor to the same extent. Both employer and employee are liable to judicially imposed orders for damages, etc, and ultimately to coercive enforcement of these, if they each fail to satisfy the obligation of their own free will.[41]

Vicarious liability, however, has to be distinguished from the case in which one person is at fault in his or her own person for failing to prevent harms occasioned by another. For example, young children may foreseeably make their way onto busy roads, and their presence there may cause vehicles to swerve and to cause or suffer damage (or both). In such a case, the adult in charge of the children may rightly be held to be in breach of the general duty of care by reason of the omission adequately to safeguard against the obvious risk in the case. But, depending on age and circumstances, the children in such a case may not have or not be in breach of any legal duty of their own, and certainly very young children wholly lack capacity responsibility. The sole party at fault in that case is the adult in charge, who is the only relevant legal actor, having alone the capacity to be such.[42] The same goes for ineffectual confinement of animals—here there is no vicarious responsibility, but a breach of duty by the keeper, which the keeper must make good if the escaped animal does harm.[43]

Hence in the case of potentially wrongful acts, both under criminal law and under civil law, it is clear that capacity to act—capacity responsibility—is distinct from the passive capacity of being subject to legal proceedings, capacity for legal liability, which is a form of passive transactional capacity. Conversely, one may for some special reason have an incapacity to be held liable without its being supposed that one has no capacity to act. The case of 'diplomatic immunity' is an example of this. Those who enjoy diplomatic immunity are not deemed incapable of action or of wrongful action, but merely incapable of being made subject to civil or criminal process.[44] The same point has been taken in some cases about legislation in respect of trade unions and trade disputes. This has been held not to affect the legal quality (in English law) of certain acts, as in cases of picketing, but merely to confer on the actors an immunity from criminal or civil proceedings in respect of such acts.[45] Whether this was a sound reading of the legislative principles is more than doubtful. Beyond doubt, however, is the logical soundness of the distinction drawn.

The ability to act or abstain from acting in a legally relevant sense is fundamental to legal order as a rational ordering of rational beings. It is this ability which is

---

[41] Cane, *Responsibility in Law and Morality* 151–157, 177–178.

[42] Cf, for example, *Carmarthenshire County Council* v *Lewis* [1955] AC 549; T B Smith, 'The Age of Innocence' Tulane Law Review 49 (1975) 311.

[43] Cf P M North, *The Modern Law of Animals* (London: Butterworths, 1972).

[44] Cf E Denza, *Diplomatic Law: a Commentary on the Vienna Convention on Diplomatic Relations* (Oxford: Clarendon Press, 2nd edn, 1998).

[45] See *Broome* v *Director of Public Prosecutions* [1974] AC 587; *Kavanagh* v *Hiscock* [1974] QB 600.

essential to either being judged a wrongdoer or being deemed one who does no wrong in respect of some given act or omission. It is this which differentiates acts and omissions from mere behaviour and from mere events. Hence capacity in the sense of 'capacity responsibility' is fundamental in law and as an aspect of legal personality.

5.6 Transactional Capacity

Transactional capacity is of equal significance in developed systems of law. The concept here in view is that of ability to exercise legal power, that is, to perform some act which is deemed to bring about some valid legal effect. In what is analytically the simplest case, the effect in view will be either that of making wrongful what would otherwise be lawful, as where a person validly promises to do a certain act, whereupon performance of that act in favour of the promisee becomes obligatory (and non-performance wrongful); or vice versa, as where a person consents to what in the absence of consent would be an assault, as in a surgical operation, or where one grants a valid release from a promissory obligation. From these simplest cases of power, one can construct others more complex, as for example when one person promises another to do a certain act if requested to do so in writing delivered not later than a certain date. In this case the promisor confers on the promisee a power the exercise of which results in the promisor either having an unconditional obligation to do the act in question or being free from any obligation in the matter. Thus there can be powers to confer powers as well as powers to incur or to impose obligations; there can also be powers to create, confer, transfer, and terminate rights of all sorts, as will appear in due course (chapter 9, below).

What is in all cases crucial is the notion of 'valid legal effect' as attendant upon the due exercise of legal powers. The special significance of this lies in the judicial enforceability of sanctions for legal wrongs (this itself being dependent on the powers vested by law in judges as such), and in the judicial duty to give effect by enforcement to all validly established legal relations and arrangements. This can even be viewed as a kind of reward: to those who have transactional capacity and who choose to exercise it in the forms and conditions prescribed by law, the reward is that the arrangements thus created are enforceable by due process of law.[46]

Accordingly, legal provisions which confer powers are to be understood as prescribing that performance of a certain act shall engender a certain legal result. But one condition to which such a prescription is necessarily subject is that which determines which kinds of persons having what characteristics can bring about this

---

[46] N MacCormick, *H L A Hart* (London: Edward Arnold, 1981) ch 6.

result by a relevant act.[47] This being one essential element of power-conferring provisions in the law, it picks out that which is essential to our concept of transactional capacity. Certain powers (eg, powers to make contracts, transfers of property, declarations of trust, or wills) are exercisable by all persons who possess certain standing personal attributes (such as age, sex, soundness of mind, etc). We properly ascribe 'capacity'—*capacity for that act or transaction*—to persons with these attributes.

A different case is that in which special powers are conferred upon specially qualified persons, whether such special qualification be by succession (eg, a monarch), by election (eg, a president), or by appointment (eg, ministers, judges, members of the civil service and of boards of nationalized industries, police officers, etc).[48] In such cases there may be conditions—by way of 'passive transactional capacity'—as to who can be appointed or elected to given offices. But the fact of succession, election or appointment is what qualifies *this* person to exercise this range of powers. 'Competence', 'jurisdiction', even perhaps 'authority', are the terms we use to signify the investment of special power through such special qualifications.[49] Although the illustrations so far chosen have been from the sphere of public law, and have concerned the competence or authority of office-holders in public law, it should be observed that there can also arise special powers by way of special appointments in private law. Examples are when one person appoints somebody to be executor of his or her will, or trustee over certain property, or when a person is elected to be an official of a trade union or a director of a company, or is appointed to a particular post within a business organization, or assumed into partnership in a firm. In all such cases, no doubt, a background circumstance is the appointee's passive transactional capacity to be appointed or elected to such a position or office, and no doubt only persons with appropriate active capacities would ever be appointed or elected. But what is conferred by election or appointment is not a general capacity but a special competence at law.

To conclude these observations on capacity, then, we shall note again that possession of some at least minimal legal capacity or capacities is of the essence of personateness in law. To be a person is to be able to suffer and to act in law, to act, and to be acted upon. Capacity can therefore be differentiated into passive and active capacity. Pure passive capacity is the condition of being eligible to receive the protection of the law *for one's own sake* rather than as a means to some other end for its own sake. It is thus the minimum legal recognition that can be conferred on any being, and is that enjoyed by very young children and by incurably weak-minded persons. Other passive capacities, the transactional ones, concern rather the ability to be beneficially or onerously affected by legal acts; these are no less omnipresent a feature of law. Active capacity is either (i) capacity-responsibility, conceptualized as the ability to act rightly or wrongly, or (ii) transactional capacity, conceptualized

---

[47] There are other conditions apart from those of personal capacity that determine the validity of an act. See 9.2, below.

[48] Cf the discussion of office-defining institutional rules in D W P Ruiter, *Legal Institutions* (Dordrecht: Kluwer, 2001) 92–93.   [49] Cf Ruiter, *Legal Institutions* 15.

as being qualified to exercise some legal power or powers. The fullest degrees of legal personality involve a full range of passive and active capacities. To be distinguished from capacities as such are special competences possessed by persons in virtue of succession, election, or appointment to special positions.

5.7 On the Capacities of Corporations

All that has been said about capacity is as much applicable to corporate persons as to other persons recognized by law. In so far as corporate status is explicitly conferred by law on particular appointed or elected bodies, and in so far as it results from incorporation by the statutory procedures (through exercises of power by persons with appropriate capacity) under legislation about incorporated companies, the corporate persons which result therefrom have in principle the full range of capacity appropriate to their corporate character. This implies some restrictions by comparison with human persons. For example, as to passive capacity, since corporations cannot in their nature be physically assaulted or killed, those branches of criminal and civil law which give protection against bodily harms do not apply—'offences against the person' are not offences against *these* persons. But property crimes and defamation are of course possible here, and companies have capacity to be wronged in these ways—even without express statutory provision. So far as concerns capacity to be acted upon by way of exercise of power, there are some types of office to which in principle companies could not be appointed, such as that of judge (though some boards, etc, may exercise judicial or quasi-judicial powers). But such private law positions as that of trustee or executor can be assumed by corporations.

In general, as to active capacity, so far as corporations can act, they can act wrongfully or within their rights, and the problems of imputing criminal intent and liability for ultra vires delicts or torts are at least theoretically resolved or resoluble. There is no reason either of conceptual logic or of legal principle why corporations cannot be considered as acting subjects, whether acting in the exercise of active rights or in the commission of legal wrongs.[50] As to transactional capacity, with such obvious exceptions as capacity to marry, to adopt children, or to make a will, corporate persons have the full range of capacities proper to the nature of commercial, charitable, or public corporations. But their special competence to act, and thus the competence of their officers to act, is in each case regulated by the incorporating statute or the incorporating instrument executed under statutory powers. How far acts beyond particular competence—ultra vires acts— are binding in the interest of third parties has been a discussed and controversial question, concerning the fair balance of interest as between shareholders and 'outsiders' dealing in good faith with a corporation. But the current resolution of

[50] Cane, *Responsibility in Law and Morality* 157–164; also ch 12.4 below.

that matter in favour of outsiders acting in good faith does not destroy the distinction between the range of transactions over which in principle corporations have active capacity, and the specific competence of any particular corporation within that range.[51]

To have stressed the capacities—including passive capacities—of corporations is important. Especially as to the fundamental rights of persons, it should be noted that the most fundamental are *human* rights and hence primarily for the protection of each and every human person. No doubt the protection of humans sometimes requires the protection of corporations derivatively, and some human interests—eg, in freedom of worship—are distinctively corporate rather than individualistic in kind. But in principle that passive protection which human rights constitute is protection for humans, and there should be no presumption of an extension of the protections thereof to corporate persons in their own right rather than as human instruments.[52]

5.8 Status

The legal concept of personal *status* is to be understood chiefly in light of the foregoing elucidation of capacity, for differences of status are to be understood primarily as the grounds for differentiations of capacity. Perhaps it would be better in modern legal systems to say that status differentials are summations of sets of qualities which ground significant differentiations of passive or active capacity among different classes of person.[53] Standing features or qualities of persons which constitute the common grounds for numerous and interrelated capacities and/or incapacities, passive or active or both, are features or qualities also constitutive of some 'status' or another. Thus a status is a summation of or ground for the legal grounds of various capacities or incapacities, as for example in the case of age: in the period between conception and birth, only passive capacities exist, and all conditionally upon subsequent live birth, so far as concerns the capacity to have action taken on one's behalf by a representative in law; then the period of childhood is a period of restricted capacity in all legal systems in which only passive capacities exist, active capacity in civil law being wholly absent, followed in the teenage years by a period of restricted active transactional capacity, but full

[51] See Companies Act 1985, ss 35 and 36, transposing European Community law into UK law.

[52] Cf Allan Hutchinson, 'Supreme Court Inc: The Business of Democracy and Rights' in G W Anderson (ed), *Rights and Democracy: Essays in UK-Canadian Constitutionalism* (London: Blackstone Press, 1999) 29–45, especially at 35–39, for a sharp critique of the extension to corporations of rights-protection under the Canadian Charter.

[53] C K Allen, in *Legal Duties and Other Essays in Jurisprudence* (Oxford: Clarendon Press, 1931) identifies status as the ground of, or summation of, capacities; likewise G W Paton, *A Textbook of Jurisprudence* (4th edn) ch 16, s 87. Cf D M Walker, *The Principles of Scottish Private Law* (Oxford: Clarendon Press, 3rd edn, 1982) vol 1, ch 3, s 2.

active capacity at any rate so far as concerns matters criminal, though often under special restrictions in relation to systems of juvenile justice. Any synoptic view of contemporary legal systems suggests that there is typically a lack of a single overall systematic view of the status—or statuses—of childhood from the point of view of private law, criminal law, and social welfare law taken all together. The status of adulthood is now typically achieved at the age of 18, whereupon the individual achieves the full range of passive and active capacities known to the law and ascribable to human persons. This full status is, however, enjoyed only by those of sound mind, and mental weakness as defined by statute or common law may be deemed a status resulting in absence of or restriction in active capacities. Bankruptcy is another status which results in substantial diminution of the active capacities normally enjoyed by adults of sound mind.

Differences of sex as between male and female have hitherto been very common grounds of differential legal status. Happily, modern statute law has almost entirely elided this. In states that recognize human rights against unjust discrimination, sexual difference, like differences of race or ethnicity or religious belief, no longer entails difference of legal status. As part of perhaps the same tendency in law, it has to be noted that familial relationships, both those between spouse and spouse and that between parent or parents and children, are nowadays barely recognizable as matters of status in the classical sense here identified. Nevertheless, since the active capacity of an adult to act on behalf of a child, especially in childhood, and the passive capacity of a child to be acted for are still largely regulated by family relationship, whether as legitimate child, illegitimate child, legitimated child, or adopted child, these remain (albeit in attenuated form) matters of status. Likewise the capacity to take legal benefits under the law of succession, both testate and intestate, depends considerably on family relationship. Since marriage bears upon parental relationships (and also upon the law of succession) it remains, even more attenuatedly, a status relation, not merely a specially regulated form of contract. The same now goes also for same-sex 'civil partnerships' in those states which have legislated for recognition of such unions as partly analogous with marriage. And, of course, the doctrines of international private law which require personal status to be determined by the law of one's domicile classically have reference to such matters of familial status, and continue so to refer regardless of the noted attenuations.

The matters discussed so far have referred exclusively to status within private law—though this has sometimes had consequences in respect of public law also. But it should be noted that even apart from public law ramifications of status as determined by and in private law, there are some distinctions admissible as distinctions of status that belong purely or primarily to public law.[54] We may here note citizenship or nationality as a status; nobility in its various grades in the few states in which legal rights or privileges remain dependent upon noble rank, and

---

[54] Cf Walker, loc cit.

the contrasting status of commoner; and the status of prisoner as against that of a person at liberty. All these statuses regulate capacities in public law, such as the capacity to cast a valid vote in elections to public office,[55] or the capacity validly to be nominated as a candidate for election to public office, or to be appointed to hold some appointive public office or position.

As is obvious, the differences of capacity and the different qualities of persons which ground differential capacities and incapacities have great importance. So also have the rights and duties directly determined by some or all of these qualities—consider here in particular those arising from family relationships. But the summation of these qualities as grounds of differential capacity into this or that named status—pupil, minor, adult; married or not; illegitimate, legitimate, legitimated or adopted; free or prisoner, and so on—these summations as such are of limited interest or importance as a topic in contemporary law. 'Status' *as such* has declined in interest as a legal concept, notwithstanding the importance of the matters which we can sum up under 'status' as a rubric.

One may speculate why this is so. Sir Henry Maine argued that the movement of 'progressive societies' up to his time of writing (in the late nineteenth century) had been 'from status to contract'.[56] This is perhaps best taken as implying that the whole of a person's legal position (rights, etc) was in earlier periods determined largely via status as regulating above all the capacity to order people about—an active transactional capacity—or the (passive) capacity to be validly ordered about. One's rights and duties, so far as not simply determined by custom, were settled by decision of familial or feudal superiors, not by one's own freely under-taken engagements. In turn, a move to contract implies an equalization of status and with it of transactional capacities such that, in the end, one's rights and duties arise largely from the contracts one makes rather than from other legal grounds. The status of different persons becomes assimilated and the range of capacities—or of rights—determined by any particular status-defining quality is reduced. Hence status dwindles in interest and importance as a legal topic. At the same time, however, differences both perceived and real in market strengths or social standing or ascribed gender roles may contrast with the equalized legal capacities whereby all persons are enabled to participate in the market. So a whole series of special and inexcludable terms comes to be implied into contracts in favour of the presumptively weaker party (in terms of economic strength), whether as passenger or consignor in relation to carrier of persons or goods, or as insured vis à vis insurer, consumer vis à vis producer, employee vis à vis employer, shareholder vis à vis company or member vis à vis trade union. Or women and members of

[55] But the prisoner's incompetence to vote in elections has been challenged, with partial success, by a recent judgment of the European Court of Human Rights, so far as concerns states party to the European Convention. See *Hirst* v *the United Kingdom (No 2)* ECHR 26 October 2005 (application no 74025/01).

[56] H S Maine, *Ancient Law: its connection with the early history of society and its relation to modern ideas* (with an introduction by CK Allen) (London: World's Classics, 1931) ch 1.

ethnic minorities gain statutory protections against discrimination in favour of men or majorities. Whereas in earlier systems of common law (or in civilian systems of law) a small range of general and standing personal features qualified one in respect of a large range of capacities, nowadays a multiplicity of legally significant roles exists, each person playing several roles and enjoying rights or restrictions accordingly under some statutory scheme. Likewise in such fields as children's law a series of statutory schemes directed at furthering each child's well-being creates a patchwork of different systems for the protection of those under incapacity, without any single age or other decisive qualification having general application. Childhood is a legal condition overlaid by a multiplicity of statutory provisions with a variety of age-qualifications and need-related criteria for intervention. Gone is the relative—and perhaps excessive—simplicity of the older all-purpose civilian concepts of pupillarity and minority—or infancy in English common law and the other systems that derive from it.

Such developments have sometimes been said to amount to a new form of status, and thus to betoken a swing back from contract to status. But, as at least hinted above, statutory roles into and out of which one may step perhaps many times in a day or a fortiori in a lifetime are a far different thing from status. It would seem better to give Maine's apophthegm a further updating. Of societies which consider themselves progressive, the modern development has been from status to statute.

6
Wrongs and Duties

6.1 Introduction

Earlier chapters have insisted on a certain assumption about the normative character implicit in 'institutional normative order'. We have said that 'ought' is the signal of the normative. The moment one enters the domain of talk about what people ought to do, as distinct from what they actually do, one enters the domain of the normative. Normative discourse is a discourse of the 'ought', descriptive discourse is a discourse of the 'is'. The discussion of the queue or line that occupied chapters 1 and 2 points to a helpful suggestion. Where there are informal normative practices and, all the more, where there is some sort of formalized practice, involving explicit or implicit rules derived from authoritative decisions, there exists one kind of basis on which to judge what a person ought or ought not to do in a given context. The law-state is a context in which there is a formidable institutionalization of normative order. This focuses very particularly on attempting to discourage various kinds of conduct that is harmful to persons or injurious to good order or to the state's own institutions, and on making provision for remedial action in case of harms done. Reasonable success in this attempt is a condition for securing the condition of 'civil society' among the citizens or subjects of the state, indeed all its residents.

Law is thus sometimes said to rest on a fundamental binary distinction, that between right and wrong, *Recht* and *Unrecht*.[1] The present chapter commences with reflection upon this distinction of right and wrong. Subsequently, it will try to tease out some particular juridical usages of the ideas of 'duty' and 'obligation', to show that we might not wish to treat these as fundamental in the same way, but as having somewhat specialized functions in denoting particular kinds of normative position or relation.

6.2 Rethinking the Normative

The introductory proposal just put forward announces a deviation from one of the most celebrated tenets of twentieth century jurisprudence. According to this, law is essentially about the imposition of duties. Legal 'primary rules' as

---

[1] N Luhmann, *Das Recht der Gesellschaft* (Frankfurt am Main: Suhrkamp, 1993), trans by K A Ziegert as N Luhmann, *Law as a Social System* (Oxford: Oxford University Press, 2004), makes

H L A Hart put it, are 'duty-imposing rules' or, as he put it in other words, rules that lay down the obligations of the persons that are subject to the legal order in question.[2] Hart stated this thesis in conscious opposition to the approach of Hans Kelsen, for Kelsen had suggested that the primary legal norm is one which stipulates that a sanction be exacted on the occurrence or non-occurrence of a certain event (the act or omission of a person). The act or omission in question is then a 'delict' (that is, a legal wrong), and the legal duty (to refrain from acting, or to take positive action) is its mere logical converse. The 'duty' is the content of a secondary norm indicating what the subject ought to do, the primary norm being that which says what the official ought to do by way of sanction should a delict be proven to have occurred.[3]

Hart's and Kelsen's observations about these matters belong to their general theories of law. They thus purport to present an enhanced understanding that encompasses and makes intelligible in an overall way the particular and local speech and terminology of those concerned to administer the law, or to legislate, or even to produce commentaries on the detail of particular branches of particular legal systems. They do not necessarily reproduce in their theories, or test their theories against, the language (or the 'semiotic systems') found in the various discourses of legislators, judges, legal practitioners, or doctrinal commentators.[4] This is perfectly legitimate. General theory is, after all, a meta-linguistic enterprise which aims to capture in simpler and more immediately intelligible terms the dense and particularized languages of the various practices involved in, and surrounding, the law in its concrete everyday life.

Nevertheless, it remains open to regret if theory recycles and stipulatively re-defines for its own purposes the very terms that are also current in the specialist terminology of legal dogmatics and legal practice. Concepts like 'duty', 'rights', 'liability', and their cognates are very much a part of the working language of lawyers. Theoretical re-definitions of these terms may be more confusing than helpful, if usages are stipulated for them in the context of theorizing that differ from those that obtain in the first-order languages of the practice. Theoretical

'Recht/Unrecht' his basic legal distinction. See 145: 'The design of schemes such as right/wrong, acceptable/unacceptable, normal/deviant, or eventually legal/illegal already lies *within* the social order containing both sides of the distinction'. 'Right/wrong' seems to me more meaningful than 'legal/illegal' for many purposes, though Ziegert's usage as translator mostly favours the former. Hector MacQueen's fascinating essay 'Some Notes on Wrang and Unlaw' in H MacQueen (ed), *Miscellany V*, Stair Society Vol 52 (Edinburgh: Stair Society, 2006) 23–26 traces the concept 'unlaw' (etymologically equivalent to German *Unrecht*) and the substantial synonymy of 'wrang' (modern English 'wrong') in mediaeval Scots law, comparing also English usage.

[2] This is, of course, the central idea developed in the first five chapters of H L A Hart, *The Concept of Law* (Oxford: Clarendon Press 1961, 2nd edn, 1994); see especially ch 5.

[3] See Hans Kelsen, *Introduction to the Problems of Legal Theory* (trans B L Paulson and S L Paulson) (Oxford: Clarendon Press, 1992) ch 3, s 14 (b); cf Hart, *Concept* 35–36.

[4] Cf B S Jackson, *Semiotics and Legal Theory* (London: Routledge & Kegan Paul, 1985) 283–304.

attempts to prescribe reformations of ordinary legal usage to conform to the pattern set by theory are perhaps even more confusing, and have rarely if ever succeeded in procuring a change in the common speech and writing of the legal community.

In search of a more fundamental terminology for universal theorizing, it will be profitable to start from the concept of what is 'wrong'. Wherever there is normative order, there are kinds of conduct (either action or abstention from action) that count as wrong with reference to the postulated order. Conformity to the order involves omitting whatever is wrong (jumping the queue is wrong, and conforming to the queuing norm requires that one not queue-jump). Whatever is not wrong is at least in a weak sense permissible. This is a line of distinction worthy of further pursuit.

6.3 Differentiating Wrong and Not-Wrong

What is the difference between the wrong and the right? It is a difference intelligible only to a being capable of conscious and intentional action, somebody endowed with 'capacity responsibility' as discussed in the preceding chapter. Such a being confronts choices all the time, between different acts, different courses of action, different ways of carrying out one or another course of action. An act's being wrong is a reason not to do that act, a reason for choosing not to do it, but to do something else, or to do nothing. It is a reason of a particular kind. This can be shown by contrasting the idea of the wrong with the idea of wants and desires as reasons for acting. That I want or desire something is always a reason in favour of doing acts that will (tend to) make it possible for me to have that thing. The wrongness of an act is a reason not to do it even though it would get you something you want. It resembles what has been called an 'exclusionary reason',[5] in that it excludes acting in what would otherwise be a perfectly reasonable way (doing *x* to get *y*, which I want). An act's being wrong places what has been called a 'side constraint' on our acting.[6] For considering a particular act to be wrong does not in itself give a person a reason to do anything, but it sets a constraint alongside one's doing whatever one has positive reasons for doing. Whatever we do, for whatever reasons we are acting, we must act without straying into committing any wrongful act or omission. We, as it were, 'draw a line' separating what is wrong from every other possible action, and then set ourselves to avoid crossing that line in all that we do. Not to cross the line is categorically required, regardless of the balance of

---

[5] J Raz, *Practical Reason and Norms* (London: Hutchinson, 1975) 40–45; I somewhat differ from J Raz in the use of this term, which he subsequently withdrew (see *The Authority of Law* (Oxford: Clarendon Press, 1979) 18, 21–23) in favour of 'protected reason'. As I argue below, it is our judgments based on norms rather than norms themselves that give reasons for particular actions. This is, perhaps, an important point of difference.

[6] Compare R Nozick, *Anarchy, State and Utopia* (Oxford: Basil Blackwell, 1974) 30–35.

our wishes apart from this consideration. Crossing it cannot be excused by the strength of our desire for whatever motivates us to cross it.

The judgment that an act is wrong always requires some context. An act can be wrong morally, or wrong legally, or wrong because a sin, or wrong in the context of a game or practice, or wrong as a breach of professional ethics, or as a breach of proper standards of scholarship, or politeness, or as a breach of conventional social practice like queuing, and so on. It is then wrong, we may say, 'from a point of view'.[7] From the moral point of view, or the legal, or the religious, or the sporting, or the professional, or the academic, or that of good manners, this contemplated act is wrong. Then, also from that point of view, the act is ruled out as unacceptable (morally, or legally, or whatever). Somebody who is (perhaps only at this very moment) fully committed to a certain point of view treats as conclusive judgments of what is wrong from that point of view. Such a person rejects the admissibility, for that context of decision, of any reason present in the given situation that would otherwise weigh in favour of the act in question.

Only someone who has at least on occasion had a full commitment to some judgmental point of view such as that of law or of morality can understand the concept 'wrong' adequately. But someone who does understand it can pass judgments concerning what is wrong from a given point of view without being fully, or at all, committed to that point of view at the time of judgment. To do so is to pass a detached[8] or uncommitted judgment. Such a judgment is then parasitical on the possibility of full commitment, but remains perfectly sound as a judgment despite the absence of that full commitment. One can be detached, but still minded to act upon such a judgment: 'If, or in so far as, I have reason to take seriously the legal point of view, I have reason to treat as excluded from choice any acts which are legally wrong; and since this act is legally wrong, I have thus far a reason to treat it as excluded'. But such a detached judgment of wrongness has a hypothetical character (compare with it: 'if I want y, I should refrain from doing x, since x would make y unobtainable'). By contrast, from the fully committed standpoint the judgment of wrongness has the categorical character noted above: the act's being wrong is an overriding or 'peremptory' reason[9] for not performing it.

What then of the right? Is right simply the contradictory of wrong? Unfortunately, it is not so in common speech. That an act is not wrong means that it is not excluded from the relevant point of view, but not necessarily that it is endorsed positively as the right thing to do. Of course, if it happens that all one's options of action are wrong save for a single one, then that single course of action marks out the only right thing to do, for not to do it would be wrong. Otherwise, we would

---

[7] Cf Raz, *Authority* 153–157.

[8] Raz uses the term 'detached statement', but this is to confuse a linguistic entity with a mental act, hence I prefer 'detached judgment'.

[9] Cf H L A Hart, *Essays on Bentham: Jurisprudence and Political Theory* (Oxford: Clarendon Press, 1982) 255–261.

at most say that x is 'all-right', that is permissible, but not required. It is permissible, but not positively endorsed.

The wrong/not wrong dichotomy seems fundamental to practical thought, and might even be considered more elementary than the famous contrast of 'is' and 'ought'. That I 'ought' or 'ought not' to do so and so expresses what is usually an overall balance of judgment, taking account of all relevant reasons for and against, and reaching an advisory or indicative conclusion. While it is true that, if x is wrong, I ought not to do x, that does not say enough. On this hypothesis, the truth is that x is something I *may not* do. For x is not merely inadvisable, it is impermissible. Refraining from x is obligatory. The idea of the normative (certainly in the institutional context) is in my view focused primarily on this line of exclusion that splits the permissible and impermissible, dividing that which is (however grudgingly) 'all-right' from that which is wrong.

How then are we to understand this most fundamental of practical distinctions, that between wrong and not-wrong? The answer is in terms of human values, and thus in terms of our understanding of our own human nature. We conjectured in chapter 1 that queuing as a practice expresses an orientation to the egalitarian value of treating everyone on equal terms, as this applies in relation to some opportunity. To generalize: some states of being and states of affairs appear to us good, in that they seem fit towards, or even essential to, living well. Living well is something humans can do only in community with others, and thus each person's living well is conditioned on others being similarly well-off. There is a common good, the general circumstances required for successful communal living. And there are individual goods, all the ends that individuals can desire to pursue within the framework of a secured common good.[10] Human dispositions that tend to realize or constitute common or individual goods are therefore valued, and considered 'virtues'. Dispositions tending in the opposite direction are objects of justified disapproval. They are 'vices'. As to vice, however, a further distinction has to be drawn between vice in the sense of mere absence of disposition towards the good or indifference towards it and an active hostility to the good. In cases of such active hostility, mere vice shades over into viciousness, wickedness, or depravity.

Thus as to states of being and of affairs, as to human dispositions, and as to human conduct we find a plurality of possible values or goods and of their opposites. In terms of these, we can grade or evaluate on scales from the best or most admirable to the worst or most deplorable or reprehensible. To regard something as good is to regard it as worthy of pursuit and to suppose that pursuit of it is worthy of approval or even praise. By contrast, indifference to it is to be disapproved

---

[10] I am here very much indebted to J Finnis, *Natural Law and Natural Rights* (Oxford: Clarendon Press, 1980), and see his *Fundamentals of Ethics* (Oxford: Clarendon Press, 1983) 26–56; cf also discussion in 9.2 below.

and activities hostile to it are blameworthy and reprehensible. All the more so are activities that pursue what is opposed to the good.

Badness is a matter of degree, and often something a long way less than wholehearted dedication to the good has to be tolerated for the sake of peace and quiet, and for the sake of the civil liberty that can nurture moral autonomy. But where do we draw the line? And how do we draw a line? In our personal moral life and in our private affairs we need not draw all or perhaps any of our lines exactly in advance, but can think through to a judgment of each situation in all its detail.[11] It is otherwise in institutional contexts, where problems of mutual co-ordination between people are encountered. Then lines do need to be drawn that are capable of being understood in advance. This is very obviously exemplified in the law of the modern state, where government is maintained, in the last resort, through coercive means, within a determined territory. A state's constitutional law supplies processes for making general abstract values more determinate and concrete, setting terms whereby government can be conducted in a coherent, orderly, and predictable way. The broadest level of determination is the enunciation of explicit principles by commentators and judges. More determinate are rules enacted in structured legal texts by a legislature or sub-ordinate legislator. Yet more determinate are rulings or precedents issued by judges to settle problems of interpretation in the application of law to particular cases.

In such a system, the line between wrong and not wrong (from the viewpoint of the state's law) is determined by reference to the principle, or statute, or inter-preted principle or statute, or interpreted-and-applied principle or statute revealed in some precedent. Such progressively more determinate norms perform the task of drawing a relatively clear line, and whatever is in breach of such a norm is not just bad to some discussible degree of badness, but more or less clearly wrong. This of course links up to the process of sanctioning wrongs, either by penal sanctions invoked by state prosecuting authorities or by civil remedies granted by courts to injured parties, or by some public law process that orders a public body to fulfil a duty imposed on it by law.

There is here no suggestion that questions about the good, both common good and particular good, are other than highly controversial among human beings. Nor is there any suggestion that agencies of state are incapable of gross error and even criminal wickedness in what they represent as values to be given determina-tion through law, or through other governmental activities and practices. Many indeed are the examples that prove they are fully capable of error and evildoing in the name of the good. But law-determining acts and processes are intelligible only to the extent that the participants purport to be oriented towards some

---

[11] Cf J Dancy, *Ethics without Principles* (Oxford: Clarendon Press, 2004) 130–132 on the absence of any master rule-book for morality.

conception of societal good, however inadequate, partial, or depraved a view they may in truth have.[12] And in that context law-determination involves the drawing of the wrong/not-wrong line.

Where governance includes the use of a legislative process, the norms enacted through that process include rules that draw the line between what is wrong and what is permissible. In the developed form familiar in the legal systems of contemporary states, wrongs take two distinct forms according to the forms of judgment and sanction involved. On the one hand, wrongs that are 'crimes' or 'offences' (or 'felonies', 'misdemeanours', or whatever) entail liability to penal sanctions, punishments of one kind or another, after proof by an established process (involving a stringent standard of proof) that an accused person has committed an offence. On the other hand, there are civil wrongs. These are wrongful acts that are injurious to some person other than the wrongdoer, and that result in liability to a prescribed restitutionary or compensatory remedy (payment of damages, usually). Where the wrongdoer fails to make satisfactory amends voluntarily, the injured party may by a prescribed process take legal action against the former, and, if successful both in proving the facts alleged and in showing their legal relevance, may obtain an appropriate remedial order from the tribunal. This order may in due course be coercively implemented if not voluntarily fulfilled.

Here, the idea of wrongful conduct has been explained in terms of normative order, in the light of particular judgments, based on rules and principles, that can be made about the conduct of persons. In the background are relevant values, with norms of one kind or the other marking a cut-off point in the way of minimal required respect for this or that value. So understood, a wrong, or rather the commission of a wrong, provides a good reason for the imposition of sanctions, of one or another kind.

Criminal punishments can be invoked at the instance of public officers (or at least persons acting in the name of the public authority) who frame accusations (complaints or indictments or whatever the relevant term in a given legal system may be). These are then tried under appropriate procedures before a court of criminal jurisdiction. The decision whether or not to prosecute is either discretionary, but guided exclusively by a view of the public interest, or non-discretionary in any case in which the prosecutor considers that there is adequate evidence to justify seeking a conviction.

Civil remedies, by contrast, lie purely in the discretion of the party affected by a presumptive wrong. That party, or some trustee or guardian acting on that party's behalf, has a choice whether or not to seek a remedy for the wrong. Such a remedy can be obtained initially by voluntary action of the (alleged) wrongdoer, but in default of that by litigation with the ultimate prospect of a coercively enforceable

---

[12] Cf R Alexy, *Begriff und Geltung des Rechts* (Freiburg/Munich: Verlag Karl Alber, 1992) 201–204; also *The Argument from Injustice* (trans B Litschewski Paulson and S Paulson) (Oxford: Clarendon Press, 2002) 35–40. See also ch 14 below.

order being issued by a civil court against the wrongdoer. The steps between initiating a civil action and finally enforcing a judgment against the other party are many and various in all legal systems. State coercion is the long-stop guarantee of the efficacy of rights, but the idea that the law is coercive because of the threat of sanctions in the wider sense of punishments or remedial rights seems well wide of the mark.[13] Coercion by the state underpins the law, but does not constitute it as a normative order.[14]

This physically coercive enforceability of state law is material to the process of drawing a line between what is unlawful and what is licit. For it can at least be said that the right and reasonable place to draw the legal line between what is merely un-praiseworthy or un-admirable and what is to be deemed actually wrong is the point at which such forcible sanctioning or other coercive measures can be considered justifiable. It should be added that not all conduct that escapes legal sanctioning is to be considered fully acceptable from a legal point of view. For example, wagering contracts or contracts for sexual gratification do not fall under the threat of civil or penal sanctions, but in most legal systems they are unenforceable as contracts. There are not a few cases of such shadowy quasi-illegality, disapprobation through withholding of legal validity rather than by direct sanctions. Thus we must recognize a grey area of what is 'licit' but not wholeheartedly lawful.

From the point of view of a state's legal order, that which is wrong is typically wrong because it involves infringing an enacted rule either criminal or civil in character. In civil contexts at least, however, there can also be judgments concerning wrongs as breaches of general principles rather than enacted rules. But such cases involve determination through a judicial ruling upon the interpretation of relevant principles and the entitlement of an injured party to reparation of injuries in the light of relevant principles. Enacted law can also take the form of the enunciation of a broad principle, as in the case of Article 1382 of the French *Code Civil* ('Any act whatsoever of a person that causes damage to another creates an obligation in the one through whose fault it occurred to make reparation'). So it is not only in common law countries that there may be a process of *determinatio*[15] whereby judges make a ruling on the concrete applicability of a general principle in more particular circumstances, considered both as particulars and as defining a potentially repeatable type of case. But certainly the common law in relation to torts (or 'delicts'), breaches of contract and of trust, and such like provides frequent illustrations of such a process of *determinatio*.

---

[13] Cf G Lamond, 'The Coerciveness of Law' Oxford Journal of Legal Studies 20 (2000) 39–62.

[14] This position is established by argument in N MacCormick, 'Coercion and Law' in *Legal Right and Social Democracy* (Oxford: Clarendon Press, 1982) 232–246, and this argument, though rejected by Lamond, is by no means refuted, taking coercion in the sense there defined.

[15] This concept here (and above) is borrowed from Thomistic philosophy via the work of J Finnis; see Finnis, 'On "The Critical Legal Studies Movement"' American Journal of Jurisprudence 30 (1985) 21–42 at 23–25.

It is sometimes said that rules and principles constitute reasons for action simply by virtue of being rules or principles. In the domain with which we are concerned, it is clearly incorrect to consider the rule or principle to be directly in itself a reason for action. It is a standing ground for judgment, by reference to which, in the presence of further relevant circumstances, we are able to judge that some contemplated or performed act is or was wrong. Suppose that a particular rule or principle is binding from a certain point of view. Suppose further that a person's factual situation satisfies the conditions of the rule, and that an act v[16] is possible and in contemplation, but counts as wrong under the rule or principle. That v is wrong (legally/morally/as a matter of proper scholarly practice) is a reason to refrain from doing v. That a contemplated act is wrong is (from the committed standpoint) a categorical reason for not doing it. The judgment based on the rule, not the rule itself directly, is what actually guides, that is, gives reason for, acting or not acting.[17]

There are other terms in which such judgments can be expressed, for example, using the terminology of what is 'obligatory'. To refrain from wrongdoing is obligatory. That not v-ing is obligatory is just another way of saying that v-ing is wrong, and so likewise when it is obligatory to refrain from v-ing, this means no more and no less than that v-ing is wrong. What is obligatory is also what in one sense we 'must' do or 'have to' do; 'ought' is somewhat weaker, and lacks the categorical sense of 'obligatory', or 'wrong'.

6.4 Of Duties

Duties concern what it is wrong to refrain from doing, or to do (if you have a duty to v, then it is wrong to refrain from v-ing; if you have a duty not to v, then it is wrong to do so). Yet in general terms and in accordance with common usage, especially the usages of the law, it does not seem correct to consider everything that is wrong to be a breach of duty. On the contrary, breaches of duty are one species of wrongful acting. Having a duty is being in a position that makes it wrong to do something, indeed, to do anything that involves failure to perform the duty.

One can give a very good illustration of this point by referring to the common law (and Scots law) conception of civil liability for harm caused through carelessness or 'negligence'. According to law, a person who causes harm to another by an act of carelessness may have to compensate for the harm caused, but only if the harm-doer owed a 'duty of care' to that victim. To give a somewhat over-simplified statement of law, the test for the existence of such a duty, that is the test for deciding whether one party owes such a duty to the relevant other, is two-fold. First, is it reasonably foreseeable that the former's conduct could cause harm of the kind in

---

[16] Here, and in later chapters, the symbol v is used to signify any verb—it is a 'verb variable'. For noun variables, 'n' is used.   [17] Cf n 5 above.

question to persons in the position of the victim? Secondly, is there a relationship of 'proximity' or 'neighbourhood' between them such that it is in all circumstances fair, just, and reasonable for a duty to be imposed, with resultant liability in damages for its breach?[18] There are many time-hallowed statements of the general underlying principle, such as Lord Macmillan's:[19]

The duty to take care is the duty to avoid doing or omitting to do anything the doing or omitting to do which may have as its reasonable and probable consequence injury to others and the duty is owed to those to whom injury may reasonably and probably be anticipated if the duty is not observed.

There are many precedents, and clusters of precedents, and rules of statute law that give more concrete or determinate effect to this general principle. Thus there is a set of legally determined situations or relationships that actuate this generally stated duty in more concrete terms that help to specify both the degree of care that is in the given context reasonable and the range of others toward whom a duty is owed. This in turn determines who is or are entitled to a remedy if they do suffer harm through a careless act. To quantify the abstract duty of taking such care as is reasonable in principle accordingly requires at least two things. It requires first of all a consideration of the role or position occupied by the person in question (eg, financial adviser, architect, driver, surgeon, occupier of premises), and secondly a view of the particular circumstances of any given case of alleged negligence. The bearer of the duty has then to conduct him- or herself in accordance with the standard that a reasonable person or person of ordinary prudence bearing that role or position would observe, having regard to the various values and interests at stake in the given case. This necessitates the exercise of value judgment by the agency responsible for trying issues of fact in the case, but this is not a value-judgment at large. It is a judgment that ought to be informed by reference to prevailing standards in the community, especially that of the members of any relevant calling. Such prevailing standards, though relevant, are not decisive and may, for example, be found to require less care than is properly deemed reasonable.[20]

This way of characterizing and conceptualizing 'duties' in one very important branch of law connects interestingly to a conception of duty that has been commented on by moral philosophers, from at least as long ago as F H Bradley's seminal paper 'My Station and its Duties'.[21] 'Duties' typically attach to 'stations in life', or 'roles', or 'positions', and are frequently set out explicitly in such

---

[18] *Caparo Industries* v *Dickman* [1990] 1 All ER 568 at 574, per Lord Bridge of Harwich. In the discussion of duties (and, later, rights) in relation to the law of torts/delict, I am much indebted to A Halpin, *Rights and Law: Analysis and Theory* (Oxford: Hart Publishing, 1997) 138–158.

[19] *Bourhill* v *Young* [1942] 2 All ER 396 at 403; 1942 SC (HL) 78 at 88.

[20] Cf N MacCormick 'On Reasonableness' in Ch Perelman and R Vander Elst (eds), *Les Notions à Contenu Variable en Droit* (Brussels: E Bruylant, 1984) 132–156; see now also *Rhetoric and the Rule of Law* (Oxford: Oxford University Press, 2005) ch 9.

[21] F H Bradley, *Ethical Studies* with additional notes by the author (Oxford: Clarendon Press, 2nd (revised) edn, 1927) ch 5.

contractual documents as 'job descriptions'. Some relevant 'stations' are inherently relational, like that of a parent, with duties toward children, or that of an employer, with duties toward employees, or that of a trustee, with duties toward beneficiaries. What the courts, certainly those of the UK and such Commonwealth countries as New Zealand, Australia, and Canada, have elaborated in relation to negligence liability in the law of torts or delict is a rich and detailed array of relationships in which the law imputes a duty to take care. Wherever there is such a duty there is a corresponding liability to having to pay remedial damages in favour of a proximately-related other who suffers harm through carelessness ('negligence'), and a right to such damages in the harmed party.

Statute law is most often explicitly concerned with the imposition of duties when it comes to the establishment and dictation of functions to public bodies exercising statutory power. 'It shall be the duty of the Board to . . . ' says such an act of legislation. Private law roles such as those of trustee or company director may similarly be specified in terms of the duties that have to be performed as well as the powers the role-holder can exercise, and indeed, most crucially, the duties they have in respect of the exercise of their powers. Especially in the case of the duties of public bodies, imposed by public law, difficult questions can arise concerning their enforcement. It is generally possible, as a matter of public law, to obtain a remedy (in the case of countries within the English common law tradition, based on what were originally 'prerogative writs' such as mandamus) whereby a court requires a body in neglect of duty to perform it. The conditions for intervention may, however, be subject to fairly strict conditions about standing (or, as the Scots lawyers put it, 'title and interest to sue'). Yet more problematic has been the question how far private law reparation ('tort damages') may be claimed by someone who claims to have suffered loss from a faulty performance of, or a failure to perform, some such public duty.[22] It is not enough that a public body have an explicitly conferred duty, say, to inspect building plans and approve them only if satisfactory; that duty must be shown to be 'owed to' particular members of the public, or a particular section of the public. Only someone held to be within the range of those to whom the duty is owed by deliberate intendment of the legislature is entitled to reparation by way of damages.

By contrast with private law and public law in relation to the powers and duties of public authorities, the criminal law is a branch of law in whose practical discourse at the level of law-making and law-applying the concept of 'duty' plays only a small part. When it comes to determinations of what is criminally wrong, legislators legislate in more or less clear terms what shall be crimes or offences (or felonies or misdemeanours), by what process these are to be tried, and what are the penalties (within what range of judicially determinable variation) that are to be imposed in cases of conviction. Prosecutors charge persons with the commission

---

[22] For a masterly and authoritative discussion, see Lord Browne-Wilkinson's speech in *X (Minors)* v *Bedfordshire County Council* [1995] 2 AC 633 at 730–741.

of (alleged) criminal acts specified in a formal complaint or indictment, and at the trial adduce evidence purporting to prove guilt as charged. The court's decision concerns whether any charge has been proved to the required standard, commonly 'beyond reasonable doubt', and if the verdict of guilty falls to be pronounced in that light, and is pronounced, the sentence is then imposed. In short, persons standing before the criminal law are charged with, convicted of, and punished for the wrongs (the crimes or offences) they commit, not for acts characterized as breaches of duty of a legal subject[23] that they necessarily commit in doing wrong. As Tony Honoré has remarked[24], there is only one duty imposed by the criminal law, the duty to commit no offence. This sounds trivial, but in fact it may be linked back to the conception of role-based duty. In a just and well-ordered state, it is a part of the duty inherent in citizenship to respect the law as it regulates the public order of society. A law-abiding person is one who makes a point of respecting the limits (or 'side constraints') imposed by the criminal law.

Apart from this, there are two more special respects in which the concept of duty and its breach plays a significant part in the criminal law, for there are some points of the criminal law where the commission of criminal wrongs presupposes acting in breach of a duty which itself exists apart from the criminal law. Thus, for example, one person's omission to take steps to save the obviously endangered life of another will in most jurisdictions constitute neither murder nor manslaughter (culpable homicide). But there is an exception to this if the former owed some duty to take care of the latter, eg, as a parent for a child, or had previously voluntarily undertaken such a duty. In the case of embezzlement or breach of trust, the criminal act necessarily involves an act in breach of the duty to use entrusted property only for another's benefit. Conversely, acts which would otherwise involve the commission of a crime against person or property are lawful when justifiably done in pursuance of a duty of public or private law. And even where such act exceeds the scope of the relevant duty, its having been done in pursuance of duty is a mitigating circumstance and may, for example, reduce what would otherwise be murder to some lesser form of homicide only.

That the criminal law and statutes criminal or quasi-criminal[25] in character do in a trivial sense engage the duty to omit unlawful actions ceases to be trivial in connection with the civil law of reparation of injuries. As we have seen, there is a common law right to the reparation of any injury caused by another's act provided that such act involves breach of a duty owed by the actor to the injured party, and provided that the breach of duty was a sufficiently proximate cause of the injury inflicted. For this purpose, the duty may be a duty created by statute or delegated

---

[23] One role which life under law imposes on all persons is that of the 'legal subject', and that is a role whose duties amount to whatever is involved in being a law-abiding person. Compare Z Bankowski, *Living Lawfully: law in love and love in law* (Dordrecht: Kluwer, 2001) 135–141.

[24] T Honoré 'Real Laws' in P Hacker and J Raz (eds), *Law, Morality and Society* (Oxford: Clarendon Press, 1977) at 117–118.

[25] P Devlin, *The Enforcement of Morals* (London: Oxford University Press, 1965) ch 2.

legislation rather than simply one arising under the principle discussed above. This can be so even where the statute expressly provides only that failure to observe the statutory requirement is to constitute a crime or offence subject to prescribed punishments or penalties. In case of such 'breaches of statutory duty', a key question is whether the statute is purely penal or can properly be regarded as imposing a duty whose breach may also give rise to a civil remedy. What is decisive on this point is the intendment of the legislation, or the intention about its application reasonably imputable to the legislature in the light of the words of the statute. What is crucial is whether the intention (in this sense) is not only to procure some common public benefit or good, or to protect some common public interest, or to avert some common public mischief, but also to procure for individuals affected by the legislation some benefit, or some protection of interest, or protection from harm. Wherever such an element is within the Act's intendment, civil remedies properly exist at common law for breach of the duties it imposes.[26]

In the light of all this, it seems that what is constitutive of duty is the imposition of requirements upon persons as holders of roles, positions, or offices, not the presence of any specific or direct sanctioning mechanism. In so far as legal duties are what categorical requirements of law require one to do, their breach or neglect is wrongful in law. Under various conditions such misconduct may be variously sanctioned or otherwise productive of adverse legal consequences. But what is essential is the notion of the requirement as partly definitive or constitutive of the position, role, or office, or annexed to the powers thereof. The sanctioning measures belong to the particular mode of wrongfulness of particular types of breach or neglect of duty; they are not constitutive of the concept of duty.

This account of the concept 'duty' is somewhat narrower than that adopted by those jurisprudents who consider every legal requirement to be a duty and thus every legal wrong a breach of duty. It is, by exactly the same token, the more faithful to the common usage of lawyers. It is a further point of importance that not every duty is imposed by a legal rule as such. For a particularly important legal duty, viz, the general duty of care, depends rather upon considerations of principle than upon any particular rule or rules, relevant though these may be to specifying its content in given instances. As one much indebted in many ways to the thought of H L A Hart, I nevertheless think we should reject the supposition that the concept of legal duty can be fully elucidated in terms of a set of 'primary rules' that are 'duty-imposing' in Hart's sense. The analysis of legal systems simply as systems of 'primary' and 'secondary' rules[27] will not do, though it contains many suggestive and fruitful insights for various purposes, as will be seen in due course.

---

[26] See again Lord Browne-Wilkinson's speech in *X (Minors)* v *Bedfordshire County Council* [1995] 2 AC 633 at 731–732.

[27] See *Concept*, ch 5; cf N MacCormick, 'The Concept of Law and *The Concept of Law*' (1994) Oxford Journal of Legal Studies, Vol 14, 1–23.

6.5 Of Obligations and The Obligatory

The concept of that which is obligatory may (as was noted above) be taken as converse in sense with that which is wrong. If it is wrong to *v*, then it is obligatory to refrain from *v*-ing; and if it is wrong to omit to *v*, then *v*-ing is obligatory, and vice versa. These are tautologies. The concepts of the obligatory and of that which is wrong are fundamental to any normative order and are not susceptible of further analysis, though explicable in the manner pursued above. The primary level of law is that at which it is determined that certain lines of action or omission are wrong and unlawful or (to put it in simply converse terms) that certain lines of omission or action are obligatory. Not surprisingly, there therefore also exists a manner of speaking according to which whatever is obligatory is 'an obligation' and one is 'under an obligation' to do or refrain from all that the law categorically requires one to do or refrain from. This conception of obligation is perhaps especially common among moral philosophers, many of whom treat 'obligation' in ethics as signifying whatever it is morally obligatory for a person to do. Nor is so wide a usage unknown to jurisprudence. Hart, in a famous passage, treats the distinction between 'being obliged' (in the sense of coerced under danger or threat) and 'having an obligation' (where a rule requires some action of a person) to be fundamental to jurisprudence. Correspondingly, he sometimes refers to the rules which in his view constitute the primary level of law as 'primary rules of obligation'.[28]

This broad use of the term 'obligation' commonly goes hand in hand with a broad use of the term 'duty', in which light 'duty' and 'obligation' become synonyms for each other, distinguishable only through established preferences for traditional phraseologies. There is also, however, a more specialized use of the term 'obligation', one which retains a certain vitality in the discourses of doctrinal lawyers, especially those concerned with the branch or branches of private law known as the 'law of obligations'. In this usage, the term 'obligation' simply translates the Latin term *obligatio*, which the classical Roman sources characterize as a *vinculum iuris*, 'a legal tie by which we may be necessitated or constrained to pay or perform something' or (one might add) to refrain from some action or way of acting. The standard students' text-book of Scots law in the twentieth century remarks that 'Taking an obligation in the narrower sense of the word . . . [it is] a legal tie by which one is bound *to a specific creditor or body of creditors*'.[29] In this sense, an obligation is necessarily a two-way link between persons, indeed

---

[28] Hart, *Concept* 84–88; cf H L A Hart, 'Legal and Moral Obligation' in A I Melden (ed), *Essays in Moral Philosophy* (Seattle: University of Washington Press, 1958) 68–75.

[29] W M Gloag and R C Henderson, *An Introduction to the Law of Scotland* (9th edn by A B Wilkinson, W A Wilson et al) (Edinburgh: W Green & Son, 1987) para 3.3; so also in previous editions; the original is, of course, found in Justinian's *Institutes* III.13.Pr.

between ascertained persons. One of these, the creditor, has in principle discretion to call for, or to waive, or to let lapse the performance, payment, or abstention required by law of the other party, the debtor or *obligatus*. This entails a different-iation from the concept of duty, which is a concept that looks only to the occupant of a role or station or position, and specifies what has to be done and what omitted by the role-holder as such. Where a role is intrinsically relational, the content of the duty is one side of an obligation that links the two parties to the relationship. But, as we have seen, there can be other contexts in which it is clear from the outset that one party is bound by a certain duty, but not certain that this duty is owed to a specific other party in the position of the plaintiff in a legal action. Obligations in this sense are specific legal relations between ascertained parties. Discussion of them continues in the next chapter.

7

Legal Positions and Relations:
Rights and Obligations

7.1 Introduction

In this chapter, we shall start from consideration of 'obligations' in the sense of 'legal ties' or '*vincula iuris*', that is, in the sense involved in discussions of the 'law of obligations'.[1] Such a 'tie' links together two (or sometimes more) legal persons, one of whom has a right to some performance or abstention by the other, that other being subjected to a corresponding duty. When obligations are bilateral, each has both rights and duties, with corresponding duties and rights incumbent on the other—as when, in a contract of sale, the seller must supply the relevant thing to the buyer, having the right to receive the price for it, while the buyer has a right to be given the thing and has a duty thereupon to pay the price (and there may be all sorts of ancillary rights and duties of each party both under the terms of the contract and by virtue of the general law concerning sales of things of the relevant kind).

These points established, we shall proceed to consider rights in relation to duties, with a view to showing when rights exist and how they correlate with duties, in particular whether or not some element of choice about or control over another person's fulfilment of a duty is necessarily involved. Passive rights to performances or abstentions by others are considered first, then active rights—what one may do or not do oneself—are reviewed. Finally more complex rights of the kind involved, for example, in human rights instruments are explained in a preliminary way.

7.2 The 'Law of Obligations'

Obligations have necessarily some degree of temporal endurance. This starts with some particular institutive act or event and continues until some terminative act or event, such as performance, express waiver, express substitution under some

---

[1] Cf R Zimmermann, *The Law of Obligations: Roman Foundations of the Civilian Tradition* (Cape Town: Juta & Co, 1990) 1: 'As far as the Roman terminology is concerned, "obligatio" could denote

new agreement ('novation'), prescription by lapse of time, or (in certain cases) death of one or other party.[2] They are capable of being reified, that is, considered as a species of incorporeal thing. As such, they may be subject to assignation by the creditor to a third party, and they may be transmissible on the death or bankruptcy of either party, save in the case of obligations involving purely personal services. (For example, if *A* owes *B* a certain sum of money, *B* may assign to *C* the right to payment by *A*; or if *B* becomes bankrupt, *B*'s trustee in bankruptcy automatically becomes entitled to payment by *A* at the due date.)

It has been customary to classify obligations according to the nature of their institutive act or event. 'Voluntary obligations' are those which are instituted by an act of the person who assumes the obligation. Such an act is typically performed with the actual or presumed intent to create the legal obligation in question, and is normally effective to determine wholly or in part the nature of the performance, payment, or abstention which is to be its content. Unilateral binding promises in many legal systems require some formality (such as a seal) in order to constitute them as legally binding, or require some special mode of proof such as a written document of some kind. They can be binding either on condition of being accepted by their addressee, or at least on condition of not being rejected. Another more important sub-class of voluntary obligations is found in conventional or consensual obligations. These require wills of two or more parties to an exchange of rights or to the incurring of reciprocally beneficial obligations. Their content is determined by the will of the parties and by any general legal provisions concerning compulsory or implied terms, or required conduct of parties to contracts of particular kinds. Contracts are, of course, the most important species of consensual obligation.[3]

In contrast to such obligations arising by acts of human will, it is common to contradistinguish obligations imposed by law without regard to will or consent. Non-voluntary obligations are those that are instituted on the occurrence of a legally-determined event, such as the birth of a child, that engages parental obligations toward the child. Obligations can arise as a result of acts that are neither actually nor presumptively intended to create an obligation. For example, a payment of money under error gives rise to an obligation of restitution in the payee towards

---

the vinculum iuris viewed from either end'. See generally, Zimmermann, 1–6, and compare Ruiter's institutionalist discussion of the point, and of Zimmerman's approach, in D W P Ruiter, *Legal Institutions* (Dordrecht: Kluwer, 2001) 112–113.

[2] N MacCormick 'Law as Institutional Fact' LQR 90 (1974) 102–125, and compare N MacCormick 'Norms, Institutions, and Institutional Facts' Law and Philosophy 17 (1998) 301–345 at 332–336.

[3] D M Walker, *The Law of Contracts and Related Obligations in Scotland* (London: Butterworths, 1979) 1–41; differentiation of the 'law of obligations' from other parts of private law, and classification of obligations as voluntary, conventional, or obediential is much more characteristic of civilian than of Anglo-American common law thought, but the difference has diminished under the influence of great common law scholars also learned in the civil law, such as the late Peter Birks.

the original payer. Again, there may be a conferment of benefit by one person upon another that gives rise to a non-contractual obligation in the beneficiary to recompense the benefactor to the extent of any gain received. Most important of the class of non-voluntary obligations are obligations of reparation. Here are involved both an act, viz, some wilfully wrongful act or some breach of duty (for example, a duty of care) or of obligation (for example, a contractual obligation), and an event, viz, the consequential occurrence of injury, damage, or loss to a person other than the actor. The act in question may in such cases be an intentional one, but it neither needs be, nor characteristically is, one intended to generate the consequential obligation. As was indicated above, the occurrence of injury, damage, or loss proximately caused by the wrongful act or breach of duty is essential to the existence of the obligation to make reparation for that injury, damage, or loss. This occurrence may arise some considerable time after the act in breach of duty. For example, a negligently manufactured article may lie in a store for some time before being incorporated in a machine which might in turn be put to use only after some space of time and only subsequently cause injury or damage.[4] The release into the market of supplies of a teratogenic drug like thalidomide must antedate by some time any doctor's decision to prescribe it to a pregnant patient. Some further space of time will elapse before actual harm is done to any developing foetus, and that harm may become known only at the birth of the child. In this case, as previously observed, no obligation of reparation arises until the live birth of the child.[5]

Sometimes, by a fiction, it is said in these cases that the breach of duty itself takes place only upon the occurrence of this injury, damage, or loss, or the birth of the child, or the time at which latent injury was first reasonably discoverable. Resort to such a fiction[6] may be necessary to overcome infelicities in legislation on prescription and limitation of actions or for other purposes.[7] But it would be preferable for a clearer conceptual structure to be sustained in the law, eg, by better drafting of relevant legislation. Properly speaking, what is subject to prescription or limitation is not the original breach of duty, but any obligation of reparation to which it gives rise. Another way to put this point would be to say that the justice served by prescription and limitation of actions is that of not permitting persons to sleep upon rights of action, that is, remedial rights. An injured party's right to a remedy should be exercised or abandoned within a reasonable time, or be deemed to have lapsed. And the length of time should be the same for all persons who have a similar right grounded in a similar injury. But the space of time between

---

[4] *Watson v Fram Reinforced Concrete Co (Scotland) Ltd and Winget Ltd* 1960 SC (HL) 92 especially at 106–107.

[5] Scottish Law Commission, *Liability for Antenatal Injury* (Edinburgh: HMSO, 1973 Cmnd 5371 (Scottish Law Commission; No 30)).

[6] 'Fiction' here means a violation by the law of the normal criteria for applying a concept, adopted in order to achieve better the proper end of the law.

[7] A case in point is the Prescription and Limitation (Scotland) Act 1973 (ch 52) s 17.

the breaches of duty that are actually committed by wrongdoers and resultant occurrences of injury can be various. So if the statute happens to date prescription from the moment of a breach of duty, the law has to have recourse to fiction in order to secure the essential justice of the statutory scheme.

To have restated the matter in this alternative way is to have introduced the concept of 'right' to the present discourse. Plainly, the position of the creditor of an obligation is exactly that of the holder of a right according to the analysis of 'rights' favoured by legal theorists such as Wesley N Hohfeld, Carl Wellman, and many others.[8] The other party, the debtor, owes to the creditor that payment or performance to which the latter has a right. Here, indeed, it is normally the case that such a creditor is in a position of choice, choice whether or not to exercise the power of calling for performance of what is owed. Where there is failure to perform, the creditor has consequential remedial rights, enabling her or him to take legal action against the debtor. Again, it is normally a matter of free choice whether or not to exercise any such remedial rights in case of breach. According to a powerful body of scholarly opinion, the very idea of a 'right' depends on the existence of such choices. These subject to the will or control of the creditor the issue of calling or not calling for performance either of the primary obligation or, if there is default in that, of the secondary remedial duty. Theories that identify the concept of right with this kind of 'power over duty' have been called 'choice', or 'will', or 'control' theories. This is a matter to be considered further, in some more extended reflection on the concept of a right.

7.3 Rights in General and in Regard to Conduct

Rights necessarily belong to or 'vest in' persons. They vest in persons on account of some feature (being party to a contract or victim of a tortious harm, for example) that makes it appropriate for a relevant constraint to fall on another person, and in favour of the former party. Rights are thus normally positions of benefit or advantage secured to persons by law.[9] One kind of benefit or advantage arises in the context of obligations, where one party has to make some payment or perform some act or omission in favour of the other. More generally, legal requirements concerning a person's conduct may have their principal point in the fact that they

---

[8] W N Hohfeld, *Fundamental Legal Conceptions* (New Haven, Conn: Yale University Press, 1919); C Wellman, *A Theory of Rights* (Totowa, NJ: Rowman & Allanheld, 1985) in particular at 102–105; see also C Wellman, *Real Rights* (Dordrecht: Kluwer, 1995); consider also, eg, M H Kramer, N E Simmonds, and H Steiner, *A Debate over Rights* (Oxford: Clarendon Press, 1998); M Stepanians, *Rights as Relational Properties—In Defense of Right/Duty-Correlativity* (Habilitation thesis, University of the Saarland, 2005); G W Rainbolt, *The Concept of Rights* (Dordrecht: Springer, 2006).

[9] The argument for this general view derives from N MacCormick, 'Rights in Legislation' in P M S Hacker and J Raz, *Law, Morality and Society* (Oxford: Clarendon Press, 1977) 189–209, and N MacCormick, 'Rights, Claims and Remedies' in M A Stewart (ed), *Law, Morality and Rights* (Dordrecht: D Reidel, 1982) 161–181.

protect another or others from some harm or disadvantage or take account of some other feature that supports a constraint on the acting person's conduct as a 'justified constraint'.[10] Conduct in violation of such a requirement is not just wrong in the abstract, but wrongful towards the particular person or persons affected. Where one party has to act or abstain in a certain way and where failure in this respect is a wrong against the party affected, the latter has a right that the former not so act or fail to act. The one has a right, and the other has a corresponding duty.

The 'choice' theory mentioned above defines rights in terms of the faculty or power conferred on persons by law to exercise choice over others' duties, entirely at their own discretion.[11] This approach, however, appears to err in defining something normally ancillary to a right as an essential part of the right itself. One can draw an illuminating analogy with those theories of personality which say that personateness in law cannot properly be ascribed to beings such as very young children who wholly lack active legal capacities. In chapter 5 arguments were deployed to show why that theory about legal persons and personality should be rejected.

Consider the case of a serious and permanently disabling injury inflicted on a month-old child by some careless act of a medical practitioner. In such a case, the law would grant two distinct remedies against the doctor. On the one hand, the parents, who would incur both extra costs in rearing and looking after the child and grief over their child's disability would have a right to compensation and whatever compensation the law allows for distress and other emotional damage—'*solatium*' in civilian terminology. On the other hand, there would be payable in respect of the child compensation for damage done and *solatium* for pain and suffering and loss of the normal amenities of life. But these damages are not merely 'in respect of the child'—that phrase better characterizes the rights of the parents to their reparation for their losses and suffering *in respect of* their child, as an object of their obligations and their affections. One could get similar damages in respect of one's domestic animals or even one's land or house. No. These damages and *solatium* are due *to* the child, and have to be held on trust for him or her. They compensate the child's suffering for its sake, not as a ground for someone else's suffering. This is quite unintelligible save as a right *of the child* to reparation for injury. Moreover, whoever has the duty to look after the child's best interests has a duty to pursue any available remedy—this is not a matter of complete discretion, as is the case where one chooses to enforce or not some right of one's own.

---

[10] I adapt this concept of 'justified constraint' from G W Rainbolt, *The Concept of Rights* (Dordrecht: Springer, 2006). Rainbolt's work appeared shortly before the present work went to press, so it may be by virtue of too hasty a judgment that I interpret his 'justified constraint' concept as adaptable to my present purpose.

[11] Hart, Wellman and others favour the notion of choice, or 'power over duty', or dominion; Stepanians in *Rights as Relational Properties—In Defense of Right/Duty-Correlativity* suggests that what all have in common is some from of 'control' exercised by the right-holder, and on that account proposes calling them 'control theories'.

Further, as was discussed earlier, no reparation at all is due save in case of injuries, etc, proximately caused by acts or omissions in breach of a relevant duty. But what makes a duty relevant? Only that it is *owed to* (not merely owed in respect of) the party whose injuries are supposed to be legally reparable. It is logically absurd to suppose that such a duty could be *owed to X* without its being the case that *X* has some right, viz, the right to be treated with reasonable care to avoid injury or damage of this kind. So, at least passively, *X* must here be deemed to have some right; and *X* as a legal right-holder is necessarily also a legal person.

To say this is to stress again the significance of the passive capacities of persons, which are indeed nothing other than capacities to have passive rights. What makes such passive rights intelligible is this: that even beings incapable of performing legally relevant acts (though acts of others can be imputed to them) are capable of being recognized as having interests which it is wrong to invade and wrong not to respect. As sufferers albeit not (or not yet) as doers, such beings can come within the law's protection. Respect for persons in such cases is satisfied by acknowledging various goods as constituting the good of that person and securing that each such person's good receives due attention. This is done at the most basic level by treating as legally wrongful any act that is substantially detrimental to the good of a person. Such a wrong is a wrong to the person affected, and that is a significant part of what makes it wrong, even if it is at the same time also counted as a punishable public wrong, a crime or offence.

What sometimes makes this view seem unconvincing is that rights in the absence of any ability to take remedial action in cases of infringement seem to be inert and useless. To this, however, the simple reply is that legal systems do make provision whereby parents, guardians, and the like—persons of full (active) capacity—are enabled to take legal remedial action on behalf of the person who lacks the necessary active capacity. Obligations of reparation owed to minors (and other persons of restricted capacity) are enforceable at the instance of whoever has the appropriate tutelary role; and damages paid have to be held in trust for the benefit of the person of restricted capacity. What this shows, however, is not that the *incapax* lacks rights, but that special means have to be used to make effectual the rights of the *incapax*. Since such means are used, however, the idea that rights of such beings are inert and useless is evidently false.

Proponents of the control theory take this as support for their view. It shows, they say, that what is truly constitutive of a right is the existence of a power to enforce it at the discretion of a relevant enforcer.[12] The weakness of this view is, simply, that the powers in question are powers *to enforce someone's rights* (as distinct from, eg, powers to prosecute wrongs in their character as criminal offences).

---

[12] C Wellman has most recently stated this in the following way: 'I believe that a legal right is best conceived as a system of Hohfeldian legal positions that confer dominion upon the right-holder in face of some second party in some potential confrontation' (*Medical Law and Moral Rights* (Dordrecht: Springer, 2005) at 83). On 'dominion' in its narrower sense concerning ownership, see ch 8 below.

They should not be considered as constitutive of that to which they are ancillary. That a motor car would be practically useless without fuel in the fuel tank does not make fuel constitutive of cars; that rights would be practically useless without remedies does not make remedies constitutive of rights. Remediless rights might well, however, be deemed radically 'imperfect' rights, at any rate in the sense of legal rights. This is something of a point in favour of the control theory. So in the end one must perhaps look to both theories for a full understanding, even if the benefit theory is the more fundamental, and both may perhaps be subsumed for what they are worth within the 'justified constraint theory', according to which any constraints imposed on persons for the sake of some significant feature or attribute possessed by another person create the relevant sense of a duty that is owed to the other.[13] Rights are legal positions of a normally advantageous kind, hedged around with remedial rights and powers to obtain enforcement of them. In the case of persons of full active capacity, the rights and powers vest in the same person, but in other cases the remedial powers may vest on behalf of the right-holder in some other private person or public official exercising a tutelary role. Such a tutelary role, so far as it involves discretion, involves a discretion which has to be guided by the best interest of the right-holder, not being simply a free discretion of the tutelary role-bearer.

However that may be, it is certainly true that in the case of any fully self-conscious rational agent, proper respect for that being includes recognition of it as a person capable of effectual action. A part of the insult historically offered to slaves and (only a little less grievously) to women was precisely a withholding of such recognition either entirely or in large measure. Among the most basic goods of personality is that of one's being recognized as a responsible acting subject. This indicates the significance of facultative provisions of law that either simply acknowledge one's free and responsible agency, or that also enable one effectually to engage in and accomplish legal transactions. These are properly considered to be right-conferring provisions. In this sense, indeed, the choice theory correctly identifies a feature central to the rights held by persons of full status. But still it mistakes part for whole in that it overlooks the purely passive aspect of the rights vested even in persons of full status and capacity. It would surely be Pickwickian to suppose that a sane adult's right to life is constituted by the power to demand (or waive) remedies in the event of wrongful actions causing death. Or is it thought that there was no right to life in the days when the maxim *actio personalis moritur cum persona* ('a personal action dies with the person') ruled and no remedy for wrongful death could vest in the wrongfully killed person's estate and thus transmit to successors?

This discussion of passive and active aspects of rights indicates that rights can always be considered as bearing on conduct. They may bear on the conduct of persons other than the right-holder, and here rights are passive in form: rights to

[13] Rainbolt, *Concept of Rights* 147–156.

be treated in certain ways, rights not to be treated in other ways. Sometimes rights of this sort have been called rights '*stricto sensu*', or 'claims', or 'claim-rights', or 'rights of recipience'.[14] Of these, 'claim-right' is predominant in most current discussion, though it is subject to certain objections.[15] We shall observe this usage, while insisting that in truth what is involved here is actually a purely passive right, to which active remedial and other rights are normally conjoined, in persons of full capacity, or through tutelary substitutes in other cases. The point is that such a right is a right that some other person act or refrain from acting in a certain way towards the right-holder. Necessarily, for the other person, the relevant act or abstention is obligatory. But it is not necessarily the case that a relevant other person is ascertainable whenever a right of this sort[16] vests in a given person. For example, under the Succession (Scotland) Act 1964, the children of an intestate deceased have from the moment of his or her death a right to be given equal shares of the intestate estate. This right has in due course to be honoured by an executor. But until an executor is confirmed, there is no individual upon whom it is yet obligatory to pay out the shares to the children. Where no executor has been named (in a case of partial intestacy, there might well be an executor-nominate), any one of the beneficiaries, if of full age and capacity, would be entitled to seek confirmation as executor, and therewith to acquire the duty to ensure proper distribution of the estate among all beneficiaries.[17]

It is sometimes said that passive rights always have 'correlative' duties.[18] But the example just given shows why any such thesis about correlativity has to be taken with some caution. Sometimes, when rights are conferred expressly by legislation on persons fulfilling certain qualifying conditions, we must envisage the exaction of duties from relevant others as consequential upon conferment of the right. In other cases, it is the general prohibiting of some kind of conduct—eg, conduct wilfully, recklessly, or negligently endangering life—that entails the existence in persons generally of a right not to be killed by wilful, reckless, or negligent actions of anyone else. And sometimes, where statutes impose statutory duties, it becomes

[14] 'Rights *stricto sensu*' is Hohfeld's preference; on 'claim-rights', see W J Kamba, 'Legal Theory and Hohfeld's Analysis of Legal Rights' Juridical Review [1974] 249; on 'rights of recipience' see D D Raphael, 'Human Rights: Old and New' in Raphael (ed), *Political Theory and the Rights of Man* (London: Macmillan, 1967) 54–67.

[15] A R White, *Rights* (Oxford, Clarendon Press, 1984), and compare A Halpin, *Rights and Law, Analysis and Theory* (Oxford: Hart Publishing, 1997) 97–100.

[16] M Kramer challenges my identification of a right 'of this sort' as effectively a Hohfeldian claim-right. Perhaps it should be considered in a similar right to the complex rights discussed in section 4 of the present chapter. See Kramer/Simmonds/Steiner, *A Debate over Rights* 28–29.

[17] G W Rainbolt, *The Concept of Rights* (Dordrecht: Springer, 2006) at 143 suggests that my reading of this matter involves my being 'led astray because [I do] not individuate rights as finely as they need to be individuated'. My response to this is sufficiently indicated in the next following paragraph of the main text.

[18] See Hohfeld, *Fundamental Legal Conceptions*; M Stepanians, *Rights as Relational Properties— In Defense of Right/Duty-Correlativity* (Habilitation thesis, University of the Saarland, 2005); G W Rainbolt, *The Concept of Rights* (Dordrecht: Springer, 2006) 28–29.

a matter of anxious inquiry whether the aim of the legislation properly understood was to confer rights as well as imposing duties. What should be said is that essential to the existence of every passive right ('claim-right') is either a prior or a resultant requirement on classes or individuals to act or abstain in favour of persons who hold such a right. It is in this way that passive rights are properly seen as rights in regard to conduct, for that to which they have regard is the obligatory character of acts or abstentions by others. Typically, this is necessary to securing some good for, or interest of, the right-holder, or, perhaps, where some other feature of a person's character or situation is conceived to justify a certain restraint upon another. They are also relational, in the sense that some other person or persons is or becomes subject to a duty to do, or refrain, in favour of the right-holder.

To summarize the points taken so far: 'obligations' are relations between persons one of whom has a right to certain conduct by the other, while that other owes a duty to the former. Rights and duties in this context are relational attributes, referring to either side of the obligation relationship. In the case of bilateral obligations, like many contracts, A both has rights against B and owes B duties, while B has rights corresponding to A's duties and duties corresponding to A's rights.

Next, we must note that rights may have regard to conduct in another way. This obtains when they have regard to the conduct of the right-holder himself or herself. Rights to do and rights not to do, rights to do or not do as one pleases, are obvious types of such active rights.[19] The simpler form of active right is that sometimes called a 'liberty' or (by W N Hohfeld) a 'privilege' or (misleadingly in legal terms, by D D Raphael) a 'right of action'.[20] Essential to the existence of such a right is the possession of capacity-responsibility together with either absence of any legal provision making it obligatory to refrain from the conduct in question, or possession of a specific exemption from such a provision. My having a right to refrain from v-ing is conditional on its not being obligatory for me to v. My having a right to v is conditional on its not being obligatory for me to refrain from v-ing. In both cases, my possession of capacity-responsibility is also a condition of its making sense to ascribe such a liberty-right to me. For given instances of a right to v, further conditions and qualifications may have to be satisfied in order for it to be *my* right to v; eg, *my* right to admit visitors to a particular building.

It is sometimes said that the law does not in any sense confer a right to v if all that is the case is that the law is completely silent about the matter in question.[21] This entails the absence of any legal requirement in the opposite sense, so to refrain from v-ing is not wrong. To put this alternatively, it is 'all-right' to v. Scots

[19] Cf M Dalgarno, 'Reid's Natural Jurisprudence: the Language of Rights and Duties' in V Hope (ed), *Philosophers of the Scottish Enlightenment* (Edinburgh: Edinburgh University Press, 1984) 13–31.
[20] D D Raphael, 'Human Rights: Old and New' in Raphael (ed), *Political Theory and the Rights of Man* (London: Macmillan, 1967) 54–67.   [21] Cf Rainbolt, *Concept of Rights* 6–17.

law contains no provisions whatever concerning entry upon the Moon, neither forbidding it nor enjoining it. Can it on this ground be said that Mr Neil Armstrong had under Scots law a right to land upon the Moon and walk about it as he chose? If he has such a right, in what sense can it possibly be said that the silence of this legal system on this matter amounts to 'securing' a 'good' to Mr Armstrong or anybody else? It seems as if the characterization of a right offered at the top of this section is running into difficulty.

Such objections, however, overlook certain points of some importance. First, they overlook the point that recognition of a person's active capacity is a precondition of anything's being deemed any sort of a legally cognizable act of a person. This recognition of active capacity is undeniably a positive matter of positive law, so there is actually no complete legal silence here. The issue of recognition can arise, for example, where it comes in question whether a non-citizen's acts count in the same way as those of a citizen. This is often important in the context of discussion of fundamental constitutional rights. Above all, they overlook the fact that any act whatever may be in principle open to challenge in some court of law. If we envisage some crank suing Mr Armstrong in a Scottish court for damage done by trespass upon the Moon, the absence of any prohibition in Scots law entails a (passive) right in Mr Armstrong that the action against him be summarily dismissed by the Scottish court. But precisely this passive right is what 'secures' it to him that he may if he chooses—so far as Scots law goes—land on and walk about the Moon just as he likes.[22] And so in all less fanciful or trivial cases. The liability of a person of full capacity to be judged a wrongdoer in case of committing a legal wrong and to be subjected to sanctions on that account is quite properly balanced by that person's having a right to do whatever is not prohibited. Likewise, in the converse case of refraining from whatever it is not obligatory to do under legal rules and principles. The protection which law does and should grant here is one's entitlement to a judgment in one's favour whenever some act is seriously but incorrectly challenged as wrongful. Further, the law does and must recognize one's active capacity (capacity responsibility) precisely as being a capacity to have and to exercise active rights, and to have them declared as such when appropriate.

Whatever verb one substitutes for *v*, then, having a right to *v* or having a right not to *v* is conditional upon its not being legally obligatory respectively to refrain from *v*-ing or to *v*. It does not follow, of course, that everything one does within one's (active) rights is a proper or admirable thing to do either morally or even legally. A part of the point of insisting upon the legal existence of active rights is that they create an area of personal discretion within which one cannot be called to account for doing what some may consider undesirable things. Indeed, one cannot be called to account for doing what is obviously undesirable when it is

[22] A Halpin argues that the existence of an associated passive right of some kind is always what makes it appropriate to conceptualize a mere absence of duty as being a case of an active right— (*Rights and Law: Analysis and Theory* at 261). Cf G W Rainbolt, *The Concept of Rights* 30–34.

clearly not legally prohibited.[23] All that is essential is that there be no contrary requirement. In a given case, this may be quite compatible with one's having a duty to do what one is not required not to do. It is a far from trivial truth that I can and should have a right to do whatever it is my duty to do. One must, however, note that this holds good only provided that my duty in a given case is not overridden or cancelled by some higher order requirement. A soldier has no right to commit murder even if ordered to do so by his commanding officer. For in this case the normal duty to obey one's commander is overridden by the prior requirement of respect for human rights. Since the duties of an office are often accompanied by a sense of the honour of fulfilling that office, it is by no means surprising to find people so often speaking of what it is their 'right and duty' to do or—even more commonly, perhaps—to say.

Furthermore, where *v* is a verb signifying some legal transaction or act-in-the-law, one is properly said to have a right to *v* only if one is the person or a person authorized or empowered in law to *v*, and if one infringes no legal requirement in doing so. (We must note that some exercises of power can be valid but wrongful. For example, *A*, having validly contracted to sell a piece of land to *B*, proceeds to convey the same piece of land to *C* under a subsequent contract of sale, *C* acting in good faith and with no notice of *B*'s prior right. Here *A* acts wrongfully towards *B*; but the conveyance, albeit not rightfully executed, is valid and effectual in *C*'s favour. There can be other cases in the sale of goods where a person has power to transfer property in goods without having the right to sell them, eg, on account of having acquired them by fraud, and thus under a voidable title.[24] This sufficiently indicates that powers are not themselves rights, although one can only have a right to exercise a given power provided one has that power, and provided that the exercise in question is not on some ground a wrongful one.)

The idea of being or of acting 'within one's rights' pertains to active rights. So long as one exercises any available legal powers in observation of all the conditions and hypothetical requirements governing the exercise of the power, and so long as one avoids committing any legal wrong, one is 'within one's rights'. This was, for example, said of Sir Stephen Gatty when he called up his bond on MacLaine of Lochbuie's estates in Mull, Lochbuie being then on active service in the trenches in Flanders. 'I confess I think the case a hard one,' said Lord Dunedin,[25] 'but I think the pursuers are within their rights'. Lord Atkinson in similar vein said: 'I do not think . . . that the conduct of Sir Stephen Gatty is very commendable, but at all events he cannot be deprived of his rights'.[26] These observations tie back

---

[23] Jeremy Waldron in his 'Introduction' to J Waldron (ed), *Theories of Rights* (Oxford: Oxford University Press, 1985) makes the similar point that, morally, having a right to do something would be an empty idea if this did not make it possible for one to act in a morally wrong way without being legally called to account.

[24] Cf Raz, 'Voluntary Obligations and Normative Powers' Aristotelian Society Supplementary Volume 46 (1972) 79–102 on wrongful but valid exercises of power.

[25] *Gatty* v *MacLaine* 1921 SC (HL) 1 at 10.   [26] 1921 SC (HL) 1 at 11.

in with the opening section of the previous chapter, in which the point was made that the law is primarily concerned to settle minimal requirements of conduct rather than the higher or even the most mediocre levels of what is 'commendable'. It is an important protection of a significant human good that one should be free from the law's coercion and entitled to exercise one's rights provided no wrong is done, and even if one fails to act commendably.

How is the concept of active right and of 'acting within one's rights' connected with the concepts of 'freedom', 'liberty', and 'privilege', with each of which it has occasionally been identified? When speaking in normative terms, one can certainly use the idea of 'being free to *v*' in a sense which is practically equivalent to that of 'having a right to *v*'. I am not free (in law, in morals, or by whatever normative standard one is judging) to do whatever I have no right to do; that is, whatever it is obligatory on me or required of me not to do. Being free to *v*, accordingly, is governed entirely by the absence of contrary requirement, and no element of power enters into this concept. What I am free to do is not the same as what I am able to do, and vice versa. Sometimes 'being at liberty to *v*' is used as identical with being free to do it. But 'liberty', notwithstanding the contrary opinion of Glanville Williams,[27] normally implies an element of choice, even in law. To be at liberty in respect of *v*-ing requires being free either to *v* or to not-*v* as one chooses. Furthermore, both freedom and liberty have vitally important non-normative senses. The constraints of legal requirement are one kind of constraint, but there are others, such as physical or psychological coercion or captivity. Being a free person, or being at liberty *sans phrase*, implies an absence of the actuality of coercion and captivity, and also an absence of threat of or liability to them. Hence to be (left) at liberty is the possible subject matter of a fundamentally important passive right. The use of 'liberty' in a plurality of senses, sometimes as the name for an active right and sometimes as the subject-matter of a passive right, is inevitably misleading, and hence is not here recommended.

As for 'privilege', this would again be misleadingly used if used as denoting an active right simpliciter. Privileges, as Alan R White remarks,[28] are positions of special advantage or favour, the content of special legal provisions for people in special positions. Some privileges are indeed special exemptions from legal duties, as in the case of qualified or absolute privilege in defamation, or in the case of evidentiary privileges, where one has a right to withhold items of evidence production of which is normally compellable. But other privileges, such as some of the privileges of each House of the Parliament of the UK and its members, are in the way of exceptional passive rights. Breach of parliamentary privilege in such cases involves infringing such a right, with resultant exposure to some form of remedy or punishment.

---

[27] See G L Williams, 'The Concept of Legal Liberty' in R S Summers (ed), *Essays in Legal Philosophy* (Oxford: Blackwell, 1968) 121–140.
[28] A R White, *Rights* (Oxford: Clarendon Press, 1984) ch 11.

Whether or not there are correlatives of active rights is a discussable question. Hohfeld, who analysed the present topic in terms of person-to-person relations, supposed that whenever some individual *A* has a privilege to *v* there must be some other individual *B* who has no right that *A* refrain from *v*-ing.[29] This involves misreading a positional attribute as though it were always a relational one. Necessarily, if someone has a right that *A* refrain from *v*-ing, it is wrong for *A* to *v*, and if it is wrong for *A* to *v*, then *A* cannot have a right to *v*. In such a case, it will be commonly said that *A* has 'no right to *v*'. So then conversely if *A* does have a right (active right) to *v*, no one can have a (passive) right to *A*'s abstention from *v*-ing. But to say that nobody has such a right is surely different from ascribing to each or any of *B, C, D, . . . X, Y, Z*, etc, a distinct 'no-right' that *A* should not *v*. Legal usages which do violence to the common sense of ordinary speech should be adopted only where some striking gain in conceptual clarity is achieved. Here, nothing could be farther from the case.

To recapitulate a point taken earlier, one should remark that passive rights can be conjoined with active rights of choice. In the case of persons with full active capacity, it is normally the case that when one has certain passive rights one also has matching active rights of choice. For one is free in one's own unfettered discretion to choose whether to demand or to forgo demanding observance by another or others of one's passive rights. Similarly, when rights have been infringed, it is normally a matter of free choice whether to demand a remedy from the infringer, or to let the matter pass. If the demand is made and rejected, or ignored, one has the right and power to take legal action before a court, calling for it to impose a suitable legal remedy. Here we return to points taken by proponents of the choice theory of rights, which suggests that the passive right is not really a 'right' unless it is protected by such active remedial rights. The error of this view has already been explained. Nevertheless, it is important to take account of the array of active remedial rights and powers (see chapter 9) that are needed to make any passive right fully effectual. In the case of persons of restricted active capacity, and all the more in the case of persons with only passive capacity, it is essential that provision be made for substitute guardians or other agents who are legally empowered to obtain remedies on behalf of the person under incapacity. They have to have the right and duty to intervene and exercise power to ensure that adequate remedies can be implemented for the protection of the rights of the persons under incapacity. From a legal point of view, passive rights without any adequate remedial powers held either by the right-holder or by somebody else on the right-holder's behalf would very properly be classed as 'imperfect rights'.

In connection with the choice theory, one needs also to reflect on the possibility of what are sometimes called 'inalienable rights'. It is a highly significant feature of normative orders in which rights are taken seriously that the legal protection of a right-holder is not subject to being divested save by the right-holder's free consent,

[29] *Fundamental Legal Conceptions* ch 1.

or otherwise in exceptional circumstances.[30] This depends on an absence of power on the part of other persons, even those holding official positions, to divest the right-holder of either the primary right or its ancillary and remedial rights. In the case of constitutional entrenchments and international treaties guaranteeing human rights, such disempowerment is either absolute and universal, or at least subject to suspension only on very stringent conditions. In other cases, all rights may become subject to divestment, for example by legislation, or by judicial order in civil proceedings, or by way of a criminal penalty. But the range of persons able to bring about such unilateral divesting is small and the conditions for allowing divestment fairly strict, and hedged in by constitutional conventions and interpretative presumptions.

'Immunity from divesting' is thus a general feature of the legal protection of the interests of individual persons which is functionally of the essence of rights. One could even grade the relative strength of rights according to the difficulty attached to overriding or cancelling immunities from divesting without the right-holder's consent. In the case of 'inalienable rights', this goes a step further and deprives the right-holder him- or herself of any power to waive either the immunity from divesting or the right itself. In most cases, persons of full status can normally waive or enforce their rights according to their own choice. People are presumed to be the best judges of their own interests, and a vital aspect of liberty lies in the upholding of this presumption even when people may act foolishly. Even so, in liberal states there are some rights which right-holders simply may not waive, or abandon, or alienate. Such are the fundamental right not to be enslaved, and the statutory right to safe conditions of work in various forms of employment.[31] Absolute disempowerment of this kind does restrict liberty, but restricts it for the sake of liberty, and actually strengthens protection of the rights in question. This is a further, and important, ground for dissent from any variant on a 'control' theory of rights when this is offered by way of defining 'rights' rather than by way of explaining what other relations normally accompany simple rights against others or in respect of one's own conduct.

7.4 Rights in Regard to States of Being and States of Affairs

Hitherto, we have considered rights as they have regard to the conduct of the right-holder (active rights) or to the conduct of another person or persons (passive

---

[30] A M Honoré, 'Rights of Exclusion and Immunities against Divesting' Tulane Law Review 14 (1959–60) 453.

[31] See N MacCormick, 'Rights in legislation' in P M S Hacker and J Raz (eds), *Law, Morality and Society* (Oxford: Clarendon Press, 1977) and see Rainbolt, *Concept of Rights* 44–6. That one cannot waive the right to safe systems of work does not mean that one is forced to sue whenever a breach occurs—but inspectors of factories and the like can be empowered to take enforcement proceedings even when an employee might be hesitant to do so.

rights). All such rights can be stated in relatively specific terms. Suppose one has specified the person or class of persons in whom the right vests, and the act or type of act to which it is a right, and the person or persons or class of persons against whom it avails. In this case, the right is as exactly specified as it can be, allowing for the omnipresent possibility of vagueness or open texture[32] in the language used to specify acts and persons. All such rights are rights to v or to be $v\text{-}ed$ (or their negations), where v is a verb denoting some kind of act or action.

Often, however, rights are rights to something that can be denoted by a noun or noun-phrase—'rights to n', rather than rights to act or be acted on. Obvious examples drawn from the commonplaces of everyday discourse in and about law are the 'right to life', or the 'right to a job', or the 'right to holidays with pay', or the 'right to freedom of conscience', or the 'right to freedom of association', or the 'right to respect for one's language and culture', or the 'right to privacy', or the 'right to fairness'. Most such rights are rights to, or in regard to, states of being— being alive, being in employment, being free to hold and act on one's own moral convictions, being free to associate with others of one's own choice, being free to speak one's own language and engage in traditional cultural practices, being able to enjoy seclusion from prying by others into one's affairs. Others are rights to certain states of affairs, for example the state of affairs in which employers are under some statutory obligation to make provision for annual paid vacations for their employees, or the state of affairs in which legal proceedings or other significant legal arrangements proceed on fair principles.

On closer inspection, there is an obvious connection between such rights and what we have called active and passive rights bearing on acts of certain kinds. Having the right to freedom of conscience may include the active right to visit a place of worship and to live in accordance with the precepts of one's religious conviction, and also the passive right not to be obstructed in these pursuits. The right to free speech is exercised by speaking, but it may also include some right to be heard by others, the right that others listen, or (eg, through access to media) be given the opportunity to listen, and perhaps the right not to have what one says shouted down by aggressive hecklers. The right to n (a state of being or affairs) may thus be a complex right, involving one or more rights to v or to be $v\text{-}ed$. In addition, it is likely to be much more open-textured and subject to rival interpretations than the simpler active or passive rights to v. Specific claims to act in a certain way or be treated in a certain way may be advanced as necessary implications or consequences of the asserted 'right to n'. So any full specification of the latter would have to indicate what rights to v it is deemed to entail in the given context of appeal to it. To make this better intelligible, let us consider some examples.

[32] See H L A Hart, *The Concept of Law* ch 7; N MacCormick, 'On Open Texture in Law' in P Amselek and N MacCormick (eds), *Controversies about Law's Ontology* (Edinburgh: Edinburgh University Press, 1991) 72–83; B Bix, *Law, Language and Legal Determinacy* (Oxford: Clarendon Press, 1993) 7–35.

The 'right to life' is itself ambiguous. What does it call for? Consider A H Clough's famous couplet:

Thou shalt not kill but needst not strive
Officiously to keep alive . . .

Is this acceptable as defining the right to life—effectively no more than the passive right that nobody kill one? Or should some active interventions by others be regarded as essential minima for respecting the right to life? If so, what interventions, and by whom? In the context of the state or of the international community, does the right to life entail some duty on the state or on foreign states to ensure medical treatment and some minimal income? Does it entail a duty to secure access to basic necessities for all persons in acute need of them, or in any need of them? How far does it involve a right that one's government act to diminish ordinary liberties of persons who are suspected of plotting acts of terrorist violence?

Consider again such a provision as this from the Charter of Fundamental Rights of the European Union, on the 'Right to an effective remedy and to a fair trial':

Everyone whose rights and freedoms guaranteed by the law of the Union are violated has the right to an effective remedy before a tribunal in compliance with the conditions laid down in this Article. Everyone is entitled to a fair and public hearing within a reasonable time by an independent and impartial tribunal previously established by law. Everyone shall have the possibility of being advised, defended and represented. Legal aid shall be made available to those who lack sufficient resources in so far as such aid is necessary to ensure effective access to justice.

Plainly a complex set of legal provisions is needed to make such a 'right' effective in any jurisdiction, and there are many and various ways in which the right might be infringed or insufficiently protected by institutions of a state. In terms of specific passive or active rights against officials or a state, it would be a long and tedious task to break this down into all its possible implications. This is, indeed, why it is easier simply to declare such a right in the 'right to *n*' mode, leaving it for concrete decision from case to case what the full implications are for given contexts. The Charter is not itself a legally enforceable instrument justiciable before courts of law, but it is (in this particular and others) based on the European Convention for the Protection of Human Rights and Fundamental Freedoms, which is fully legal and justiciable. It is implemented by the courts of member states of the Council of Europe, with a final back-up in the European Court of Human Rights. Over the years, in a series of contested cases, that court has built up a substantial body of case law interpreting the articles of the Convention and thus giving body to the specific implications of the various rights it protects. 'Human rights law' is a substantial body of jurisprudence. We shall further consider the legal and political implications of this in chapter 11 below, and again in chapter 15.

It would be unprofitable therefore to say much more in detail at this stage. Suffice it to note that 'rights' of the kind protected by human rights law tend to have the character of complex rights belonging to the class of 'rights to n' as that has been analysed here.[33] The instruments that confer or protect them are themselves complex and polysemous, and the business of practically guaranteeing implementation of or respect for the rights calls for a substantial body of interpretative decision-making by appropriate courts or other authorities. In terms of the simple, perhaps 'atomic', person-to-person right-duty relationship these appear as large complex molecules, where a single 'right' may imply a myriad of rights-and-duties, and indeed other legal relations or positions. When thinkers like Ronald Dworkin advance the thesis that 'taking rights seriously' is a defining feature of liberal societies,[34] they are contemplating complex rights to states of being and of affairs such as constitutional Bills of Rights and International Conventions declare. Dworkin appears to define rights, indeed, in terms of their status as 'trumps' over other aspects of the public good.[35] It is thus a necessary corollary of his position that 'rights' are always subject to interpretation, for it is critically significant to determine in light of implicit constitutional values what exactly in a given case the molecular (or 'abstract') right is to be interpreted as entailing in the way of particular atomic (or 'concrete') rights against particular officials or the state itself. It is a somewhat disappointing feature of Dworkin's work that he leaves rather vague the relationship between his own discourse of rights and the large body of work done over many years by jurists and philosophers who have elucidated the concept of 'right' in its full complexity.

---

[33] This is also true of constitutional fundamental rights, for example in Germany. See the analysis by R Alexy in *A Theory of Constitutional Rights* (trans J Rivers) (Oxford: Oxford University Press, 2002) 120–138, dealing with 'rights to something', and how to unpack these.

[34] R Dworkin, *Taking Rights Seriously* (London: Duckworth, 1977). See especially ch 4.

[35] R Dworkin, 'Rights as Trumps' in J Waldron (ed), *Theories of Rights* (London: Oxford University Press) 153–167; for critique, see Rainbolt, *Concept of Rights* 189–94.

8

Legal Relations and Things: Property

8.1 Introduction

The previous chapter explained certain rights and duties as essentially paired relations between two persons. This is the case of passive rights, where one person's right is a constraint on the other. Active rights do not have to be in this way relational, since they involve absence of the constraint of duty on a particular person, whether or not this is envisaged as relating to any particular other. (Active rights are sometimes called 'liberties' and sometimes 'privileges', though, as was noted in chapter 7, neither such usage is completely free from difficulty). These passive and active rights can be considered as simple or atomic rights by contrast with more complex or molecular ones, such as the fundamental rights of constitutional charters or bills of rights or international conventions. These are typically 'rights to states of being or affairs', discussed in the closing section of the previous chapter. Now, in the present chapter, attention shifts to a different type of complex right, that involved in the ownership of property, and in other related forms of proprietary right, or 'real right'. What kinds of legal relationships are involved in owning something? What kinds of things are susceptible to being owned? What are property rights as distinct from other kinds of rights? What are real rights as distinct from purely personal rights?

Two warnings should be stated at the outset. First, the phrase 'real rights' is not here a synonym for 'rights as they really are', by contrast with one distinguished contemporary.[1] 'Real' in this chapter has a significance akin to that used in the English and American expressions 'real property' or 'real estate'. But, in common with civilian usage, we do not treat the 'real' or 'thingly'[2] character of certain rights as applying only in the case of immovable things. Movable and immovable things, corporeal and incorporeal things, can all be subject to rights that belong in the class of real rights. A further word of forewarning: the phrase 'right *in rem*' is not

---

[1] C Wellman, *Real Rights* (Oxford: Oxford University Press, 1995).

[2] 'Real' means 'pertaining to a *res*', for '*res*' is Latin for 'thing'. My use of the civilian idea of real rights, and of the distinction between 'rights to things' and 'rights in things' derives from reflection on unpublished lecture notes about rights by A H ('Archie') Campbell, my predecessor in the Regius Chair of Public Law and the Law of Nature and Nations in the University of Edinburgh. See also K Reid, 'Rights and Things' in T B Smith and R Black (eds), *The Laws of Scotland: Stair Memorial Encyclopaedia, Vol 18* (Edinburgh: Law Society of Scotland and Butterworths, 1993) paras 1–17.

used here.[3] This usage, found sometimes in English and American legal writing, is a misuse of a Latin phrase originally adapted to the Roman law of actions, some of which were formulated 'against a thing' (*in rem concepta*) while others were formulated 'against a person' (*in personam concepta*). It is bad grammar and bad Latin to wrench these terms out of context, and the inconclusive character of writings about 'rights *in rem*' is itself enough to justify steering clear of that phrase.

8.2 Things and Rights to Them

Hitherto, in considering 'rights to *n*' where '*n*' stands for a noun, we have considered only instances of abstract nouns that signify states of being or of affairs. But what about rights to things? What if '*n*' signifies some thing, for example 'Shergar' (a racehorse), or 'a block of 100 shares in ICI', or 'the dwelling House at 44 Scotland Street, Edinburgh' or the like. These are indeed 'things' in the eyes of the law, or '*res*' in Latin. What is the difference between a thing and a state of affairs? The answer is that things are conceived as durable objects existing separately from and independently of other objects and of persons, subject to being used, possessed, and enjoyed by persons, and capable of being transferred from one person to another without loss of identity as that very thing.[4] 'Durability' means at least endurance in time, that is, having a continuing identity over some period of time. There are some things that only have endurance in time, not necessarily location in space. These are incorporeal or intangible things. Your share certificates are corporeal, tangible things, and you can specify where they are at any time, whether in your bank safe deposit, or in your desk drawer, or wherever. The shares whose ownership they certify do not in the same way occupy space—they merely endure in time. Corporeal things that are 'movable' can, as the term implies, be in different places at different times. Corporeal things that are 'immovable', like houses and plots of land, have an unchanging terrestrial position (though in some legal systems certain items that do not have unchanging position are included among 'immovables' for reasons of legal policy that favour their being subjected to the same regulatory regime).[5]

It is easy to suppose that corporeal things exist in nature while incorporeal things exist only fictitiously, or by 'legal fiction'. Fiction, however, is in this context a concept more misleading than helpful, though it has been used by distinguished jurists.[6] As

---

[3] Cf fn 10 below, and accompanying text.

[4] Cf J Waldron, *The Right to Private Property* (Oxford: Clarendon Press, 1988) 38 on 'the idea that resources are on the whole separate objects each assigned and therefore belonging to some particular individual'.

[5] This can generate awkward mismatches between systems in the context of the conflict of laws. J Carruthers, *The Transfer of Property in the Conflict of Laws* (Oxford: Oxford University Press, 2005) 1.04–1.11.

[6] Compare ch 7, n 6 above and Carruthers, loc cit, and see L L Fuller, *Legal Fictions* (Stanford, Ca: Stanford University Press, 1967); J C Gray in *Nature and Sources of the Law* (ed R Gray)

will be further discussed in a later section of this chapter about intellectual property, we must recognize that the existence, identity, and mutual separateness of things such as copyrights, patents, company shares, or servitude rights, being legal institutional facts, depend on acts, events, and states of affairs and on their interpretation in the light of legal rules. Incorporeal things are things that completely depend for their existence on human rules and conventions. It should not, however, be supposed by contrast that the identity and separateness of corporeal movable things is entirely independent of human rules and conventions—think of what makes it possible for there to be cars, or knives, or sacks of potatoes. This is even more obviously true of items of corporeal immovable property, each lot of which is identifiable only by recourse to elaborate rules of land-measurement, boundary-drawing, and mapping. '44 Scotland Street, Edinburgh' is actually a fictitious address, indeed one used in a recent novel,[7] but we can understand what it means because we know how it is possible for really existing houses or flats ('apartments') in tenement blocks to be identified in such a way. 'Fiction' is a term that should be used to designate objects existing only for imaginative purposes, not objects whose existence depends on actually functioning rules in actual, practical life.

The individuating, naming, or describing, and in some cases the manufacturing, of movable things also depends on rules and conventions. This is most obvious in the case of those corporeal movables that are 'fungible', that is, subject to being weighed and measured out, and bought or sold in specified quantities under specific descriptions. A ton of Bilston Glen coal can be handled and burned or stored away. It comprises lumps of real pieces of coal. But it satisfies the description we give it by virtue of our conventions for naming and our rules for weighing, and these take their place in a wider world shaped by distinctively human interests. The presence of carboniferous strata in the earth under Bilston Glen in Midlothian, Scotland, is a completely natural fact, wholly independent of human interest and convention. Coal dug out from there, weighed, and placed in containers does not in the same way exist as pure matter of nature, though it is neither miraculous in its provenance nor unusual[8] in its collocation. But the same naturalness is to be found in a block of shares in the Royal Bank of Scotland. All the 'things' of the law have their 'thinghood' or 'reality' defined by or under law, and, beyond law, by very basic conventions deeply rooted in human cultures.

(New York, NY: Macmillan, 2nd edn, 1921) distinguishes 'historic' from 'dogmatic' fictions, the latter of which, he argues, are an essential part of legal thought. Since such fictions are, in substance, institutional facts in the present terminology, this argument is acceptable. But the term 'fiction' is misleading for the reasons explained here. On Bentham's (unacceptable) view that every use of nouns for purposes other than to refer to physical objects involves a reference to fictitious ones, see C K Ogden, *Bentham's Theory of Fictions* (London: Taylor and Francis, 2nd edn, 2002).

7 Alexander McCall Smith, *44 Scotland Street* (Edinburgh: Polygon, 2005).

8 Regrettably, it has become decidedly unusual as a result of the closure of Bilston Glen Colliery some years ago.

In law, as already noted, distinctions are drawn between corporeal and incorporeal things, and between movable and immovable things. These differentiate the modes of existence and identity of things of these different kinds. It is certainly the case that corporeal things, both movable and immovable, are part of the material world and count as some of the constituents of that world. Thus among 'institutional facts' they differ significantly from incorporeal things, for the latter are non-material. As noted, this is not a difference well captured by resort to the contrast of 'fact' and 'fiction'. Blandings Castle is a fictitious castle, but Edinburgh Castle is not. Shares in the Drones Club Ltd are fictitious, but shares in the Royal Bank of Scotland are real shares in a real company. The Empress of Blandings was a fictitious pig, unlike the fine sow Portia that my Aunt Elizabeth reared during the War of 1939–45, thereby securing a source of excellent bacon during a time of food shortage. It is true of legal things of every kind that the way they are identified as specific and distinct things runs parallel with the way they impinge on specifically human interests and with the way human rules or conventions serve these interests.

It is in their mutual separateness, their susceptibility to human possession, their durability, and their identity through time despite changes of possession, that legal 'things' differ from abstract states of affairs. Hence rights to them and rights 'in' or 'over' them can have a much sharper specificity and exactness than are to be found in the case of rights to states of being or of affairs, what we have called 'abstract rights'. There is, however, a resemblance in that real rights are also complex. That is, they can be the ground for sets of simpler active and passive rights in regard to conduct. I turn to considering how this is so.

If you own something, for example a blue Honda Accord car with a certain number plate, I might offer to buy it from you and you might agree to sell it, conditionally on my satisfying you that I have sufficient funds to pay the agreed price. Once I have so satisfied you, I have a right to your car—that is, a right that you will transfer the car to me. Then it will be mine. The right that you will transfer the car to me is an instance of what we have called a 'passive right' or 'claim-right'. Sometimes the idea of a 'right to a thing', *'ius ad rem'* in Latin, was used to signify this kind of right held by one person against another that s/he hand over the thing to that other. This right is purely personal between the two parties. A has a right that B transfer the car at the agreed time—A cannot call upon C, or D, or any body else to do the transferring. Only B can transfer, and only B has the duty to transfer, the car into A's possession. Perhaps in some legal systems A has an active right to take it non-violently out of B's possession in case B fails to transfer it voluntarily. But this again is a matter of relations exclusively and personally between A and B. Personal rights of this kind in relation to things and their possession or use commonly arise out of obligations, especially contractual or quasi-contractual ones.

8.3 Real Rights—Acquisition and Title

Real rights stand in contrast with such personal rights. Real rights are rights *in* things rather than merely *to* them. Once *A* does receive the car and acquires ownership of it, *A* no longer has a right that avails only against *B*, *A* has a right that avails against anybody, a right in or over the thing such that anyone who interferes with it infringes a right of *A*. A person has to have appropriate transactional capacity to be able to hold or acquire rights to things. But capacity is only necessary, not sufficient—there must be some particular title, some act, or event, or occurrence that has the effect in law of vesting the right in *A*. The making of a contract and fulfilling of relevant contractual conditions is one case. Many other such cases exist—for example, in the law of succession, when a testator's death may give rise first to personal rights against an executor of a deceased person's estate, and subsequently to ownership of an asset bequeathed by the deceased, by transfer from the executor. Another example is bankruptcy, which may have the effect of vesting property in the bankrupt person's assets in a trustee or other official. Things (as distinct from limbs and bodily parts, which become things only on being severed from the living body[9]) do not have intrinsic links to any specific person. Hence the constitution of a legal link by way of a right to a specific thing, or a right in it, requires the existence of a specific title.

The issue of title is at its most salient in the case of 'rights in things', or 'real rights', such as ownership. Rights of this kind do not attach to persons naturally, nor do the things themselves. Even one's gloves, unlike one's hands, have to be put on, and can be just as casually taken off. One owns one's gloves, but not one's hands. Only given some suitable title does a real right in or over any particular thing vest in any particular person. By 'title' again is meant some act, event, or state of facts (or some combination thereof) implicating a particular person endowed with relevant capacity in respect of a particular thing. Institutive legal provisions, ones which may in this context be given the particular name of 'investitive' provisions,[10] are to the following effect:

- For any Person *P* having capacity *c* and
- for any thing *T* of type *t*,
- if an act of type *a*, events of type *e* and/or facts of type *f* are carried out or occur come to pass, by or in respect of *P* with reference to *T*,
- then a real right of type *rr* vests in *P*.

[9] But compare C Fabre, *Whose Body is it Anyway? Justice and the Integrity of the Person* (Oxford: Oxford University Press, 2006). See also J K Mason and G Laurie, *Mason & McCall Smith's Law and Medical Ethics* (with a chapter by M Aziz) (Oxford: Oxford University Press, 7th edn, 2005) 511–538.

[10] On 'investitive' and 'divestitive' provisions of law, see J Raz, *The Concept of a Legal System* (Oxford: Clarendon Press, 2nd edn, 1980) 175–183.

We may ask what constitutes title to a particular type of real right (such as ownership, tenancy, mortgage, pledge, or servitude) in a thing of a particular type (movable or immovable, corporeal or incorporeal). The answer is that it is nothing other than the legally prescribed set of acts, events, or facts that suffice to vest that right in such a person.

The simplest type of title conceptually is that of initial acquisition by taking a thing into one's possession, for example, catching a fish in the sea. *Occupatio* (to use the Latin term for this) requires an act of taking possession, in the sense of taking physical control with intent to act as owner of the thing. This act must occur in certain circumstances, viz, those of the thing being of a type admitting of possessory title and of its not being currently in another's ownership. The act necessarily relates to the specific thing, that of which possession is taken, and to a particular person, the one who so takes possession. The act can be performed by anyone with capacity-responsibility, and provided capacity for ownership exists, the person becomes owner by the act of *occupatio*. The same goes, subject to somewhat more complexity, in the case of other original modes of acquisition.[11] Of these, legal systems typically recognize: accession, as where ownership of the new-born foal goes along with that of the mare; alluvion, where new soil is gradually washed on to land by a river or by the sea; specification, where a new article is made by irreversible alteration of raw materials, ownership going to the maker; and confusion or commixtion, inextricable mixing of liquids or solids, giving rise to joint ownership of the mixture. Initial acquisition of an incorporeal thing such as a trade mark may be achieved by registration in statutory form. This both brings the trade mark into legal existence and vests ownership of it in the person registering it.

Derivative modes of acquisition concern acquisition of a thing or some right in it from another person who is already its owner. In this situation, obviously, two parties are involved. So here two persons have to have appropriate capacity, and in addition the transferor has to have good title to transfer the right in issue.[12] There may be legally stipulated procedures (eg, writing, registration of deeds or of title) that must be observed. There must be an absence of such vitiating circumstances as fraud, force, and fear, or error; and all required background circumstances must hold good. So establishing title may require establishment of complex acts and facts in such a case. In cases of acquisition by intestate succession, if ever that operates to transfer rights automatically, title is constituted by facts—of the deceased's lawful ownership, and of the successor's relationship to the deceased—and events, viz, that person's death.

---

[11] Justinian, *Institutes* II.1.12. Some things change slowly in human affairs. For modern (western) legal systems, common law and civilian alike, the contemporary law on the 'original' acquisition of things is little more than a gloss on Justinian, and before that on Gaius.

[12] Many legal systems recognize situations in which a person, acting in good faith, acquires a thing from one who is not in fact its true owner, or who has some defect of title; such acquisition can, in defined circumstances, result in full ownership vesting in the good faith acquirer. Such provisions serve the public interest in there being definiteness of ownership whenever possible.

8.4 Real Rights—their Content

The issue of title concerns the mode of acquisition of real rights. A separate issue concerns the content of the right one acquires. As to their content, one may make first a general and then some special points. The general point is that real rights entail a specific legal relationship between one person and a thing, in a way that entails consequential rights against unspecified third parties, or specific third parties who in some way interfere with the thing to the detriment of the right-holder. Stair puts this pithily in saying that real rights concern things directly, but persons indirectly, so far as they have meddled with things.[13] Although he stated it specifically in relation to ownership, Stair's point holds quite generally. Real rights are beneficial legal relations as between particular persons and particular things. They are beneficial in that they imply that the holder of the real right thereby enjoys certain active rights to the use and enjoyment of things, coupled with passive rights not to be impeded in or deprived of that use and enjoyment by anyone else. The benefit extends also to the right holder's having some degree of immunity against unilateral seizure of the thing or overriding of the right by public authorities or private persons—we may call this 'immunity from unilateral divesting' of the right.[14]

What then is to be said of the relationship to persons 'indirectly, as they have meddled with things'? Clearly there is always a risk or a possibility that somebody may invade the real right-holder's passive right by taking the thing or impeding access to it. Or somebody might challenge his or her active rights (as in the case of a prohibition to pass along a right of way). Or somebody might purport to override the immunity against divesting (eg, by a purported act of 'compulsory purchase', or confiscation). Each such invasion, challenge, or attempted override cannot but be invasion, challenge, or override by some distinct other person, or group of ascertainable persons. Against that person (or those persons) there must then be remedial rights to damages, interdict, or injunction, or some form of declaratory order. Without that ability to obtain some state-backed remedy against someone who 'meddles' in one or another objectionable way, real rights of any kind and ownership in particular would be a mere mirage. The holding of a real right in law must have among its consequential legal provisions such rights and powers to obtain legal remedies. These are remedies against any person who, as Stair puts it, meddles in any way with the thing (or, indeed, with the right, as in purported overriding of immunities against divesting). The relationship between person and thing is normatively significant only because of its logical connection to possible relations between person and person in a context where one 'meddles'

---

[13] J V Stair, *Institutions of the Law of Scotland* (ed D M Walker) (Edinburgh: Edinburgh University Press, revised 2nd edn, 1980) I.i,22. Cf J E Penner, *The Idea of Property in Law* (Oxford: Clarendon Press, 1997) 25–31.

[14] A M Honoré, 'Rights of Exclusion and Immunities against Divesting' Tulane Law Review 34 (1959–60) 453. For discussion of 'immunity', see 9.4 below.

with a thing that belongs to another. But these possible relations work in law as consequential to the person-thing relation that is a real right. Another way to conceptualize this was proposed by Jeremy Bentham. In relation to things that are subject to ownership (*res intra commercium*, things within commerce), the law concerning civil and criminal wrongs in relation to these things should be understood as a set of universal prohibitions qualified by systematic exceptions. Such prohibitions are what Jim Harris suggested calling 'trespassory rules'.[15] They say, in effect, that no one may use, or appropriate, or damage, or otherwise interfere with any thing except if he or she is the owner of that thing, or is acting with the permission or authority of the owner. (For completeness, though of no real importance here, one should nod in the direction of such other exceptions as: use in emergency situations; seizure by a public official under some express power conferred by public law; forfeiture in bankruptcy or by virtue of a court order.) In this light, the owner has a privilege (an active right) that no one else has, for everybody other than he or she is subject to the 'trespassory rules'. Thus ownership always includes an element of what Adam Smith called 'exclusive privilege'.[16]

All that has been said so far concerns real rights in general. Next, it is proper to consider briefly what is the specific difference of real rights that belong to different types. By its nature, each real right, whether ownership, tenancy,[17] security, or servitude entails among its consequences the holding of specific active and passive rights in or over the thing, differentiated according to the right in question. Each also entails powers to regulate and license its use by others (exercise of which powers may involve investment in others of rights *to*, but not *in*, the thing in question). Each real right has its own special set of consequential active and passive rights and powers. What makes it a *real* right is that each of the consequential active and passive rights with ancillary remedial rights holds good against anyone simply upon proof that the right-holder has title to the real right in that thing.[18] There does not have to be proof of any special title that obliges the given party to act in such or such a way towards the right-holder. Further, however, the consequences of holding a real right do not themselves all have the character of rights or

[15] J Harris, *Property and Justice* (Oxford: Clarendon Press, 1996).

[16] A Smith *Lectures on Jurisprudence* (ed R L Meek, D D Raphael, and P G Stein) (Oxford: Clarendon Press, 1978) 81–86.

[17] In some systems, tenancy is deemed a real right, in others it is considered merely a personal right of the tenant of property against its owner, which can give rise to complications if the current landlord sells the property subject to the tenancy.

[18] It is this feature of real rights that is highlighted by discourse about so-called 'rights *in rem*', especially within the Hohfeldian tradition that analyses these simply as bundles of rights with identical content between the right-holder and indefinitely many correlative bearers of duties or no-rights; see Hohfeld, *Fundamental Legal Conceptions* 69–81. Once this step is taken, it becomes possible to treat all such 'multital rights' as rights *in rem*, regardless of whether any 'thing' is the subject of the right. George Rainbolt, for example, discusses a person's right not to be assaulted, which is a right against everybody else, as a 'right *in rem*' in the sense of a Hohfeldian multital right. Such an approach cannot begin to tackle the true complexity of property rights. Rainbolt, *The Concept of Rights* 22, 86. For a demolition of the 'bundle' theory, see Penner, *The Idea of Property in Law* at 23.

powers. Some of them are burdens, having the character of duties and liabilities, that is of restrictions upon active rights of use and abuse. These might be imposed under planning or zoning laws, or under sumptuary laws prohibiting conspicuous consumption. There can also be restrictions upon, or exceptions in given cases to, the powers consequential upon the holding of a real right in some type of thing. Examples here are provided by restrictions upon alienation, as for example under certain forms of entail of landed property, or under the laws imposing strict conditions upon hire-purchase and credit sale agreements. Despite such burdens and restrictions, however, it remains the case that the holding of real rights is on the whole and on strongly predominant balance advantageous to the right-holder in all normal and ordinary circumstances and cases.

Nevertheless, for any given generic real right, the specific and detailed consequential provisions in the way of rights and powers (including remedial rights and powers) and in the way of duties, liabilities, and disabilities can be made subject to variation by law. When variations occur, for example by means of legislation, they do not change either the conceptual quality of the real right nor the vesting of it in particular persons over particular things. Owners of land in Scotland did not cease to own the very pieces of land they owned in the preceding moment when at a given moment in time the Town and Country Planning (Scotland) Act 1947 came into force. Nor was land ownership then abolished in Scots law. Existing rights of ownership remained undisturbed; but some of their consequences, or incidents,[19] were altered. Specifically, active rights of use of land were restricted to existing modes of use of given pieces of land; but owners were empowered to seek from local planning authorities permission for changes of use, permissions which these authorities were then empowered to grant under statutory conditions.

It can reasonably be said that such legislation constitutes a shift in the legislature's conception of the proper rights and responsibilities attaching to land ownership. It cannot reasonably be said that the concept of (private) ownership of land is thereby excised from Scots law, or any other legal system which has introduced some form of restrictive zoning or environmental-protection law. This exhibits why the theory of real rights as specific 'bundles' of other rights, or of personal rights, one each against every other citizen of the world, is not a satisfactory notion. Real rights are grounds for a variable and shifting set of consequential rights, powers, duties, liabilities, and disabilities, the rights being at least in reasonable measure hedged around with immunities against unilateral divesting. The ground remains conceptually the same even as the consequences vary, either by legislation or by private act of the right-holder, exercising one of her/his powers to change (active) rights of use of a thing, as when a landowner licenses another to enter her/his property.

[19] A valuable term suggested by A M Honoré. See 'Ownership' in A G Guest (ed), *Oxford Essays in Jurisprudence* (Oxford: Clarendon Press, 1961) ch 5.

What can be invested in a person can be also divested from that person. Divestment takes two forms. The first is transfer of the right from one person to another, so that *A's* divestment is *B's* investment. The second is termination of the right, which may occur by abandonment or dereliction of the thing and of the right in it, or by death (eg, of a farm animal), destruction, or other cessation of the thing, or by reason of the right having come to the end of a fixed term. (Sometimes the termination of the right at its term calls for the exercise of some power or powers by one or more parties, for example where a landlord must give notice to quit prior to the end of a tenancy, without which it continues by implication of law from year to year, or on some other basis. Sometimes it occurs simply by operation of law.) It is in terms of modes of divestment or termination that one can best distinguish rights of ownership from other real rights. For it is of the nature of such rights that they are divested only either by voluntary abandonment or by transfer to another, whether by a voluntary act as in gift or sale; or by an involuntary event, as on death or expropriation. Also, they are terminable only upon destruction of the thing or abandonment of the right. These reflections enable us to state in a general way what are the conditions for the existence of private property as one institution within a given legal system.

This exists in any system that provides for real rights in things of a given class, with consequential active rights. These are typically rights of use and enjoyment and power to regulate use and enjoyment by others. They have an open-ended, enduring quality, being subject only to eventual passing in the way signified by divestitive and terminative provisions such as those just noted. Any thing of the given class can be an item of someone's property. Such rights of ownership over private property contrast with rights, such as tenancies, which, albeit conferring rights of use and enjoyment and at least some powers to regulate use by others, have fixed terms. That means that they terminate at a fixed date and then divest from the holder without transference to another. Certainly, this effect may require also notice to quit given by the owner of the property, as was remarked above. They contrast also with liferents, life estates and other 'usufructuary' rights which, although lacking a fixed term, necessarily both divest and terminate upon death of the right-holder, leaving the owner of the thing previously subject to that right with full unencumbered enjoyment of previously overridden property rights.

A further contrast is with rights by of real security ('mortgages', 'hypothecs', 'pledges' of movables, etc). These rights presuppose some obligation owed by a debtor *D* to a creditor *C*. For securing this, *D* grants *C* appropriate rights in security over some property owned by *D*. Sometimes such a security right is, and sometimes it has to be according to law, one that endures for a fixed term within which *D* must fulfil the obligation in question. Whether or not that is so, it is always the case that upon some stated default of *D's* in respect of the obligation, *C* has a right to realize his/her security. This may either invest at once in *C* what were previously *D's* rights of ownership (now free of the encumbrance created by the security right). Alternatively, it may enable *C* to exercise such powers over the property as will enable him/her to secure satisfaction of the full pecuniary value of the defaulted obligation. Such events necessarily terminate the security-right, divesting *C* of it; while at the same time *D* is either divested of ownership of the property, or holds it only subject to such liabilities rights as are required to satisfy *C's* security right.

It is clear that all tenancies, lifetime rights, and real securities presuppose ownership in two senses: first, that they are all created by exercise of powers vested in owners as such; secondly, once created they constitute encumbrances upon property. For they restrict, qualify, or cancel rights of use and disposal that the owner would have but for the encumbrance in question. On the other hand, among the economic advantages that ownership secures in commercial societies are the capabilities to let out property to tenants at favourable rents and to borrow money for investment upon the security of the property. That one who has reaped the advantage of property in these ways may have fewer advantages left to reap is scarcely a cause for grief or concern; or for amendment of our definitions.

Finally, let it be noted that servitude rights of way, of light, of support, and the like, so-called 'praedial servitudes', are necessarily also real rights and do also presuppose ownership of landed property. For the duty to afford persons free passage along a path or way, or to refrain from impeding the flow of light, or to sustain the support of an adjacent building, is in each case an incident of owning the servient tenement whoever be the owner of it. The right to pass and re-pass freely upon a path or roadway, or to receive light unimpeded, or to have one's building supported is conversely a right conditional upon ownership of the dominant tenement. It is not capable of being severed therefrom save at the cost of becoming a purely personal right in favour of its current holder as against its present granter. Further, it is a particular feature of servitude rights that they are automatically terminated as such if dominant and servient tenements both come to be owned by the same person.

To summarize: in distinguishing various types of real right, one must look at each in a broad way, to see what sort of legally-secured advantage is involved. Ownership, tenancy, and lifetime rights all have in common that they look to securing a person in enjoyment and use of some thing or asset—or 'property', as we commonly say and have said here. Ownership is differentiated from the latter two by an absence of specific term, as indicated in what was said above about provisions for divestment or termination. Once that distinction is grasped, one can see how tenancy and liferent are derivative rights, created by exercise of pro-prietorial powers. Rights of real security in effect conditionally secure to the right-holder the economic value of the use and enjoyment of the subjects of the security. For the security-holder will have a prior right to them (deriving from the real right he has) in the event of default and (in particular) bankruptcy of the owner. Servitude rights enhance the beneficial incidents of ownership of one piece of land at the cost of an exactly equal increase in the burdensome incidents of ownership of adjoining land, the 'servient tenement' or *praedium serviens*.

The concepts of ownership, tenancy, liferent, real security, and praedial servitude (as of other real rights, if any) are thus to be elucidated in terms of their consequential incidents in the way of rights and powers over, and duties, liabilities, and disabilities in respect of, any thing owned. As to their acquisition, each depends upon some *title* determined by institutive/investitive provisions of law, and each is protected by some relative immunity from unilateral involuntary divesting. Voluntary divesting is a different matter, and depends on divestitive/terminative provisions to which each is subject. These determine the voluntary acts and involuntary events whereby persons may be divested of the given right, with or without its transfer to another, or whereby the right itself may be terminated.

As this suggests, just as there are acts, facts, and events which, under law, constitute titles to rights of ownership *in* things, making particular persons owners of particular things (and likewise, *mutatis mutandis*, for other real rights), so too in effect ownership and other real rights constitute titles to particular rights *to* things, or are conditions of such titles. I have the right now to mark this paper with this pen, because each is mine. You can get a right to use my pen only by securing my agreement, as its owner, to lend or sell it to you. The consequential provisions of real rights are far-reaching and ramified, and most particular rights to particular things are dependent on them. These reflections, it will appear in the next section, also apply to 'intellectual property'.

8.5 Some Observations on Intellectual Property Rights

Clearly, property is always dependent on norms. Having rights of property in some physical object, or over some (normatively demarcated) piece of land entails being protected by rules that require others to leave you unimpeded in possession and use of the thing or the plot of land. This presupposes that you acquired the rights in normatively regulated ways that constitute a good title to this right over that kind of thing. In ordinary everyday thought, all this is overshadowed by awareness of a factual social state of affairs, your physical control over the thing or land and over access to it, and your sense of psychological security and easy familiarity with the place.[20] There is likely to be an equally unreflective acceptance by others, at any rate others who also have some things to call their own, that this is yours and you have the say about what goes on here, how this car or computer is used and by whom.

We have established in previous sections of this chapter that the rules or other norms that define property always establish a three-place normative relationship: the relationship is between one person, who owns; a thing, which is owned; and other indeterminate persons as against whom the owner's ownership prevails. Ownership is the most extensive real right known to the law. There are other,

---

[20] Cf Penner, *The Idea of Property in Law* at 2–3.

lesser rights in things, such as servitude rights, but ownership is the fullest or most complete of such rights. It is a right of a peculiar kind in that it is itself the ground of a set of more particular rights and other incidents possessed by or incumbent on an owner by virtue of her/his being owner. At the centre of these is the idea captured in the concept 'use-value' by Marx and other economists under his influence. The point of owning a thing is that you can use it as you wish, and others cannot. That is, they cannot save with your permission, or in their exercise of a right to or in the thing specifically conferred by you in the exercise of one of your powers or rights consequential on ownership. How is this so?

In this picture, as we saw, an owner has the benefit of non-subjection to a duty that binds everyone else: the duty not to use the thing. An owner has the active right to use a thing which everyone else is duty-bound to leave alone, what Hohfeld called a 'privilege', in this case an exclusive privilege. To generalize: ownership entails exclusive privilege. This means both the privilege to use the thing to the exclusion of others and the privilege to exclude others from using the thing. This is quite easy to grasp in the case of physical objects both movable and immovable, and perhaps some others as well. But contemporary law and the contemporary economy accord great importance to yet more exotic objects, 'intellectual property rights', abbreviated as 'IPR'. How can the present account accommodate patents, trade marks, copyrights, design rights, know-how? What about the very idea of 'intellectual property', indeed? Must this be dismissed as no more than an oxymoron akin to the notoriously suspect phrase 'military intelligence'? Or can we make any sense of the idea that here there exists property just as genuinely as there may be ownership of shoes, ships, sealing wax, or cabbages?

In one way, it looks easy. Ownership, we have seen, implies exclusive privilege, the privilege of use of the thing in question. Copyrights and patents likewise imply exclusive privileges, the privilege of reproducing a certain ordered set of meaningful words or symbols or images, with copyright, and with patent, the privilege of carrying out a certain creative process that makes use of particular knowledge in a particular way. But where is the thing? In this case, surely the privilege is not *about* some thing. The privilege seems to be the very thing itself.

The law prohibits every person except the original author or the registered inventor (or persons who have obtained a licence from her/him, or have acquired the copyright or patent itself from her/him) from commercially reproducing that string of intelligible symbols, or from manufacturing a particular commodity using that process. Hence the author or inventor (or the licensee or transferee) has a legal privilege to do that which no one else may do, and this is an exclusive privilege. But which printing press or factory is bound by this universal prohibition? Which factory or other work-place? The answer is 'any one at all'. The prohibition is indeed universal, subject to the exclusive exception. Nor on the other hand is the privileged party privileged in respect of anything in particular. Any printing press can be used, any typeface, any factory anywhere. You cannot exercise the rights of intellectual property-holding save by bringing about effects in the physical world, using movable and immovable things as you do so. But the intellectual property right is not itself a right of property over the things you use or things you produce, though they may indeed be yours as well. The intellectual property right focuses on and seems almost to be exhausted in, the very privilege itself. It is almost so, but not quite: the conceptual structure on careful analysis will prove to be one according to which you have the privilege as a consequence of your ownership of the copyright or the patent.

Here we see the law at the work of reification, thing-making. Some commentators, especially within the Critical Legal Studies movement have taken reification to be a particular vice of traditional jurisprudence.[21] They are half right—jurisprudence abounds in reification; but half wrong also—there is nothing intrinsically vicious about this. We must consider: what is the thing that is constructed here? It is, plainly, a thing existing in the contemplation of law, a 'copyright', or a 'patent', or a 'design right', or a 'trade mark', or a 'brand name', let us say. How is it that these words name things? According to the institutional theory of law, they name institutional facts—and this is unremarkable given the institutionalization involved in all the classifications of things that can be owned under law. That I owned the copyright of the present book but have assigned it for a period to Oxford University Press is a fact of the relevant kind. The judgment we pass in such a case concerns not just physical facts—such facts as that over several years I have worked and re-worked attempts at exposition of an institutional theory of law, eventually creating a master data file accessible on my computer, then printed everything in that file on certain sheets of paper, and delivered these to a publisher's editor, leading to their eventual printing and binding in the form of the book now in the reader's hands. As well as these physical facts, you must add a judgment in terms of an understanding of the facts and relationships involved. These are humanly meaningful because imputable to shared human norms of conduct. The existence of a copyright, like the existence of a queue in the book's introductory example, is a matter of 'institutional fact', not simply one of 'brute fact', though in this case the relevant norms of conduct concerning copyright crucially include norms of state law.

The 'property-character' of the norms in question depends on their including norms that facilitate transferability. This may be transferability between persons either of the property-item, some particular copyright or particular patent itself, or of some of its incidents, as in the case of licences to print copies of the literary work or to manufacture goods by means of the patented process. Transferability implies contract, and contract implies payment in return for total or partial transfer. The reification of exclusive privileges of this kind, by making them into durable and interpersonally transferable entities, at the same time commercializes

---

[21] Cf W Twining and D Miers, *How to Do Things with Rules* (London: Butterworths, 4th edn, 1999) 143–146, 372. The advantage of reification becomes clear in the light of, eg, K Reid 'Rights and Things' in T B Smith and R Black (eds), *The Laws of Scotland: Stair Memorial Encyclopaedia, Vol 18* (Edinburgh: Law Society of Scotland and Butterworths, 1993) paras 1–17 at 16.

authorship and invention, making them processes of new wealth-creation as marketable objects.[22]

To conclude: intellectual property rights are necessarily artificial creations of state law—'institution things', in the terminology of this book. There have to be laws in place that make three different kinds of provision, exhibiting the triadic rule-structure that is characteristic of legal institutions according to the approach taken in this book. First, they must prescribe in what circumstances and on the occurrence of what acts or events an instance of some named IPR comes into being and vests in a particular person as his or her property. Secondly, the law must provide what privileges and other rights belong to the holder of the IPR as such, including powers to license other persons to use the IPR upon specified conditions. Conversely, the trespassory rules will prohibit all persons other than the IPR-owner or licensees of the owner from acting in ways it characterizes as infringements of the right. Finally, the law must specify how and when any particular right is extinguished, eg, by the passage of time, and how it can be transferred from one person to another, either voluntarily or by operation of law.

8.6 Splitting Ownership: The Trust

Trusts are a legal device for splitting the legal ownership of some asset or assets from the right to beneficial enjoyment of the asset and its fruits. Legal ownership of the trust property is vested in a trustee or trustees on a legal title appropriate to the thing(s) in question. But the trustee(s) have the duty to manage, use, and conserve these things, the trust assets, only for the benefit of the persons for whom they hold the property on trust, the 'beneficiaries' of the trust. A trust is normally created by a specific deed whereby an owner of assets passes ownership to named trustees to hold the assets for the benefit of named individuals, or for the general public benefit, in the case of a charitable trust. There can also be situations in which a trust comes into existence by operation of law, where the law specifies, on the occurrence of certain events, assets held or acquired by one person will be subject to a trust in favour of another.

The trust originated in English law as a result of an historic division between the common law, administered in the ordinary law courts, and equity, which was administered by the Lord Chancellor in the Court of Chancery. The roots of the Chancellor's jurisdiction lie in the proposition that there may be uses of property which are within the strict legal powers of an owner, but which that owner ought not to exercise in good conscience. One example would be if somebody about to undertake a hazardous journey entrusts some property to a friend to look after for the sake of his or her children, and the friend then uses the property for his own

[22] H L MacQueen, *Copyright, Competition and Industrial Design* (Edinburgh: Edinburgh University Press/David Hume Institute, 2nd edn, 1995).

purposes to the detriment of the children. The Chancellor could be petitioned to intervene in such cases and enforce more conscientious conduct. The Chancellor's jurisdiction was thus an 'equitable' jurisdiction, in the classical sense according to which the strict provisions of law ought sometimes to be overridden to achieve a more fair or equitable result. For the enforcement of equitable duties, there were equitable remedies, which imposed burdens up to and including physical imprisonment on those subjected to them, thereby forcing them to exercise their legal powers in accordance with the requirements of equity as determined by the Chancellor.

The upshot of this division of jurisdictions between the common law and equity was to facilitate the evolution of two parallel sets of rules, one of which regulates the ownership of property at common law, the other of which regulates its beneficial enjoyment according to the dictates of equity. Thus within a single legal system, that of England and Wales, there evolved a form of split ownership, whereby legal and equitable titles to a given asset can be held by different persons. From the point of view of one who has legal ownership of many things of all kinds, it may be the case that some belong to him or her both in law and in equity, as a full beneficial owner, while others belong to him/her only as a trustee in favour of someone else. That latter then has the equitable ownership of the things that are subject to the trust. There are consequential problems about third parties— what if one person gives or sells an asset which he/she holds as trustee to a third party? Does that person now hold the asset on trust for the original beneficiary, or can he/she become beneficial owner, leaving the trustee in possession of the purchase price, held on trust for the beneficiary?

The general rule in relation to third parties is that only a third party who purchases an asset in good faith without any knowledge or imputed knowledge ('actual or constructive notice') of the trust, and who pays full value for it, acquires it free of the trust. In that case, the original trust relationship continues between trustee and beneficiary in relation to the purchase price paid, and any assets into which it is subsequently converted. Otherwise, the new owner becomes subject to a trust in favour of the original beneficiary. (Alternatively, a trust deed may confer on trustees powers of management, including powers to acquire and to dispose of assets in ways that seem advantageous to beneficiaries. In this case, of course, a purchaser in good faith from a trustee who is exercising such a power in good faith acquires the asset free of the trust.) All this is in principle a simple picture, but it need scarcely be said that the parallel systems of law and equity—since 1873 managed within a single unified court system in England and Wales, and in most of the other common law countries too—have acquired great complexity in details. They have also facilitated developments in the law of property that have had huge economic impact, in facilitating many and versatile ways of disconnecting the enjoyment of economic value from technical aspects of legal ownership.

The particular division of law and equity achieved in England and countries with legal systems derivative from the English was a unique one, and other systems struggle to achieve the kind of internal split in real rights that it involves. Yet the advantages achieved through a developed law of trusts are plain to be seen. Some civilian (or mixed) systems accordingly developed versions of the trust, especially those which came strongly under the influence (direct or indirect) of English law, as in Scotland and other civilian jurisdictions in the Commonwealth and the United States. There are problems of making this work where there is no historical trace of a split of jurisdiction between courts of law and courts of equity—how can there be trusts without equity, in the sense of a separate equitable jurisdiction?[23]

The problem is that a conceptual division of rights into real rights and personal rights such as that proposed in the present chapter has difficulty in accounting for the position of a beneficiary of a trust. Certainly, the beneficiary's rights against the trustee are in principle personal rights, rights against the trustee 'to' things, but not 'in' them. In respect of the rest of the world, the trustee holds the real rights in the things which are subject to the trust, and hence any transfer by the trustee to a third party must in principle be effective in that person's favour. If, however, the third party takes the thing knowing of the trust, there is no reason at all why the personal rights of the beneficiary should not continue to encumber the property by binding the new owner. They clearly should do so, unless steps have been taken to ensure that the trust relationship now governs new assets held by the original trustee in substitution for that which has been sold to the third party. So a beneficiary's personal rights may be no more than rights *to* a thing, but may nevertheless run with the thing and bind each successive owner of the thing except an eventual good faith purchaser for value who acquires it with no notice of the trust. Thus the beneficiary's personal right acquires much of the economic significance of a real right even without changing its fundamental legal character.

It is easier to account for this in the original systems within which the trust is at home. If there are parallel systems of property ownership within a single entire legal order, it is possible that there are real and personal rights in each of these. The equitable owner of an asset has a real equitable right in it; the owner at common law has a real right in it at common law. How then do these relate? The answer is that the equitable real right overrides that at common law so far as concerns ensuring beneficial enjoyment of property, except in the case of the person who acquires the real right at common law for full value and without actual or constructive notice of any equitable rights encumbering the property. In that case, the equitable real right is defeasible in favour of the common law right. Because equitable rights, although defeasible,[24] are defeasible only in stringently defined contexts they are quite properly to be considered as a species of property rights.

---

[23] G Gretton, 'Trust without Equity' (2000) International and Comparative Law Quarterly Vol 49, 599–620.
[24] On defeasibility generally, see 9.4 below, and MacCormick, *Rhetoric and the Rule of Law*, 237–53; also R H S Tur, 'Defeasibilism' Oxford Journal of Legal Studies 21 (2001) 355–368.

8.7 Conclusion

Property in all its forms is norm-dependent, and legal property depends on and is defined by the norms (rules, principles, etc) of particular legal systems, structured in the ways explained here. What kinds of property to recognize, and how extensively to recognize different kinds, is a question of politics, guided by economics and perhaps moral philosophy. This is particularly obvious, and sometimes quite controversial, in the case of intellectual property, for reasons to which we shall return in chapter 13. For the present, suffice it to say this: in principle, at least, one could abolish every form of private property, and prohibit every use of every thing save particular uses licensed by public licensing authorities to particular persons. Since that is in principle possible, it follows that a full socialization of property is possible, and could still allow of the necessity that the actual use of particular things be by particular people. Such an 'administration of things', however, could hardly involve any 'withering away' of the state, for a vast apparatus of public law would be called for, and a vast variety of public institution-agencies regulating the administration of things would have to be set up. To whatever extent that private property is recognized, ownership of it involves a devolution of power over the use and enjoyment of things to the discretion of each member of a multitude of persons in ways that constantly vary in the context of markets wherever these exist. Whether it is desirable to eliminate such a devolution of power is a different question from that concerning its possibility. Aside from complete socialization, it can confidently be asserted that all legal systems allow of some forms of private property exercisable by some classes of persons (governed by status and capacity) over some types of things. And all forms of property and associated real rights can be understood in terms of the analysis here stated.

9

Legal Powers and Validity

9.1 Introduction

The idea of change is an idea essential to the discussion of power. Power in general is the ability to cause or prevent change in some prevailing state of affairs. As between human beings, power of one over another is the ability within some given context to take decisions that bring about changes affecting that other's interests regardless of their consent or dissent. People frequently do, and always have reason to, act in accordance with their interests. Hence, when one has power over another in the sense of being able to affect that other's interests regardless of consent, this amounts to having the ability unilaterally to affect the other's reasons for action. Someone who has power over another is able to impose on that other reasons for action or inaction that would not otherwise have existed. Since people often act in accordance with the reasons they have for acting, it follows that having power means being able to get people to do things, to act as they might not otherwise have acted. Conversely, it can mean being able to get them to refrain from doing things they would otherwise have done. Exercises of power affect the way in which it is rational for people to act.

Interpersonal power is hence a factor in practical reason; it is a factor relevant to the practical deliberations of both the power-holder and the person subjected to the power. Sometimes an exercise of sheer physical power, or psychological compulsion through the exercise of outstanding charisma, may simply overwhelm another person's will or reason. But in general terms, and setting aside such exceptions, interpersonal power operates through reason, and makes it possible to understand human action and behaviour in the context of some kind of rational and motivational account of it. Power of a purely mechanical kind is different. To say that the power of the moon's gravitational field causes the tides to rise and fall does not imply that anyone thinks of the sea as responding to the moon's demands. Some would argue, with Michel Foucault,[1] that social structures are endowed with an analogous form of power extraneous to practical reason. This is

---

[1] M Foucault, *The History of Sexuality, Vol I* (trans R Hurley) (London: Allen Lane, 1979) 93; *Power/Knowledge: Selected Interviews and Other Writings* (ed C Gordon) (New York, NY: Pantheon, 1980), and see R Cotterrell, *The Sociology of Law* (London: Butterworths, 1992) 297–298.

a power which, like mechanical power, operates without regard to reason and deliberation, and enables us to explain social events and outcomes in terms of the operations of the social structure regardless of individual motivation or decision. Power in that social-structural sense can be borne in mind as one possible source or ground of the interpersonal power that is here analysed. For if we were to ask how it comes about that one person is able to act in ways that affect another's interests regardless of consent, it seems probable that some account of social-structural aspects of the situation of the parties would be highly relevant.

This discussion of power so far looks at power-in-fact, power actually to change the factual situation so that another's interests are affected, and thereby his or her reasons for action or inaction altered. When we turn to consider normative order, the focus switches to the possibility of bringing about change concerning what it is right or wrong to do. Since ideas of right and wrong belong within the range of reasons for action, it follows that we must acknowledge the possibility of normative power as a special form of interpersonal power. This exists when one is able to change ways in which it is, within a certain normative order, right or wrong to act, or able to change possibilities of change of that simpler sort.

Normative power is, then, the ability to take decisions that change what a person ought to or ought not to do, or may or may not do, or what a person is able or unable to do, in the framework of some normative order.[2] Sometimes, as will appear, these changes call for the consent of the person or persons affected, sometimes not.

It is worth repeating that such power, as normative power, remains distinct from power-in-fact. This provides the ground for the distinction of legal power from a closely related, and indeed intertwined form of power, political power. Political power is power over the conditions of life in a human community or society. It is the ability to take effective decisions on whatever concerns the common well-being of the members, and on whatever affects the distribution of the economic resources available to them. The taking of such decisions has important bearing on the reasons that guide the actions of people in their social intercourse with each other. Political power is power-in-fact, concerning what can actually be brought about by the decisions of power-holders.[3]

However, since the ability to do such things depends to a considerable extent upon the opinion of members of a society, especially their opinion concerning the legitimacy of a decision-maker's decisions, it follows that political power is rarely independent of legal power. For legitimacy is largely dependent on the possession of power or authority conferred by legal order, so far as it is not a matter of purely

---

[2] Cf N MacCormick, 'Voluntary Obligations and Normative Powers' Aristotelian Society Supplementary Volume 46 (1972) 59–78, and reply by J Raz in same volume, 79–103.

[3] M Loughlin, *The Idea of Public Law* (Oxford: Oxford University Press, 2003), at 89–90, rightly says that I regard political power as a species of 'power-in-fact', but, as the present argument makes obvious, there is no merit in his suggestion that in my view this depends on something other than the 'relationship between rulers and ruled'.

traditional respect for the order of things as they have always been, or of responding to the personal magnetism or charisma of a political leader.[4] Conversely, the stability of any institutional normative order must be dependent to a considerable extent on the possibility of exercising power-in-fact in the political setting. Hence, although it is important to distinguish political from legal power, it seems improbable that either can endure without the support of the other; certainly not in any society whose members aspire to co-exist in a law-state (or 'constitutional state') organized under the rule of law.[5]

9.2 Law as Enabling

It is an obvious and important truth that law has as much to do with enabling as with obligating. In large part, H L A Hart's *The Concept of Law* is an exploration of the theoretical significance of this truth.[6] Law gives powers as well as imposing duties. These can be powers exercisable as a private person, for example, contracting a marriage, forming a partnership, making a will, or buying and selling stocks and shares. Or they can be powers exercisable as a holder of some public office, for example, as a member of a legislature voting upon legislation, as a judge hearing and deciding a lawsuit, as a tax official issuing a notice of demand for some due payment of taxes, as a local authority granting planning permission for property development under a zoning law, or as an official issuing payment of a social security benefit. The difference between public and private powers is fully explored in chapter 10 (the next chapter).

The empowering aspect of law can be envisaged as involving a legally conferred capability to alter the legal situations or relationships of legal persons. Powers in law in their simplest form are powers to vary in some way what it is right or wrong to do. For example, by consenting to take part in a boxing match with *B*, *A* (validly) waives the right not to be assaulted by *B*, though only so far as concerns those forms of physical attack allowable under the rules of boxing. Deliberate blows to head and body are not wrongs in a properly supervised and conducted boxing-match, though assaults of the kind involved would certainly be wrong in almost any other context. Since it is also possible to change the ways in which to make such changes in what it is right or wrong to do, there can be much more complex powers. Such complex powers include power to confer, vary, or restrict powers and cognate relations as well as powers to impose, confer, vary, or restrict duties and rights.

---

[4] M Rheinstein (ed), *Max Weber on Law in Economy and Society* (trans E Shils and M Rheinstein) (New York, NY: Simon and Schuster, 1967) xxxi–xxxv. Cf Cotterrell, discussing Max Weber's theory of 'legitimate domination', in R Cotterrell, *Law's Community* (Oxford:Clarendon Press, 1995) 137–139.

[5] Cf Loughlin, *Idea* 88–89 on the mutually interactive and mutually supportive interaction of legal and political power. He differs from me less than he thinks.

[6] *The Concept of Law* (Oxford: Clarendon Press, 1961; 2nd edn, 1994), especially at 27–42.

In Hart's conception of law, and others derivative from his, powers are con-ceived as conferred by a particular kind of legal rules. These are rules that guide both conduct and judgment of it by prescribing what must be done in order to exercise a certain power, whether a private one or a public one. Legal power con-cerns bringing about change in the legal situation. To bring about an intended change, one must act in ways prescribed by the power-conferring law. If one does, one's act is valid and the change takes place; if not it is invalid and thus ineffectual, or at best imperfect in its effects.[7] So far as concerns the exercise of judgment, power-conferring rules make it possible to differentiate valid and invalid results of acts performed with a view (actual or imputed) to bringing about certain legal changes which would not otherwise take place. Valid exercises of power are effective in changing the legal situation in some way, and indeed they often bring about complex sets or series of changes. Whatever reason one has for bringing about such changes, these are reasons to observe the law's requirements for validity. Therefore such requirements are in the Kantian sense hypothetical in character, at least in the case of private powers. There are things you have to do if you want to bring about certain legal changes, but not otherwise. By contrast, though many public powers involve a broad discretion concerning their exercise, they are always to be exercised according to a con-scientious judgment of the public interest.[8] Others may be less widely discre-tionary, and some may even be exercisable only where there is a duty to exercise them, eg, when a valid request or complaint of some kind is made through some person's exercise of private power.

A complete understanding of any particular power (and, generalizing, an adequate understanding of the concept of 'power' in its normative sense) depends on adequate awareness of the whole range of circumstances required for validly exercising power.[9] The conditions of legal empowering are always in some measure complex, and in each case must cover the following elements:

(a)   What person or persons, having
(b)   *either* what active capacity *or* what competence based on some position or appointment,
(c)   in what required circumstances, and
(d)   in the absence of what vitiating circumstances or factors,
(e)   by what if any special procedures or formalities, and
(f)   by what act
(g)   in respect of what if any other persons
(h)   having what general capacity
(i)   can validly bring about a certain legal change?

---

[7] Hart, *Concept*, 92–97; J Raz, *The Concept of a Legal System* (Oxford: Clarendon Press, 2nd edn, 1980) 156–166 and 224–230.

[8] This is discussed further in ch 10; public powers are powers to act in the general interest.

[9] Cf MacCormick, *Rhetoric and the Rule of Law* 249–251.

Points (a) and (b) draw attention to the qualifications required for having and exercising any legal power. Private powers depend upon those general characteristics of persons (such as age, soundness of mind, gender, citizenship, more generally 'status') that determine 'transactional capacity' in the various ways discussed in chapter 5. One can make a contract only if one has the necessary active capacity, and only (point (h)) with another party who also has this capacity. Public powers depend on some particular competence, based on the holding of some legally defined office or position, normally through a process of valid election or appointment, the validity of exercise of powers being dependent on the validity of the office-holder's position. Such powers involve the exercise of 'authority', in so far as they may involve a capability to change the legal situation without the necessity of obtaining consent from other parties affected.

Elements (c) and (d) draw attention to the way in which powers may be exercisable only given the presence of certain conditions (c). Their exercise may still be (d) defeated or vitiated by the presence of adverse circumstances such as mistake, intoxication, or duress, or bribery, or bias, or invalidity of appointment to office, in the case of public powers.

Elements (e) and (f) draw attention to the fact that exercising a power requires the performance of some act, possibly attended by some solemnities or formalities of procedure or execution. Points (g) and (h) draw attention to something particularly important in the case of private powers, namely that it is common for such powers to be exercisable only in respect of other persons who themselves have appropriate capacity. Indeed, they often have a reciprocal power, that of acceptance or rejection of an arrangement proposed by the first party's initial power-exercising act: for example, where *A's* offer of marriage or of some other contractual terms must be matched by *B's* acceptance of the offer on the same terms. Where there is both valid offer and valid acceptance, the joint act of the parties is effectual to set up validly the arrangement in question. Powers of this kind are, in an obvious sense, essentially bilateral, and contrast with powers that can be exercised by one person in respect of another without any requirement of that other's consent ('unilateral' powers).[10]

This draws attention to the question in exactly what way powers need to be conceptualized in relational terms as having some form of 'correlative'. Are powers 'relational attributes'?[11] As we have just seen, it is normal that private powers are bilaterally relational in the sense that their full exercise requires the consensual or reciprocal interaction of two or more parties, each having requisite capacities. On the other hand, public powers of a law-making or executive decision-making kind do not characteristically require any such consensual or reciprocal interaction, and

---

[10] Even in the case of bilateral powers, someone always has to make the first move, and in doing so unilaterally changes the legal position of the other party. If I make you a certain offer, even an unwelcome one, I thereby confer on you the power to reject or accept it. Only if you do accept, of course, does a valid contract come into existence.

[11] See above, Introduction to Part II, at n 2, on 'relational attributes'.

are thus not in this way bilateral. Still, it can always be a question whether a particular person is or is not subject to a particular power exercisable by another. Perhaps a police officer purports to arrest a person who has refused to give certain information requested by the officer. Or, more spectacularly, a federal judge purports to issue an order to the president requiring that certain tapes in the president's possession be surrendered to the court. In each case it is a question whether the given purported exercise of power is indeed valid against that other person in the given circumstances. Another like question is whether a legislature whose powers of legislating are subject to defined limits can validly pass legislation to ban or restrict abortions, or indeed to remove restrictions on them.

On this account, since power-exercising acts purport to change the legal position in some way, and since this must affect some person in some way, there is always a relational aspect to the exercise of power. For it is always open to question which persons can legally have their legal situations altered in the given way by that act of that power-holder. Hohfeld used the term 'liability' to denote exposure to the valid exercise of a certain power. Although this is a potentially misleading use of a term in common use in another sense,[12] it has become so well-established a term in this context as to be incapable of substitution by some potentially preferable term such as 'susceptibility'.

It is, in any event, clearly not necessary always to have in contemplation the relational character of a power. When contemplating a parliament's legislative powers, we rarely take note that everyone subject to the legal system is susceptible to the impact of new legislation, though this is so. Only the above-noted bilateral private powers and others like them have to be contemplated in these terms for all purposes. But for any power, there can be some circumstances when the relational view of it becomes salient. With any power, one may always have reason to ask in the case of a particular person towards whom a purported exercise of power has been directed whether or not this person is indeed susceptible to this exercise of this power. And on a certain widely-held conception of fairness, any such party affected should be given the opportunity to raise any grounds of objection to the exercise of power that he or she thinks provable and appropriate to defeat the effectiveness in law of the purported exercise of power in the given case.

This observation brings us back to the point about vitiating conditions that defeat the validity of an otherwise proper exercise of a power. Points (c) and (d) on the above list of matters to be determined for the full specification of a power were:

(c) subject to what required circumstances, and
(d) in the absence of what vitiating circumstances.

---

[12] W N Hohfeld, *Fundamental Legal Conceptions as Applied in Judicial Reasoning* (ed W W Cook) (Newhaven, Cnn: Yale University Press, 1919) 50–59; on the normal sense of 'liability', see MacCormick, *Rhetoric and the Rule of Law*, 75–76.

As we have seen, the exercise of a power requires that there be a person with appropriate capacity or competence performing a specified act in a specified form or by an appropriate procedure. In addition, however, there have to be appropriate background circumstances. These might, for example, be prior possession of a property right one proposes to transfer, or the giving of due notice, eg, in the case of marriage, or having an appropriate intention, eg, intention to create legal relations (contract), intention to create an irrevocable trust (trust), or the like. Such 'positive' conditions are within the knowledge and, to a degree, the control of the party who seeks to exercise a power. To some extent they contrast with the 'negative' conditions envisaged in (d). These are circumstances whose absence is a prerequisite of the valid exercise of power. They are circumstances whose presence vitiates the otherwise valid exercise of power, such as mistake (error) of one or both parties, or fraud, or unintended contravention of some collateral provision of the law, or illegal or immoral purpose of one or both parties. This kind of vitiating factor may depend upon a background principle of law, not necessarily on an explicit rule, or explicit condition, or exception specified in a rule-formulation. Where a widow claims a widow's pension on the ground that her husband is dead, it may be contrary to principle (not to any specific rule of the pensions legislation) for this to be granted if the cause of the husband's death was manslaughter by his thereby-widowed wife.[13] Characteristically, such vitiating factors are often of a sort which lie outside the control, and thus even the knowledge or reasonably obtainable knowledge, of the person who exercises the power. Difficulties of a similar sort might affect questions of capacity both of the power-exerciser and of the other party in the case of a strictly bilateral power. Whenever a person acts with a view to exercising a certain power, he or she (and his or her legal advisers) can take all possible steps to secure regularity in matters within his or her own control or knowledge, and can exercise considerable diligence to check on the absence of vitiating circumstances. Yet even so there remains some risk, often only the faintest risk, that events as they unfold will reveal some defect. This may render the ostensibly valid exercise of power defective. This in turn may mean that it has been either a nullity *ab initio* or that it has become nullifiable (voidable) in its effects as from the moment of discovery of the defects or some earlier or later date determined by appropriate legal provisions.

What more has to be said about the legal changes that power-exercising acts bring about? Very often, these relate to and flow from the making of some arrangement of an institutional kind.[14] Typically, powers are powers to bring about some arrangement, some new constellation of legal relationships. Particular arrangements are instances of general abstract 'institutions' of private or commercial law, such as marriage, contract, trust, property transfer, or incorporation of a company.

---

[13] Cf the discussion of *R* v *National Insurance Commissioner, ex parte Connor* [1981] 1 All ER 770, in MacCormick, *Rhetoric and the Rule of Law*, 242–243.

[14] N MacCormick, 'Institutions, Arrangements, and Practical Information' Ratio Juris, 1 (1988) 73–82.

In public law, particular Acts of Parliament are instances of binding legislation; particular judicial decisions instantiate forms of legal judgment and remedy, or criminal conviction and sentence, or public law order; revenue officials issue demands for payment consequential on tax assessments; local government bodies grant particular instances of planning permission for particular building developments in particular places under stated conditions—and so on. Particular arrangements, as instances of such institutions, endure in time from the moment of their valid establishment until some later date when they are terminated either by a further exercise of power or by some other legally stipulated event (for example, somebody's death). During their valid existence (and sometimes even after it) they function as the conditions of other ulterior legal consequences, including duties and rights of particular persons or persons in general, and also various forms of power. This accounts for the way in which valid exercises of power amount to effectual changes in legal relationships. What is valid or invalid is the particular arrangement (or institution-thing, or institution-agency, eg, an incorporated company) that some person sought to establish. Given that such arrangements are normative in their content, altering duties, or rights, or powers of other persons, the validity of the arrangement entails the validity of the norms it brings into being.

All these considerations add up to a strong reason for dissenting from Hart's idea that each power derives from a single 'power-conferring rule', one per power, so to say. Contemplate for a moment the law about the formation of contracts, or about the incorporation of companies as legal persons, or about the creation of trusts, or in relation to practically any significant legal institution. Here, to be sure, many rules and principles attested in many precedents, and often in codes or statutory provisions as well, interact in determining the matters we summarised in the list (a) to (h) above. The power/liability relationship depends indeed upon the law, but not because just one rule confers or creates each legal power. The possibility of establishing arrangements validly within an institutional framework entails the possession of power by persons having appropriate capacity. It endows them with the ability to change the normative situation of themselves and others that we have identified as conceptually central to the idea of normative power. Such relationships result from the application of legal rules and principles to particular persons in particular situations. They are not established by single discrete rules.

9.3 Validity

The idea of validity thus relates to the conditions for the existence of institutionalized norms of all kinds. Similarly, Kelsen considers validity to be the 'specific existence' of legal norms.[15] There is a connected opinion of Kelsen's, or perhaps of his

---

[15] H Kelsen, *The Pure Theory of Law* (trans M Knight) (Berkeley and Los Angeles: University of California Press, 1967) 213 on validity as existence; *General Theory of Norms* (trans M Hartney) (Oxford: Clarendon Press, 1991) 2–3; also at 28, 171–172, where Kelsen ascribes to norms an '*ideell*'

translators, to the effect that 'valid' and 'binding' are synonyms.[16] To be valid is to be binding and vice versa. Being valid or binding is what makes some putative norm exist as a norm of law.

This is not convincing in relation to the idea of what is binding. Validity concerns satisfaction of the conditions for correct and successful exercise of a power. The marriage, or the contract, or the trust is valid if the parties have done everything correctly in the sense of (a) to (h) above. Correctly performed acts in the exercise of some public competence result in a valid planning permission, or local by-law, or tax demand—or Directive of the Council and Parliament of the European Union, to take a much grander example. Appraisal on the dimension of validity/invalidity concerns satisfaction of stipulated conditions governing the exercise of a power. To be binding is, however, not the same thing as to be valid, but is one of the consequences of validity. Because a certain contract is valid, the parties are bound to fulfil their mutual obligations under it. Further, in the event of dispute, a court which upholds the validity of the contract is bound to award a suitable remedy to a party that can show it has suffered, or apprehends, damage as a consequence of the other's breach. Because a valid planning permission has been granted, the developer has an active right to proceed with the development under whatever conditions have been validly attached to the grant. Courts would be bound to uphold his/her right to do so in the event of physical obstruction or legal challenge. A valid Directive binds all the member states of the European Union to amend their domestic law to give effect to the terms of the Directive, and the law thus amended binds citizens, courts, and officials alike. In general terms, binding arrangements are ones that must be fulfilled by those whose obligations they determine, and must be respected by courts, and by other public officials in fulfilment of the duties of their office.

Not all that may be binding upon private persons or public office-holders acquires its binding character by virtue of a specific deliberately established arrangement of the kind we have been discussing. In the case of a purely functional constitution like that which obtains in the United Kingdom, the ultimate basis of some, though not all, of the fundamental rules and principles of the constitution is custom rather than formal establishment. Even in countries which have adopted a formal constitution, the act of adopting the constitution and the principles that guide its reasonable interpretation do not themselves derive from valid institutional exercises of any previously conferred power. This is especially obvious when the functional constitution of such a country works on the basis of reasonable interpretations of the formally adopted constitution, guided by appropriate principles. The customary observance of a non-posited and

---

[in German] existence, which is the equivalent to existence as a matter of 'institutional fact' in the usage proposed in the present book.

[16] Kelsen, *Pure Theory* at 193: 'A norm referring to the behaviour of a human being as "valid" means that it is binding—that an individual ought to behave in the manner determined by the norm'.

non-institutionalized norm that the constitution must be respected by those who hold the offices it defines is what gives any constitution its binding character and guarantees its existence as a functional constitution, in ways discussed in chapter 3. All formal normative order rests on a foundation of custom, that is, on informal normative order.

There is doubtless a strictly theoretical point of view from which all putative or purported rights and arrangements in law either have perfect and valid existence or do not (or are already subject to valid nullification on appropriate application). Such a theoretical view concerns itself solely with questions about existence and non-existence and the conditions relevant to that (that is, it is concerned only with pure ontological questions). But in the practical world of the persons who seek to act within and under the law, this viewpoint is normally unavailable in pure form. People act within the limits of available information and foresight, both as to matters of fact and as to questions of law of the kind which demand careful and reflective deliberation on issues of legal principle. They do, and they have to, take a great deal upon trust. The practical human view of the world is not *sub specie aeternitatis* but moment by moment, becoming aware of events as they unfold, and responding as best one can in the light of current information and deliberation. As suggested in chapter 4, rules become depressed from consciousness, and habits become the bases of action.

A particular virtue, indeed, of legal institutions and legal arrangements is that they procure a certain degree of through-time stability in one's normative position. A common aim of many power-exercising acts is to achieve arrangements with this kind of trans-temporal (or 'diachronic') security. This does not always work out successfully. However hard one tries, there is always a risk of disappointment, of failure.

Nevertheless, it remains in general true in legal practice that someone who relies on the validity of arrangements made through the exercise of power is able to trust in their presumptive validity on account of the satisfaction of positive conditions about capacity, background circumstances, and formality. Unless someone raises an objection and can establish by appropriate proof that there was/is a vitiating factor present, the arrangements will stand. Quite often, ulterior arrangements subsequently made in good faith relying on the validity of the prior arrangement will not be vitiated by a discovered defect of the prior arrangement. Pragmatically, the question whether an ostensibly valid and working arrangement is somehow vitiated has to be raised by a challenger, rather than there being some requirement for absolute proof that no possible vitiating circumstance actually exists. This is the law's compromise between the need for reasonable security in human plans and the need to uphold principles of deep importance in a given view of socio-legal order. There is no standing presumption that existing arrangements violate principles, yet there is always some possibility of challenge in case they do.

9.4 Defeasibility

To say that many legal arrangements are challengeable draws attention to the concept of defeasibility.[17] What was set up with all the appearance of validity may in due course be challenged and found defeasible, indeed defeated. Local authorities set up interest rate swapping arrangements with banks, hoping thereby to neutralise the effect of fluctuations in interest rates. They act in good faith and on advice, thinking that their statutory powers extend to transactions of this kind. The local government auditor, however, takes a different view and challenges the swap arrangements. Finally, the courts uphold the objection. What the participants had thought was valid turned out not to be so, according to the authoritative interpretation of the law laid down by the superior judiciary.[18]

The same goes for legal positions and relations more generally. Most of the rights we rely on (to whatever extent, indeed, we consciously rely on them at all) are very much background features of the situation. A person drives her car to her house. In the background, there is an insurance policy covering the car and third party liability, there is a registration document for the car, and a certificate from the Vehicle and Operator Services Agency that it has been adequately maintained and is in a safe condition. The house is jointly-owned, subject to a mortgage, and is also insured. Here is a great web of personal and real rights arising from presumptively valid legal arrangements made quite long ago and not the subjects of day-to-day conscious thought, except when something starts to go wrong.

How then can we be so confident that these taken-for-granted arrangements are valid, that these active and passive rights hold good? What are the foundations of this? The answer is indeed that it is by applying rules and principles of law to concrete situations, and by exercising powers to establish appropriate arrangements under sundry rules and principles, that we justify our assertions about the rights, etc, that we have, and the basis on which we enjoy them. To put this another way, it is by an interpretation of our given situation against an assumed background of institutional normative order that we can consider ourselves to have various particular rights. Such a way of interpreting one's situation is of comparatively little conscious importance to most people most of the time, though it may become salient when disputes arise with neighbours, family members,

[17] Defeasibility is also discussed in N MacCormick, *Rhetoric and the Rule of Law* ch 12, with particular reference to its role in legal reasoning. A starting point for recent discussion has been H L A Hart, 'The Ascription of Responsibility and Rights' Proceedings of the Aristotelian Society 49 (1948–49) 171–194, re-appraised in G P Baker, 'Defeasibility and Meaning' in *Law, Morality and Society*, (ed P M S Hacker and J Raz) (Oxford: Clarendon Press, 1977) 26–57, notwithstanding Hart's own retreat from the 'Ascription' paper announced in the Preface to H L A Hart, *Punishment and Responsibility* (Oxford: Clarendon Press, 1968); R H S Tur, 'Defeasibilism' Oxford Journal of Legal Studies 21 (2001) 355–368. [18] *Hazell v Hammersmith and Fulham LBC* [1992] 2 AC 1.

employers, business partners, or whomever. This is probably as true of lawyers in their private life as of everybody else, but in their professional work lawyers are attuned to this interpretative approach. In tasks like advising people on the making of wills with arrangements to minimize the impact of inheritance tax, or on the purchase of a house and the effecting of a conveyance from the previous owner, or on forming and floating a new company, the aim is to minimize risk of subsequent defeasance. So far as possible they seek to foresee and forestall possible vitiating circumstances, and usually they succeed. In other situations, concerning litigation in private law or prosecutions in criminal law, they take the situation as it has presented itself and consider what interpretation is most favourable to their client's case from among the range of seriously arguable possibilities. Lawyers professionally view the world in terms of legal positions and relationships in the context of legal institutions. Few other people do this, except those who are for some reason caught in the toils of the law. Likewise, few people ever reflect on the maze of sewers beneath a great city, or of the connectedness of their domestic facilities to it. But if damp patches or bad smells appear, they take sudden interest. They seek assistance from a plumber, one whose professional life is geared to advising on and intervening in the drainage system to make it work properly.

Some will reject this analogy as far from perfect. Whether or not anybody thinks about them, the physical drains are there where they are. The same does not seem to be true of legal relationships. These exist as a matter of institutional fact, by virtue of the interpretation of acts and events in the light of a system of rules. But we have conceded that these have a built-in defeasibility. Whatever care we have taken, events may turn up that defeat the arrangements we have made, or that lead to some radically new interpretation of the rules we thought it safe to rely on. Not merely do these 'things' not exist in the physical realm like drains and sewers, they seem to have a fragile kind of existence—now you see them, now you don't. That is the meaning of defeasibility.

The first response to this objection is that most things that are defeasible never in fact get defeated. Vitiating circumstances never appear, and/or nobody with any interest bothers to challenge what might in fact have been challenged. Moreover, the arrangements people make have real-world effects. I do not just divest myself of ownership of my previous residence in favour of the purchaser, then acquire ownership of the new residence through a conveyance by the seller of that property. I also move house, and dig the garden, and decorate the walls, and put up a garage in the garden, or whatever. However hazily aware of the legal background, people do rely on their rights and derive psychological security from them, and they do their duty and abstain from criminal acts—most of the time. This is not, after all, so shadowy an existence.

It is important, picking up a point from Kelsen, to note that defeasibility has two possible forms. In one kind of situation, a legal arrangement that is found to be vitiated is nullified, but only with prospective effect. Whatever was done up till now on the faith of an arrangement stands and is not now subject to invalidation.

But no future normative effects can be derived from this now nullified arrangement. In the other kind of situation, the voidness or nullity of the arrangement applies from the very beginning. Whatever consequences were derived from it in the way of rights, duties, powers, or whatever were always falsely derived, and must be deemed wholly ineffectual.[19]

Kelsen's point is to deny that there is here a radical difference. The same technique is being applied through judicial decisions or otherwise. Nothing now can change facts in the world that have already taken place. The arrangement was treated as valid and relied upon. Now it is being set aside. Legally, there is a choice between two forms of nullification as of this date—one which does not authorize the undoing of whatever has hitherto been done under this arrangement; the other which does authorize or even require that. In pragmatic terms, this is an attractive way of conceptualizing these matters. For it makes it unnecessary to deny that arrangements really took effect with all the appearance of validity over a certain space of time. Something that was defective in its constitution did exist over a period of time and did form a basis for some people's practical reasoning and corresponding conduct. The fact that lawyers characterize it as having been 'void *ab initio*', and thus never really existent, is a feature of legal rhetoric.

Is this, however, a reliable proposition of legal ontology? Surely, even when we deal with institutional facts rather than physical ones, we must be able to say that they are valid and existent, or invalid and non-existent, whatever anyone actually thinks. Once a flaw or mistake is discovered, we realise that the attribution of validity on the basis of which practical courses of action were undertaken was all along a mis-attribution. In the same way, if medical science establishes and works with a hypothesis according to which (for example) poliomyelitis is treated as a water-borne disease, it may subsequently appear that this is a causal mis-attribution, and that the disease was communicated to and from the respiratory tract. Refutation of a causal hypothesis does not change the fact that people did act on that hypothesis, and administered treatments and took precautionary measures accordingly. These pragmatic truths do not force any ontological conclusion such as that, while it was believed in, the hypothesis was valid. It was invalid all along if invalid now. The same, surely, must obtain in relation to institutional facts and arrangements.

It is necessary to differentiate different sorts of failure or imperfection in power-exercising acts. Some involve attempts to make arrangements that never achieve even presumptive validity, for example, because purportedly carried out by persons wholly lacking relevant capacity or competence. Some are carried out by competent persons, but with defects of procedure or form of a grave kind. Such arrangements are sometimes simply ignored because of their obvious defectiveness, but sometimes it may be more prudent to treat them as valid, or possibly valid, until the fact of the defectiveness is established and appropriate judicial

---

[19] Kelsen, *Pure Theory of Law*, 276–278. Cf the discussion in D Ruiter, *Legal Institutions* (Dordrecht: Kluwer, 2001) 138–170.

declarations have been granted indicating the nullity *ab initio* of the purported arrangement. Some are cases of legal imperfection rather than radical defectiveness. In law, this can justify a nullification of the act or arrangement from the moment at which the complaint of imperfection was first raised. Looked at in the perspective of normative ontology, norms and normative arrangements of the former two kinds are not valid and do not exist, though in respect of the second kind it is pragmatically prudent to treat them as at least possibly existing until they have been declared non-existent. Imperfect arrangements do exist until such time as they are revoked or nullified.[20]

9.5 Immunity

If the rules and principles of institutional normative orders can confer power, they must also restrict it, at least impliedly. Someone who seeks or who purports to change my legal position in a certain way has to be able to show some legal provision by which he/she is so empowered. If the provision does not exist, or cannot be properly interpreted as empowering that person to make this change, the purported power does not exist. Where power ends, disability commences.[21] 'Immunity' is the most accepted term for the correlative position of the person whose position is not susceptible to the envisaged change.[22] You are minded to order me off the pathway that leads past the front of your house. But I am your neighbour, and there is an established right of way (a 'servitude right' or 'easement') in favour of my property and incumbent on yours. In this case you cannot unilaterally impose on me a duty to keep off. I am immune from (have an immunity from) losing my right of way by your say-so. This can be taken in the first instance as a simple tool of analysis. For every possible legal arrangement or change in some existing arrangement, any person either has power to bring this about, or does not. Where a person has power, the other(s) in the relevant relationship are susceptible to the consequential changes in their situation. Where the power is lacking, the former party is under disability, and the latter enjoys immunity in respect of this change.

When coupled with principles of civil liberty, the analytical tool can become a veritable shield against overweening interventions by one person in the life of another, especially by officials over citizens. It is an important principle of liberal legal order that powers other than those bilaterally exercisable by mutual consent can only exist by virtue of clear statutory conferment or constitutional provision.

---

[20] This account follows that of Ruiter in *Legal Institutions* at 169 and preceding page—note his distinction between 'revocatory, voiding, suspensive, and invalidating legal acts'. These are subtle and useful distinctions in the context of an analysis more detailed than appropriate to the present work.

[21] 'Disability' is the useful term coined by Hohfeld to signify a position of non-power: see *Fundamental Legal Conceptions* 60–64; G W Rainbolt, *The Concept of Rights* (Dordrecht: Springer, 2006) 38–39. [22] Compare Rainbolt, *Concept* 44–46.

The rights of a citizen under the general law (whether common law or codified law) cannot be divested by unilateral act save under clear positive enabling provisions. Such provisions are commonly interpreted restrictively by courts. Hence citizens of free societies enjoy a general immunity against interference with their rights except where clear authority exists for this. This is, in fact, a part of the meaning of the concept of a 'free society'.

Such a position can be further strengthened by means of a constitutional or other process of entrenching fundamental rights. This forms the subject matter of a later chapter (chapter 11). For the moment, suffice it to observe that entrenchment has the effect of protecting certain rights not only against encroachment by officials acting without clear and adequate statutory warrant, but yet more securely. For the supreme legislature itself is put under a disability to enact laws that take away rights to life, to liberty, or to a fair trial (for example) from any citizen, indeed any person within the jurisdiction, and this extends to all minorities or classes of suspected public enemy. There is a general immunity from derogation from basic rights, especially from discriminatory acts of this kind. Whether the powers of the state and its institutions can safely be subjected to stringent limits of this kind in cases of, for example, war or terrorist threats is a controversial question. Not controversial is that it is possible to erect such protections and that currently they receive powerful underpinning from various international declarations and conventions.

PART 3

LAW, STATE, AND CIVIL
SOCIETY

So far we have considered in part 1 the basic ideas of normativity, normative order, and then the institutionalization of normative order with special reference to legal orders under the constitutions of states or confederations. Then in part 2 we have examined the kinds of positions, relationships, and arrangements that can exist when we interpret human affairs against the backdrop of such a legal order. Especially in part 2, the discussion has been relatively abstract and without systematic reference to the context and point of the constitutionally established legal order of a law-state. The time has come to remedy this defect, by showing that the contents of legal order are not arbitrary, though there is a great range of choice among different ways to flesh-out the basic forms of law.

Law of the kind we are mainly considering is a feature of a certain kind of state, and of transnational organizations established by such states to institutionalize a basis of supranational collaboration. In this light, we need to consider the main divisions of law as these have been traditionally conceived—public law (chapter 10), criminal law (chapter 12), and private law (chapter 13). We also need to consider (chapter 11) how both internationally and nationally fundamental rights instruments have been adopted that seek to place limits on possible abuses of state power. Taken in a broad and summary view, these branches of law supply the frameworks in which we can understand how law contributes to shaping the state and creates within the ambit of the state the conditions for the existence and flourishing of civil society. This follows out the suggestions made at the conclusion of chapter 4. We do well in this context to remember the following observation by Adam Ferguson: 'Where men enjoy peace, they owe it either to their mutual regards and affections, or to the restraints of law. Those are the happiest states which procure peace to their members by the first of these methods: but it is sufficiently uncommon to procure it by the second.'[1] This well sums up the contribution law can make to the civility of civil society, though civility is never achieved through law alone.

---

[1] A Ferguson, *An Essay on the History of Civil Society* (1767: ed, with introduction by Duncan Forbes) (Edinburgh: Edinburgh University Press, 1966) at 154.

10

Powers and Public Law: Law and Politics

10.1 Introduction

Public law comprises constitutional law and all those other parts of law that establish and empower the executive branch of government and other agencies of government. Such agencies may be part of a state's central government or may appertain to regional or local levels of government. Laws that confer power also subject it to limits and direct it towards certain purposes. As we shall see in the following chapter, there may be further general limits imposed in the name of fundamental rights. There may also be important duties of public authorities requiring them to exercise their powers in certain specified conditions or in ways that exhibit due care towards those affected by the exercise of a given power (this was discussed in 5.4, above).

Government in the contemporary law-state covers a great range of domains, with appropriate powers derived from constitution or from legislation (thus governmental power depends on the constitution and, under that, on grants of power by the legislature). Domains of public law include at least the following: taxation; social security; economic policy; policy on trade and industrial development; policy on labour relations and on consumer protection; policy on agriculture, fisheries, and food standards; policy on housing; policy on environmental protection, on town and country planning, on water supplies and sewerage, and on transport and communications infrastructures; education, cultural, and media affairs; health services; police; internal security of the state; external relations and defence. In relation to all such topics, it is perennially disputable how far governments should be involved at all. In respect of various services, it is particularly controversial whether they should restrain themselves to a primarily regulatory role, leaving provision of the services to private initiative, or should to some greater or lesser extent actually provide them. In relation to most, there are further options, and attendant controversies, in the matter of assignment of powers to local or regional authorities, or maintaining them at the level of the central government of the state. Howsoever these controversies are resolved and options exercised in different places and from time to time, government in all such domains involves the exercise of powers. To understand public law one must therefore reflect upon the special character of the powers of governmental authorities.

10.2 Public Powers

All legal powers are both relational and relativistic. They are relational in the sense that any person's exercise of a power involves a change in the normative position of some other person. They are relativistic in that they operate relatively to particular legal institutions, whose existence or termination one can bring about or whose normative consequences or contents one can determine or vary. An important difference exists between powers whose exercise is essentially bilateral, and powers whose exercise is essentially unilateral. In the former case, valid exercise of power by P requires for its completion some matching act or some signification of consent or assent by the other. In the latter case, even if the occasion for P's exercising a power requires to be triggered by some form of application or request by another, the validity of the exercise of the power is independent of any matching act or signification of consent or assent by the other. Another important difference exists between what may be called 'powers for private good' as against 'powers for general good'. The former are powers which may properly be exercised by the power holder P for P's own benefit, or for the benefit of others whom P chooses to benefit according to P's own free will. The latter are powers whose exercise must be for some distinct end or interest other than that of P and other than that of persons arbitrarily chosen by P on the basis of personal preference.

Within the constitutional framework of a law-state, the governmental authorities set up to perform legislative, executive, or judicial functions typically are clothed with powers of the unilateral kind. The legal validity of any particular act of legislation, for example, does not depend upon consent to that particular act given by any of the persons to whom it is to apply.[1] Nor does the legal validity of most exercises of executive power. No act of consent by any person affected is required to validate a minister's grant of approval for the use of a certain drug after it has been tested for safety, or for a minister's grant of permission for a certain building development to go ahead under some piece of zoning law, or for any other ministerial decision taken as authorized under appropriate legislation. In the case of judicial decision-making, it is indeed necessary for the courts to be activated by some form of intimation of some claim by a litigant, or by the presentation of a valid criminal complaint or indictment by a competent prosecutor, in the case of criminal law. But the validity of the decision in civil proceedings or of verdict and (in case of guilt) sentence at the conclusion of criminal proceedings does not depend at all on the consent of those whom the decision addresses, or those whom it affects.

The powers of such governing authorities are also typically powers for general good. They are conferred with a view to ensuring good government in the relevant

---

[1] This is not to deny that, politically speaking, the legitimacy of a legislature may well depend on its enjoying the general consent of the citizen body, in the sense of an acknowledgement that this legislature has law-making power, and thus one ought to respect its enactments by complying with them.

domain. It is thus an abuse of power if *P*, as a minister, or judge, or member of a legislature, acts from a motive of personal advantage or for the advantage of (say) *P's* own family or friends, or any other particular group whom it pleases *P* to favour (co-religionists, or political sympathisers, or whomever). That is so, whether or not any remedy exists to correct such an abusive act. That such powers are powers for the general good does not, however, entail that they may not be used for the benefit of particular classes of persons. Quite possibly the legislature may on occasion choose to legislate for the benefit of trades unions or trades unionists, or for the benefit of agriculturists, or small farmers, or small- and medium-sized enterprises, or consumers, or company shareholders. In the implementation of such legislation ministers belonging to the executive branch, or civil servants or agencies acting on their behalf or at arm's length from them, may quite properly have to exercise delegated powers for the benefit of the relevant class. 'General goods' are thus not necessarily universal goods, to the benefit equally of all citizens all the time. The point, however, is that there must be an absence of any sense of personal favouritism in the identification of classes to be benefited, at any level of government, including even the highest legislative level. Also, holders of delegated power have to use their discretion in favour of those whom the legislation was designed to benefit, to the extent of that design, read reasonably in the light of other standing values recognized by law.

The principle at stake here is that constitutionally-conferred powers ought to be exercised for the good of the state taken as a whole or, in a well-attested phrase, 'for the common good'. The common good requires the just treatment of all persons within the state's jurisdiction, according to some statable idea of justice, and requires otherwise that government be conducted with a view to sustaining or enhancing the welfare of all. As was remarked in chapter 6,[2] 'There is a common good, the general circumstances required for successful communal living. And there are individual goods, all the ends that individuals can desire to pursue within the framework of a secured common good'. John Finnis defines the common good as the 'set of conditions which enables the members of a community to attain for themselves reasonable objectives, or to realize reasonably for themselves the value(s) for the sake of which they have reason to collaborate with each other . . . in a community'.[3] It is not incompatible with this that different sectors of industry, economy, or society be separately dealt with by separate acts of legislation or overseen by different ministers and ministries. Different elements of general good should, however, be capable of being represented as somehow meshing together into an over-arching common good in the above sense. To identify this requires invocation of some reasonable (though probably also controversial) political principles, including principles of justice. Legislation favouring farmers at

---

[2] At text accompanying n 10.

[3] John Finnis, *Natural Law and Natural Rights* (Oxford:Clarendon Press, 1980) 155; cf Michael S Moore, 'Law as a Functional Kind' in Robert George (ed), *Natural Law Theory* (Oxford: Clarendon Press, 1992) 187–242 at 215–216; for a general response to Finnis's position, see MacCormick, 'Natural Law and the Separation of Law from Morals', in George (ed), op cit 105–133.

a time of crisis in farm incomes is not objectionable in the way that legislation aimed at differentially increasing resources available to a governing party against opposition parties is objectionable. Ministerial interventions to ensure that all passport applications are dealt with as speedily as possible are not objectionable, whereas an intervention by a minister to secure speedy handling of a passport application by his mistress's nanny is thoroughly objectionable.[4]

It is important not to define the idea of a law-state in a way that would proscribe or seem to proscribe any reasonable political ideology or programme. Differences about what is for the common good are inveterate among human beings, and the point of representative politics is to secure fair equality of opportunity for all those who wish to advance any set of policies and principles relative to the good governance of the state. Which shall prevail at any given time then depends on election to office through fairly conducted elections. Where democracy prevails, those elected as representatives are elected on a basis of universal adult franchise. There is then a reasonable basis for claiming that the election is the best possible representation of majority opinion. This is of value in circumstances in which it can be universally acknowledged that majority legitimation is preferable to any alternative, provided that no specific electoral majority may close the door to the subsequent formation of a different majority. It is on some such assumptions as these that we can conclude not only that constitutionally conferred powers of government typically are, but also that they ought to be, powers for general good, and ought to be exercised accordingly.

Their unilateral character is a kind of corollary of this. However contestable may be particular policies that purport to favour some aspect of the common good, controversies cannot go on forever, and decisions must be taken.[5] To say that decisions then have to meet with specific consent by those affected would simply be a way of saying that no governmental decisions can bring about closure of controversy, even for the time being, and even though the possibility of reversal remains open after a subsequent election. In extreme cases, civil disobedience may even be legitimate, but that does not affect the validity of any decision taken. If there is to be effective government at all, there must be some powers of unilateral decision-making both about general rules and about individual cases.

10.3 Differentiating Public Law

The features of orientation to general goods and of unilateral character, when taken together, enable us to differentiate public from private powers, and therewith

---

[4] Cf the resignation of David Blunkett MP from the office of Secretary of State for Home Affairs in the UK Cabinet, *The Times* (London), 15 December 2004.

[5] Cf Jeremy Waldron, *Law and Disagreement* (Oxford: Clarendon Press, 1999) eg at 106; Svein Eng, *Analysis of Dis/Agreement with Particular Reference to Law and Legal Theory* (Dordrecht: Kluwer, 2003).

public from private law. Public law concerns chiefly public powers that are unilateral in their exercise and that are powers for general good. The sphere of private law, sometimes also referred to as that of 'civil society', is that of powers that are bilateral, or multilateral, and that are powers for private good. This sphere is one in which persons of full age and capacity confront each other as the bearers of equal legal status, or of equivalent status, as in the case of corporations, incorporated partnerships, and the like. This means that none is legally superior to any other, however different they may be in personal characteristics or acquired assets. Hence any legal arrangements that are to become binding on them through an act of private will must be ones to which they mutually consent, so far as concerns any change in the legal position between them. Of course, that you have a certain holding of property is not something that requires my consent, nor vice versa. But any dealings between us from any particular starting position have to proceed by agreement between us, or by some other form of voluntary arrangement, such as pooling some of our assets to form a limited company. Even a (unilateral) gift cannot take effect without the recipient's acceptance of the thing given. Private law obligations are based on voluntary acts, including both conventional obligations, like contracts, and those obligations of reparation that arise from the commission of wrongful acts by one person to the injury of another. Duties imposed under public law do not exhibit this voluntary quality.

State agencies do, however, exercise certain powers in a manner akin to that of private law, as when contracts are made for the provision of public services, or employment offered in the public service. Ownership of movable and immovable property, both corporeal and incorporeal, can be vested in the state itself or in subordinate public authorities. States and their internal public authorities can be required, eg, under the European Community Treaty, to fulfil their requirements for the provision of certain goods or services only by a process of competitive tendering set up on fair terms as prescribed by relevant European law.[6] In this light, it must not be asserted that all powers of public authorities have both characteristics of being unilateral and being oriented to general good. (But the latter feature has indeed a particular urgency in the case of, eg, required competitive tendering, one point of which is, precisely, to exclude improper favouritism in allocations of public funds.) Nevertheless, the special position of all public authorities entails that, whatever be the system of courts or tribunals before which they are answerable, their responsibility under contract law or the law of delict or torts has certain special features. These differentiate public authorities' responsibilities from the responsibilities of persons in general under private law. Not all the powers of public authorities are both unilateral and for general good; but all public authorities are identifiable by the fact that their core powers do have both these characteristics, and almost all have at least the latter.

---

[6] Cf Office of Government Commerce (OGC), *The New Public Procurement Directives* (London: OGC, 2004).

Speaking generally, public law, comprising constitutional law and all those other parts of law that establish and empower agencies of government, assigns to them specific powers that are unilateral and for the general good, and other ancillary powers, including powers to hold property and to make contracts. The terms on which power is assigned also necessarily imply, and sometimes expressly state, the limits of the power so conferred. As already mentioned, and as we shall see in the following chapter, there may be further general limits imposed in the name of fundamental rights. There are also important duties of public authorities requiring them to exercise some at least of their powers in certain conditions or in ways that exhibit due care towards those affected by the exercise of a given power.

Public law differs from private law in the kinds of power it confers, this being explicable in terms of the need for effective government and governance. Both private and public law, however, are elements in a contemporary state's realization of institutional normative order taken as a whole. Hence public law is not law in a different sense from private law.[7] They are both law in the same sense, but they have different domains of application and different subject matter. One would therefore have to reject any claim concerning the 'autonomous' status of public law that tended or was intended to deny that private and public law are two parts of the single normative order of a state or other polity.[8] A legal system would be incomplete if it lacked either part, and each part is law in the same sense of the term 'law', for all the difference in the kinds of powers they confer on persons of different kinds having different functions.

10.4 Public Law and Politics

In constitutional states that have at least representative forms of government, and all the more so where representation involves a fully democratic franchise under which all adult citizens have equal votes, public law provides both the framework

[7] M Loughlin (*The Idea of Public Law*, Oxford: Oxford University Press, 2003, 153 ff) argues that public law is quite distinctive and deserves recognition as an autonomous discipline. As long as such a claim does not amount to saying that public and private law are 'law' in different senses of the term, it is not objectionable, since it only amounts to proposing a sensible basis for division of labour among legal scholars. Loughlin's argument on this depends on the interpenetration of public law with the business of governing; this specificity is here explained in terms of the special character of public powers. Peter Morton, *An Institutional Theory of Law* (Oxford: Clarendon Press, 1998) treats criminal law, civil law, and public law as three distinct 'legal Practices', in his own special sense of that term. He argues that: 'The crucially important relationships between the Practices, the various subtle interconnections between these discrete forms, do not warrant the assumption that legal norms add up to a unified system' (p 63). This seems to me to be seriously mistaken, given the institutional account of the unity-in-diversity of legal systems advanced from chapter 3 of the present work onwards.

[8] In different ways, both F A Hayek (*Law, Legislation and Liberty: Vol I Rules and Order* 131–4 and 141–3) and M Loughlin (loc cit) assert the autonomy of public law—the former to denounce it, the latter to celebrate it. H Kelsen (*Pure Theory*, 280–1) for his part exaggerates the sameness of public and private law. The difference is akin to that of two species within a single genus, such that neither can be understood without study of the other.

for and a substantial part of the subject matter of politics. Politics concerns the exercise of governmental power within a polity, exercised with a view to some conception of a common good for the whole. This includes, as was said recently, some defensible conception of justice among persons over whom the state has jurisdiction. In political contests, what rivals seek is to gain the positions of predominance in the legislative and executive branches of government. That is, they seek positions in which they can exercise unilateral powers that are powers for general good.

The point of doing so, apart from personal self-aggrandisement and the pleasures of being in high office, is to put into effect the conception of justice and the common good laid down in the political programme of the winning party, faction, or coalition, or otherwise in accordance with its general principles and ethos.[9] This may indeed be no more than a cloak for sectional advantage or class interest. But it cannot openly proclaim itself to be such, for reasons that are explored in chapter 15. The actual implementation of a political programme in turn requires the exercise of public powers of a legislative kind and an executive kind, and also subordinate administrative powers. Does this then mean that public law and politics simply collapse into each other? Certainly not.

A highly influential and persuasive sociological theory of law—the 'system-theory' of Niklas Luhmann[10] as further developed by Gunther Teubner[11]—goes so far as to insist that social systems (or sub-systems) like law and politics or economics are systems of communication that are in a certain sense sealed-off from each other. Each system continually makes and re-makes itself according to its own internal logic and working with its own basic binary distinctions such as the law's differentiation of right and wrong,[12] as we discussed it in 6.3 above. Each system is part of the environment of the others, and there are mechanisms of 'structural coupling' that facilitate their interaction. Yet the information that enters each from all the others assumes a system-determined character in the process of its being assimilated. Legal agencies read outputs of the political system (eg, acts of legislation) in legal terms. Political actors view outputs of the legal system, eg, judges' decisions about the validity of governmental acts, as politically relevant constraints on the manner in which desired effects can be achieved

---

[9] The distinction between the express principles or doctrines or manifesto commitments of a political party or faction and its 'ethos' is a very important one. See H M Drucker, *Doctrine and Ethos in the Labour Party* (London: G Allen & Unwin, 1979).

[10] N Luhmann, *Law as a Social System* (trans K Ziegert, ed D Nobles and others) (Oxford: Oxford University Press, 2004).

[11] G Teubner, *Law as an Autopoietic System* (trans R Adler and A Bankowska, ed Z Bankowski) (Oxford: Basil Blackwell, 1992).

[12] Luhmann uses the terms '*Recht*' and '*Unrecht*' and their derivative adjectives in the German original of his work. The standard translation is 'legal/illegal', which however makes the binary coding by law seem trivial in English—(legally) right versus (legally) wrong seems to me a binary opposition that makes better sense. Whether or not it is more faithful as a translation of Luhmann's text, I wish to adopt his idea in this sense, or with this modification, if that is what it is. See *Law as a Social System* 94 ff.

through governmental action. Both law and politics receive inputs from the economic system (see the discussion in 13.4, below), and generate inputs for it while each in its own way somehow adjusts in response to information from the others. This is a continuous and dynamic interaction.[13]

As noted, statute law enacted by the legislature in the exercise of its constitutionally predominant law-making role is one output of a political system. Few legislators, however, are legal experts, and legislative debates are organized on programmatic party political lines. The members of the legislature may have only a relatively limited understanding of the details of the laws they enact, and their reasons for voting may not include much or any reference to these details. Legal experts (drafters) employed by the legislature or the executive may be employed to ensure that the actual words enacted will be likely to bring about the consequences their authors intend. Having such experts is necessary, because the legislature's output is input from the point of view of lawyers and courts. Statutory interpretation is a topic of considerable importance, much discussed by those interested in the processes of reasoning characteristic of systems of law-application, through the courts and otherwise.[14] Only somebody who understands well the practice of statutory interpretation is in a position to ensure that statutes are written in such a way that the interpretation applied by the law-applier is likely to match reasonably closely what was intended by the promoter of the legislative proposal. This might be a minister, or a parliamentary committee, or even an individual legislator, for, although only the full legislature can enact laws, it always does so in response to some specific proposal of such a kind.

A statute represents a new input into an already ongoing legal system. So to make sense of the newly-enacted law one has to read it in the light of the existing legal system to see what it has changed and how the new rules enacted can best make sense in the light of the continuing-but-altered legal system. Not surprisingly, a lawyer's or a judge's understanding of the enacted law may well be different from that of the politicians who participated in enacting it as law. It will certainly be formed in a different general context, based on awareness of the law more than on attention to a particular political programme. All the more will this be so in the case of statutes which fall to be applied long after the particular lawmakers who promoted them or enacted them have moved on to different concerns, suffered electoral defeat, or even retired altogether.

Moreover, anyone interested in the rule of law is well aware of the importance of insulating the courts and the judiciary from improper political pressures by

---

[13] Luhmann, *Law as a Social System* 381–385 discusses 'structural couplings' between law, politics and economics, drawing on work by Humberto Maturana in the domain of the epistemology of the biological sciences, though it remains controversial whether this sociological use of the concept is a satisfactory form of analogy.

[14] See, eg, N MacCormick and R S Summers (eds) *Interpreting Statutes: A Comparative Study* (Aldershot: Dartmouth Publishing Co, 1991) for a broad comparative consideration by a group of legal theorists from different jurisdictions; cf N MacCormick, *Rhetoric and the Rule of Law* ch 7 for an account of this set in the context of the (present) institutional theory of law.

members of the executive government or of the legislature. Even where they are in fact disappointed by the interpretations the judges give of the laws they pass, politicians undermine the rule of law to the extent that they interfere or put pressure on judges or lawyers to take a particular political line in legal interpretation. Once the law has been made, it is entirely up to the courts to figure out what it means and apply it according to their own reasons and reasoning. If legislatures are dissatisfied with the results, their only legitimate recourse is to return to the drawing board and draft a new version of the law that will be yet clearer in pointing the way to the desired outcome.

Such considerations are fully compatible with the system-theoretical account of the separateness of these different systems from each other. It must of course be stressed that this is not a radical separation that cuts off all effective interaction. Indeed, Luhmann suggests that 'the state' functions (at least conceptually) by way of what he terms a 'structural coupling' between the legal and the political systems.[15] This is because the constitution is, in a political perspective, the framework for political action and yet at the same time, in a legal perspective, the source of legal power and the ground of legal validity. Hence, as already noted, there is a sense in which the law is a target for politics. A party that thinks the state has grown too powerful, and taxes citizens too heavily, interfering too much with individual and local discretion, will seek election to office in order to pursue a reform programme. If it is elected to the majority position in the legislature, its leadership will assume or be appointed to leading roles in the executive branch of government, and will bring forward the instruments of reform. These will necessarily be legislative proposals, parliamentary bills aimed at reducing tax burdens and divesting central government agencies of some of their powers, and so on. To implement the policy, they must get the bills enacted into law.

Conversely, a party with a more socialistic conception of the common good might aim at a programme opposite in sense to the foregoing, and might seek reforms that would tend towards greater equalization of welfare through public services and higher taxation. It too would have to include in its pursuit of these policies proposals for relevant law reform, and would have to enact suitable reforming laws if it succeeded in being elected. There are several ways in which a reform programme either of the latter or of the former kind might fail. One of them would be if the legislation were so botched that it could not be interpreted in such a way as to have the effects intended by the proponents of the political programme. Another would be if the courts set their faces against fairly interpreting the enacted law to pursue the values its makers intended to embody in it. The latter would be an abuse of judicial office, even though there might well be no constitutional remedy available for this.

The same goes for environmental concerns or for worries about civil liberties as affected by criminal law and the law-enforcement authorities. Whatever one

---

[15] *Law as a Social System* chs 9 and 10, especially at 408–409.

perceives as a deficiency in the political ordering of the state, its remedy is likely to include exercising legislative power. This remedy works only if the legislation so enacted is interpreted both with a view to securing coherence in the legal system and to implementing the values implicit in the legislation, namely the values that have been argued out in the political process.[16] A different tension between law and politics follows from the difference of time-scale within which they operate. Legal systems take many years to process cases from the first raising of a complaint to the final decision of the ultimate appeal court in cases important and controversial enough to 'go the whole way' and yield a final highly authoritative ruling on the correct interpretation of law on the point in issue. The imperatives of political life, and sometimes (eg, in environmental matters, or urgent issues of national security) also the practical urgency of some kind of harm-prevention make the difference of legal and political time-scales politically problematic. Partly on that account, the executive may frequently in such matters seek the enactment of legislation for the purpose of setting up some kind of proactive public body. This might, for example, be an environmental protection agency with powers to intervene proactively in relation to the activities of economic actors such as industrial corporations with a view to speedier prevention or rectification of apprehended damage. Such an agency may come into existence (within the sub-branch of public law commonly known as 'administrative law') and accelerate the effective legal implementation of political solutions to perceived environmental problems. The authoritative legal interpretation of their powers and duties, and the legitimate use thereof, will however await the outcome of comparatively slow-moving legal processes in the event of disputes arising. Eventually, the highest courts may be called upon to rule authoritatively on the validity of the grant of power, or of some particular exercise of the power granted.[17]

10.5 The Political Value of Judicial Impartiality

Judges do not only risk becoming involved in politics through some actual or attempted exercise of improper influence by ministers or other powerful political actors. They can themselves become embroiled in politics if they actually or apparently set out to resist or denature political reforms after these have been successfully embodied in legislation. Some schools of legal theory go so far in a direction opposite to that of system theory as to deny that there is any gap at all between law and politics, precisely because of the role the courts play in implementing the law. 'Critical' theorists point out that judges are always having to

---

[16] This is substantiated in N MacCormick, *Rhetoric and the Rule of Law* at 139–141.
[17] On the problem of differences of time-scale between legal and political systems, compare Luhmann, *Law as a Social System* 372–374.

choose whether to pursue values akin to those that currently prevail in legislative programmes, or values opposed to them.[18]

According to the institutional theory of law as expounded in a companion volume to the present one,[19] this 'critical' thesis about law-application is itself grossly overstated if it denies that there really can be objective legal arguments that give better or worse interpretations regardless of personal preferences among judges. It is indeed possible to have such objective grounds of preference. Of course, it does not follow that judges never make mistakes or that they never take sides in an improper way. It is, however, possible for judges to avoid political partisanship in carrying out their office and in that sense to steer clear of politics.[20] One does not have to adopt the full panoply of sociological system-theory of the style of Luhmann or Teubner to be grateful for the strong corroboration it offers on this point.

Yet again, in another sense, this very non-partisanship of the judiciary is itself a precious achievement of politics when and to the extent that it is realized. The very idea of a polity under the rule of law, a constitutionalist state, or law-state, is that of one in which there is a successful separation of powers such that different functions are carried out by different agencies. It is not then the case that judges and courts are in every sense non-political—of course they ought to be non-partisan, refraining from taking sides overtly in matters of inter-party dispute in the ongoing political struggles of the day. But achieving non-partisan impartiality is itself a particular political role, one of inestimable value in securing constitutional balance. It is by participating in this way that judges contribute most to sustaining the common good of the polity.

There are other significant interfaces between the legal and the political. Politicians in all forms of representative government and *a fortiori* in democracies compete to achieve power in the sense of a practical ability to make changes in the way people live and the relative well-being of citizens and a fair balance of welfare among them. But in a law-state (the very term is redolent of 'structural coupling'), the power they seek requires the acquisition and exercise of an aggregate of powers under law, that is, legal powers.

A minister's powers, exercisable by virtue of her/his investiture in this public office at the apex of the political system, are either powers directly conferred in the constitution or powers conferred under legislation enacted by virtue of constitutionally-conferred powers of law-making or subordinate rule-making. Or (most likely in relation to defence and external affairs) it may possibly be the

---

[18] Compare generally D Kennedy, *A Critique of Adjudication* (Cambridge, Ma: Harvard University Press, 1997); A Norrie (ed), *Closure or Critique* (Edinburgh: Edinburgh University Press, 1993), especially ch 7 (P Goodrich, 'Fate as Seduction').

[19] N MacCormick, *Rhetoric and the Rule of Law* (Oxford: Oxford University Press, 1995).

[20] N MacCormick, *Rhetoric and the Rule of Law*, ch 13. But contrast, for example, J Balkin, 'Ideological Drift and the Struggle over Meaning' Conn Law Rev 25 (1993) 369.

kind of residual power vested in the head of state under the concept of executive prerogative (in monarchies, 'royal prerogative') exercised on behalf of the head of state by a minister. Powers to direct the conduct of civil servants or military personnel, to authorize the expenditure of public funds, to require citizens to respond to demands issued in the name of the state, to grant them special permissions by way of one or another form of licence—quite generally, the whole panoply of public powers—are conferred by law. This remains a significant fact even in cases of powers whose exercise permits of a wide discretion exercisable by or on behalf of a minister. Accordingly, it is normally a justiciable question, one capable of being raised before some independent court or tribunal, whether a given exercise of a ministerial power was a legitimate use of the power on its proper legal interpretation, or was ultra vires or otherwise an abuse of discretion, or *détournement de pouvoir*. To the extent that there are powers whose validity-conditions depend solely on the say-so of those exercising them, to that extent the rule of law is violated.

10.6 Political Power above Law?

To be sure, political success is not guaranteed by mere legality, and occasionally, as with Nelson's blind eye, violations of strict legal requirements can have brilliant results. Politics sometimes calls for that sort of bold stroke. It also requires leadership, and vision, and teamwork to realize commonly defined policies, goals, and ideals. Law establishes public powers and sets their limits. How they are exercised within these limits is the very business of politics, and it is a matter of political vision and understanding to bring it about that a multitude of exercises of a multitude of powers in the legal sense amounts to a coherent and beneficial exercise of power in the political sense. It goes without saying that the law does not contain a recipe for political success or for good political conduct. But without some legal framework, there would not be a political system at all, nor indeed a state.

Yet curiously the converse also seems to be true. For it takes political will and political organization to sustain a state and to keep it in being as (however imperfectly) a law-state. Moreover, it can be argued that every polity, including the best ordered of states, can find itself in a condition of crisis, perhaps through political or industrial conflicts internal to itself, or through natural catastrophes or through external pressures. The normal decencies of the separation of powers have to be set aside and some crisis-solving decision taken. According to Carl Schmitt[21] and contemporary followers of his, this need for a decision in 'the state of exception'

---

[21] C Schmitt, *Political Theology: Four Chapters on the Concept of Sovereignty*, trans G Schwab (Cambridge, Ma: MIT Press, 1988; original German edition, 1922); cf Schmitt, *The Concept of the Political* (trans G Schwab) (Chicago: Chicago University Press, 1996; original German edition, 1932).

provides the benchmark for ascertaining where lies the ultimate sovereignty that always underlies any successful polity.[22] 'The sovereign is: He who decides on the case of exception'.[23] Such cases are ones where nothing succeeds like success. A seizure of ultimate power may lead to disastrous failure and the collapse or overthrow of the state. Where it succeeds, however, the state is preserved, and its true character revealed, in respect of the real ultimate power-relations that hold it together, however little the normal and superficial, legally correct, conduct of affairs may make this apparent.

What shall we say about this? It is worth repeating that power is always a relational attribute, as argued in chapter 9. That which has power has it in relation to something or someone. Power is revealed in the changes the one which has power can bring about so as to affect the one over which power exists, and the scale of power can be graded according to the degree of change that can be wrought, and the amount of resistance overcome. Legal power as a form of normative power is the ability of one person or agency to change the legal situation of some person or agency, creating some new duty or expansion of an existing duty, or making wrong that which was not previously wrong, or conferring, or extending, or restricting, or annulling some other power. Political power is better conceptualized as power-in-fact rather than normative power. It is not about changing what in some way people ought to do. It is about changing what they actually do, but in a law-state this can only be achieved through what is also an exercise of legal power.

To the extent that citizens are motivated to, and do, act in a law-abiding way, they will tend to be responsive to legal changes of any of the kinds we have mentioned. To that extent, the exercise of legal powers can be a highly effective strategy in the exercise of political power. Moreover, the legitimacy of the conduct of political actors is an important element in the standing or aura they have or acquire. Achieving what one achieves by constitutional and legal means enhances one's legitimacy, hence contributes to the responsiveness of citizens to political exercises of power. There is a clear conceptual difference between political power and legal power. But in real life they go hand in hand and can only be prised apart in exceptional moments—perhaps, indeed, in the 'state of exception'. Surely, indeed, it is of the character of states of exception to be indeed exceptional. To derive a thesis about the normal and proper working of the state from the conditions of its survival in extreme conditions that may never come about seems simply perverse.

People who stress the politics-shaping character of public law, the way in which it defines and at the same time necessarily delimits public powers (however

---

[22] M Loughlin's stress on the ultimate character of political power owes something to Schmitt, though he by no means goes the whole way with him. See *Idea of Public Law* 33–35, 155–156.

[23] This is the opening sentence of *Political Theology*, as rendered by D Dyzenhaus, *Legality and Legitimacy: Carl Schmitt, Hans Kelsen and Hermann Heller in Weimar* (Oxford: Clarendon Press, 1997) 42.

broadly and vaguely) can be criticized for lack of realism. Martin Loughlin, for example, scolds such thinkers (the present author included) for ignoring the fact that public law is ultimately about government.[24] It is concerned with what makes government possible, preferably good government, but at least some government rather than chaos and disorder, or even mere anarchy. It is therefore worthwhile to underline the commitment of the institutional theory of law to a stress quite as firm as any by Loughlin upon the facultative aspect of public law. But it has to be said again that law only facilitates, while politics carries out—anyway, politicians as members of the executive branch, assisted by the state's civil servants, carry out—the business of government.

Whether or not this is well done is commonly judged by outputs, or imputed outputs. Are the crime statistics satisfactory, showing a downward trend and helping to allay fears of possible victimization? Is monetary policy maintaining satisfactory control over price-inflation? Is the economy growing or shrinking? Is unemployment high or low, rising or falling? Is the educational system producing well-educated pupils and students, able and willing to integrate themselves into productive work? Is the health service delivering satisfactory health care to those in need, and supporting effective prevention of preventable disease? Is foreign policy being conducted in a way that tends to promote the conditions of peace and the maintenance of satisfactory economic and military security for the state? Are the armed forces adequately recruited, equipped, and armed for their necessary tasks, and is the subordination of military to civil power successfully upheld?

It is deeply controversial how to answer such questions, and, all the more, how to design the conduct of government so as to secure a satisfactory answer to all such questions. The rivalry of parties in representative systems (the more so, the more democratic) is a rivalry about claimed superiority in bringing about satisfactory outcomes in such domains as those mentioned. Different political philosophies point to different approaches both to the choice of means and to the definition of ends. What are the demands of political and economic justice? What is for the common good, not merely for sectional good, and how can it be realized? It is even controversial whether such questions admit of any reasonable answer or are merely the cloaks of ideology and false consciousness.

What all this shows is that law and politics are certainly not and cannot possibly be opaque to each other. A reading, or misreading, of Luhmann and Teubner that attributed to these authors the view that they are mutually opaque would render these authors wholly unpersuasive. Mutual respect for the difference of roles in a constitutional regime of separated but mutually interactive powers is not only (in a trivial sense) essential to the security of such a regime; it is essential to a well-secured rule of law. The conceptual difference must be fully acknowledged

---

[24] Cf M Loughlin, 'Ten Tenets of Sovereignty', in N Walker (ed), *Sovereignty in Transition* (Oxford: Hart Publishing, 2003) especially at 82–83; for a response, see N MacCormick, 'Questioning "Post-Sovereignty"' European Law Review 29 (2004) 852–863.

between law as a normative order of right and wrong versus politics as a domain of statecraft guided by considerations of prudence. These are to be understood as concerning what is more or less effectual to some postulated common good, or indeed considering the political elaboration of a new understanding of the common good by means of political debate and discourse. Politics, however, depends upon the constitutional-cum-legal order, and politicians have to utilize the roles of executive and legislature within a constitutional separation of powers to achieve their ends legitimately. Their doing so is, in turn, essential to the ongoing viability of the state as a law-state operating under a functional constitution that remains fully in sympathy with the text of the formal constitution (wherever such a constitution exists) on some reasonable interpretation of it.[25] Law and politics are conceptually distinct but reciprocally interactive in the dynamic processes of government and of law-application and interpretation.

[25] On 'functional' in contrast with 'formal' constitutions, see ch 3 above.

11

Constraints on Power: Fundamental Rights

11.1 Introduction

The powers of the state's governing authorities are typically unilateral. They include power to deploy the use of physical force through rules and orders issued to institutionalized agencies of law-enforcement. The criminal law, as is well known, and as will be explored more fully in the next chapter, includes provisions that prohibit the use of physical force by anyone other than a state officer (in police or prison service, exceptionally in armed forces) acting reasonably to uphold law and order. This prohibition on the private use of force is subject to exceptions only for narrowly defined domains of self-defence, or defence of others in case of extreme necessity. Thus do the state's governing authorities assert its monopoly of the use of lawful force—every use of force by one human being against another is either a legal wrong or a legally authorized enforcement measure or sanction, as it might be said, though in a slightly exaggerated way.[1]

The pretension of the state, or its governing authorities, to monopolize force in this way clearly points to certain obvious dangers. May not supreme normative power to authorize force lead in fact to concentrations of force, and use of that concentrated force in ways that are inordinate, cruel, and unfair, even unwarranted? There is certainly an abundance of evidence that this can happen. Out of the high culture in literature, the humanities and social sciences, natural science, music and the arts that characterized nineteenth-century Germany, there nevertheless emerged dire evil. Defeat in war and the collapse of the monarchy led to the foundation of an unsteadily democratic republic under the Weimar constitution. Its collapse was brought about by the way it enabled Hitler and the Nazi party to take power. They then undertook progressively worse abuse of the resources of the state, descending into deeds that have become a byword for inhumanity, cruelty, racism, and mass murder. There are many lesser illustrations of essentially similar evil processes.

---

[1] Cf Kelsen, *Pure Theory of Law* (trans M Knight) (Berkeley and Los Angeles: University of California Press, 1967) 42.

It is perhaps too easy always to refer to gross and unforgivable evil in raising problems. Sometimes one may also look uncomfortably closer to home in time, space, and sentiment, to remind oneself how grave situations may call forth problematic responses. In this spirit, one might reflect upon the reaction of two of the longest-established democracies, the United States of America and the United Kingdom, to the dastardly attacks of September 11th 2001 on the World Trade Center in New York and the Pentagon in Washington and to subsequent events. The first response was an all-out assault on the Taliban government in Afghanistan and the initiation of procedures aimed at establishing a new constitution for a democratic state in Afghanistan. Alongside this went a continuing determined and ferocious series of actions aimed at rooting out the leadership of the al-Qaeda organisation responsible for the '9/11' attacks. Next came a massive military intervention in Iraq on the pretext of preventing development or deployment of weapons of mass destruction and with the ulterior aim of deposing the tyranny of President Saddam Hussein and facilitating the establishment of a working democratic constitution in Iraq. The levels of violence and destruction that accompanied this, and that arose in response to it through various forms of insurgency and eventual sectarian violence among Sunni and Shia Muslim communities, led many commentators to dispute the wisdom and justice of the Iraq intervention, and many indeed contended that it was in execution and conception illegal under international law. Moreover, conditions in which prisoners were kept in Iraqi jails, and those prevailing at Camp Delta (previously Camp X-Ray) in Guantánamo Bay, Cuba, housing captives from the Afghan campaign suspected of involvement with al-Qaeda, appeared to violate basic rules of United States constitutional law.[2] They also failed to comply with the Geneva Convention on Prisoners of War, until such point as the US Supreme Court asserted the legal bounds within which the President could handle matters.[3] The fact that the detainees were classed as 'enemy combatants', not captured soldiers of a recognized state, had been cited in justification of this way of proceeding, but it was one that shocked the conscience of many Americans and yet more citizens of other countries, to whom the reassertion of the rule of law by the US Supreme Court came as a huge relief.

Meantime in the United Kingdom, especially following cruel suicide-bomb attacks on the London Underground and bus service in July 2005, the Prime

---

[2] Relatively junior military personnel have been tried and convicted for offences against Iraqi prisoners; and prisoners in Guantánamo have successfully challenged aspects of their detention. In *Rasul v Bush* 542 US 466 (2004) 321 F. 3d 1134, the Supreme Court held that foreign nationals imprisoned without charge at the Guantánamo Bay interrogation camps were entitled to bring legal action in US federal civilian courts challenging their captivity.

[3] In *Hamdan v Rumsfeld* 126 S Ct 2749 (2006) the Supreme Court held 'that the military commission convened to try Hamdan lacks power to proceed because its structure and procedures violate both the UCMJ [Uniform Code of Military Justice] and the Geneva Conventions' (Opinion of the Court, *per* Justice Stevens). Owen Fiss argues that foundational principles of the US Constitution remain seriously damaged even after these cases. See O Fiss, 'The War against Terrorism and the Rule of law' Oxford Journal of Legal Studies 26 (2006) 235–56.

Minister, Tony Blair, declared that 'the rules have changed' and proceeded to introduce a series of anti-terrorist measures. These include an ill-defined offence of 'glorification' of terrorist acts[4], and increases in the power of ministers—members of the executive branch—to order the detention of individuals or to place 'control orders' restricting their ordinary freedoms. These were subject to only limited forms of judicial control. Further legislative proposals claimed for ministers a general power to amend or repeal existing legislation by statutory instruments with minimal effective parliamentary control. Again, in the UK, the Courts have set limits to the freedom of action of the executive in matters touching human rights and fundamental civil liberties.[5]

Thus can executive authorities in countries with proud constitutional traditions of respect for the rule of law and with a long-standing regard for the basic rights of human beings within their jurisdiction find themselves derogating alarmingly from these traditions when faced with the challenges of organized terrorism. It is a real problem to find ways that enable power to be exercised for the sake of public safety without creating scope for its abuse, initially perhaps at the margin but always with the prospect of ever-greater incursions into previously banned fields of discretion. It is also a serious question who should finally decide to what extent safeguards against abuse are necessary, and which safeguards.

The reflections of the preceding paragraph about developments in the USA and the UK in the first decade of the twenty-first century concern developments

---

[4] See Terrorism Act 2006 s 1:

(1) This section applies to a statement that is likely to be understood by some or all of the members of the public to whom it is published as a direct or indirect encouragement or other inducement to them to the commission, preparation or instigation of acts of terrorism or Convention offences.

(2) A person commits an offence if—
  (a) he publishes a statement to which this section applies or causes another to publish such a statement; and
  (b) at the time he publishes it or causes it to be published, he—
    (i) intends members of the public to be directly or indirectly encouraged or otherwise induced by the statement to commit, prepare or instigate acts of terrorism or Convention offences; or
    (ii) is reckless as to whether members of the public will be directly or indirectly encouraged or otherwise induced by the statement to commit, prepare or instigate such acts or offences.

(3) For the purposes of this section, the statements that are likely to be understood by members of the public as indirectly encouraging the commission or preparation of acts of terrorism or Convention offences include every statement which—
  (a) glorifies the commission or preparation (whether in the past, in the future or generally) of such acts or offences; and
  (b) is a statement from which those members of the public could reasonably be expected to infer that what is being glorified is being glorified as conduct that should be emulated by them in existing circumstances.

[5] See *A* v *Home Secretary* [2004] UKHL 56, [2005] 2 WLR 87; *A* v *Home Secretary (No 2)* [2005] UKHL 71, [2005] 3 WLR 1249.

directed by democratically elected political leaders, acting with the authority of resolutions by Congress in the one case and Parliament in the other. The ancient question 'Who guards the guards themselves?' may only bump forward into the question 'Who judges who should judge of that?'. Where is the line to fall between judicial and executive responsibilities? The present chapter will discuss first the background to and evolution of the idea that there must be recognition of fundamental rights that no government can legitimately overthrow or undermine. Then it will consider the level of institutionalization such rights have achieved in the contemporary world. Finally, it will return to the question just raised, and the doubt expressed about the desirability of institutionalizing fundamental rights in certain ways.

11.2 Rights as Possible Limits on Government

Fidelity to the rule of law is one condition for the protection of liberty against unwarranted incursions by agencies of government. Insistence on the character of a *Rechtsstaat* or law-state is a way of stipulating that the force of the state must always and only be deployed under general rules that can be interpreted quite strictly and in universalistic ways that preclude unjust discriminations. But this does not itself seem enough. General rules can confer extremely wide discretion on particular officials—a case in point is the law under which Hitler was granted the power to rule by decree in Germany after 1934. Examples of abusive grants of broad discretionary powers abound in other states both in Europe and beyond it, though few as egregious as that of the Nazi terror. One must even point with regret at the Legislative and Regulatory Reform Bill brought forward by the Blair government in the UK in 2006.[6] Moreover, there is a risk that, even when power is formally limited, these limits can be ignored with impunity in practice and dire deeds can then be done. We do have always to be asking 'Who is to guard the guards themselves?'.

Taken by itself, the rule of law, albeit essential, seems likely to be in some contexts insufficient to protect against evil doing by agencies of the state. It is a real virtue but, taken on its own, a formal one.[7] Perhaps we need also some substantive limits as well as purely formal limits to state power? Recognition of fundamental rights is one candidate for providing such limits. It is one which has gained great contemporary prestige as a result of the various international instruments and

---

[6] Clause 1 of the Bill proposed conferring on ministers, that is, on the executive, extensive general powers to make and amend law subject to quite weak parliamentary scrutiny. Amendments introduced by Parliament seem likely to restrict these powers very strictly to matters dealing with administrative simplification and, in that sense, 'deregulation'. Still, the powers conferred on the executive branch by this means are a remarkable derogation from the separation of powers as commonly understood.

[7] Cf J Raz, 'The Rule of Law and its Virtue' in *The Authority of Law* (Oxford: Clarendon Press, 1979) 210–229.

national constitutional safeguards adopted in the aftermath of the World War of 1939 to 1945, and devised in response to the horrors revealed by that period of human history.

The idea is an old one, having roots in the philosophical ideas of the period in which modern forms and conceptions of the state began to emerge. Feudal kingdoms and empires appealed to ideas like immemorial right and custom, or the divine right of kings, to justify their pretensions to rule. After the Reformation and the wars of religion of the sixteenth and seventeenth centuries, such ideas came to seem more and more threadbare. Anyway, no taken-for-granted legitimacy could any longer be ascribed to kings or emperors, just because they were there and had been around for a long time in one form or another. What could justify royal rule? How could it or some alternative be established if it had broken down in the confusion of civil strife and religious enmities? On what footing?

One line of thought postulated that humans living outside an established legal order would necessarily be in a 'state of nature', having nothing to guide them or enable them to trust each other except whatever basic precepts of morality might be binding on them. Thomas Hobbes considered that the basic precepts in such a situation would be minimal. All people would face the imperative to secure the means of their own survival and that of immediate kin; none would have strong ground for trust in any other. In the absence of any organized and effective prohibition on the use of violence, each would be naturally at liberty to use whatever force was necessary to preserve life and make it as comfortable as possible in the circumstances. But that would be grim, since the circumstances would be a war of all against all, even if actual fighting were only intermittent. The imperative of self-preservation would therefore yield a subsidiary imperative, to seek peace with everyone else on terms that everyone could accept. Any peace agreement, however, would itself be precarious if there were no force to back it up ('covenants without swords are but words'). So the agreement would have to contain some provision that would make it enforceable. This could be done if the 'social contract' instituted a sovereign to whom (or to which—it might be an assembly of persons, not an individual) everybody transferred all their 'natural right' to use force. In return they would have to accept the protection, but also the burden, of laws imposed and enforced by this sovereign.[8]

'Natural right' in this form would be but a poor protection against state arbitrariness. For the only fundamental natural right is to use all the force necessary for one's own survival, and that is given up by the social contract. Thereafter there can be all manner of rights of property and rights to regulated liberty, fair trials, and everything else of that kind. But these come from the positive law laid down by the sovereign, hence could not provide an independent substantive ground for limiting the sovereign power. Enacted law, in the Hobbesian picture, is the only

---

[8] T Hobbes, *Leviathan* in Sir W Molesworth (ed), *The Collected English Works of Thomas Hobbes* (London: Routledge/Thoemmes, 1997) vol 3, chs 12–17.

standard of objective justice available to humans among themselves. There can be no independent criteria of justice whereby to criticize laws for failing in justice. (There can, however, be a set of precepts about the wise use of sovereign powers, and Hobbes gives a careful account of these prudential guides to good rulership as a kind of supplementary 'natural law'.[9])

A different view concerning the moral precepts that are binding in a state of nature would be needed in order to generate a different conclusion. Such a different view was advanced by John Locke. He argued that a state of nature would be one of liberty, not licence, since there would still be a law of reason binding on humans as rational creatures designed by a benevolent deity. Given the equality of humans as creatures of God, none could have the right to slay or offer violence to another, and each must respect the liberty of every other, having no right to enslave anyone else. Each would have equal access to the fruits of the world, and by mixing one's own effort in cultivation or in going to the trouble of hunting and gathering, one could acquire a right to possessions. Others would have no right to take these save by consent, for example, in an agreed exchange of some kind. Thus even in a state of nature, humans would have rights to life, liberty, and to hold property legitimately acquired.[10]

The problem, however, would be that there could be no mechanism for enforcing one's natural rights except through self-help. What I might regard as legitimate punishment of you for some infringement by you of my right—say, to property in some gathered fruit—you might in turn regard as a violation of your right to bodily security. For if you denied that I had acquired the fruit legitimately or indeed had any exclusive right to it at all, you could not possibly consider my violence to be a just punishment, rather than a kind of violent seizure of ownerless goods. I might call on my friends to back me up in this condition of potential conflict, but you might do likewise. A spiral of violence is the likely outcome. The situation of everyone in a state of nature would thus be unstable, and the hoped-for peacefulness of life in a state of nature under the law of nature would prove illusory. So what might be done about this?

The answer is not wholesale transfer of all one's natural rights to a single sovereign person or assembly, but only a transfer of one's 'executive power of the law of nature', that is the right to enforce one's own rights and exact remedies or punishments for breach of them.[11] A social contract to remedy the insecurity of a state of nature would provide for establishing a government. The government would have to be capable of making general rules to express basic principles of natural right in clear positive terms, capable of adjudicating about alleged breaches of law and invasions of rights, and capable of organizing external and internal defence against

<hr>

[9] *Leviathan*, ch 14. I am indebted to Garrett Barden for reminding me of the importance of this aspect of Hobbes's thought.

[10] J Locke, *The Second Treatise of Civil Government* (ed J Gough) (Oxford: Basil Blackwell, 3rd edn, 1966) especially ch 2.   [11] Locke, *Second Treatise* ch 7, paras 87–90.

violence. Governments so established would remain bound to respect those very natural rights whose insecurity in a state of nature would lead people to contract into forming a society under effective civil government. Governing authorities which seriously violated subjects' rights would forfeit their own right to be obeyed as legitimate rulers—for indeed in violating natural rights, they cease to be legitimate. A security against violation would be to ensure that the different powers of government resided in different hands.[12]

Doctrines of this kind were involved in the 'glorious revolution' of the various British kingdoms of 1688–89 (Locke's *Treatise* was written earlier, but not published until 1690; it expresses a contemporary spirit rather than being an assignable cause of revolution) and again in the American Revolution of 1776. After adoption of the American Constitution proposed by the founding fathers in Philadelphia in 1787, a first set of ten amendments was proposed and adopted in 1789. These constituted what has come to be known as the 'Bill of Rights' enumerating rights that the federal authorities were bound to respect in favour of citizens. The Fourteenth Amendment, adopted after the Civil War of 1861–65 completed the catalogue of rights, writing in the right to equal protection of the laws for all citizens, and extending the reach of the Bill of Rights to cover state as well as federal governments. In the second half of the twentieth century this became a powerful weapon in the battle for equality of black citizens with their white co-citizens.[13]

'Social contract' doctrines did not only help shape the US constitution, but they continued to be popular during the eighteenth century, and were developed in different forms, that of Jean-Jacques Rousseau being particularly influential in the francophone world.[14] The French Revolution of 1789 saw the adoption of the *Déclaration des droits de l'homme et du citoyen* as a statement of fundamental natural rights that were superior to any laws of the state, even the revolutionary state, or, finally, republic. This declaration was repeated in the Constitution of the fifth French Republic in 1958, and thus remains in force as a constitutional limit on public power. However, the French conception of the separation of powers precludes the possibility that judges in the ordinary courts of law could have a power to review legislation for conformity with constitutional restrictions, since this would involve an intrusion by the judicial power into the sphere reserved to the legislature. The *Conseil Constitutionnel*, which oversees the constitutional validity and propriety of legislative and regulatory acts is considered to be an integral element of the legislature, not of the judiciary.[15]

---

[12] Locke, *Second Treatise* chs 8–14.
[13] See, eg, A E Dick Howard (ed), *The United States Constitution: Roots, Rights and Responsibilities* (Washington, DC and London: Smithsonian Inst Press, 1992).
[14] Jean-Jacques Rousseau, *Du contrat social* (ed with an introduction and notes by R Grimsley) (Oxford: Clarendon Press, 1972).
[15] R C van Caenegem, *An Historical Introduction to Western Constitutional Law* (Cambridge: Cambridge University Press, 1995) 200–217.

In the hands of Immanuel Kant and later thinkers like John Rawls[16] or Timothy Scanlon,[17] and, more qualifiedly, Jürgen Habermas[18] in the late twentieth century, the 'social contract' underwent a revival in the form of what Kant called 'an idea of reason'.[19] This envisages a social contract not as an actual historical agreement ever made by any persons, but as a model whereby to test whether and which institutions of a state might be such as could command the assent of all persons affected. For we ask whether these could be accepted if they were being proposed for adoption by everyone in a position of mutual equality. Such imagined equality in a 'state of nature' enables us to abstract from the many pressures that are inevitable in actually functioning states and societies, with all sorts of adventitious socially determined inequalities affecting life-chances and bargaining capabilities. So the question of what would be acceptable in this case can provide a critical template for assessing actual institutions in the light of an ideal alternative that attempts still to be grounded in truths about human nature.

However that may be, from the late eighteenth century and through the nineteenth century and much of the twentieth, theories about the social contract and natural rights ceased to be of much practical political or juridical influence in the United Kingdom. Thinkers like David Hume[20] earlier and Jeremy Bentham later[21] derided the idea that a contract that never happened anywhere could be a basis for criticizing or improving, far less for founding, legal institutions and institutions of government. Custom and usage accounted for the institutions that had evolved, and the principle of utility provided a far better test for the quality of laws than any appeal to conjectural and contestable natural rights. Laws, as Bentham and his follower John Austin insisted, were whatever the actual sovereign person or body laid down by way of general commands in a functioning 'political society', that is, one in which people in general habitually, though not by any means universally, obey some such commander.[22] Rights are, they agreed with Hobbes, the consequences of sovereign legislation, not the preconditions of legitimate sovereignty. Good law is that which is most useful in promoting the greatest happiness of the greatest number of persons in society. The rights we should have are those that would be conferred by the most generally beneficial

---

[16] J Rawls, *A Theory of Justice* (Oxford: Oxford University Press, revised edn, 1999).

[17] T M Scanlon, *What We Owe to Each Other* (Cambridge, Mass and London: Belknap Press of Harvard University Press, 1998).

[18] J Habermas, *Between Facts and Norms: contributions to a discourse theory of law and democracy* (trans William Rehg) (Cambridge: Polity Press, 1995).

[19] J Ladd (trans), *Kant: The Metaphysical Elements of Justice* (Indianapolis, Ind: Bobbs-Merrill, 1965) at pp xxx and 80–81.

[20] D Hume, 'Of the Original Contract', in *Essays Moral, Political and Literary* (Oxford: Oxford University Press, 1963) 452–473.

[21] J Bentham, *A Fragment on Government* in *A Comment on the Commentaries and a Fragment on Government* (ed J H Burns and H L A Hart) (London: Athlone Press, 1977).

[22] Bentham, *Of Laws in General* (ed H L A Hart) (London: Athlone Press, 1970); J Austin, *The Province of Jurisprudence Determined* (ed W E Rumble) (Cambridge: Cambridge University Press, 1995).

laws. Reflection on the Terror that developed out of the French Revolution and led into Napoleonic imperialism discouraged any nostalgia for ideas about the social contract.

Alongside utilitarian political theory, though not always in anything like full agreement with it, runs a tradition of looking to common law as the source of the most fundamental rights to life, liberty, and security of property and possessions. According to A V Dicey, for example, the best security for protecting citizens' rights from unjust exactions by state agencies is to ensure that Parliament's sovereignty is respected through the ordinary courts of law. The process is one of subjecting all decisions between state and citizen or citizen and citizen to the same courts, interpreting new legislation in a context of established common law rights that Parliament is presumed to uphold except if it very explicitly legislates to the contrary.[23] Even that view came under criticism for its assumption about the benign quality of judicial decision-making. For it was argued, especially on the left wing of politics, that judges typically took a rather conservative line, for example tending to favour employers against trades unions even in the face of legislation attempting to free unions from some of the strictures developed through the common law. Hence any proposals that would tend to give judges power to review legislation, for example for conformity with a bill of rights, were viewed with great suspicion, both from the left and from the more conservative Diceyan attitude to common law. During the Second World War, however, and from quite early on in it, opinion in the UK began to shift. The atrocities of Nazi Germany were not yet fully exposed, but enough was known to trigger grave alarm. Certain intellectuals began meeting in London to try to work out a statement of the basic requirements of human decency such as might become the basis for an international code of human rights to be established after the war.[24] This activity, together with that of other like-minded persons, drawing also on the American and French traditions of constitutional rights, resulted in major developments concerning human rights in the post-war period.

11.3 Institutionalization of Rights

In December 1948, the recently established United Nations adopted and proclaimed the Universal Declaration on Human Rights, to which all members of the UN must subscribe. Subsequently (in 1966) UN Covenants on Civil and Political Rights and on Economic Social and Cultural Rights were produced, and there

---

[23] A V Dicey, *An Introduction to the Study of the Law of the Constitution* (ed E C S Wade) (London: Macmillan, 10th edn, 1964) 183–205.

[24] G Robertson, *Crimes against Humanity in International Criminal Law: The Struggle for Global Justice* (London: Allen Lane, 1999), for a description of this process. Cf Lord Irvine of Lairg, *Human Rights, Constitutional Law and the Development of the English Legal System* (Oxford: Hart Publishing, 2003) 17–22.

have been several more specialized conventions dealing with such matters as racial discrimination, discrimination against women, children's rights, and the like. The total effect is to concretize in greater detail the grand-scale commitments expressed in the Universal Declaration, and to establish a set of Committees and Commissions of the United Nations that can actively monitor improvements or deteriorations in the general situation, or specific instances of abuse, and in some cases adjudicate in a quasi-judicial way on complaints made to them.

In Europe, institutionalization has proceeded yet more deeply. The Council of Europe was established in the aftermath of war (on 3 August 1949) to create a common forum for democratic states, and it propounded a European Convention for the Protection of Human Rights and Fundamental Freedoms ('ECHR'),[25] to the drafting of which much was contributed by lawyers from the United Kingdom. In trying to state basic rights clearly, the ECHR goes into considerably greater detail than most such instruments. It lays down the various limitations that are to apply to particular rights, where a balance has to be struck with competing rights or other aspects of the public good, and the circumstances in which, by reason of emergency, a state may validly derogate from some (but not all) of the rights. An important innovation in the European context was that the Convention also made provision for considering complaints about violations of rights, and eventually submitting unresolved complaints to a Court of Human Rights with judges from all the participating states. Initially, this involved a somewhat roundabout process involving a Human Rights Commission that tried to reconcile disputes with states, only sending a case to the Court if reconciliation did not produce a satisfactory result.

With the passage of time, however, the Court and the judicial role have grown more robust, with individuals enjoying a right to take complaints directly to the Court once they have exhausted domestic remedies inside the relevant member state. States that ratified the Convention originally on terms that precluded individual petition have relented and the right of individuals to take cases to the Court is all but universal. At the same time, developments in the European Community and now the European Union have added further strength to Convention obligations, for entry into the EU and continuing membership of it is conditional upon a commitment to due observance of human rights as laid down in the European Convention and the constitutional traditions of the member states. There now exists a substantial European Human Rights jurisprudence based on the judgments of the court and on judgments of national courts. The latter deal with human rights issues, for example by way of constitutionally entrenched Fundamental Rights as in Germany since the Basic Law was adopted in 1949, or by applying the Declaration of the Rights of Man and Citizen through administrative tribunals and the *Conseil Constitutionnel* in France, or by

---

[25] This was opened for signature by the members of the Council of Europe, in Rome, on 4 November 1950.

'domestication' of the European Convention, as in the UK since the Human Rights Act of 1998.

Clearly, this amounts to a very substantial institutionalization of fundamental rights, both internally to states and through regional-international organizations (like the Council of Europe and its Court of Human Rights) or transnational confederations like the EU. The forms this institutionalization has taken transform the old 'natural rights' debate. It can—and it does—remain as controversial as ever whether there are universal natural rights based on fundamental and universally valid moral principles, rights that might indeed be binding in a 'state of nature', if such a thing ever existed or can even be credibly imagined. Various schools of thought in different ways argue about objective bases on which to assert basic moral rights and duties binding on humans simply by virtue of human nature and/or the nature of things. Others oppose this, but need not oppose the institutionalization of human rights. Utilitarians, for example, might well argue that the virtue of institutionalized human rights is that, by the common accord of many states, they lay down rules that would not otherwise exist at all. These rules, given the interests they help to protect, have the quality of tending to maximize human happiness. Yet more plausibly stated, they set real and substantial obstacles to notorious and historically well attested ways of inflicting misery and degradation on humans. Utilitarians can nevertheless also engage in critique of rights instruments and regimes if or to the extent that the obstacles they set prove to be inexpedient in the cause of promoting the common good of a community. This can be seen vividly, if not always in a well-argued way, in some contemporary critiques of the 'rights culture' with which the developments we are considering are bound up.

All such issues remain open at the level both of philosophical foundations and in the context of current and continuing substantive moral and political debate in the contemporary world.[26] Yet institutionalization of rights remains an established element in institutional normative order both within states and among them, one that erects substantive as well as formal limits to the powers of state authorities. Legislatures violate serious obligations of their state, and may also simply fail to achieve legal validity,[27] when they make laws that cannot be interpreted in any such way as to achieve compatibility with human rights according to the governing

---

[26] See A J M Milne, *Human Rights and Human Diversity: an essay in the philosophy of human rights* (London: Macmillan, 1986) for a critique of the cultural biases inherent in many of the human rights instruments currently in force. Cf Tom Campbell, *Rights: A Critical Introduction* (Abingdon, Oxon: Routledge, 2006), who argues that over-attention to rights in legal and political practice can foster all four of egoism, legalism, dogmatism, and elitism—see particularly his summary of the argument at 199–205.

[27] Not, for example, in the United Kingdom, where the Human Rights Act 1998 enables courts to issue a 'declaration of incompatibility' of UK legislation with the Convention Rights; this does not take effect to invalidate the offending legislation, but may lead to executive or legislative rectification of the problem. There is a radical contrast here with the situation prevailing in, for example, Germany, where basic rights were written into the Basic Law of 1949, and have been strongly upheld by the federal Constitutional Court. See R Alexy, *A Theory of Constitutional Rights* (trans J Rivers) (Oxford: Oxford University Press, 2002).

interpretation of these. Subordinate rule-makers and executive decision-makers, law-enforcement officers and others, can find their conduct and practices exposed to scrutiny concerning respect for rights, decisions being valid only to the extent that they do observe these restrictions. Citizens have a simple immunity against being deprived of rights by such subordinate rule-makers or decision-makers.

That conduct is wrong or is lacking in legal validity does not, of course, entail that no one indulges in it. Rogue officials can violate duties of their office, and get away with it. Rogue states can to a degree successfully defy international public opinion, and violate declared rights of human beings and their own acknow-ledged international obligations. Genocide still stalks the planet, sixty years after the full discovery of the supreme criminality of the Holocaust. Bodies like the International Criminal Court are still a long way from securing remotely effective universal enforcement of punishments for those who violate the most basic of the piously proclaimed universal rights. Nevertheless, one can say that contemporary law-states now observe not only a formal 'rule of law' that insists on basic formal minima in the exercise of public power. They have also come to share a body of overlapping if not identical substantive limits on the legitimate use of public power through an institutionalization of human rights. This has transformed credible but contestable moral principles into established and normatively effect-ive limits on public powers, though always subject to the interpretative decisions of whatever agencies are charged with considering and deciding complaints about violation of rights.

This is not a work primarily about human rights, so no detailed account of the various charters, conventions, constitutional fundamental rights clauses, or of their implementation, is needed. We may take it as a currently established article of belief that governmental power has to be limited power, because there are cer-tain fundamental human goods that no-one should be denied.[28] These goods are enshrined in rights instruments, and institutions of government erected among us to serve the common good should never be able to cancel or ride roughshod over these fundamental rights of individual people.

Nevertheless, a brief conspectus may be offered as a mere reminder of the main themes in the contemporary institutionalization of human rights. The basic idea is that all humans are to be treated as persons and all persons must be treated with due respect. The value of respect for persons in its contemporary understanding brings one of Kant's fundamental ideas to a kind of positive realization.

A particularly clear and straightforward summary of the terms of current human rights instruments and the conception of respect for persons that they encapsulate can be found in the Charter of Fundamental Rights of the European

---

[28] This established belief, however, does not preclude disagreement with utilizing the mechanism of conventions, bills, or charters of rights, coupled with judicial enforcement of these, to secure fundamental goods in contemporary states—cf Campbell, *Rights*.

Union. The Charter was adopted in 2000 under the Treaty of Nice, though only with the force of a 'political declaration'. The legally binding text for Europeans remains the European Convention. The Charter elucidates these rights, and others derived from the European Community treaties and other more recent conventions on special topics, by expounding them under the headings of individual dignity, personal liberty, interpersonal equality, social solidarity, political citizenship, and proper administration of justice under law. This is a valuable way of summarizing the matter.

To start with dignity—there may be marginal disputes concerning what exact forms of treatment are inhuman and degrading, depriving a person of his or her dignity as a person, treating him/her as a mere thing or a sub-human animal. The Kantian imperative to treat rational nature as an end in itself, never simply as a means, captures the central sense of this. Continuing to liberty, imprisonment, or physical confinement of any kind always calls for justification. Other ways to deprive an individual of autonomy, of the ability to be a self-determining member of a 'kingdom of ends', are inevitably objectionable. Interference with freedom always needs affirmative justification and can only be tolerable to the extent that any particular form of interference is covered by pre-announced laws that are proportional to an end that is itself a part of the fundamental values we are discussing. Freedom of opinion and of speech, of conscience, and the free exercise of religious observances come under this head, too.

It is an affront to dignity to the extent that fundamental goods are differentially protected for different categories of persons, except in so far as strong affirmative justifications can be provided for such differentiation. The idea that discriminatory laws are wrong is in play here—but it is only discrimination without affirmative justification, and discrimination to a degree that is disproportional in the light of such justification, that is absolutely excluded. This is the sense of 'equality' that we embrace in embracing fundamental rights. Social solidarity looks to outlawing a different kind of differentiation. No doubt liberty requires and includes liberty to acquire to use and to dispose of property. But inequality of an extreme kind in access to material goods is itself an unjustified form of discrimination that in turn spawns others. All property is acquired under law, and property regimes that enshrine unacceptable discrimination between rich and poor cannot be justified. The remedy lies in taxation and redistribution. The human rights end of this concerns the right of everyone to have a decent minimum of the world's goods, whether personally acquired or achieved as a result of a deliberate distribution of part of the overall social product. All this concerns solidarity.

Political citizenship entails the right to participate in democratic political activity, to vote in elections and to stand for elections, and to have the right of free departure from and entry into the country of one's citizenship. Arbitrary removal of voting rights, for example, even from persons serving prison sentences, were held in 2005 to be incompatible with the European Convention—even in this case there must be due proportionality between any forfeiture of such a right and the other provisions of the penal system.[29] So far as concerns rights to the proper administration of justice, these call for standard provisions like the right to fair notice of any charge or accusation, and a fair opportunity to answer it and defend oneself in a judicial proceeding, with adequate access to professional advice and assistance. They also require that the tribunal before which one is tried be a genuinely independent judicial tribunal, and they exclude forced self-incrimination.

The Charter itself indicates that it is to be interpreted as laying down rights in conformity with the European Convention and the established jurisprudence of the Human Rights Court, except if a more extensive protection is given by the Charter. This is very important. Any claim that there are proper limitations on governmental power by virtue of fundamental rights that stand outside state law is weakened to the extent that there are too many different texts, all of them purporting to be authoritative, that enunciate these rights in different terms. If there are real differences, the claim to 'fundamental' character is weakened for all. Moreover, there is a risk of widely diverging judicial interpretations of similar terms in different instruments. The institutionalization of fundamental rights inevitably involves a certain degree of arbitrariness in the choice of words used to delineate a right and the exceptions or limitations to which it is subject, and the possible permissibility of derogating from it in situations of emergency. But the legitimacy of the institutionalization in question, and of the recourse to tribunals of an international character, where limits are thus placed on the legislative powers of the democratically established organs of states' governments, is precarious. The credibility of the institutions thus depends on consistency and coherence of a high degree in the substance of judgments passed concerning rights and the limits on legislative power that they entail.

It cannot be said that there is any single uniformly authoritative institutional formulation of fundamental human rights, though special respect is surely due to the 1948 Universal Declaration. But in different places, different standards prevail. The US Constitution and the US Supreme Court afford the longest-standing example of a domestic entrenchment of rights, with justiciability of any allegation concerning a violation of rights. Yet the content of the Bill of Rights is by no means equivalent to that of the European Convention or the EU Charter, or the UN Declaration or Covenants. The French Declaration is different again as are the *Grundrechte* entrenched into the German Basic Law of 1949. Only the Irish Constitution treats the human foetus as a person entitled to constitutional protection. In the United States, the death penalty is permissible under the currently prevailing interpretation of the prohibition on 'cruel and unusual punishments', whereas in Europe it is now generally outlawed in the name of the self-same human rights tradition as was so precociously developed in the United

---

[29] *Hirst* v *the United Kingdom (No 2)* ECHR 26 October 2005 (application no 74025/01).

States. Canada, a latecomer to the establishment of 'Charter Rights' in its constitution, tends more to the European than to the US model.[30] India is different
again.

It would seem unreasonable to assert that any one institutional version of fundamental rights captures their essence in absolute preference over all others, or to
say that only this benchmark provides a solid test for enacted human instruments
to participate fully in the quality of being 'law'. There are different institutional-
izations of rights in different political and constitutional settings. There is a growing international consensus on the need to set limits on states' powers, including
powers of legislation, for the sake of upholding human dignity, liberty, equality,
and solidarity, along with entrenched rights of political citizenship and to the fair
administration of justice. Governmental systems which fail in these regards fall
short of some of the essential virtues of legal order, even if they succeed in sustaining some form of institutional normative order, and to this extent of law. But one
cannot say that there is a single specific institutionalized set of 'fundamental',
'human', or 'natural' rights that has highest authority for all purposes.

11.4 Problems about Rights: Who is to Judge?

It seems plain that there is a large and overlapping consensus about the need to
take rights seriously.[31] The devil, as usual, lies in the detail. Once you start trying
to define the rights in question, you may state them too broadly, or too vaguely, so
that they either catch far too much or have to be worked out in more concrete
terms by courts comprising judges from many different legal and judicial traditions. Surprising and unwelcome interpretations may emerge from this process,
taking a form that is much harder to amend by democratic decision than it was to
adopt the rights-text in the first place, for all institutional versions of fundamental
or human rights belong in the category analysed in chapter 7 as 'rights in regard to
states of being or of affairs'. Hence they are polysemous, and can be read as entailing different sets of active and passive rights, powers, and immunities. The task of
human rights jurisprudence has been and is to concretize relatively vague and
abstract statements of rights into more exactly understood and specified legal
relations between individuals and states, and, to some extent, individuals *inter se*.

It follows that agreement about the need to safeguard fundamental rights can
mask quite deep-going disagreement about what exactly is covered by such rights
as the right to life, or the right to a fair trial, or the right to privacy in one's home
and correspondence. There can be parallel disagreement about any qualifications
or exceptions to the core right—how extensively to read the exception or the

---

[30] G W Anderson (ed), *Rights and Democracy: Essays in UK-Canadian Constitutionalism* (London:
Blackstone Press, 1999).
[31] The phrase, is, of course, Ronald Dworkin's: *Taking Rights Seriously* (London: Duckworth, 1977).

qualification? One principal point about institutionalized law is that it provides means to make authoritative rulings about practical issues that arouse disagreement.[32] There are two possible ways of doing this. One is the method of adjudication. Provided some rule or principle has been laid down or is otherwise recognized, judges can decide disputes about how the rule or principle is to be applied in an individual disputed case. This always has at least some exemplary value in relation to other individual disputes, and in many traditions the individual decision taken by a high-level tribunal is acknowledged as a precedent containing a rule or ruling that is applicable to future cases. The other method is that of legislation. Once it is clear that the implications of some acknowledged right—the right to a fair trial, say—are disputed, a legislature can legislate in more precise terms to clarify the disputed point (and, after that, it will be for judges to carry on the process of concretization). Where the legislature is a democratic and representative body, the ultimate authority is that of the electorate, the whole citizen body. As between the legislature and the judiciary, dealing with ordinary matters, the last word concerning general rules rests with the former. Judicial precedents that are found unsatisfactory under democratic scrutiny can be corrected for the future (though only very exceptionally in a retrospective manner) by new legislation.

In the case of human rights tribunals and supreme constitutional courts, however, the situation is reversed. For once the court or tribunal has declared an authoritative interpretation of a fundamental right, it would involve violation of that right were the legislature to reverse the precedent, even prospectively. At any rate, it would be for the court or tribunal subsequently to rule on whether the new statute violated the right as declared by the court or tribunal. Only a revised international convention or a constitutional amendment could change the interpretation once it had been authoritatively given. Of course, under criticism from commentators and after hearing fresh arguments in later cases, the tribunal or court might adopt a different ruling about interpretation of the right. Even so, that still leaves the question open whether it is courts that should have the last say about these matters,[33] or whether a democratic alternative is possible and preferable.

This should not be characterized as a simple issue between the protection of rights on the one hand and the protection of institutions of majority rule on the other. The point of democracy, as Jeremy Waldron has argued, is that it depends on 'the right of rights',[34] that is, the right to participate in deliberation and voting

---

[32] See ch 14 below; cf J Waldron, *Law and Disagreement* (Oxford: Oxford University Press, 1999) 119–122, 149–151; S Eng, *Analysis of Dis/Agreement with particular reference to Law and Legal Theory* (Dordrecht: Kluwer Academic, 2003).

[33] Consider again Tom Campbell's critique of the elitism inevitably involved in the judicial determination of human rights; *Rights* 152–156.

[34] Waldron, *Law and Disagreement* 232–254, 282–283; but see, for a powerful rejoinder, C Fabre, 'The Dignity of Rights: Jeremy Waldron's Law and Disagreement' Oxford Journal of Legal Studies 20 (2000) 271–282.

on all issues of what is (to be) legally right or legally wrong. Democracy in relation to rights would mean that citizens have the right to decide about all the rights everyone is to have. Such rights would no doubt have to include the basic rights without which everyone's democratic participation is impossible—for example, the rights in the Universal Declaration, or the European Convention, or EU Charter. But any decision that these are to be taken out of the ongoing democratic process and entrenched in such a way that, for the future, they are reserved for judicial decision and interpretation, not re-opened to democratic debate, has an odd effect. It involves trusting a previous democratic majority, which adopted or signed up to the rights charter, while mistrusting the present majority to keep faith with the same rights, or—and here is the rub—to determine upon a restatement or re-interpretation of the inherited stock of rights. Alternatively, it can be said to involve preferring 'aristocratic'[35] decision-making by judges chosen for their exalted practical wisdom to democratic decisions that rely on such practical wisdom as everybody can bring to bear on an issue. Tom Campbell has argued in similar vein that: 'A regard for humane values, and even a commitment to the ideal of autonomy which underlies much of the human rights conception, point definitively to the need for keeping the power of defining the content of human rights with the mainstream of democratic politics'.[36]

These are not trivial issues, and it needs to be underlined that there is no single model that sets the manifestly correct way of handling fundamental rights. Germany and the United States have constitutional courts with power to review and set aside any unconstitutional legislation. France builds the safeguard of the *Conseil Constitutionel* into its legislative, not its judicial, process.[37] The UK has a Human Rights Act that gives the force of law domestically to most of the ECHR rights, directing its courts to interpret all legislation 'so far as possible' to ensure that there is no conflict with the Convention rights. But in the last resort, in cases where the courts find an Act of Parliament that simply cannot be so interpreted as to conform with Convention rights, they have to issue a 'declaration of incompatibility'. That in turn transfers the problem back into the political system, for ministers and Parliament have then to decide whether to amend the offending legislation to bring it into line with the Convention rights, or to leave it as it stands.

Beyond all such domestic arrangements, there remains the appeal to international or European human rights law. Especially for European states, there are considerable disadvantages to be faced by a state that opts for open violation of the Convention (and, possibly, the Charter in future), in the face ultimately of a

---

[35] Waldron, *Disagreement* 264–265.

[36] T D Campbell, *The Legal Theory of Ethical Positivism* (Aldershot: Dartmouth, 1996) 185.

[37] See C Fabre, *Social Rights Under the Constitution* (Oxford: Clarendon Press, 2000) 138–141, rightly arguing that different models for adjudication and upholding constitutional rights affect the question of how fundamental rights mesh together with democratic decision-making procedures. The UK's Human Rights Act is yet another example of this.

judgment by the European Court of Human Rights. Few other national or international tribunals have the full weight of authority attaching to the European Court's judgments, but in all cases there is a possibility of some objective judgment with at least some morally persuasive force. None of this was enough, for example, to prevent the establishment of Camp Delta in Guantánamo Bay and the detention there without trial of many persons over several years. Once the Supreme Court had pronounced on the legal obligations of the United States towards prisoners held there, President Bush announced (on Thursday 13 July 2006) his decision to effect its closure. Yet subsequently, on 28 July, the President put forward fresh proposals for legislation by Congress to authorize forms of detention substantially the same as those the Supreme Court had held unlawful. Here is a focus of continuing legal conflict.

It was at one time a standard feature of books on general jurisprudence that they had to review the question whether international law is really 'law' at all. Doubts about this were attributable, for example, to the absence of any supersovereign who could command all the states to behave appropriately or else suffer some sanction. For all that the present work is focused mainly on the laws and institutions of states, the theory of law offered here fully endorses the legal character of international law. It is quite clear that public international law fully fits within the concept of an 'institutional normative order'. None of the institutions of international law, indeed, have greater importance than those charged in various ways with upholding and protecting internationally established standards of decent and civilized behaviour, with human rights at the very heart of this.

Especially in times of stress and crisis, and in the face of shocking atrocities, democratic governments can find themselves precipitated into sudden and extreme measures, by way of response both to public outrage and to their own sense of duty to protect innocent lives and punish guilty persons. There are international courts and agencies of various kinds that can over the longer-run be called on to judge about and call for correction in the practices of states that have gone too far in bending rights of some with a view to better protecting rights of others. There is thus a long-run blending of objective judgment chiefly by outsiders to the state, working as insiders to sustaining agreed international standards about minimum acceptable conduct by states, and of democratic responses within a state to judgments of this kind when they go against the state.

This is never enough to guarantee that rogue states and pariah governments can be halted in their tracks. Hunger is not bread,[38] and the wrongfulness of cruelty

---

[38] Jeremy Bentham's critique of the 'natural rights' tradition in the form it took in his day included attacking it for creating a cruel delusion—appeals to rights can give a comforting illusion that these are already positively established—but that is exactly what natural rights are not. '[A] reason for wishing that a certain right were established, is not that right; want is not supply; hunger is not bread' (J Bentham, 'Nonsense Upon Stilts' in P Schofield, C Pease-Watkin and C Blamires (eds), *Rights, Representation and Reform: Nonsense Upon Stilts and Other Writings on the French Revolution* (Oxford: Oxford University Press, 2002) 330.

and genocide is not a security against their ever happening. Obstacles to abuses of power can never be absolute guarantees that all such abuses can be prevented, nor that all abusers will repent of what they do. One can say with confidence, however, that no state is properly counted as a law-state unless it succeeds in erecting genuine obstacles to abuse of power and then observes both the internally-determined boundaries and those that can also be subject to adjudication from without.

Legal power is never unlimited power.

12

Criminal Law and Civil Society:
Law and Morality

12.1 Introduction

Whatever else is credible or otherwise in Locke's depiction of the 'state of nature', he is surely convincing on the topic of a universal right to punish. If everyone were in the position of having to defend her or his own rights against all comers, and having to take her/his own steps to obtain some remedy from, or to punish, anyone who invaded their rights, the prospects for civil peace would be slim. Even without recourse to fables about the state of nature, one can learn much from the history of blood feuds in clan-based societies,[1] and even from contemporary examples of vigilante justice or historical accounts of 'frontier justice' during the westward expansion of the United States or during the wild days of the Anglo-Scottish border.[2]

The comparatively modern development of a specialized body of criminal law, backed-up by organized police forces and related law-enforcement agencies, working alongside a system of public prosecution before specialist courts, has been a condition of a progressively greater civility in civil society.[3] This has depended on successfully restraining the exercise of police powers within the rule of law, where the law has insisted upon restrictions of the police power for the sake of civil liberty, and, in later years, for the sake of the full panoply of human rights. This was explored in the last chapter. But such powers exercised with restraint can facilitate relative peacefulness and mutual trust even among complete strangers. Self-protection, or resort to pre-emptive disablement of potentially threatening persons, becomes less attractive and less necessary the more there is an effective maintenance of public order and substantial discouragement of crime. Of course, this mainly depends on the voluntary and reciprocal self-restraint of citizens in

---

[1] J Cairns, 'Academic Feud, Blood Feud and William Welwood: Legal Education in St Andrews, 1560–1611' Edinburgh Law Review 2 (1998) Parts 1 and 2, 158–179, 225–287.
[2] G M Fraser, *The Steel Bonnets: the story of the Anglo-Scottish border reivers* (London: Barrie and Jenkins, 1971).
[3] V A C Cattrell et al (eds), *Crime and the Law: the Social History of Crime in Western Europe since 1500* (London: Europa Publications, 1980).

their interactions with each other. But the collective sense of security and solidarity in a relatively peaceful society is likely to depend on a fairly high degree of confidence among law-abiding persons that those who do not abide by the law, engaging in violent or dishonest behaviour, will be effectively restrained. It also requires a degree of confidence that efforts will be made to detect wrongdoing, and then to bring detected wrongdoers to trial, with an adequate punishment meted out in the case of a conviction after due process of law.

Thus the civility of civil society is partly dependent on the state's establishing or maintaining an adequate body of criminal law, and sustaining adequate institutions for securing its observance, judging on allegations of crime, and carrying out the punishments to which convicted persons have been sentenced. These are necessary, but of course not sufficient, conditions to secure civility. Other conditions such as adequate education, shared though far from identical moral convictions that certify the state's institutions as reasonably just in the eyes of most citizens, religious communities, and institutions, and many other institutions of civil society must play a part in upholding a common willingness to observe the restraints of the law.[4] But these are the less effective to the extent that it can credibly be supposed that those who do not willingly abide by the law's constraints can successfully prey upon those who do, without effective intervention by public officials.[5]

All this indeed helps to establish a sense for the much-used but often pretty vague term 'civil society'.[6] Human life is always, as Aristotle observed, social. We cannot live in complete isolation, and the full flourishing of human potentialities depends on our coexisting in relatively extensive social groups, or groups of groups. Warlike societies interact on the basis of strong internal solidarity within clan groups (or the like) but with regular bloodshed and long-running blood feuds among clan groups. Civil society exists to the extent that peaceful interaction prevails among persons who trust each other to observe a common set of legally-established constraints, mainly on a voluntary basis, but with coercive state institutions in the background, as everyone is aware. Resort to violent self-help can then be effectively excluded to a very considerable extent, though a residual right to reasonable self-defence continues to be acknowledged by law in cases where other help cannot be forthcoming in a timely enough way. In the circumstances of civil society thus

---

[4] Conversely, David Garland draws attention to the fact that governmental policies that enhance social stratification and undermine solidarity actually lead to enhanced crime and a felt need for stronger crime control. See D Garland, *The Culture of Control* (Oxford: Oxford University Press, 2001) 101–102.

[5] Cf Hart, *Concept of Law* 197–198 on the necessity for 'voluntary co-operation in a coercive system'.

[6] 'It is in conducting the affairs of civil society, that mankind find the exercise of their best talents, as well as the object of their best affections' (A Ferguson, *An Essay on the History of Civil Society* (Edinburgh: Edinburgh University Press, 1966) at 154). See also M Krygier, *Between Fear and Hope* (Sydney, NSW: ABC Books, 1997) 44–63 on 'The Uses of Civility'; also *Civil Passions* (Melbourne: Black Inc, 2005) 163–176.

understood, the development of an extensive market economy becomes possible, as will be discussed in the next chapter. These background reflections, however, suffice to introduce some reflections on the character of criminal law within the broader framework of the type of institutional normative order that is state law.

12.2 Crimes and Wrongs

Chapter 6 established the thesis that the differentiation of right from wrong (more strictly, of wrong from not-wrong) is the basic binary opposition on which law is founded. Crimes are a species of wrongs, distinct from delicts (torts), breaches of contract or of promise or of trust, and other civil wrongs. Their distinguishing mark is that they are punishable wrongs. That is, properly, a crime which merits the imposition of a state-imposed punishment on one who commits it. That is actually a crime which in a given system of state law (or, nowadays, also under the rules of international law constitutive of the International Criminal Court), is prohibited under liability to a state-imposed or internationally-administered penal sanction.

Not all punishments are state-imposed or internationally-administered. Parents punish children, schools punish pupils, employers punish employees, football associations punish footballers, and so on. Punishment is an intentional reaction to conduct for which a person is held responsible, aimed at expressing a sense of the wrongfulness of that conduct and the blameworthiness of the actor for it. It thus seeks to impress on the actor the seriousness of his/her misdeed with a view to encouraging better behaviour in the future, and to serving as an example to like-minded others. The intentional reaction takes the form of imposing some form of 'hard treatment' on the actor.[7]

The state claims and seeks to exercise a monopoly of physical force, and this therefore entails restrictions on the forms of hard treatment non-state authorities are entitled to use in the imposition of their own punishments. Apart from whatever (if any) forms of 'reasonable chastisement' are permitted in domestic or educational contexts, the use of physically coercive force is reserved under law to the state's own civil and (under tight restraint domestically) military agencies concerned with crime and its prevention, with the frontier security of the state, with public order, and with the safeguarding of public revenues.

Thus practices of physically coercive punishment are substantially reserved to the state's authorities concerned with criminal law and certain other branches of

---

[7] J Kleinig 'The Hardness of Hard Treatment', in A Ashworth and M Wasik (eds), *Fundamentals of Sentencing Theory*, explores the concept of 'hard treatment', and ascribes the original use of the phrase to Joel Feinberg's 1968 paper 'The Expressive Function of Punishment', reprinted in Feinberg, *Doing and Deserving* (Princeton, NJ: Princeton University Press, 1970) 95–118. See also A Duff, *Trials and Punishments* (Cambridge: Cambridge University Press, 1986) 240–246, 260–261, and *Punishment, Communication, and Community* (Oxford: Oxford University Press, 2001). Cf V Tadros, *Criminal Responsibility* (Oxford: Oxford University Press, 2005) ch 3.

public law (environmental protection, health and safety at work, customs and excise, taxation, for example). In countries that observe the European Human Rights Convention, physical coercion nowadays involves only incarceration, other physical punishments such as flogging, beheading, or hanging having been abolished as incompatible with human dignity, though many other contemporary states take a different view. Incarceration for substantial periods of time is itself a serious matter for ordinary human beings, and because it is imposed as a punishment it also carries a heavy element of stigma. Under the rule of law and by virtue of entrenched rights (or common law rights) to fair trials, punishments can be imposed only by the order of an independent judge or bench of judges after a fairly conducted trial on the basis of a specific charge or set of charges, and only if the accused person has been found guilty as charged. The charge itself must specify an act that was defined as criminal under a clear pre-existing legal rule.[8] Under some systems, trial must be by a jury of the accused person's peers if any serious charge is involved. Punishment may only be for an offence charged and proven in this way (or judicially admitted by the accused through a freely-made plea of guilty to the charge).

The constraints that surround the practices of detection, prosecution, trial, conviction, and finally punishment of a person for a crime indicate the moral gravity attaching to the whole process. It would undermine the sense of security that is essential to life in civil society if it were credible that the forms of trial and punishment were no more than show-trials involving essentially arbitrary accusations and verdicts. On the other hand, they underline that punishment would be misused if it were applied otherwise than to cases of serious and wilful wrongdoing. This is a thought which sometimes gives rise to concerns about the growth of a body of 'regulatory law' or 'quasi-criminal law', offences against which apparently involve little moral stigma.[9]

At this point, it may be protested that the present account has strayed too far from a sensibly 'positivistic' account of the matter in hand. Such a protest would take the following lines:

Crimes are those deeds that the state does prohibit under threat of punishment, and does punish when the prohibition is violated. If the state chooses to criminalize smoking in places of public resort, or burning coal fires in homes within smokeless zones, or driving defective motor vehicles, even when the defect is unknown to the driver, such things become crimes along with all the others. And wherever the state abolishes a prior prohibition, what was a crime ceases to be so—as in the case of homosexual acts between consenting adults. Punishments cause pain, and are designed to cause it. Therefore it is indeed a moral issue when and how much such imposed pain can be justified. But 'ought' should not be

---

[8] See, eg, Art 5 of the European Convention for the Protection of Human Rights and Fundamental Freedoms.
[9] See P Devlin, *The Enforcement of Morals* (London: Oxford University Press, 1965) 26–34, on 'quasi-criminal' law.

confused with 'is'. Crimes exist relative to specific legal systems at specific times, and to know what is a crime you must study the relevant body of law and find out what it prohibits. What the criminal law does say and what it ought to say are different things that should not be conflated.

There is, of course, an important kernel of truth in this robustly relativistic and positivistic protest. Even where broadly similar lists of crimes and offences are found in the legal systems of different states, they are defined differently in different places and the whole catalogue of offences differs quite a bit from place to place. You can't tell what is a crime in France or Latvia or Japan without consulting someone expert in French or Latvian or Japanese law, or learning the relevant body of law for yourself. Nevertheless, the protest does in its blunt form ignore the significant truth that there are conceptual limits to what can intelligibly be done using certain kinds of institutional means, and this applies in particular to crime and the institutions of criminal law.[10] It is possible to believe or disbelieve that all acts of homosexual intercourse are wicked perversions of the human sexual faculty. It is possible to believe or to disbelieve that acts of homosexual intercourse, even between two adult and fully consenting parties ought to be punishable as crimes. What is not possible is both to believe that such acts are morally innocent, and either harmless or harmful only to the participants, and to believe that they should be punishable as crimes.

To punish, and thus to prohibit upon the pain of some threatened punishment, is to stigmatize morally the conduct prohibited and the persons punished for engaging in it.[11] This is unintelligible without some presupposition about the moral character of the act in respect of which the punishee is punished. Such a presupposition is contestable, as most moral positions are, and sometimes we may be convinced that historical examples of such prohibitions were based on a false or corrupt moral judgment. For example, laws that made it an offence in the pre-1861 USA to assist a fugitive slave to escape into freedom nowadays seem very obviously to have been based in a perverse morality about the legitimacy of chattel slavery applied to people of African birth or ancestry. Indeed, they were based on a perverse set of moral values, even if some who held them did so honestly.

In this sense, criminal law is always and inevitably expressive, or perhaps it would be better to say constitutive, of a prevailing social morality adopted and enforced by the state. Some even argue that it is the fact that some people violate the law and expose themselves to punishment that helps to build and sustain a kind of social solidarity. The punishment of the guilty reinforces the collective virtue of the innocent, at any rate of those whose wrongdoings have not (yet) been

---

[10] N MacCormick, 'A Moralistic Case for A-Moralistic Law?' Valparaiso University Law Review 20 (1985) 1–41 at 28–29.
[11] Duff, *Trials and Punishments* 233–41, also his *Punishment, Communication, and Community* at 79–82; J Feinberg, *Doing and Deserving: Essays in the Theory of Responsibility* (Princeton, NJ: Princeton University Press, 1970) ch 5.

exposed.[12] Others argue, in morally more fundamental terms, that the criminal law is justified by the very fact that it facilitates public expression of condemnation for wrongdoing through a process of trial and conviction that establishes by public means public knowledge that a wrong has been done.[13] On this view, a 'public wrong' is a wrong that it is right for the public to be concerned about, and to show an interest in. It is not one that is done *to* the public. In any event, on some such grounds we may conclude that there is always some kind of moral substratum beneath the surface of the positively established criminal law anywhere.

This thesis of the moral substratum of the criminal law is likely to be taken as more or less incontestable in the case of what are sometimes called '*mala in se*' (crimes wrong in themselves). These are deeds that are serious moral wrongs, and that are also prohibited as crimes, but without being wrong just because prohibited. The traditional typology of serious crimes makes this obvious. There are crimes of violence against the person, which exhibit malevolent and wilful disregard for life, bodily integrity, and safety, including also personal integrity. There are crimes such as kidnapping that directly attack liberty, and much criminal misconduct has the effect of inhibiting the liberties of persons in the vicinity (many people are 'imprisoned' in their homes at night by fear of street crime). Rape insults human equality as well as bodily integrity. Crimes of dishonesty violate solidarity and wrongfully take from people what it is their right to keep. Public order crimes undermine social solidarity. Electoral intimidation and electoral impersonation violate rights of citizenship to the general detriment of democracy. Offences against the proper course of justice, such as perjury and suborning of witnesses, attack institutions that are vital to a secure regime of rights. Not surprisingly, one can map the crimes that are wrongs-in-themselves against the very same values that we track through the developed system of institutionalized rights. In the case of the criminal law, the point is to discourage and discountenance actions that intentionally subvert the values in question as these are enjoyed by other persons, in particular the person attacked, robbed, or whatever. No intelligible moral code gives blanket permission for killing, maiming, raping, assaulting, cheating, deceiving, housebreaking against, or stealing from other people. No intelligible criminal code fails to include such items in its catalogue of most serious crimes. To punish people for other deeds while condoning such actions would be radically incoherent.

But what about merely regulatory offences? What about so-called *mala prohibita*—deeds which are wrong because they are prohibited, not prohibited because they are wrong? What becomes of the moral substratum thesis in this case? We need not assume that all cases of existing prohibitions in this category are justified prohibitions in moral or any other terms, but we can say with some

[12] See E Durkheim, *The Division of Labor in Society* (trans G Simpson; Glencoe, Ill: Free Press, 1933) 108–110, discussed in R Cotterrell, *Emile Durkheim: Law in a Moral Domain* (Edinburgh: Edinburgh University Press, 1999) 68–78.   [13] Duff, Tadros: n 7, above.

clarity what does justify those that are justified prohibitions. All of them look to some state of affairs which is considered either seriously disadvantageous to the state or civil society and the citizens or members thereof, or to have significant value for them. The circumstances are such that no individual would have sufficient reason to act in ways that counter the disadvantage or procure the positive value, save in the context of a relevant, universal, and reasonably well-enforced prohibition. Environmental damage often arises from certain activities of many persons, any one of whom could carry on in that line of conduct without doing any measurable harm. The burning of coal fires in city houses affords an obvious example, or the use of cars generating toxic gases through exhaust systems, and even some cases of quite large-scale industrial pollution might be tolerable if there were few enough polluters on the scale in question. So everyone faces a situation in which an optimal outcome would be if everybody else stopped the damaging activity, leaving oneself able to carry it on in a much pleasanter environment. So nobody does stop, except if a suitable general prohibition is adopted, whereby nobody is suckered into compliance in favour of non-compliant others.[14]

Similar considerations apply in relation to legislation about healthy and safe working practices in factories and other workplaces, legislation about conduct that creates risks to public health, or about safety in transport systems and the due construction and maintenance of vehicles for use on public roads, and to most legislation concerning road traffic. (But offences like speeding, dangerous driving, and drunk driving belong among *mala in se*, even if there is an element of the conventional or arbitrary in statutory definitions of maximum speed limits, or safe blood-alcohol levels.) Laws concerning taxation belong in public law, and seek to establish distributively just burdens of contribution to the revenues of the state relative to the scope of tasks it is considered right for the state to undertake, also according to some scheme or theory of distributive justice. Such a scheme being in place, necessarily tax evasion is made a punishable offence, on the basis that the sustenance of a properly financed state is a public value to which all must contribute to the extent required by law. These considerations apply to all forms of taxation, including Value Added Tax or sales taxes, and customs and excise duties, as well as taxes on income. The justice of such impositions is frequently contested and differences concerning distributive justice lie at the heart of electoral politics in democratic political systems. But no system of revenue that depended on voluntary giving would be workable in the circumstances of any contemporary state, therefore the compulsions of the criminal law are everywhere needed to support whatever system and rates of taxation have been determined upon by the legislature.

Prohibitions which are justifiable under the type of argument indicated here can therefore quite properly be supported and enforced by the institutions of

[14] See D Parfit, *Reasons and Persons* (Oxford: Clarendon Press, 1984) at 56–66, 88–91 on 'prisoner's dilemma' problems of the kind regulatory law can help to alleviate. Cf Duff, *Trials and Punishments* 210–211.

criminal law and punishment. The act which attracts punishment has not the same in-itself wrongful character as murder, rape, assault, or theft (for example). But in the context of a justifiable statutory scheme aimed at forestalling some common evil or fostering a prized element in the common good, violation of the law evinces unjustifiable self-preference.[15] It is on that account morally objectionable to a greater or lesser degree depending on the circumstances of the case; it is in some measure a public wrong, meriting public attention and concern—and, given appropriate proof, condemnation and punishment. Each act of wilful non-compliance weakens a scheme from which all, including the violator, draw benefit. At least in some contexts, moreover, there are kinds of activity that are obviously dangerous and therefore demand special care—driving a car is an obvious and hackneyed case. There can also be activities that are undertaken professionally or in pursuit of a trade in circumstances of known or obvious risks to private or public goods. In all such cases, it is reasonable to prohibit conduct undertaken without due care, or even in some cases care of the most exacting kind, and hence to make legislative provision for forms of strict criminal liability.

Someone might argue that this is just a typical piece of utilitarian reasoning, in the light of which one should do as Jeremy Bentham did, and view the whole criminal law in the same light, as a set of prohibitions justified if at all by their contribution to public utility.[16] Murders cause pain and unhappiness, and so do accidents at work. The self-same considerations of preventing avoidable human misery apply in both cases, and apply also to the practice of punishment. To distinguish *mala in se* from *mala prohibita* is to obfuscate the matter. It also misses the point that the just measure of punishment in all cases is the lowest level of pain-causing that will suffice to prevent a greater amount of pain arising from criminal acts and the fear of them. Hans Kelsen in like vein said that from the standpoint of his non-moralistic Pure Theory of law, all wrongs in law are prohibited wrongs and are thus wrong in the same way and for the same reason—because prohibited.[17] The reply to the utilitarians is that, whether or not their ethical theory is sustainable at the deepest level, even a utilitarian morality does and can stigmatize certain kinds of acts as wrong because of their directly and inevitably—and seriously—harmful character. These are genuinely distinct, under a reasonable utilitarianism, from other cases in which a larger scheme of co-operative pursuit of benefits or of the avoidance of detriments justifies a scheme of prohibitions against a threat of punishments. So the distinction between wrongs-in-themselves and prohibited wrongs is not in itself anti-utilitarian. So far

---

[15] See J Finnis, *Natural Law and Natural Rights* (Oxford: Clarendon Press, 1980) 262–263 on unjustified self-preference.

[16] See J Bentham, *A Comment on the Commentaries and a Fragment on Government*, (ed J H Burns and H L A Hart) (London: Athlone Press, 1970) 63–66, 381, 386–387, attacking the differentiation between *mala prohibita* and *mala in se* drawn by Sir William Blackstone.

[17] See H Kelsen, *The Pure Theory of Law* (trans M Knight) (Berkeley and Los Angeles: University of California Press, 1967) 112: 'there are no *mala in se*, but only *mala prohibita*'.

as concerns the moral purity of the Pure Theory of law, it is bought at too high a price when it makes impossible the identification of internal relationships between legal practices and moral values. If we really want to purify law of any moral element, we have to avoid recourse to the ineluctably morally-laden concept of punishment altogether, whereupon the important difference between crimes and civil wrongs such as delicts/torts, or breaches of contract, or trust disappears from view.

12.3 Legal Moralism

'Legal moralism' has been the subject of quite long-standing controversy, ever since the nineteenth century.[18] The controversy concerns the legitimate uses of the criminal law in a free society. It belongs to the domain of what is sometimes called 'critical morality', that is, moral principles established by rational arguments for applying to the critique of actual existing law and current social attitudes to law.[19] The 'harm principle' proposed in John Stuart Mill's celebrated essay *On Liberty* of 1859 argues against the use of criminal law to enforce moral virtues, contending that the only proper use of state force is to prevent people harming others.[20] Contrarily, supporters of 'legal moralism'[21] argue that it is a legitimate function of the criminal law to restrain and stigmatize any grossly immoral conduct, including harmful acts, but potentially including non-harmful ones as well. Although this dispute primarily concerns legislative policy and the establishment of moral principles to guide good legislation in the field of criminal law, inevitably a certain amount of interpretative description of the actual law is involved as well. This arises, for example, in discussion of the issue whether laws against shamelessly indecent conduct are covered by the harm principle, since it is hurtful to be exposed to grossly offensive displays or performances.

The present thesis concerning the moral substratum of criminal law excludes the possibility that the criminal law can ever be considered, even in a purely

---

[18] The earliest shots in the conflict are perhaps to be found in John Stuart Mill's *On Liberty* (ed D Spitz) (New York and London: Norton, 1975), originally published in 1859—this is the *locus classicus* of the claim that the law can only be legitimately used to prevent or deter one person from harming another—and J F Stephen *Liberty, Equality, Fraternity* (ed RJ White) (Cambridge: Cambridge University Press, 1967) from 1873, a spirited rebuttal of Mill's claim. The controversy resumed in the 1950s following the publication of the Wolfenden Committee *Report on Homosexual Offences and Prostitution* (London: HMSO, 1957 Cmnd 247) with Lord Devlin's response in *The Enforcement of Morals* (London: Oxford University Press, 1965) and H L A Hart's rejoinder in *Law, Liberty and Morality* (London: Oxford University Press, 1963).

[19] H L A Hart, *Law, Liberty and Morality* (London: Oxford University Press, 1963) 17–24, on 'critical' as distinct from 'positive' morality.

[20] Hart, as cited above, revived and slightly qualified the 'harm principle', allowing that it could embrace an element of paternalism, applying legal restraints to deter self-harming behaviour. See also J Feinberg, *The Moral Limits of the Criminal Law* (New York: Oxford University Press, 1984–1988), which covers the field exhaustively in four volumes: I *Harm to Others*; II *Offense to Others*; III *Harm to Self*; IV *Harmless Wrongdoing*.   [21] Stephen and Devlin as cited above, for example.

descriptive-interpretative way, in purely non-moralistic or a-moralistic terms. Crimes are punishable wrongs and punishment is a morally-loaded practice, as are the institutions for the public prosecution and punishment of crimes. The question cannot be whether the criminal law should be morally-loaded, but, rather, what moral load it should bear.[22] For sure, the 'harm principle' seems unsustainable either descriptively or critically. A corollary of the harm principle understood as prescribing that conduct should only be treated as criminally wrongful if it is also harmful to persons other than the acting subject is that, broadly speaking, degrees of wrongfulness should depend on degrees of harmfulness. Punishments provided for in law should be carefully graded to match the severity of the harmfulness of different crimes, as well as, possibly, the degree of wilfulness or premeditation exhibited in a particular harm-causing act. Descriptively, this principle and the corollary do not sit well with the institutions of criminal law as we have represented them here. The branch of law that deals with harmful behaviour and with attempts to make good the consequences of harmful conduct, also to provide disincentives to harmful activity, is the law of obligations, most particularly the part dealing with reparation for civil wrongs (torts, delict). This was discussed earlier in chapter 6 and will be further considered in the next chapter. The actual criminal law of constitutional states quite properly deals with acts that do no harm,[23] including criminal attempts and conspiracies, and insists normally on the presence of an element of wrongful intention, at least where *mala in se* are in issue. Grounds of liability can quite reasonably be drawn more broadly in the case of regulatory offences that are *mala prohibita*, for reasons that were noted a while ago.

Any general theory about the moral grounds of criminal law (and it may be that no general theory is possible) should take its clue from the essential contribution a functioning criminal law makes to the civility of civil society. Peaceful relations among persons who can trust relative strangers to avoid violating their persons or their property are the fundamental conditions of civility. This can be enhanced by collective schemes concerning environmental and other common goods such as were discussed in relation to *mala prohibita*. What is wrong about committing crimes is that it involves some wilful form of behaviour that violates the conditions of civil peace. This is the sense of public wrongfulness that, in my submission, should be taken up by those who argue for the intrinsic worth of public condemnation of public wrongs. Such conduct shows wilful disregard for peace among persons, and it is therefore seriously alarming and seriously to be deplored, however much or little harm ensues in a particular case. In feudal kingdoms, each lord up to and including the king as highest lord of all lords had their own 'peace',

---

[22] For a full argument in favour of this view, and relevant other sources, see N MacCormick, 'A Moralistic Case for A-Moralistic Law?' Valparaiso University Law Review 20 (1985) 1–41, reinforcing 'Against Moral Disestablishment' in MacCormick, *Legal Right and Social Democracy* (Oxford: Clarendon Press, 1982) 18–38.   [23] See Feinberg, *Moral Limits*, Vol IV *Harmless Wrongdoing*.

their own domain in which maintaining the peace was their special concern. Hence for a time in England (for example) all actions that were competent in the King's Bench court were ones in which it was recited that the defendant had acted violently and in breach of the 'king's peace'.[24] It seems not too fanciful to think that the evolution of modern states out of feudal kingdoms depersonalized the peace, so that we are left with the idea of 'breach of the peace' as a matter of common concern, not layered into different pieces of peace. Peace, to the extent that the state's institutions succeed in securing it without infringing the fundamental right to and interest in personal liberty, is the common asset of, and common ground of, civil society.

This suggestion helps one to see why so much of the debate about morality in the criminal law has focused on issues concerning sexuality and its expression, and issues concerning the commencement and termination of life. The wrongs that are apprehended in these domains do not so clearly as others exhibit the public character, the peace-threatening character that is in other cases so obvious. People's sexual activities conducted in private with genuine and un-coercive mutual consent do not bear directly on civil peace at all, and in this way differ from public displays of a sexually explicit kind. They can lead to unrest and violence in some circumstances, where injury to family ties or insult is apprehended. But in relation to such insult and injury, there is a possibility of an expanded tolerance and an expanded regard for liberty. This would seek to bring about a consensus that readiness to be provoked is as much a part of the problem for civil peace as is the provocation that people complain is caused by certain kinds of private activity. The same goes for the use of images and visual media in the context of political and theological debates. Laws of blasphemy, and related laws, may in some contexts be essential to keep the peace and avoid intercommunal violence. The prospect of such violence was graphically illustrated by the response in early 2006 throughout the Muslim world to certain cartoons originally published during late 2005 by a low-circulation Danish newspaper from Jutland, though subsequently republished by other sections of the European press. Several Danish consulates were burned to the ground by protesting mobs in various countries. A regard for human rights and in particular for freedom of opinion and expression supports the right of writers and artists to push the frontiers of taste and to express controversial opinions. Yet in some situations of high tension, the conditions of communal peace must also be taken into account.[25]

Whether or not a human foetus can or should be recognized as a potential or actual bearer of any rights and thus as enjoying already a kind of inchoate personate

---

[24] A Harding, 'Rights, Wrongs and Remedies in Late Medieval English and Scots Law', *Miscellany Four* (Edinburgh: Stair Society vol 49, 2002); cf D Garland, *The Culture of Control* 29–30.
[25] Philip Selznick in *The Moral Commonwealth* (Berkeley/Los Angeles/London: California University Press, 1992) 391–392 contrasts 'civility' with 'piety' in a way that is perhaps material to this point.

status is a matter already discussed. There seems no reason to doubt that against persons other than the pregnant mother the foetus is worthy of regard in its own right and not just as (in effect) part of the mother's body. On the other hand, a foetus is much less credibly than even a day-old baby a participant in civil society and its peace. Hence laws that prohibit a mother from choosing on grounds that seem to her sufficiently compelling to terminate her pregnancy, at least in its earlier weeks, can be characterized as unjustly intrusive into a matter of private liberty. Likewise laws that prevent close relatives and medical practitioners in assisting a terminally-ill patient to commit suicide, or actually taking steps with the known prior consent of the person to end her or his life when she/he has lost all capacity to do so for her/himself, can come into controversy as depriving persons of the right to a peaceful and dignified death. The counter-arguments mainly concern the 'slippery slope', and the risk of coercion of old and vulnerable people. To focus on what are truly the requirements of civil peace in the light of our doctrine of human rights may help to clarify deliberation, well short of dictating a single obvious answer.

A serious objection might be that the stress on the 'requirements of civil peace' is compatible with failing to treat persons—in particular 'natural' persons, that is, human beings—as ends in themselves. Criminal processes and punishments simply use the suffering of those condemned as a means to secure the good of others, according to some kind of utilitarian calculus. A justifiable system of criminal law would not do this. Such considerations should lead towards trying to establish the conditions in which the imposition of punishments of an appropriate kind in the context of appropriate processes has intrinsic value. It could have this simply by being a vindication of public justice through the condemnation of public wrongs, while effectively communicating this both to the subject of punishment and to the wider society. Securing civil peace might then be a valuable side-effect, but should not be the justifying aim of criminal law and punishment.

This view is worthy of respect, but it seems that there may be a better case if the order of priorities is inverted. To achieve morally exemplary effect, there must already be peace and civility. Justice among citizens is a crucial part of the common good, and unjust uses of punishment are therefore in principle excluded. Those practices of criminal law and punishment that can genuinely contribute to civil peace and the common good have to have, or at least genuinely aspire to, the kinds of values for which Duff, and Tadros, and others argue. But if peace and civility cannot be secured and sustained, there is no prospect of progress in the direction of a properly refined system of criminal law and punishment.

12.4 Corporate Crimes

Too much emphasis upon the moral aspect of crime and punishment might come under suspicion for diverting attention away from the contested issue of corporate criminal responsibility. If the paradigm case of crime and punishment is always that of the fully-rational individual intentionally committing an act which is manifestly criminal, this shifts attention away from ill-doing by anything other than the human being as natural person. This would be a profound mistake. We have earlier said a little about the capacity responsibility of groups and corporations. It is time to say more. What needs to be challenged is any assumption that corporations cannot be meaningfully considered morally or legally responsible for wrongful acts.

It is remarkable how many verbs and verbal phrases cannot be inserted in a sentence that has a singular person as subject. I can play a symphony on my CD player, but only derivatively; it takes a whole orchestra to play the symphony live, and a whole lot more agencies are involved in recording, issuing and marketing a CD. I cannot manufacture a Ford car or a Hewlett Packard computer, nor can anyone else acting purely individually do so (though somebody could perhaps make one, or build it from a kit). It takes a large organization to run a ferry service between ports on an island and others on the adjacent mainland. One person may edit, but only a team can produce, a mass-circulation newspaper.

Even from the point of view of a tightly focused concern on rational, intentional, and purposive action, the fact of the intrinsically many-handed character of huge parts of distinctively human activity demands attention. Symphonies (as distinct from CDs) are never played accidentally, or inadvertently, or without rational planning and practising. Newspapers are quite deliberately published, as are ferry services maintained, and manufacturing operations carried on. These are not odd or substandard instances of intentional activity. They are paradigmatic examples of it in a contemporary market economy grounded in large part on legally sustained forms of corporate capitalism. It would surely be a seriously erroneous form of ontological individualism to maintain that they are odd examples of intentional activity, even though no single human being is or could be acting in just that way. A concern with intentional activities, and their intended and unintended consequences, should surely have a central and not a peripheral regard for these massively important forms of intentional action.

This is not to deny that analysing the ideas of agency, rationality, and intentionality must start from and give a special place to the individual human being, the autonomous moral agent; but it cannot stop there. We can ascribe intentions to corporations on much the same grounds as we can ascribe intentions to individual agents. Both deliberate about what to do. This is always interpersonal deliberation in the corporate case, not necessarily so in the individual. For both, deliberation may conclude in decision, usually by some relatively formalized procedure for making and recording decisions in the corporate case, rarely so with the individual. We can also ascribe physical actions to corporations as to individuals, namely those acts that implement corporate decisions and those activities that are a necessary element of, or are necessarily incidental to, their implementation.

It is all too easy to produce or presuppose a highly individualistic conception of the responsibility of persons, and thus to distort the significance of collective or corporate forms of agency, with corresponding forms of responsibility for injurious results or consequences of corporate activities.[26] This comes to light in the many confusions surrounding the ascription of civil, and even more of criminal, liability to corporations. A ferry company, for example, which organizes a ferry service from England to Belgium, and which aims for maximum speed of turnaround at the ports on either side, is deliberately and indeed quite legitimately seeking to maximize profits by optimizing the employment of its capital equipment. In competitive circumstances, this also benefits passengers by keeping fares low, and by enhancing speed and frequency of journeys. But it also entails risks that are obvious to any reflective person and which must be particularly well known to those who are operationally involved in running a ferry service.

These are not slight or fanciful risks, nor are they risks of unusual or improbable harms. There are completely obvious risks of death by drowning of passengers and crew whenever any vessel engages in this trade while in an unseaworthy condition, whether temporarily (eg, while bow or stern doors are not closed and watertight), or more permanently owing to design defects or maintenance failures. Some of these risks are exacerbated by speed of operation unless specific safeguards are built in to operating systems to counter the special risks inherent in fast turn-around times. Whose responsibility, other than that of the ferry company, could it be to ensure that such systems are in place, and adequate to their purpose? Why would it not constitute manslaughter or culpable homicide by the company through its own gross negligence if there were a failure to discharge this responsibility? There might be excuses, and there might be accounts of what was actually done in any given case (compare the *Herald of Free Enterprise*[27]) that might provide a satisfactory defence to such a charge. But legal systems that fail to recognize such a responsibility on the ground of its being unintelligible, or to acknowledge such a charge as competent in law, appear to be mired in grave conceptual confusion, with resultant retributive injustice unduly favourable to shareholder interests over those of travellers.

Clearly, there is a two-way linkage between concepts or conceptions of personality (personateness) and responsibility, and this gives powerful backing to the case for introducing new provisions of criminal law concerning 'corporate killing'.[28] Even better might be an attempt to re-cast company law so as to purge from it misunderstandings built up over many years through unreasonable ways of drawing contrasts and analogies between natural and juristic personality. A different error on the other side is the interpretation of human rights as directly protecting corporate interests. The real character of corporate personality does not

---

[26] Cane, *Responsibility in Law and Morality* 145–168.

[27] S Crainer, *Zeebrugge: Learning from Disaster: lessons in corporate responsibility* (London: Herald Charitable Trust, 1993).

[28] See Cane's discussion of proposals by the Law Commission for England and Wales, *Responsibility in Law and Morality* 160–161.

warrant including corporations in the class of human beings for the purpose of ascribing human rights directly to them as legal persons. This is not to say that some ways of interfering with corporations might not quite genuinely infringe human rights of persons involved in corporate activity, or owning shares in a company.

12.5 Conclusion

The present work is not an essay in descriptive criminal law nor in critical moral philosophy. As an interpretative account of the most essential functions of law, including criminal law, within a contemporary constitutional state, it suggests that the most basic demand citizens ought to make of criminal law is that it contribute to securing the conditions of civility and social peace, thus sustaining civil society. This, however, cannot be a function of the criminal law alone, for without social justice the conditions of solidarity and civility are not capable of being achieved. Criminal law and public law have to work in tandem, and cannot work at all to these ends without background social conditions that the law does not establish, but which it can damage.

13

Private Law and Civil Society: Law and Economy

13.1 Introduction

We said earlier that the sphere of private law, sometimes also referred to as that of 'civil society', is that of powers that are bilateral, or multilateral, and that are powers for private good. It is one in which persons of full age and capacity confront each other as the bearers of equal legal status, or of equivalent status, as in the case of corporations, incorporated partnerships, and the like. This means that none is legally superior to any other, however different they may be in personal characteristics or acquired assets. Hence any legal arrangements that are to become binding on them through acts of private will must be ones to which they mutually consent, so far as concerns any change in the legal position between them.

The main point of this chapter is that, just as law interacts especially closely with politics when public law is in focus, so it interacts especially closely with economics when private law is in focus. The legal system, the political system, and the economic system together sustain, or perhaps constitute, the state and civil society. Structural couplings between law and economy are most saliently visible when the legal discourse is of private law, at least if one takes private law in a wide sense. This chapter has five main sub-themes. The first concerns private law in its narrower sense, as the law of private life and private relationships. These relationships themselves belong within a broader set of concerns, those relating to the 'private sector' of the economy. Private law in this broader sense is considered in section 13.3. Following from that, it is appropriate to consider how law and economy interact (13.4). Then follow (in 13.5) some general reflections on the institutions of private law, with particular reference to the law of torts or delict and the forms of corrective justice involved in that. Finally, in 13.6 there is a discussion of law, economy and information, focusing particularly on the topic of intellectual property.

13.2 Private Law and Private Life

'Private law' has a narrower and a broader sense. In its narrower signification it concerns only the relationships of private life, that is, the family and the institution of marriage and analogous forms of civil partnership, and the obligations of spouses or partners between themselves, and of parents towards children. Related to this is the law of succession and the institutions of testate and intestate succession. The latter includes rules concerning what rights family members have in the estates of deceased members in the event of intestacy, or even in cases of testate succession in those legal systems that confer on children indefeasible rights to a fixed share in some part of a parent's estate.[1]

It concerns also the institution of the trust, whereby some property can be dedicated to specific purposes for the benefit of individuals, or for public purposes. This requires a kind of 'split patrimony', whereby property held by a trustee is considered to be separate from his/her personal patrimony or estate.[2] The historic separation of the court of equity from courts of law in England made this division relatively easy, in facilitating emergence of a distinction between legal and equitable ownership, or a concept of bare legal ownership as distinct from beneficial ownership.[3] Other systems of law, which never split law and equity in the English way, have found it harder to adapt the trust to the available conceptual framework, but some have succeeded after a fashion.

Private relationships require private space, hence ownership of immovable property or some form of reasonably secure long-term secure tenancy rights over property occupied as a family home, taking 'family' in its contemporary extended sense to include all sorts of partnership-based life. The acquisition of a home either by acquiring ownership or by taking a tenancy requires the institution of contract, that is, the means of establishing consensual obligations among persons having adequate transactional capacity. The persons of private law are 'natural persons', though in their private activities they may be involved in various sorts of voluntary association or club. Typically, such clubs are organized on a basis of a multilateral contract of membership, with any common assets being held through some kind of trust. Such associations do not need the trappings of corporate personality

Nevertheless, 'juristic persons' in the form of corporations great and small also have a strong bearing on the lives even of the most private of private citizens. They acquire, package, and retail his/her food. They manufacture the drugs she/he takes for sickness; or the telephone, the computer, and the software she/he uses

---

[1] Cf N MacCormick, 'Discretion and Rights' Law and Philosophy 8 (1989) 23–36.

[2] See G Gretton, 'Trust without Equity' (2000) International and Comparative Law Quarterly Vol 49, 599–620.

[3] Cf A Hudson, *Equity and Trusts* (London: Cavendish, 4th edn, 2005) chs 1 and 2.

to communicate with family and friends or the car he/she uses for shopping. They provide insurance against loss of or damage to property and against liability for car or other accidents, and life insurance in the context of a pension package of some kind. They afford him/her employment wherewith to pay rent, meet mortgage payments and insurance premiums, and buy clothing, food, and drink. They bank her/his money and provide credit for purchases, or electronic means of payment of bills and accounts. Part of his/her savings is almost certainly tied-up, either directly or indirectly, through insurance policies or pension funds, in corporate stocks and shares. The capability of commercial corporations to provide all this on the interface between commercial and private life depends also on a large nexus of relationships of corporations among themselves.

13.3 Private Law and Commerce

Private law in its wider sense thus embraces not only the private relationships of private persons as natural persons, but also the whole connected congregation of commercial relations of business corporations with each other as well as with the citizen as employee or as consumer, and with institutions of government. Private law in this wider sense embraces the law of the private sector as well as the law of private life. In this wider sense, 'private law' includes commercial law in respect of the private sector of the economy. It is all the law that is not public law and not criminal law. 'Civil law' is an alternative name sometimes in use, with private law and commercial law, perhaps also labour law, figuring as separate but related departments of civil law. The problem is that the term 'civil' and related expressions such as 'civilian' are so strongly associated with the historical *jus civile* of the Roman Republic and later the Roman Empire, and the successor legal systems in Europe and beyond that evolved out of Roman civil law. For that reason, the broad sense of 'private law' is used here. This broad usage has a respectable pedigree, for it can be traced back at least as far as to Justinian's *Digest*. There, the classical jurist Ulpian is quoted as contrasting public and private law: 'public law concerns the establishment of the Roman polity, while private law is the law that has regard to the interests of individuals'.[4] Commercial law in the contemporary sense is clearly included in the latter category.

---

[4] See Justinian, *Digest* I.1.2 quoting from Ulpian: 'There are two branches of legal study: public and private law. Public law is that which respects the establishment of the Roman commonwealth [*quod ad statum rei romanae spectat*], private that which respects individuals' interests [*quod ad singulorum utilitatem spectat*]' (*The Digest of Justinian* (Latin text, ed T Mommsen with the aid of P Krueger; English trans ed by A Watson) (Philadelphia, Pa: University of Pennsylvania Press, 1985) at 2). Justinian *Institutes* I.1.4 repeats this in essentially similar terms. Compare also Lord Rodger of Earlsferry, in *Davidson* v *Scottish Ministers* [2005] UKHL 74 at para 77: 'The core idea is that private law regulates relations between individuals. I therefore use the expression "private law" simply as a convenient label for that branch of the law'.

Reflecting upon the idea of civil society draws to our attention the duality of the private and the commercial. In private life our most important relationships are highly personal, and in relationships of family and friendship many people find the core of the values that motivate them in life. Nearly everyone finds in them a significant part of their system of values. In troubled times characterized by an absence of, or precariousness of, civil peace, these relationships tend to provide the outer perimeter beyond which lies the dividing line between friend and enemy that Carl Schmitt saw as the defining binary contrast of politics.[5] To the extent that civil society can come into being and acquire secure establishment, impersonal relationships can develop in importance, and enemies recede to those beyond the perimeter of these relationships, along with those intent on undermining peace from within. Impersonal trust is the foundation of extensive commercial relationships. The prosperity of private life and relationships can be greatly enhanced by extensiveness of commercial relationships, at least for all those who are admitted to the full set of active and passive capacities available to natural persons. They must also be free of the shackles of obligations inherent in ancient conceptual frameworks such as 'master and servant', redolent of status-based law, in contrast to contemporary employment law.

13.4 Private Law and Economy

We have seen that it is hard to conceive of the emergence of civil society save in the context of a constitutional state (of which the limited constitutional monarchy achieved by various kingdoms during the eighteenth and nineteenth centuries were forerunners). In such a state, successfully enforced powers of government co-exist with properly respected limits on those powers in favour of essential basic liberties. Indeed, in later circumstances, limits extend to the full panoply of human rights under various international conventions or covenants as well as through constitutional entrenchment in various states. Criminal law in its peace-securing function is crucial, as also in its support for schemes based on ideas of justice and the common good, with attached *mala prohibita*. The institutions of public law and those of criminal law are thus two of the pillars of civil society. The institutions of private law are the third. Without them, a functioning market economy is inconceivable, though rudimentary systems of exchange and various kinds of command-based divisions of labour could perfectly well exist, as for example they did in feudal kingdoms.

We return to the issue of impersonal trust. Property holdings depend upon secure real rights. Partly these are secured by criminal law; but even more fundamentally

⁵ C Schmitt, *The Concept of the Political* (trans G Schwab) (Chicago: Chicago University Press, 1996; original German edition, 1932).

they are secured through the proprietary remedies of private law.[6] These enable a person with ownership of a thing to claim it back into possession when wrongfully deprived of it, or to obtain compensatory remedies in case of wrongful damage to it inflicted wilfully or by negligence or through some form of nuisance. Without effective remedies in private law, property cannot be secure. Without security, there is little opportunity for consensual transfer of things—why buy what you can take? Consensual transfers—sales, exchanges, leases, or licences—take place within a framework of effective private law remedies. These uphold the express or implied agreements involved in consensual transfers, both by specific implemen-tation of agreed terms and by compensatory damages for breach of agreed terms where these are more appropriate to the circumstances. The development of ever more elaborate contract doctrines and rules that regulate when and how such remedies can be deployed also provide a benchmark to decide which takings by one from another are unlawful takings.

A hitherto unmentioned, but essential, institution of public law, that of coined or printed money, at once comes into view. Without sound currencies, exchange-based economies are in great trouble. Hitherto some state or states—in principle, but not in practice, all states—have established the viable currencies that facilitate trade. The development of the Euro in the EU since 2000 under the 1992 Treaty of Maastricht raises the question whether supra-national or trans-national public institutions can achieve stability and soundness of a currency within an expanded market economy. In 2006, it is too early to give any final judgment on this, though the present indications seem to ground a cautious optimism about this bold experiment in trans-national money. Anyway, trust in the currency as well as trust in other traders is necessary to support the kind of calculated risk-taking that is involved in all cases where one party invests effort and resources for the sake of a future agreed exchange with another party. It is also needed before people will see much reason to enter into impersonal bargains in the first place.[7]

For the sake of impersonal trust, there is need for an effective and reasonably efficiently enforced body of private law with judicial remedies that can be suc-cessfully invoked in cases of breakdown. The remedies are not best seen as sanc-tions enforcing good behaviour, for in the ordinary run of situations mutual co-operation in continuing relationships is much more strongly motivating. Private law is far from being coercive in that way.[8] What its remedies do is provide a background assurance that those who enter the system in bad faith, or who decide to disregard a particular obligation that seems or becomes unduly onerous, will fail to get away with unilateral non-performance. Security of expectations is

---

[6] J Harris, *Property and Justice* (Oxford: Clarendon Press, 1996) 24–26 expounds a broad concep-tion of 'trespassory rules' as fundamental to ownership of property.

[7] See, in general, C Proctor, *Mann on the Legal Aspects of Money* (Oxford: Oxford University Press, 6th edn, 2004).

[8] This position is established by argument in N MacCormick, 'Coercion and Law' in *Legal Right and Social Democracy* (Oxford: Clarendon Press, 1982) 232–246; G Lamond, 'The Coerciveness of

made rational by the fact of a background capability for remedial enforcement in case of non-performance or defective performance. In this light, it is not at all surprising that much commercial practice sits no more than loosely with doctrinal expositions of contract law.[9] Contracts are not normally entered with the expectation that judicial remedies will have to be invoked, though awareness of the long-stop availability of remedies is a condition for generalized impersonal trust.

Security of property rights and faith in contracts are the two essential cornerstones of a market economy. They are not, of course, causes of economic activity, but conditions for it. Adam Smith drew attention to the distinctive feature of human communities, that they are characterized by a division of labour that tends to grow ever more specialized.[10] Alongside this, he speculated about the universal propensity of human beings to engage in 'truck, barter, and exchange'.[11] Recent spectacular advances in human genetics suggest that Smith's empirical generalizations may indeed find a deeper explanation in elements of the human genome, the enormously elaborate code-book present in every cell of every human being as the biological foundation of our common human nature.[12] Smith, of course, did not make the mistake of supposing that 'truck, barter, and exchange' always take the same form. The simple divisions of labour and ephemeral possessions that he took to characterize hunting and gathering communities ('nations of hunters and fishermen' in Smith's terms) led to no elaborate market structures or transactions. These, and possible subsequent societies of a pastoral or agrarian form, stand in contrast with 'commercial society' as Smith saw that emerging in various parts of Europe in the eighteenth century. All human societies contain trading relationships. Only some are centred upon trade, commerce, and market relations.[13]

Karl Marx did not disagree, but thought that commercial capitalism was bound to collapse under its own contradictions, leading to a dawn of socialism and the absence of the dominion of human being over human being. From a Marxist point of view 'truck, barter, and exchange' were not universal human propensities, but themselves the products of commercialism and the capitalist mode of

---

Law' Oxford Journal of Legal Studies 20 (2000) 39 argues for a different position, on the basis of a more extensive but, it is submitted, less convincing, conception of 'coercion'.

[9] See S Macaulay, 'Non-Contractual Relations in Business: a preliminary study' American Sociological Review 28 (1963) 55–67; *Law and the balance of power: the automobile manufacturers and their dealers* (New York: Russell Sage Foundation, 1966).

[10] A Smith, *An Inquiry into the Nature and Causes of the Wealth of Nations* (ed R H Campbell, A S Skinner and W B Todd) (Oxford: Oxford University Press, 1976) Book 1, ch 2.

[11] *Wealth of Nations* Book 1, ch 2: 'Among men [by contrast with other animals] the most dissimilar geniuses are of use to one another, the different produces of their respective talents, by the general disposition to truck, barter, and exchange, being brought, as it were, into a common stock, where every man may purchase whatever part of the produce of other men's talents he has occasion for.'

[12] M Ridley, *Nature Via Nurture: Genes, Experience and What Makes Us Human* (London: Fourth Estate, 2003) 258–260.

[13] On all this, cf N MacCormick 'Law and Economics: Adam Smith's Analysis' in N MacCormick, *Legal Right and Social Democracy* (Oxford: Clarendon Press, 1982) 93–125.

production. The belief that they were an element in a universal human nature was itself an element in the false consciousness generated by the capitalist system.[14] For the moment, Smith and his supporters appear to have had the better of the argument and to have been surprisingly supported by new discoveries in the life sciences. But even if that is not so, it is certainly true that so long as commercial societies based around free markets exist, the persistence of property and contract and the remedial agencies of private law are an essential element in it.[15] They are so for the reason stated, namely as being a condition of the impersonal trust that markets require. The motivating factor in economic behaviour is not, however, the law, but the advantages derived by persons from exchanges that facilitate a more and more thoroughly specialized division of labour in the use of available resources. This leads to enhanced cheapness and plenty of commodities desired for human use.

It is arguable, anyway, that both Smith and Marx, the latter more than the former, distort the relationship of law and economy by treating the law as a mere adjunct to or reflex of the economic forms within which it operates.[16] The version of 'system theory' suggested in chapter 10, by way of a reading of the work of Niklas Luhmann and Gunther Teubner, casts matters in a somewhat different light. The activities of human beings proceed within subsets of the whole social system that are themselves ever more specialized systems of communication and of corresponding action. Each has its own basic concepts in the light of which it makes the surrounding world intelligible, and responds to inputs from it, and none of these conceptual frameworks is perfectly translatable into any of the others. The idea sometimes ascribed to Marx that law belongs to the 'superstructure' of society, while economic relations form its 'base'[17] is then clearly in error. We are dealing here with interacting systems each of which is self-sustaining in its own conceptual terms (this is so-called 'autopoiesis') yet is connected with the others

---

[14] K Marx, *Capital* (trans E and C Paul, introduction G D H Cole; addendum by M Wolfson) (London: Dent/Everyman's Library, 1972) 47–58 (ch 1, last section); for a text actually using the phrase 'false consciousness', see the letter to Mehring: 'Ideology is a process accomplished by the so-called thinker. Consciously, it is true, but with a false consciousness. The real motive forces impelling him remain unknown to him; otherwise it simply would not be an ideological process. Hence he imagines false or seeming motive forces' (F Engels in D Torr (trans and ed) *Karl Marx and Friedrich Engels, Correspondence 1846–1895; a Selection with Commentary and Notes (an enlarged edition of the selection by V V Adoratsky)* (London: Martin Lawrence, 1934)). Compare R Cotterell, *Law's Community* (Oxford: Clarendon Press, 1995) ch 6 on 'Law, Ideology, and Power: The Marxist Tradition', and H Collins *Marxism and Law* (Oxford: Oxford University Press, 1982) 35–40.

[15] Compare R Kinsey, 'Karl Renner on Socialist Legality' in D Sugarman (ed), *Legality, Ideology and the State* (London: Academic Press, 1983) 1–36, discussing K Renner *Institutions of Private Law and their Social Function* (ed with introduction, O Kahn-Freund) (London: Routledge and Kegan Paul, 1949).

[16] But see R Kinsey, 'Marxism and the Law: Preliminary Analyses' British Journal of Law and Society 5 (1978) 202–27, at 207, on the supposed 'base/superstructure' model of the relationship between relations of production (economic relations) and law in Marx's thought.

[17] See the discussion in B Z Tamanaha, *A General Jurisprudence of Law and Society*, (Oxford: Oxford University Press, 2001) 40–43.

through what can be called 'structural coupling'.[18] Hence they have reciprocal interactions and effects, not a relationship of super- and sub-ordination one to another.

In this light, it is not surprising that the 'economic analysis of law' proposed by Richard Posner[19] and others has produced such interesting if also controversial results. Especially in areas of private law like torts and contract, it is a significant question to consider what rules of law, or rulings on the law in contested cases, would be productive of the most efficient outcomes judged in economic terms (or, at least, more efficient than available alternatives). It is right to apply an economic critique to those parts of the law which have the—or a—function by way of establishing frameworks for interactive economic activity, and by way of rectifying disturbances to the existing framework or positions of particular persons within it. In respect of legal reasoning in problem cases, at least to the extent that consequentialist reasoning is acceptable in the justification of decisions,[20] argument concerning the most economically satisfactory, that is 'efficient', is clearly relevant. Much less convincing is the application of similar reasoning to other domains, such as the criminal law.

13.5 Property and Obligations: the Institutional Analysis

It makes sense at this stage to pause and offer some theoretical reflection on the main institutions of private law, building on the positions already established. Property and contract are examples of what we have called 'institution-arrangements'. Property is the institution whereby rights in things ('real rights') can be vested in individual persons. This gives them power over the possession, control, and use of the things in question, including normally the power to transfer the real right they hold to another person by way of sale, exchange, or gift, and the power to lease or license use of the thing to another person or persons. The most extensive of the real rights recognized within the institution of property is that of ownership.

Property is thus the institution whereby the value of things, both their value in use and their value in exchange, is made available for enjoyment by individual persons, natural or juristic. The things in question can be either corporeal things, existing quite apart from the law but institutionally defined as specific movables or immovables, or they can be incorporeal things, that is, 'institution-things' existing solely by virtue of legal provisions, as was highlighted in the earlier discussion of intellectual property (chapter 8).

---

[18] Luhmann, *Law as a Social System* 381–5.

[19] See R A Posner, *Economic Analysis of Law* (Boston, Ma: Little, Brown & Co, 1972); A Halpin, 'The Methodology of Jurisprudence: Thirty Years off the Point' Canadian Journal of Law and Jurisprudence 19 (2006) 67–105 at 72–73.

[20] Cf N MacCormick, *Rhetoric and the Rule of law* (Oxford: Oxford University Press, 2005) ch 6; R A Posner, *Frontiers of Legal Theory* (Cambridge, Mass: Harvard University Press, 2001).

Contract is the legal institution whereby persons are able to make legally effective transactions with others, thereby undertaking obligations and/or making transfers of rights on the basis of unilateral or bilateral acts directed to the other and subject to consent or acceptance by the other. Power to make contracts is vested in persons with the appropriate transactional capacity acting in respect of things or actions over which they have sufficient powers, without vitiating circumstances such as error, undue influence, duress, or fraud. This is subject to the consent of the other party or parties, also acting with appropriate capacity and in the absence of vitiating circumstances. Contractual obligations consist of all the duties and reciprocal claim-rights and all the powers and reciprocal liabilities to which the parties expressly or impliedly agree, or that are imposed or implied by operation of law. The terms of a contract are to be found in any instrument adopted by the parties as a record of their transaction, or that otherwise sufficiently evidences what they have agreed. There are many different specialist forms of contract that are subject to specific frameworks of statutory regulation, many deriving from international agreements or transnational law (European Community law in particular). Contract is a universal institution of commercial societies, necessary to all forms of commerce. Contract law is subject to local variations on such doctrines as that of the 'consideration' or '*cause*' needed to make a contractual obligation binding, or that of privity of contract, and the extent to which third party rights are recognized as enforceable, or that of the evidentiary or other requirements for recognition of the legally binding character of unilateral promises. There are also specialities within all legal systems in the way of special statutory regimes governing particular forms of contract (eg, contracts for the sale of immovable property), or contracts with particular subject matter (eg, sale of goods, or insurance, or carriage of goods by land, sea or air), or contracts having particular parties (eg, consumer contracts).

It may not be quite true to say that without contracts people would not be able to rely on each other—people who were not willing to rely on others would never develop an institution of contract at all. What is true, however, is that the legal enforceability of contracts in the circumstances defined by law is a powerful security in facilitating trust and reliance even in the impersonal circumstances of civil and commercial society. Thus contract is the institution by virtue of which it is possible to ascribe to things exchange value as well as use value.[21] Neither economists nor indeed traders or commercial persons have to be experts in law. But that in respect of which they are expert could not exist save with the background of the fundamental institutions of property and contract, and related satellite institutions such as trusts, succession, and bankruptcy.

Obligations of reparation and of restitution are also fundamental in private law. Obligations of reparation are not, like contractual obligations, created by acts

---

[21] The distinction between the value something has in use, and its value as an item in exchange, was drawn most explicitly by Karl Marx in *Capital*, Vol 1, Part 1, ss 1–3.

intended to create them. They are created when persons act in ways that inflict harm either wilfully or unintentionally, being harm to another person's bodily or psychic well-being or reputation, or to his/her property or the environment in which it is situated. The law of torts, or of delict or (in some systems) quasi-delict (*délit, quasi-délit*), identifies and regulates the kinds of conduct that give rise to the obligation to make financial or other reparation to compensate for harm caused, and even in some cases provides for aggravated or punitive damages beyond the mere measure of compensation. Of great importance here is the idea of causation.[22] The law must determine what constitutes a causal link between a harm suffered by one person and some act or omission of another sufficient to enable the harm to be imputed to the actor as a legally relevant result of the act or omission charged.

Obligations of reparation in law, requiring one person to make good harm caused to another, are justified by the principle that persons should have common rights not to be harmed in person and property, and not to suffer invasion of whatever property rights the law ascribes to them.[23] These are formally and qualitatively the same rights for everybody, though in content they can exhibit considerable inequality in quantitative terms. This depends on different property-holdings of different people, and differences of reward gained through the elaborate network of contracts that knit together the market economy and the employment of persons in various tasks in it and ancillary to it. Distributive justice (a core concern of many institutions of public law) is called in to diminish or rectify inequalities of that kind. According to prevailing principles of law, and, arguably, of morality as well, neither inequalities nor the interventions of public law in favour of distributive justice justify departure from the formal equality secured by the regime of legal corrective justice[24] constituted by the law of torts. Nevertheless, legislation that introduces new provisions of (for example) consumer law into the private law do amend tort law (also contract law) with a view to taking fair account of differences of bargaining power and economic muscle.[25] The same goes for some elements introduced by legislation into landlord and tenant law, and there are other relevant examples in other departments of private law.

Private law rights secured by tort law relating to negligence would lack the desired feature of formal equality if the standard of care to avoid harm were a subjective one, such as 'everybody to take the best care of which that individual is capable'. Greatly preferable is an objective standard such as the test of the care

---

[22] H L A Hart and T Honoré, *Causation in the Law* (Oxford: Clarendon Press, 2nd edn, 1985); A Peczenik, *Causes and Damages* (Lund, Sweden: Juridiska Föreningen i Lund, 1979).

[23] N MacCormick *Legal Right and Social Democracy* (Oxford: Clarendon Press, 1982) 214–219.

[24] E Weinrib, *The Idea of Private Law* (Cambridge, Mass: Harvard University Press, 1995) on corrective justice as the basis of private law. Cf MacCormick, *Legal Right and Social Democracy* ch 11 on 'obligation of reparation'.

[25] Cf P Cane, *Responsibility in Law and Morality* (Oxford: Hart Publishing, 2002) 186–190.

taken by a reasonable person (erstwhile reasonable man) to avoid a certain kind of harmful conduct.[26] This is operationalized by postulating a duty to take reasonable care to avoid foreseeable harm, coupled with liability to compensate for the sufficiently proximate harmful consequences of any breach of that duty, whether or not intentional. That is, of course, the standard applied by contemporary Scots and English law and in the common law more generally in other countries within that tradition. Implementation of this standard is achieved principally by way of awards of damages. These are quantified solely by reference to the successful pursuer's or plaintiff's relevant and recoverable loss, not in any way (like a penalty) proportioned to the defender's fault, which might be slight indeed or even non-existent from a moral point of view. Third party insurance to cover such liabilities is encouraged, and is indeed in some cases (eg, car-driving) compulsory.[27] By contrast, the law wholly discountenances insuring oneself against the risk of criminal penalties. To permit it would deprive criminal law of its function in aiming to achieve retributive justice in the manner discussed earlier.

Sometimes there is an inclination to speak and write as though those who do harm and those who suffer it (eg, drivers and pedestrians, or producers and consumers, or occupiers of premises and those who come on to the premises) were different classes of people. It can then be (mis-)represented that the law has to hold a balance between these different classes. This is fallacious. Most people at different times participate on one or another side of such paired roles. Sometimes we drive and sometimes we walk; everyone consumes, and most people are in some way active in, or at least financially interested in, some aspect of the production of goods and services; nearly everyone is sometimes an occupier and sometimes a visitor. Over a lifetime, unless very unlucky, we are neither exclusively victims of harm nor actual or potential agents of its causation. We are both. Human beings have interests both in the freedoms necessary to their character as rational intentional agents, and in protection from reasonably avoidable harm as well as strict respect for such property rights as the law deems vested in them.[28] These are actually two sides of the same coin. For free rational agency requires (as Kant fully recognized) effective protection from external interference with the conditions of being able to act at all and to participate in civil society.

Legal corrective justice concerns holding and establishing a balance, but not principally a balance between different classes of people. Rather, the balance struck, whether well or ill struck, is between different aspects of the interests of every human being who participates in the life of civil society. States whose political and

---

[26] On reasonableness, see MacCormick, *Rhetoric and the Rule of law* ch 9.

[27] P Cane, *Responsibility in Law and Morality* 225–250 (chapter on 'Realising Responsibility') contains, as well as a realistic account of the practice of settlement of claims, an excellent account of the relationship between responsibility and liability insurance, contrasting tort liability with criminal liability (242–249). Consider also his extended investigation of issues concerning strict and vicarious liability, and the interrelation of such issues with principles of causation.

[28] Cane, *Responsibility in Law and Morality* 94, 99–100.

economic systems fall far short of the reasonable demands of distributive justice may indeed tend to embody unacceptable and oppressive forms of class discrimination, even in their systems of corrective justice. This is, however, a pathological condition, not one intrinsic to the idea of the corrective justice that is sustained through private law and the civil court system.

The protection of rights, and particularly of property rights,[29] is a project that entails strict liability, and justifies it again on grounds of equality of protection. Vicarious liability secures everybody against the increased possibilities of harm that organized activity in industrial and post-industrial economies generates, via division of labour and the employment of many hands in pursuit of common tasks, or integrated economic activities of a wide-ranging nature. This is not a case of capriciously holding people responsible for mishaps that were somebody else's fault, but not their own. It is a rectification of an individualistic bias in the private law system, adopted for distributive reasons, in order to secure continuing reasonable protection of human persons in their passive as distinct from active roles.

Obligations of reparation arise from harm-causing actions. Those of restitution arise from actions by one person that confer some kind of benefit on another with no intention that this should be a gift. To the extent that one person might in such circumstances be enriched accidentally at the expense of the other, it is right that restitution be made, though only to the extent of an actual enrichment of the obligee. The underlying principle here, that one should not profit from another's loss, underlines the values of an exchange-based market—accidentally enriching transactions do not receive the protection extended to those entered consensually in the domain of contract law.

13.6 Law, Economy, and Information

Markets are irrational, in the sense that no one does, or can, plan the moment-by-moment outcomes of all the ongoing exchanges that participants engage in. But they can be seen as information-systems, providing the fastest possible positive and negative feedback of information concerning those forms of activity and allocations of effort for which there is adequate demand to repay the effort invested. They are thus a context for rational decision-making.[30]

In an age of informatics, information itself becomes property, valued for its uses and applications, and acquiring exchange value by the very fact of being susceptible to packaging as units and then to being reified, that is, turned into varieties of 'institution-things', forms of 'intellectual property'. Reflection on

---

[29] Cane, *Responsibility in Law and Morality* 197–198; cf 85–87 and 175–177 on strict and vicarious liability.

[30] F A Hayek, *Law Legislation and Liberty* (London: Routledge and Kegan Paul, 1993) vol II, *The Mirage of Social Justice* 107–132, especially at 115–120, on markets as information systems.

intellectual property is instructive for the light it casts on the interaction of private law and the economy. The 'property-character' of the norms in question depends on their including norms that facilitate transferability. This may be transferability between persons either of the property-item, some particular copyright or particular patent itself, or of some of its incidents, as in the case of licences to print copies of the literary work or to manufacture goods by means of the patented process. Transferability implies contract, and contract implies payment in return for total or partial transfer. The reification of exclusive privileges of this kind, by making them into interpersonally transferable entities, at the same time commercializes authorship and invention, making them processes of new wealth-creation as marketable objects.

There is an inversion of the normal relationship of use-value and exchange-value here. Physical things and plots of land have use-value to human beings regardless of their exchangeability; indeed they have use-value to other animals which know nothing of exchange or of market values. Objects of that kind acquire exchange value in commercial societies on account of their ultimate use-value. Nobody would buy or sell oats if somebody did not want to feed Scots or breed horses, to adapt an (originally rather belittling) insight from Samuel Johnson's *Dictionary*.[31] Things for which people have uses can be exchanged, and the point both of contracts and of markets is that they facilitate such exchange, getting useful objects into the hands of those who most value their use. Money is also, to say the least, helpful to this end; and the introduction of coins and subsequently notes is the invention of a kind of thing whose primary use is in facilitating exchange.

Like money in this respect, items of intellectual property have use-value by virtue of the regime that gives them exchange-value. They are of course connected to useful objects—books or patent medicines, for example. But they are not themselves the object in use, rather they are the pattern of, or template for, what is produced and used. As Jim Harris observed, they are ways of capturing and rendering exclusive what is not naturally scarce, namely ideas, nor naturally exclusive, for anyone can entertain my ideas without wearing them out or preventing me from at the same time entertaining them or inviting others to do so.[32] The law, in reifying intellectual property, creates an artificial scarcity by assigning an exclusive privilege of exploitation to the person it qualifies as owner or licensee of the relevant institution-thing. Thereby exchange-value becomes possible, to the extent that there proves to be demand for the fruits of exercising the privilege. All this makes it very clear that intellectual property rights are necessarily artificial creations of state law. So how extensive are the rights of IPR-holders, and over what can they be exercised?

---

[31] S Johnson, *A Dictionary of the English Language* (London, 1755): 'Oats . . . a grain which in England is generally given to horses, but in Scotland is the support of the people'.
[32] Harris, *Property and Justice* 42–44.

On the present analysis, the answer to these questions is almost entirely contingent upon a particular legal regime. How far an IPR extends is wholly dependent on the extensiveness of the trespassory rules, and on the number and extensiveness of exceptions or qualifications thereto. For example, in the case of copyright, no one may reproduce without permission the copyright work or any part of it except in the case of various exceptions, one of which is 'fair dealing'. So what is fair dealing, and how much does it embrace? That simply depends on the rules of law you adopt and the interpretations the courts give of them in applying the rules.

Not everyone agrees with this. Especially in traditions that ground commercial copyright in the moral right of the author—*le droit morale de l'auteur*—there is a tendency to equate copyright and related rights to a natural right. Someone might argue that, just as literary or artistic creation expresses the soul of the author, so is it a kind of enslavement of that soul for others to appropriate the work. But this proves either too little or too much. Too little, since it does not show why anyone should be able to appropriate an exclusive privilege of publication; too much, since it suggests that only expressive literary work should enjoy copyright. There are of course important reasons of justice why the author's should be the primary right *if* a copyright regime is to be adopted or kept in being. You might even be able to make a case for special provisions to protect from leonine exactions by publishers impecunious authors like the Robert Burns who sold cheaply the rights to the 'Kilmarnock Edition' of his subsequently celebrated poems. But the issue remains whether and why to protect copyright at all, and the same goes for patents, trade marks, *droits de suite*, design rights, and all the rest of them.

None was more sharply aware of this than Adam Smith, who had a generally poor view of exclusive privileges. These, he thought, had no analogy in nature. (Though he did concede that a hunter who set up a deer and pursued it to near exhaustion had a natural ground of indignation if a hitherto idle bystander moved in for the kill and claimed the deer for his pot in preference to the hunter's.) Exclusive privileges, he argued should be deemed only creatures of positive law.[33] Since they amounted to derogations from the order of natural liberty, they stood in need of special justification. Incentives to investment seemed to him to provide one viable justification.

For example, in a period of agricultural improvement, it might be desirable to invest in constructing a mill to help the peasant population switch from production for subsistence to production for the market. To encourage a proprietor to get a mill up and going might call for a guarantee of a return on the initial investment, and, to that extent, suggested Smith, a time-limited monopoly right could justifiably be established. The time limit was important, for the exclusivity of the privilege involved should be seen as a derogation from the order of natural liberty, and thus as one to be extended only so far as the justification for it runs. The

---

[33] A Smith, *Lectures on Jurisprudence* (ed R L Meek, D D Raphael and PG Stein) (Oxford: Clarendon Press, 1978) 81–82.

justification is, then, essentially utilitarian. There is a public benefit to be produced by encouraging certain kinds of investment, and the minimum encouragement necessary for the maximal benefit is all that can be justified or that should be accepted by way of positive law.[34]

One does not, of course, have to buy the Smith, the whole Smith, and nothing but the Smith. But in the context of contemporary arguments, many of which are strongly driven by corporate interests, it can be important to find sound grounds for opposing inordinate demands in the way of assertions of IPR. To that end, it is at least a useful *ad hominem* argument that those who extol the economics of Smith had better attend to his jurisprudence as well. A good example was provided during the heated debates concerning the second reading of the Copyright Directive in the European Parliament that came to a conclusion in 2000, or the controversy about the proposal for allowing patents in respect of items of computer software that was finally dumped in 2005. The publishers, especially music publishers, having especially in mind the circumstances of publishing on the internet, or of copying things like CDs via the internet, were seized of the need for the most stringent restriction of any exceptions of the 'fair dealing' sort to rights of copyright-owners. The university librarians, and other public librarians, were in turn alarmed at the effect of some proposed restrictions on the ability of libraries to continue providing a reasonable service to their users without incurring, and inevitably passing on to users, massive new costs by way of copyright permission fees. There were those who argued the matter in terms effectively of theft from authors, artists, and musicians, and from their publishers. The collecting agencies touted the case for authorial reward, no doubt duly conscious of their own cut therefrom. But the argument that rightly prevailed was this: where there is not property, or where property does not extend, there is no theft.

In the case of software patents, it was argued by the smaller entrepreneurs engaged in software development that all the protection they needed was already afforded by copyright law. They further contended that patents were in any event conceptually inept in the case of software in view of its 'non-technical' character in operations of data-handling. The introduction of a patent regime would chill the development of software through small independent firms, to the advantage of large scale monopolistic producers like Microsoft.

The argument derived from Adam Smith is instructive in this context. Property rights in the domain of copyright should extend only so far as, on balance of public benefit, there is sufficient value from the extension. There is a greater public benefit in retaining reasonable rights of use in libraries open to the public in general or to the scholarly community. Therefore the fair-dealing limits should be retained in forms adjusted to some of the realities of the internet age.

---

[34] Smith, *Lectures on Jurisprudence* 85–86; cf H L MacQueen, *Copyright, Competition and Industrial Design* (Edinburgh: Edinburgh University Press/David Hume Institute, 2nd edn, 1995).

Patents pose other concerns, not unrelated. Is it too easy for great multinationals to write up fairly ordinary processes in novel terms and then apply for a patent in a way that facilitates exaction of a monopoly rent from poorer people? The development of gene research and the enormously exciting progress that is being made in and as a result of the mapping of the human genome poses further questions. On the one hand, we seem here to stray towards the domain that ought to be placed outside IPR altogether as *res extra commercium*, for the possession of the code for the individuality of each individual cannot in the public interest be made the subject of anyone's property.[35] On the other hand, we run squarely into the problem of differentiating discoveries from processes. In a world that adequately values science and scholarship, the idea of property in the knowledge of facts, even newly discovered ones, is a sin against the spirit of inquiry. Yet in what concerns a fair opportunity to recover the research and development costs of making scientific discoveries then carrying them to the point of having humanly useful applications, the arguments for a time-limited exclusive privilege in newly-developed manufacturing processes remain as good, in their limits, as Smith's argument for the miller's monopoly in a context of rural improvement.

It would not be apposite in the present context to develop any detailed practical answer to the problems about the limits of IPR appropriate to the domain of genetic research. But reflection on the conceptual framework can at least help to bring into focus the principles that are at stake in justifying, or placing limits on, extensions of the sway of intellectual property rights. Certainly, no absolute credence should be given to the argument that scientists must always depend on income generated by exploitation of IPR to finance their capability to find out matters of which knowledge is desirable (and potentially profitable). That argument presupposes what has to be demonstrated, that the knowledge in which you are dealing is of things that ought to be subjected, or may be subjected, to commercially exploitable knowledge in the commercial domain. But there are other ways of, and other conditions for, the pursuit of knowledge, and there may be cases where public investment in the public domain is more seemly, and just as efficient.[36]

13.7 Conclusion

It has been no part of the purpose of this chapter to reproduce even in summary form the massive array of scholarship surrounding topics like the law of property (including intellectual property), the law of contract, the law of trusts, corporation

---

[35] Cf J Sulston and G Ferry, *The Common Thread: a story of science, politics, ethics and the human genome* (London: Bantam, 2002).

[36] Sulston and Ferry, *The Common Thread* 260–279. J K Mason and G Laurie, *Mason & McCall Smith's Law and Medical Ethics* (with a chapter by M Aziz) (Oxford: Oxford University Press, 7th edn, 2005) 206–252.

and partnership law, employment law, consumer law, the law of delict or torts, and the law on restitution and unjustified enrichment. The law concerning civil courts and their procedures and the remedies they can award for infringements of rights or infliction of wrongs has likewise come before our attention only in the most summary form. The point is that civil society is and can be a theatre of economic activity, in particular of free economic activity carried on through markets or strongly influenced by them, only given the framework conditions established by all these institutions of private law. They are not causes of a free economy, but conditions for its existence. It is reasonable to judge the adequacy of particular provisions of private law by reference to the contribution they make, or conversely the obstacles they pose, to economic efficiency judged in terms of suitable versions of economic theory. But it must be remembered that they are not merely conditions of economic activity. They are central to the idea of a common scheme of justice that all citizens can acknowledge as broadly fair. As such a common scheme of justice they are an element in the conditions of civility in civil society. It ought not to be assumed that economic theory on its own constitutes an adequate theory of justice.

PART 4

LAW, MORALITY, AND METHODOLOGY

Whatever else part 3 establishes, it certainly discountenances the idea that law or its doctrinal exposition can be in any interesting sense 'value-free'. Inevitably, therefore, we must now confront questions about the relationship between law and morality, for it may be that the values implicit in law generally, not only criminal law as discussed in chapter 12, are moral values. It may be that these impose constraints on what can possibly count as law. Such questions have over many years been at the centre of debate between two broad approaches to jurisprudence: legal positivism and natural law theory.

Sometimes this debate proceeds on the apparent assumption that law and legality may be problematic, but morals and morality are uncontroversial in character. The reverse, however, seems more plausible. It is often easier to establish what the law requires on a given issue than to establish what morality demands. This is precisely because of the institutional character of law, with its authoritative rule- and decision-making agencies. Morality is differentiated from law above all in being normative but not institutional. According to one approach, morality has the important character of enshrining and depending upon the autonomy of moral agents. This then indicates a fundamental distinction between morality and law, even though both focus often on essentially similar questions. Chapter 14 develops an argument to this effect.

The distinction established, however, is not one that justifies the conclusion that law can have any content whatever. Disputable as most deep moral questions are, it is not disputable that some orientation to justice and the common good is, as established in part 3, essential to legitimate participation in legislative and judicial law-making and law application. Moreover, the fact, if it be one, that reasonable people can reasonably differ about many questions concerning justice, by no means entails that there are no outer limits to what can be reasonably represented as justice. There is much current disagreement as to what are the exact conditions of a just war, and as to where the line falls between inflicting unavoidable 'collateral damage' while attacking legitimate military targets and illegitimately targeting civilians. This does not mean, however, that it is reasonably arguable that violence deliberately directed at civilians is ever in itself justifiable. Genocide is not a justifiable project in any reasonably statable moral position that any reasonable moral agent could construct. It is therefore perfectly possible and reasonable to set outward limits to what can be accepted as valid law. Provisions which are unjustifiable by reference to any reasonable moral argument should not be considered valid as laws. This argument is stated in chapter 15.

Finally, chapter 16 considers, and seeks to rebut, possible objections that might be raised to the methods adopted in this book in relation to the study of law and legal concepts, and to the line it takes concerning the possibility of ascribing any kind of scientific status to legal scholarship. A case is developed that supports the methodology of interpretative analytical inquiry intrinsic to the present version of the institutional theory of law.

14

Positive Law and Moral Autonomy

14.1 Introduction

The present institutionalist account of law exposes to clear view the 'positive' character of the legal provisions laid down in treaties, constitutions, statutes, acts of delegated rule-making, and also of the decisions of courts. Where precedent is considered a source of law, we may also include the rules and principles derivable from the reasons offered for such decisions. Law's 'positive' character is nothing other than this very characteristic that it is laid down through intentional human acts aimed at regulating human conduct. For '*jus positivum*' means 'law laid down', and 'positive law' is '*jus positivum*' translated into English.

In one of the senses in which people commonly speak of 'the law', or 'the law of this country' (in any particular country), it simply means the whole compendium of such laid-down (or 'posited') legal provisions. Perhaps it would be more accurate to think of this as the whole compendium of laid-down provisions that are valid in and for that country. (They are valid for that country by virtue of criteria that are themselves intrinsic to its legal order viewed as a whole.) The institution-agencies of the legislature, authorized rule-makers belonging to the executive institutions, and members of the judiciary have the task of laying down the various relevant kinds of normative provisions. When they exercise their powers correctly, what they do is valid as law. Whatever is valid as law has to be respected by all those for whom the law is binding, that is all citizens and persons resident within the country in question. Otherwise what they do is either legally wrongful or (in the case of purported exercises of legal power) legally invalid.

The law of states, or of partly autonomous regions or countries within states or of suigeneric trans-national commonwealths such as the EU, or of international associations or organizations, is composed in great measure of positive norms, in this sense of 'positive'. Such positive norms are contained in norm-texts and stored electronically or in printed books and the like. Their physical or electronic embodiment is not a matter requiring explanation in a work of the present kind. The fact that their meaningful content is a set of norms—rules, principles or decisions—is of interest, but has already been explained at some length. It is a matter of institutional fact.

14.2 Explaining the Positive Character of Law

Positivity has sometimes been explained in terms of a political will. It is possessed by rules that are laid down through acts of will of a political superior to political inferiors and are sustained in existence by the will of that same superior, acting personally or through subordinates with delegated powers of command and coercion. However, the historical and contemporary instances that would seem best to approximate to this picture are instances of dictatorship, whether of a charismatic political figure or of an hereditary absolute monarch or autocrat. So far from being particularly central or enlightening examples of law in the sense of the law-state, or democratic constitutional state, federation or confederation, dictatorships exhibit what is only very questionably a legal rather than an arbitrary form of government. Criminal procedures are abused to repress enemies of the regime, and public law either ceases to exist or consists of grants of discretion so vague and general as to be uncheckable in practice. Private law may survive, but in a somewhat shadowy form owing to erosion through corruption and discretionary interventions that weaken confidence in contractual obligations or property rights.

One response to this objection might say that the will of dictators is not the only will that might be at stake. What about the will of the whole people of a democratic country, establishing a constitution and watching over the exercise of public powers by the various organs of state constitutionally established? Or what about the will of the elected representatives of the people in a parliament, in circumstances where parliamentarians acknowledge that they must respect the independence of the judiciary and exercise themselves some supervision of the executive? To the extent that there is some effective co-ordination of action among the constitutional agencies (institution-agencies) that exercise public power, one can reasonably impute a kind of common coherent will to the state itself, or the people of the state as a kind of corporate entity. So the positivity of the law is a matter of its being willed by the state or the people.

This is not in the least objectionable, but it has no explanatory value. A single dominating will, a real psychological will, is perhaps easy enough to detect in the case of a personal dictatorship or a tightly collaborating oligarchy. This can then genuinely be the directing impulse behind all or most state action, and explanation in terms of such a will is in principle illuminating. No such unitary real psychological will exists in a complex institutional order such as one finds in a democratic constitutional state. The will of such a state is a matter of pure imputation, imputation which makes sense in the context of coherent political action and a coherent reading of the law that emerges from such action. This depends on persons who hold institutional office conducting themselves with respect for co-ordinating norms. It also depends on persons who exercise critical observation of office-holders, that is, persons in other branches of government, and in the media and the academic world, concerning themselves with respect for those same co-ordinating norms—rules and principles of constitutional law, conventions of the constitution, and the like. Office-holders have to be already respecting these constraints before the conditions for intelligibly imputing a concerted will to the state can be realized. But if they are already respecting these constraints, they are already respecting law, so the will that we impute to the state is a consequence, not a cause, of the existence of law in a law-state.

Norm-using rather than norm-giving is the key to the understanding of normative order. Humans are by nature norm-users. They would neither be able to speak, nor to co-ordinate activities at a distance, nor therefore to have any social division of labour, if they were not norm-users. The institutional theory of law can thus give a better and more intelligible account of elaborate bodies of norms such as are found in legal systems than can theories which one way or another become bogged down in postulating 'acts of will' as the basis either of normativity itself or of the positive character of institutional norms. But this is not to say that legislative acts of will, or judicial or executive acts of will, are unimportant. They are enormously important in accounting for the positivity of law, but not at the deepest level for its normative character.

Public law is much concerned with efficient governance coupled with respect for distributive justice. Criminal law upholds through punishment and threats thereof certain moral fundamentals that have to do with securing social peace. Private law upholds the essentials of personal private life and the conditions for some variety of social market economy. Distributive justice, retributive justice, and corrective justice are at the heart of the main divisions of law. But all these are highly controversial subjects. The obvious message to derive from the partisan struggles that preoccupy all democratic systems of government is this. People care deeply about justice, demand that the law expresses a vision of justice, yet disagree about what justice demands. Disagreement of this kind can perhaps be contained within small-scale face-to-face communities, for people may consensually rub along with more or less talked-through compromises between opposed views. Even today, many extended families might be found to give examples of this, as might certain kinds of workplace community like colleges or faculties and departments within some kinds of more traditional university, or partnerships in law or accountancy firms that have not expanded on to a colossal industrial scale. But disagreement cannot usually be handled by tacit compromise in a large-scale society involving the kinds of impersonal trust and impersonal interaction we have considered especially in relation to the conditions of an extensive market economy.[1] How then can it be handled?

We already know the answer. Decision-making on points of actual or potential disagreement is entrusted to the institutional agencies of government. Legislatures must determine upon general rules, possibly along with statements of general principles that the enacted rules embody, possibly in a way that simply leaves this

---

[1] Cf J Waldron, *Law and Disagreement* (Oxford: Oxford University Press, 1999) 2–8.

implicit. Ministers and executive agencies must exercise their powers, including powers of rule-making and specific decision-making within constitutional and legislatively ordained limits on their discretion. The courts must decide individual cases according to procedures appropriate to the main domains of law (public, criminal, or private-cum-commercial), and in deciding must interpret enacted rules in order to achieve a just and reasonable application of them. The reasonableness of a reasonable decision-making procedure is not something that could, even in principle, be the subject of rule-making, for it is simply the application of general practical reason to the specific task of institutional decision-making in the context of a body of already posited law. This application of practical reason is expressed in judges' justifying reasons for their decisions.[2] Even when unconvincing or unsatisfactory reasons are given in a particular case, the decision itself remains binding on the parties. Of course, there is every likelihood of its being reversed on appeal if an appeal is launched, or of being overruled in a later decision in a case for which it is cited as a precedent. But it stands in the meantime as a binding decision.

14.3 Moral Controversy and Legal Decision

It is easy to give examples of this process of legal settlement of controversial issues. In March 1994 the *Bundesverfassungsgericht* (German Federal Constitutional Court) handed down a decision calling for more uniform practice among the *Länder* (federal regions) to ensure that a common line was taken by public prosecutors in the various *Länder*, by way of discontinuing prosecutions of individuals for possession of cannabis, in cases where the charge concerned only 'small' quantities, and these were for the individual's own use. This was required to fulfil the constitutional principle of proportionality and apply it fairly throughout the federation.[3] This attempt, still not fully successful, to ensure a common practice throughout the German Republic did not involve an outright decision to decriminalize possession on the ground that statutes prohibiting it infringe guaranteed constitutional liberty. Even so, the decision was highly controversial. Many criticized it as being excessively permissive and seriously wrong from a moral point of view, especially since young people can often be led through soft drugs into an addiction to hard drugs. Others criticized the moral timidity of the decision, as one that failed to grasp the nettle of constitutional liberty one way or the other, and failed to say flatly that personal use of cannabis lay within the citizen's constitutional liberties.

---

[2] For a full account of this from the point of view of the institutional theory of law, see N MacCormick, *Rhetoric and the Rule of Law* (Oxford: Oxford University Press, 2005), especially chs 2 and 13.

[3] BVerfG E 90, 145 at 151–153. See also L Paoli and C Schäfer, *Drug Consumption and Criminal Prosecution in Germany* (Freiburg: Max Planck Institute for Foreign and International Criminal Law, Research Report, 2005).

However that may be, the underlying moral question in such a case is one that is likely to be controversial. So far as concerns 'soft drugs' like cannabis, or perhaps, if it is 'soft', alcohol, we may all find ourselves wondering whether it is right for humans to resort to such substances. Either it is morally permissible or not, and if it is permissible, a person's indulgence, at least within some limits of moderation, may either belong to the good life or not. Whether it is permissible or not may presumably also be affected by questions of the example the use of drugs or drink may give to the young and impressionable. Or it may be affected by the extent to which a particular culture has or has not developed social practices structuring and socializing use of the substance in question. But (on a certain assumption to be discussed later), it is of the character of morality that each moral agent on whose life the question impinges as a practical issue has to make up her or his own mind on the issue. This calls for reasoning and reflection, for discussing with friends, for taking such advice as he/she thinks right, but each in the end can only come to his/her own conclusion on the issue of the permissibility of drug-use. Furthermore, since there is an issue whether the state ought to prohibit possession or permit it, there is a question for every citizen whether statutes permitting drug use, or prohibiting it under penalties, ought to be in force in the state. There is a further question whether this should be settled as a matter of constitutional right or as a matter of ordinary legislation. (Needless to say, all these are interrelated but distinct questions, with distinct answers.)

One can further dramatize such a matter by reflecting on questions of life or death. Consider the case of Anthony Bland, a victim of the disaster at the Hillsborough football ground in England in 1989, who died in 1993 after several years in a persistent vegetative state. He died because of the discontinuance of the nourishment through tubes that had hitherto sustained him. His persistent vegetative state had been long-enduring, and had been found irreversible owing to the degeneration of his brain-tissue. In this situation, it had been held according to responsible medical opinion that continued medical intervention to prolong Anthony Bland's life was not in his best interest. On these two accounts, the House of Lords held that cessation of feeding and of treatment with antibiotics was lawful.[4] The Lords therefore laid it down that, in future like cases, the same test should be applied, subject to the confirmation by the High Court in each case of the lawfulness of the discontinuance in the light of all prevailing circumstances. The Lords also specifically held that in such a case the patient must not be actively killed, for example by some quick-acting and (necessarily) painless lethal injection. At most, the patient must be let die by discontinuance of the invasive treatment by feeding and the like that no longer served any interest of the patient.

Abortion is an even more perennial example of an issue of life and death in which the law readily becomes embroiled. In 1938, in England, the surgeon Alec Bourne performed an abortion on a girl of fifteen impregnated by violent rape,

---

[4] *Airedale NHS Trust v Bland* [1993] AC 789; [1993] 1 All ER 821.

and then reported himself to the police. He was prosecuted, but the judge directed the jury to acquit if the Crown had not proved beyond reasonable doubt that the surgeon had acted otherwise than in good faith with a view to protecting the life, understood as the continuing sane and healthy existence, of the girl in question. The law's express prohibition on performing or procuring abortion was, according to the judge, subject to an implied exception of the sort indicated.[5] Mr Bourne was acquitted, and the judge's ruling in the case was somewhat precariously accepted as governing the sound interpretation of abortion law for the three following decades. But a precedent at this level of a High Court trial at first instance was only persuasively binding as an interpretation of the law. Accordingly, the law as stated in *Bourne's* case spoke with an uncertain voice to the medical profession, to women, and to any other concerned citizens. In 1967, to remedy this lack of clarity and provide more finally authoritative legal permissions and prohibitions, the Abortion Act was passed by Parliament on the initiative of David Steel, MP.[6] What was previously somewhat vague, and defeasible because reliant on a single precedent, was made more secure and more determinate, both as to the prohibition of abortion, and as to the precise conditions of the exceptions where it is permissible. The constitutional supremacy of Parliament gave a firmer foundation to the definite rules laid down. As a matter of relative legal clarity at least, the legislative reform has apparently worked since 1967 as a statement of intelligible rules of law. Nevertheless, the abortion issue, in the UK as in other industrial and post-industrial states has remained in the front line of moral controversy. For some, the law now mandates murder, foeticide, and results in annual mass-killing carried out in public hospitals paid for by all taxpayers, who themselves thus become willy-nilly accessories to murder. For others, the issue concerns the moral liberty of women ('A Woman's Right to Choose'), and the law is only a timid half-way house, still illegitimately invading the proper autonomy of women as independent moral agents. Yet others perhaps see the law as a morally satisfactory compromise through balancing of significant principles. Similar controversy proceeds in many states, whether under constitutional banning of abortion, as in Ireland or to a more mitigated degree Germany, or under more permissive legislation, or permissive constitutional interpretation as in Canada, or under conditions of ongoing constitutional debate, as in the United States.

The cases discussed have been chosen for their legal setting, but it is relevant here to reflect also on these problems in their character as moral problems. The controversial character of the cases arises from their moral salience, and they retain this same moral salience even when legal decisions settle the point within the framework of legal-institutional order. To point up the contrast, it is opportune to reflect here on the character of moral deliberation relevant to such problems. What then is the character of deliberation and decision about them when such deliberation is pure moral deliberation?

---

[5] *R v Bourne* [1939] 1 KB 687; [1938] 3 All ER 615.
[6] Subsequently the Rt Hon Sir David Steel, Baron Steel of Aikwood.

14.4 Autonomy in Morality

We return to an earlier-noted assumption about its character. Autonomy, that is, the autonomy of each moral agent, has a special place in defining morality and in accounting for the special character of moral deliberation and decision-making. Each moral agent is a law unto her/himself. More literally, the moral law for each moral agent is that which she or he reasonably judges to determine the right for her/himself. This does not, of course, mean law for herself or himself only, for what is judged to be right has to be so judged universally. If it is right that I consume alcohol, it has to be right that anyone do so; what is permissible for me has to be permissible universally. What is obligatory for me (say, abstention from hard drugs) has to be obligatory universally. (But for me-as-a-what? Is it for me as a human or for me as an adult human that alcohol is permissible? Is it true that even for me as an adult, hard drugs are absolutely prohibited, or only their non-medical use? And so on.) The point here is not to enter into deliberation about what exact conclusion of substance to reach on the mentioned, or any other, questions of morality; it is only to characterise what—upon this conception of morality and moral agency—is essential to moral thought and action as such.

Here, we may distinguish the moral questions of what is universally permissible, obligatory, or prohibited from what are sometimes differentiated as 'ethical' questions about the good life. Even if I am morally at liberty to take alcohol, or perhaps to indulge in some other 'soft' drugs, it would remain a question what part I judge them to have in the good life. Here, autonomy remains, but universality recedes. What is the good life for me is certainly that which I autonomously shape for myself, that for which I take responsibility.[7] Each moral agent then has a life-story of her/his own, and we all write the story of our own lives according to what seems to us the best pattern for the unfolding narrative we make of it. We need not, indeed should not, think it necessary or even permissible, to legislate our view of a good life for anyone else. Parents, teachers, and others do, however, have a duty to help children and young persons to learn the art of autonomous living and of self-disciplined definition and pursuit of the good within the framework of the moral law as they construct this over a lifetime.[8] At the stage of still being under tutelage and even a degree of compulsion by elders, the child remains heteronomous. Autonomy supervenes upon heteronomy as full moral agency comes into being.

This conception of the essentially 'autonomous' character of morality owes a great deal to the moral philosophy of Immanuel Kant.[9] It is itself philosophically controversial. Some would locate morality not in autonomous judgments (if such

---

[7] Cf, on 'public and private autonomy', J Habermas 'On the Internal Relation between the Rule of Law and Democracy' European Journal of Philosophy 3 (1995) 12–20 at 17–18.

[8] Cf J Nedelsky, 'Reconceiving Autonomy' Yale Journal of Law and Feminism 1 (1989) 7–36.

[9] Expressed with particular clarity in H J Paton, *The Moral Law: Kant's Groundwork of the Metaphysic of Morals* (London: Hutchinson, 1981) 36, 86–88.

exist at all) but primarily in the practice of a community. Others would locate it in a sense of virtue and of the particular virtues, perhaps as these have been transmitted in a particular tradition. Others regard moral thought as primarily an interpretative way of thinking, making the best sense of a common world-view rather as aesthetics seeks to interpret and make best sense of an artistic tradition. Some again would adhere to realism, claiming that moral judgment concerns real qualities of acts and objects independent of our deliberation or will. A possible rider to this is that such moral qualities are capable of being recognized through what is sometimes called 'intuition' when we confront them in life's practical dilemmas.

The realist line of thought can give space to autonomy, but in a sense somewhat different from the Kantian. For what is then in issue is a reinterpretation of autonomy. In Kantian thought the idea of the moral agent as autonomous is taken to be a ('transcendental') presupposition of the very possibility of moral thought as practical reason. Realism accommodates it not as a precondition but as a special moral value or virtue, that of being willing and able to take responsibility for a definition and pursuit of the good life, coupled with self-discipline in adhering to one's own conception of one's moral duties and rights.[10] The duty to act conscientiously, however, is itself a moral duty independent of our willing it, and one's interpretation or conception of duties and rights can be a misinterpretation or misconception, however firmly held.[11]

For present purposes, the difference between the Kantian and this realist version of autonomy is not important. On the former view, the truth about autonomy is a matter of meta-ethics, or even of the metaphysics of morals; it is presupposed by the very possibility of moral thought. On the latter view, the autonomy of moral agents is not an independent presupposition for all moral thought, but itself one fundamental moral truth. It is the truth that we can and ought to exercise self-discipline and must each act upon our own reflective understanding of moral duty and moral right, as well as taking responsibility for our own idea of the good life, and for trying to pursue this idea through the opportunities and contingencies of life that we happen to confront. Autonomy is on the former view metaphysically, but on the latter view morally, fundamental to our moral life. In either case, it goes to the heart of what it is to be a (fully) moral agent.

Let us take this conclusion to be true, on one or other of the grounds that can be offered for it. In either case, it reveals what is surely the core idea of 'autonomy'. Autonomy is a quality of persons, that is of conscious acting subjects, who shape their will according to reasonable judgments based on the information derived through external and internal senses and gained in discussion with others or from reading and reflecting. By that rational will they construct and act upon conclusions concerning duties and rights that are inherently universalizable.

[10] J Raz, *The Morality of Freedom* (Oxford: Clarendon Press, 1986) chs 1–3.
[11] Cf A Donagan, *The Theory of Morality* (Chicago, Ill: University of Chicago Press, 1979).

To apply the term 'autonomy' in any other setting will involve either an extension of this sense of the term, or the devising of a distinct concept to which the term ambiguously applies (but here, to avoid ambiguity, it would be better to use a different term). The extended use would be apt in cases of collective or corporate bodies to which it seems proper to impute some kind of decision-making and law-making power analogous to that which we stipulate in the case of the conscious rational agent who is also a biological human being. Given certain institutional arrangements, we can reasonably impute common decisions to all sorts of organized bodies like clubs, trade unions, sporting associations, commercial companies, partnerships, families sometimes, universities, churches, states,[12] and we can ask how far such decision-making is autonomous, how far subordinate to some extraneous or superior regulation.

Heteronomy is defined by simple negation. Where there is will, or decision-making capability, but where the rule to which the will submits is set by an extraneous or alien will, there heteronomy prevails. Where one person acts upon another's taking responsibility for the rightness of the action ('Well, if you say so, I have no choice about the matter') there is no autonomous action by the ostensible agent, though there may be by the other party. If I give up smoking, not because I reflectively decide that it is right or good to do so, but because of pressure exercised by family and peer-group, or because of some enforced unavailability of tobacco, or under pressure of a legal ban on smoking in enclosed public spaces, the resultant state (my not smoking) may be on some view better than the former, but no moral credit belongs to me for this.

To sum up on this characterization of morality, deliberation and decision as moral deliberation and decision are autonomous. One must come to a conclusion on the best view one can form of all the evidence, and in the light of the whole range of one's moral commitments and beliefs. One must bring these together into the kind of consistent and coherent set of practical principles that it befits a rational agent to possess. None of us is likely to achieve this unaided, and indeed each of us has reason to seek the views of others in framing a conclusion. Moral views on such issues impinge on other people, so one should hear their views. Most of the moral position of each of us has emerged through a taking of individual responsibility for a body of moral opinion and tradition initially acquired heteronomously, and continuing reflection on the quality of our principles therefore engages critical reflection upon inherited tradition. This again gives reason for co-reflection with others reared in the same or kindred traditions, as well as critical co-reflection with others from other traditions. Above all, the insight that one is oneself autonomous entails recognition of the like autonomy of every other, hence the equality of all moral agents as such. Any moral co-ordination of moral opinions can then only come about through the reaching of common but

[12] Cf R Dworkin, 'Constititutionalism and Democracy' European Journal of Philosophy 3 (1995) 2–11 at 3–5, on 'two concepts of collective action'.

independently endorsed conclusions, and this implies a readiness to engage in fully open and non-coercive co-deliberation with others. That is, moral deliberation morally ought to proceed through 'discourse' and can never proceed in a non-discursive way, by recourse to power-play, rhetorical tricks, or the like.[13]

An essentially discursive character, therefore, as well as an autonomous one, is crucial to moral thought, and to morality as such. Moral deliberation involves a discourse of equals, seeking some common answer to what is for all the same set of questions, to which, however, no one can lay down the answers with conclusive authority for any other consistently with sustaining the essential character of moral thought.

This leads to a third feature of moral thought that almost inevitably supervenes upon the other two. Moral opinions can be controversial. Since each of us confronts moral questions as an autonomous agent, nobody's answer is conclusive for anyone else. Given the complexity of practical life, perhaps an ever-increasing complexity, there is no *a priori* guarantee that all human beings, or even all human beings who come much into contact with each other, can come to identical conclusions in moral deliberation. In practice, as is obvious every day, conscientious and reasonable people thinking rationally and reasonably about moral issues do come to different and mutually incompatible, sometimes sharply opposed, conclusions. Issues about drugs, about euthanasia, and about abortion are no more than especially vivid illustrations of this. So we may conclude about morality: morality is intrinsically autonomous; and in consequence it is also both discursive and controversial.

14.5 Of Law: Institutionality, Authoritativeness, Heteronomy

Now let us go back to remarking that the problems most recently under discussion did in fact come from legal decisions, in Germany, in England, and in the United Kingdom respectively. The cannabis decision, the decision about the PVS patient, the decisions about abortion, were all decisions by legal institutions—a constitutional court, a highest-instance civil court, a criminal court of first instance, a parliament. From this follows another fact: that the decisions, taken as they were by legal agencies within their legal competence, were authoritative and (within a certain range) conclusive. The point of legal institutions is exactly that they exist, inter alia, to settle disputable practical issues in an authoritative way for all persons who fall under their jurisdiction or legislative competence.

Previous reflection on the character of moral deliberation reveals a positive value that may accordingly be ascribed from a moral point of view to legal institutions endowed with exactly the features of being institutional and authoritative

---

[13] Cf R Alexy, *Theory of Legal Argumentation* (trans R Adler and N MacCormick) (Oxford: Clarendon Press, 1988) 114–135, 193–194.

that we are now contemplating. For it may be necessary to live by some common public standards that are settled and determinate for all of us even while they remain highly controversial, or at least always open to controversy, at the level of pure moral debate. Issues of the kind here discussed, and many similar issues, are not subjects of moral consensus among contemporary citizens of contemporary states. Yet for purposes of social life in complex societies they are issues upon which it seems necessary to have some determinate common norm of public action.

Where there are publicly-licensed medical practitioners and publicly-licensed, usually also publicly-financed, hospitals, it must be a question what is required or permitted in the way of therapeutic practice, especially where the boundary between therapy, permitting death, causing death, or actively killing comes into question. And if there is a rule against the taking of human life, there must necessarily be a threshold rule saying when protected life begins, and with what consequences.

Hence the fact of moral controversy does not mandate avoidance of any common rule. To refrain from adopting any common rule is not a non-answer, but is one of the controversial answers to the question what rule to have, namely the answer in favour of a permissive approach to the issue in question. What the law's institutions can do is that which moral deliberation cannot itself achieve. They can lay down a common rule in relatively determinate terms, and where the rule first enunciated is insufficiently clear, there are legal practices of reasoning and interpretation that can further clarify, further determine, the law. At least for individuals, the practice of law-application can produce almost incontestable clarity at the level of an individual norm. In the *Bland* case, for example, one can say confidently that the medical and nursing personnel in whose care Mr Bland was placed had an absolutely clear declaration of the things it was their legal duty to do. If afterwards they had been prosecuted for doing them (and an attempt was made to that end), they surely had a conclusive answer to any legal indictment we can imagine. Almost the same can be said of other doctors and nurses in the meantime charged with the care of other patients who have suffered brain injuries and degenerated into an irreversible condition of PVS.

Not all legal determinations are necessarily as determinate as that. The Federal German cannabis decision said only that prosecutors' discretion should be applied to abstain from prosecuting persons found in possession of 'small' quantities of hashish or cannabis. This lays down one common rule for all the *Länder* where previously there were several conflicting practices between different ones of them; but clearly it is not yet fully determinate. This is the kind of ruling that clearly has to be further concretized in subsequent decision-making at appropriate levels. It has indeed taken some time, and several decisions in several *Länder*, to establish (still not with absolute clarity) what the line is between small amounts for own use, and larger ones for presumed uses of illicit commerce. However determinate, all case-law is to a degree defeasible—highest courts can always, and occasionally do, review or vary their own precedents.[14] (In the USA, the Supreme Court is in the process of pulling back from its own earlier rather extensive decisions about the permissibility of abortion during the first trimester of pregnancy, for example, and for the moment a degree of indeterminacy appears to prevail.) Quite apart from such review, there can always be fresh legislation altering previous legal understandings and calling in turn for new acts of interpretation in the process of further judicial application of law.

Despite all that, it remains the case that the law has institutions for establishing common rules and for rendering them progressively more and more determinate. This 'progressive concretization of norms', as Kelsen noted, reaches its maximum of determinateness when it comes to the individual norm of decision issued by a court of law to or in respect of an individual person or determinate group or set of persons.[15] It is of the character of legal institutions that their decisions have a necessarily authoritative character within the framework of the law. Sometimes, as with a first-instance court, which is subject to appeals, or with a legislature whose enactments are subject to constitutional review, this authority is provisional and defeasible upon proper challenge. But it is of the character of legal institutions that for any given line of decision and review or appeal there is some institution that has a final authority upon the given question. Then, internally to its own institutional activities, though not at the level of legal-scientific or juristic debate and criticism, the law simply admits of no other authoritative answer than that which has been given. Whoever ought to, or wishes to, or has no choice but to, act in accordance with law has to act in accordance with the determination given by the relevant institution, for it is conclusive as to the law for the time being.

Normally, this is no mere theoretical conclusiveness. States are political entities, that is, their constitutional order is sustained by power-relations, ultimately including relations of brute coercive power. They are highly organized and can dispose of power quite effectively. Where law is state-law, it has the backing of state power (though also, where a state is a law-state, it is legitimated by, and restricted in its use of power by, law as normative order; and all states have some minimal aspiration to be credible in the guise of the law-state). There are other settings in which law belongs, such as supra-statal communities or unions (particularly the EU, increasingly also the UN), churches, national and international sporting associations, commercial and educational corporations, trades unions. These also dispose of forms of power, psychological, social, or economic, but usually they have access to physical force (if at all) only through, and by permission of or with the support of, some state.

Hence it is usually the case that legal determinations are not merely institutional and authoritative in a purely normative sense. They also have the backing of

---

[14] On defeasibility, see MacCormick, *Rhetoric and the Rule of Law* ch 12.

[15] Kelsen, *Pure Theory of Law* 237: 'This process, in which the law keeps renewing itself, as it were, proceeds from the general (abstract) to the individual (concrete); it is a process of increasing individualization and concretization'.

some form of power that bears significantly on vital interests of the persons to whom legal determinations are addressed. Two significant conclusions follow. First, each addressee of law normally has some reason to comply; secondly, each knows that the same is presumptively true of the great majority of other addressees of the law, and each can accordingly form reasonably reliable expectations of others' conduct. This is because ordinary social experience gives people in all sorts of contexts and settings reasonably well-founded views of the general likelihood that others will act upon the reasons that the law gives them for acting.

Further to this, in settled situations there may well be a general acceptance that the law as laid down is on the whole reasonable. This will lead to the law's being backed by customary norms and practices according to which one ought to accord respect to the law's demands and to the constitutional order that lies behind them. Thus to any reflection on the power of the law and to any expectations of general conformity is added a normative conception of the ultimate foundations of the law. This resides in popular attitudes of support for a society's established way of organizing itself and going about its business. The weight of moral opinion as well as of coercive force and common expectations swings also behind the law's determinations. It is no wonder that so many people have such deep reservations about open disobedience to law in normal circumstances. It is a routine part of everyday morality to hold that law and order should be respected.

Yet it remains the case that there is a moral price to be paid for the utility of law as institutional establishment of common norms for conduct in society. That is, that law as well as being institutional and authoritative, indeed, precisely because it is so, is heteronomous. That is, it confronts each moral agent with categorical requirements in the form of duties, obligations, and prohibitions that purport to bind the agent regardless of the agent's own rational will as an autonomous moral being. The law's demands to the autonomous agent purport to bind the agent in a heteronomous way. Law is (in this sense) heteronomous, as well as authoritative and institutional; it thus stands in clear conceptual contrast to morality, which is autonomous, discursive, and controversial.

Thus understood, there is a clear conceptual distinction between the moral and the legal. It is a distinction that can be made clear only upon a conception of morality that holds it as essentially engaging the autonomy of each moral agent. Such a conception of morality can be based upon meta-ethical theses about the necessary presuppositions of morality (or, even, on a 'metaphysic of morals'), or on some normative moral account of autonomy as itself a fundamental moral principle available to moral intuition or established in some other way.

Of course there are other conceptions of morality that do not treat autonomy as foundational to it. On the one hand, we may think of conventional, or 'positive' morality,[16] consisting of a set of opinions that are commonly held in some

---

[16] 'Positive morality', in the sense of an actually current popular moral code, was a concept used by John Austin in *The Province of Jurisprudence Determined* (ed W E Rumble) (Cambridge: Cambridge

community on what are commonly regarded as moral issues concerning honesty, sexual continence, and mutual respect, and goodwill, and the like. This might take us back to where we started, thinking of conventions about queuing, for example. Whoever follows conventions in an unthinking and uncritical way is to that extent acting heteronomously. The problem comes when doubts arise or competing interpretations emerge of similar conventional norms. This challenges one either to develop some form of institutional authority to settle issues or forces one into the reflective mode of autonomous morality after all—one takes responsibility for one's own interpretation of the convention in question.

On the other hand, one may have an authority-based conception of morality, as sometimes can be found in the case of religious conceptions of morality. Where the authority is that of a sacred text, the Koran or the Bible, for example, there remains even for the most fundamentalist believer the need sometimes to come to a conclusion about the proper interpretation of a key passage in the text. Thereupon one falls back either on one's own interpretation or on that of a teacher. Where, as in Roman Catholic Christianity, the Pope speaking *ex cathedra* on a matter of faith and morals is held to be infallible, there is no possible competition between rival teachers. But one has now moved beyond convention into what is plainly a form of institutional normative order, a kind of positive law, grounded in the will and wisdom of God intimated through his supreme representative on earth. To a believer, it is then a positive law explication of the divine law. To a believer, such a law must be superior in authority and binding force to any merely human institutional normative order. The one autonomous choice concerns whether to embrace or reject such belief. Here, there is a contrast of content but not of form with state-law.

14.6 Mitigating the Contrast: Relative Heteronomy of Law

The argument so far faces an objection derivable from Kant's own theory of law. Kant takes account of the fact that the autonomous moral agent would face a potentially chaotic social existing of competing norms. For such an agent, says Kant, the first act of rational self-legislation would consist of submission to a social contract establishing a constitutional state along with others. Since that state is thus mandated by moral reason, the rational agent's autonomous will in relation to 'external conduct' must be willingly subordinated to the will of the law-giver expressed in a constitutional legislative process, the constitution being one to which the agent ought to submit for the reasons mentioned.[17]

University Press, 1995) ch 2. It was developed and applied in contrast to 'critical morality' by H L A Hart, *Law, Liberty and Morality* (Oxford: Oxford University Press, 1963) 17–24.

[17] I Kant, *The Metaphysical Elements of Justice* (trans John Ladd) (Indianapolis: Bobbs-Merrill, 1965) 71 (Part II, Section 42).

The argument in this form goes well beyond the points mentioned in the preceding section. There, it was suggested that a moral reasoner ought to acknowledge the factual situation constituted by a legal order as one that gives her or him strong moral reasons for going along with the law in many circumstances. Notoriously, Kant, in the course of elaborating 'laws of freedom', brought himself to conclusions about the absoluteness of a person's obligations toward state and law that go beyond anything that any mere legal positivism has ever begun to endorse. This is a sad end for a transcendentalist natural law theory to drive itself to. It is also quite unnecessary. To see why, we need to differentiate the theory of actual positive law from a theory of ideal positive law.

Actual systems of positive law in contemporary states result from politics and even from warfare. They enshrine and to a degree presuppose economic arrangements and structures of economic power that many people from their autonomous moral perspective find it impossible to endorse fully or unconditionally. Not all that is enforced as law satisfies even elementary requirements of justice. The constructing of principles of justice in the moral sense is for each of us anyway a matter for our own autonomous judgment. There is plenty of evidence that this implies not merely the already noted inherent possibility of controversy, but an actual and widespread state of deep-seated dissensus over issues of justice in most contemporary political societies. The prevalence of party politics in democratic states is but one index of this. The attempt to enforce consensus of a kind through one-party states so often repeated in the twentieth century always exacerbated dissent while momentarily masking it.

In this state of affairs, to assert any plain or simple categorical obligation to enter a political community and autonomously to endorse *ab initio* whatever is passed as (or passes for) law therein seems to go beyond anything that can be warranted by rational deliberation or discourse. There plainly are strong reasons of principle for one to uphold one's membership in the legal-political society in which one happens to be, or to seek out one and acquire membership in it. There plainly are strong reasons of principle to grant at the very least a high prima facie respect for that society's constitutional norms and derived obligations at the level of substantive civil and criminal law. But, to say the very least, the question of the nature and weight of countervailing principles in general and in particular contexts is a controversial one. Arguments for a yet more anarchical view at least deserve a respectful hearing in any pure moral discourse.[18]

The character and incidence of any obligation to obey the law is then a question upon which the sovereign judgment of each moral agent must be brought to bear for autonomous decision. Judgments about the weight attaching to any such prima facie obligation will vary according to the context of different states and politico-legal orders. There can be no theorem of the metaphysics of morals that

[18] Cf Z Bankowski, *Living Lawfully: love in law and law in love* (Dordrecht: Kluwer Academic, 2001) 13–26.

settles the matter a priori. Each of us who advances a view of the character of this opposition stakes out a position in the contestable ground of moral discourse. While this does not absolve anyone from forming an honest and well-reflected view of the answer to the question, and trying to get it right, each has to acknowledge the illegitimacy of enforced *moral* assent to one among the contested answers. This is the very fact that we allude to in acknowledging the heteronomous character of the moral agent face-to-face with authoritatively issued legal norms.

The other side of this, though, is that we can envisage a position that many reflective people might hold in quite a variety of states. This is the position of autonomously committing oneself to upholding the constitution and constitutional processes, and therefore to giving legal obligations arising under it an at least qualified endorsement. Jeremy Bentham's dictum that, faced with bad laws, we ought to 'obey punctually, but censure freely'[19] is not so far from Kant's position after all. It encourages us to engage in active legal criticism and law-reform activity as normally preferable to violent resistance or futile refusal to obey. Someone who takes this line might view legal obligation as leaving intact a kind of relative autonomy. For it is acknowledged that there are autonomous moral reasons for obedience, even while consent to the content of the obligation is only qualified, or even absent. (Consider the conscientious objector to abortion who is nevertheless willing to endorse an obligation to go along with legislative decisions democratically taken, yet who at the same time campaigns vigorously against the use of tax revenues to finance abortion clinics). This person's position would also therefore be relatively heteronomous. All the more would the law present only heteronomous motives to anyone whose considered judgment accorded less than that degree of endorsement to his/her state as currently constituted.

Unless it seemed possible to construct a substantive argument within a moral discourse to prove that even a weak endorsement of law and the state is rationally untenable, it would have to be conceded that people living under law are at best relatively heteronomous, hence relatively autonomous also. It does not seem possible to do so. But there remains a conceptual distinction between law and morality.

14.7 Doubting the Contrast: Interpretation and Argumentation in Law

Another doubt may now be raised about the contrast drawn between the moral and the legal. I have said that law's point is to render common and determinate societally that which is interpersonally controversial in the perspective of autonomous morality. Law does this by laying down rules. But the rules are not

---

[19] J Bentham, *A Comment on the Commentaries and A Fragment on Government* (ed J H Burns and H L A Hart) (London: Athlone Press, 1977) 399.

self-applying. The law therefore also has law-applying agencies, in the form of police, prosecutors, judges, juries. Law-applying practices enable citizens to take claims to courts where, assisted by counsel, they explain their claims in the light of rules and precedents, and explain the interpretation of the rules and precedents under which their claim is justified. Their opponents can, like accused persons in criminal cases, raise objection to claims or accusations on the ground either of factual untruth or unprovability, or of misinterpretation of the rules or precedents to which reference has been made.

The more these processes are probed, the more it can be argued that law always falls short of having a fully determinate character. At least at the level of general rules, and of the rulings on law laid down in precedents that we rely on to provide narrower but still general rules, the point is well-taken. There are always 'leeways' of interpretation around almost any rule one can imagine, and it has been the distinctive gift of Critical Legal Studies to jurisprudence in recent years to have issued so many salutary reminders of the difficulty we have in ever coming up with a rule so clear that no problem of interpretation can be imagined for any context of its application.[20] Even so, the contrast with morality remains worth drawing. Autonomous morality admits of no authoritative texts; law in a certain sense consists of a set of authoritative texts (statutes, or 'rule-texts', and law reports or 'precedent-texts'). These texts are commonly acknowledged as authoritative repositories of binding law. Though they have to be interpreted to be applied, they are a fixed starting-point for interpretative deliberation. While we must fully admit their lack of perfect determinacy, we must also admit their relative determinacy as common points of departure for different persons, by contrast with the radical interpersonal indeterminacy of pure moral reasoning.

We should recall also the other feature of legal processes that was considered above. Legal processes conclude in the issuance of 'individual norms'. Having heard claims or accusations, and evidence in support of their factual grounding, and debate about interpretation of relevant texts, the judge pronounces a decision, and issues orders to individuals to give effect to it (or issues declarations of their particular rights in a given matter). These individualized norms of law can even occasionally themselves give rise to problems of interpretation, but in that case one goes back to the court for further orders, and so on. In the end, the concrete legal right emerging from a legal process can be wholly determinate for practical purposes. By contrast, even where two or more people agree fully about all the moral principles applicable to a given problem, they may come to quite disparate conclusions about their duly weighted application to the case in hand. (This does not say, of course, that each moral agent for her/himself does not come to a quite determinate conclusion. Each can and should, and often does. It is not these

---

[20] S C Levinson and S Mailloux, *Interpreting Law and Literature* (Evanston, Ill: Northwestern University Press, 1988); D Kennedy *A Critique of Adjudication* (Cambridge, Ma: Harvard University Press, 1997); M Kelman, *A Guide to Critical Legal Studies* (Cambridge, Ma: Harvard University Press, 1987).

conclusions that are indeterminate, but the interpersonal conclusion as to the right or wrong of the matter.)

It might be counter-argued that the interpretative element in legal reasoning elides the difference between it and moral reasoning.[21] Now certainly it is the case that interpretative reasoning in law (and other elements in legal reasoning) form one special part of practical reasoning, and hence there is much in common between legal reasoning and moral reasoning. The attempt to do justice in the legal forum, but always justice-according-to-law, must clearly come under the guidance of some conception of justice which is always a moral, or morally defensible, conception of justice. As such, it need not be considered perfect or ideal justice, even from the point of view of the engaged legal reasoner. Thus the law as it emerges from the interpretative process addresses its demands to us subject to a 'claim of correctness',[22] making claims about the practical and moral justifiability of the duties or other legal relations it asserts. Hence it addresses us with full respect for our autonomy.

That legal reasoning is a sub-species of practical reasoning, and hence either strongly analogous to, or even a specialized form of, moral reasoning, is true. The intrinsic arguability of law is one of its salient features.[23] The cases that were discussed earlier make this very vividly clear. To decide whether or not it is legal to permit a PVS patient to die; or to procure an abortion; or to prosecute those who possess small quantities of cannabis for their own use; is clearly to take a decision which has great moral significance. To produce justifying reasons for one's decision, although these include legal norms and precedents, requires one to interpret the norms and precedents in the light of background principles and values, hence the interpretative reasoning is also in part moral reasoning. The judges in all the cases I mentioned are obviously wrestling with issues that are highly charged morally, and the reasons finally given include substantial moral elements alongside more technically legal ones. Moreover, the final utterance of the decision as a satisfactorily justified decision is an act by a moral agent who must be presumed to be satisfied that it is morally justifiable to proceed to decision on the basis of the reasons given.

All this is highly important, and a necessary corrective to a merely narrow legalism. Yet it does not resolve the distinction between the legal and the moral. If anything, it exacerbates it. Let us indeed insist that the judge or other authoritative interpreter of law is her- or himself a moral agent who must take moral

---

[21] A case for this could be based on R Dworkin, *Law's Empire* (Cambridge, Ma: Belknap Press, 1986) or, indeed on MacCormick, *Rhetoric and the Rule of Law* (Oxford: Oxford University Press, 2005).

[22] R Alexy, *Theory of Legal Argumentation* 214–220 on the claim to correctness; R Alexy, *The Argument from Injustice: a reply to legal positivism* (trans B Litschewski Paulson and S Paulson) (Oxford: Clarendon Press, 2002) applies the 'claim to correctness' argument in support of the thesis that extreme injustice is incompatible with law.

[23] MacCormick, *Rhetoric and the Rule of Law*, ch 2.

responsibility for the interpretative decision she/he issues,[24] and for the concrete decision between parties that it supports. But the more we insist on this, the more we underline the risk of disagreement from the point of view of those whom the decision addresses directly or indirectly. We come back to the problem of the conscientious dissenter. Whatever a court decides about the rights of the PVS patient or about the legitimacy or otherwise of abortion in a given setting, that decision speaks with the authority of law to the whole audience, assenters and dissenters alike. Hence there is always a possible moral point of view from which the law governs conduct in a purely heteronomous way, and this possible point of view is an actual one for many persons in any actual human society.

This consideration in fact justifies a more rather than less legalistic approach to legal decision-making. The more we take legal decision-making to be a public matter drawing on public sources, the less we force agents into the position of having to knuckle under the moral decisions of particular judges and other legal officials. That may in fact show better respect for autonomy than an excessively moralized approach to legal reasoning in concrete cases. In any event, the problem of autonomy is *the* moral problem. Law, by virtue of the way in which it addresses the moral agent *ab extra* is always at least relatively heteronomous. That is why law and morality are conceptually distinct.

[24] M J Detmold, *The Unity of Law and Morality* (London: Routledge and Kegan Paul, 1984).

15

On Law and Justice

15.1 Introduction

Law and morality are conceptually distinct. Yet they interact most intimately. On the one hand, for reasons that have been explored, there are normally good reasons to consider it a moral virtue to be a law-abiding citizen, at least in acceptably just states where the rule of law is observed. Many ordinary moral duties autonomously embraced by many moral agents concern respect for the safety and property of others, observance of speed limits when driving, honesty in making tax returns and promptness in paying taxes due, and a host of other quite mundane 'oughts'. It is good to be a law-abiding citizen in this way. On the other hand, state law by virtue of its subject matter is focused on matters of great moral concern, issues engaging political morality at its most weighty.

So far as public law deals with issues of distribution and redistribution, through taxes and expenditure allocations, and through measures to protect aspects of the common good such as environmental values, or worker protection, or consumer protection, or regulatory schemes concerning road safety, or safety at sea, or for rail travellers, it raises issues of distributive justice balanced against concern for the common good and efficient administration, all against a background of respect for the rule of law. So far as criminal law deals with the prohibition of acts which constitute *mala in se*, it deals with matters of great moral concern. Where it concerns positive or negative prescriptions arising under schemes of distribution, redistribution, and pursuit of aspects of the common good determined by public law, the *mala prohibita* that it determines are also matters of considerable moral concern. Punishments are appointed for breaches of criminal law, and are forms of hard treatment that carry moral stigma and that are deliberately inflicted by state agencies. It is therefore the more urgent that there be sufficient moral justification both for the proscription of offences and for the proportionality of punishments available in case of conviction. It is also vital to have fair systems of prosecution, with reasonable rules concerning evidence and procedure and the composition of the courts appointed to try criminal accusations—again, the rule of law is permanently in issue. In short, the criminal law engages vital questions of retributive justice. Private law defines persons and their capacities, and upholds a system of property-allocation (including succession to property) and a body of contract and related law; through laws on reparation and restitution it provides a system whereby wrongful invasions of established rights can be remedied through awards of compensatory damages or otherwise. Assuming a sufficient achievement of some acceptable degree of distributive justice, it aims to supply corrective justice to restore violations of the general scheme of rights in circumstances in which fair market exchange can proceed.

Thus summarizing the findings of chapters 10, 12, and 13, we conclude that law is necessarily geared to some conception of justice, taking account of distributive, retributive, and corrective aspects of justice, to all of which respect for the rule of law is, in the context of the state's capability for coercion, essential. It is 'necessarily geared' to it in the sense that anyone engaged in its administration, whether in a legislative, executive, or judicial capacity, can only be justified in implementing, amending, or interpreting provisions of the system given a certain condition. This is that they can give grounds for holding that some reasonable conception of justice is satisfied by the provision in question, or that it pursues some element of a reasonably assessed common good in a way that is reasonably coherent with the relevant conception of justice. A person would have to believe this condition was satisfied, and thus would have to claim that it is satisfied, before he/she could claim to be justified in actively upholding and implementing the law. To be sure, nothing precludes the possibility of such claims being made insincerely, as a mere cloak for what are in truth and in the actor's intention brutal exercises of sheer power, or corrupt diversions of the proper uses and purposes of law. But the character of the whole enterprise determines that its intrinsic ends, or 'final causes', are the realisation of justice and the common good, according to some reasonable conception of these. Hence you cannot sincerely participate in this enterprise without a serious orientation to these values, and you cannot intelligibly participate in it without at least pretending to have such an orientation.

15.2 Civil Liberty and Critical Morality

To accept all that has been said so far by no means permits complacency as to the actual realization of these values by any actual system of positive law in any actual state. People engaged in law should be, and probably many, even a majority, are trying to sustain justice in their society. But some are not trying and others may be trying but failing, or they may have conflicting but reasonable opinions about what justice requires so there may be a sad lack of coherence about the whole business. Law ought to be just and ought to serve the common good for all within the jurisdiction. But law frequently fails to be as it ought to be. What law is and what it ought to be are different things. Still, if it is true that in the conception of law as institutional normative order we must include the idea that the proper purpose of such an order is the realization of justice and the common good, this has certain consequences. First of all, it justifies a critical attitude towards actual institutions of law and state. They may be unjust in this or that way, they may fail to promote the common good in some way that is readily achievable. It is important that thoughtful citizens, commentators about public affairs and activists engaged in them, should engage in critical moral reflection about the institutions and practices of the law and the state. What H L A Hart called 'critical morality'[1] matters. Over time it can have an important influence, and can be transformed through the political system into programmes of law reform. The law has legitimate uses and unjust or illegitimate ones.

Can we offer any general moral principles that assist in the critique of law? One demand that flows from the idea of autonomous morality is rather obvious, that law should not be used in such a way as to prejudice or violate individual autonomy. Freedom of mind and judgment should be respected. This entails a jealous regard for civil liberty against encroachment by the institutions of the state. Plainly this principle does not license any and every acting-out of an individual's beliefs and convictions. The law, especially the criminal law, has the task of maintaining so far as possible civil peace, and the private law upholds existing property rights and enforces both voluntary and non-voluntary obligations through the law of contract and of delict. Conscientious refusal to comply with the law's demands may be respected. But at least to the extent that such refusal involves violating somebody else's legal rights or some clear public interest enshrined in law, the person who conscientiously breaks the law has normally neither a justification nor an excuse that the law can recognize. At best, there may be a good basis for a plea in mitigation of sentence.

In this sense law necessarily limits freedom. Does it also necessarily restrict autonomy? One traditional answer has been that the law does not do so provided it concerns itself only with the 'external' conduct of persons. I may think what I like about the speed limit that would be reasonable on a certain stretch of road. If, however, a competent authority has validly imposed a restriction of speed to (say) 20 miles per hour, and I do not observe this, I have no just complaint when I am prosecuted and fined. My physical freedom may be constrained by this, but not my freedom of mind. By contrast, attempts to use the law in ways that create 'thought crimes' are objectionable precisely because they do impinge on freedom of mind. Also, the use of psychological or physical pressures aimed at brainwashing individuals, for example, in the course of criminal punishment or during interrogation of suspected criminals is profoundly objectionable.

It would be too simplistic to take it for these reasons that all forms of 'external' prohibition are in principle acceptable, while anything 'internal' to the mind is outside the law's proper purview. The outside/inside metaphor is itself dubious, to say the least. More importantly, though, unduly burdensome restraints on what one is legally at liberty to do, and indeed unreasonable physical restraints on one's movement, deprive the autonomous agent of the opportunity to exercise free

[1] H L A Hart, *Law, Liberty and Morality* (Oxford: Oxford University Press, 1963) 17–24.

self-government in action. A man in a cage might be able to preserve freedom of mind, but this would hardly be a model of what it is like for a person to have an autonomous existence. That only external constraint should be exercised does not mean that all external constraint is acceptable. So far as concerns the 'internal', the law necessarily has regard to states of mind such as intention or recklessness in defining crimes, and may have regard to motive both in respect of mitigation and in respect of aggravation of penalties. States of mind can also be relevant in public and private law, for example where it is in question whether somebody acted in error, or where intention may be relevant in interpreting some kind of a deed.

The point is that ill-will itself is not punishable, but only ill-will that is expressed in some overt action, including unequivocal preparations to act (attempts and conspiracies). Ill-will may be a necessary but should never be a sufficient condition for coercive public intervention in a person's life. Careful attention to the drawing of this line is of high importance, never more so than when protective measures concerning terrorism and incitement to terrorist crimes are in view. Examples of points of danger are when 'glorification' of terrorist activity is made a crime, and when robust criticisms of religious tenets or practices risk being interpreted as incitements to religious hatred or insults of religion. The foundations of criminal law in the securing of the circumstances of peace and civility must be recalled here. Civility is a condition in which people trust each other to refrain from unprovoked violence, and where the excuse that some conduct of another amounts to provocation is subject to severe scrutiny. The liberty of persons as autonomous moral agents is one of the greatest achievements of civil society.

There can be problems for liberty arising from branches of law other than the criminal. Public law in its distributive functions and in schemes for protection of health or the environment may become excessively intrusive. Not all that is genuinely for the good—even the common good—need be brought within the domain of the state. For indeed subsidiarity is one important element in justice. Whatever can be as effectively achieved by individual effort or in families or through local or regional governments or non-governmental agencies as by the central agencies of a state should be left for management at the relevant 'lower' level. This amounts to a principle about how to distribute liberty of action and liberty of initiative in pursuit of the good. The principle of subsidiarity[2] is not a rival to distributive justice, but a part of it.

Another way to indicate what limits must be set to the reach of a legal system into the sphere of personal moral autonomy looks to justice itself as implying a restrictive condition. Law-makers and judges may face a perennial temptation to enforce moral duties as such. In response, it can be demanded that they restrict

---

[2] Cf K Endo, 'The Principle of Subsidiarity: from Johannes Althusius to Jacques Delors', Hokkaido Law Review 43 (1994) 553–652; J Finnis, *Natural Law and Natural Rights* (Oxford: Clarendon Press, 1980) 146, 169, 194–197; N MacCormick, *Who's Afraid of a European Constitution?* (Exeter: Imprint Academic, 2005) 62–68, on subsidiarity in the European constitution.

themselves to overseeing the fulfilment of duties of justice. Justice as a virtue of private persons consists in performing (for whatever motive) the duties one owes to other persons or, under reasonable provisions of public law, to the state. The duties in question have to be ones in respect of actions and activities, not in respect of the spirit in which they are undertaken. In this, duties of justice contrast with those of, for example, benevolence, or love (charity), or modesty. To do those things which are duties of love or benevolence cannot properly be coerced, if only because genuine benevolence and love require freely made and full voluntary commitment to the relevant other. People cannot be coerced by law into loving their neighbours, since coerced 'love' is no love at all.[3] But they can be properly restrained by law from overt actions expressive of hatred or contempt, especially where such hatred or contempt is directed at persons distinguished by such characteristics as race, or colour, or ethic, or national origin, or religious affiliation, and where the manner of expression is calculated to provoke fear and possible retaliation. The requirements of civil peace again come to the surface of attention.

15.3 Religion, Liberty, and Law

If it is not proper to use law to make people love their neighbours, can it be used to make them love God or to honour Him according to the correct form of divine worship and observance? In a quite startling way, this ancient question has assumed a new urgency in the context of religious tensions emerging in the early twenty-first century. Yet it is difficult to conceive of a benevolent and omnipotent and all-knowing divine being (Allah, or Jehovah, or Yahweh, or the Godhead in trinity) to whom the tributes of coerced acts of worship would be in any way welcome. Far less can one conceive of such a being whose divine completeness would be in any way diminished by human neglect or even active blasphemy. If sin is harmful, it can only be harmful to the sinner's own person and those in the surrounding community affected by it. Divine omnipotence could not be diminished one jot or tittle thereby.

These considerations suggest that there are strong religious arguments against the enforcement of religious belief and forms of worship. This would remain so, even if it were universally acknowledged that one particular prophetic or other revelation of religious truth and of proper religious observance was uniquely the correct one, putting all others in the shade except so far as consistent with this perfect truth. In the world as it is, no such universal acknowledgement exists. However respectfully they conduct themselves towards each other, the leaders of the great faiths and of different sects within them necessarily contradict each

[3] N MacCormick, 'A Moralistic Case for A-Moralistic Law?' Valparaiso University Law Review 20 (1985) 1–41; Z Bankowski, *Living Lawfully: love in law and law in love* (Dordrecht: Kluwer Academic, 2001).

other. Each has a revelation or insight that uniquely captures what the others grasp in some less complete or correct fashion. For each, the others see the clear truth at best only through a glass darkly.

It appears that few impulses felt by human beings are stronger than those summoned up by the demands of faith and religious loyalty. Crusades, and jihads, and wars of religion; civil wars between upholders of rival faiths or rival versions of essentially the same faith—these litter the pages of our history books and account for a distressingly large portion of the human blood humans have spilt in savage wars. In the perspective of autonomous morality, there are conclusive arguments against using coercion or brainwashing to inculcate into any person any particular religious view, or any particular anti-religious view. Regardless of autonomous morality, it is monstrously imprudent to do so, because each coercive intervention calls forth acts of bitter resistance, often against apparently overwhelming odds. God, who knows with certainty who is correct in matters of faith and religious observance, cannot be presumed to wish the slaughter of honest unbelievers, or believers in distorted versions of His truth. For this could not be the wish of a benevolent deity, who understands the honesty of those who are in honest error. And it is they who are most prone to fight to the end for their honest convictions.

Mutual tolerance of different creeds, confessions, and practices is thus not only a necessary duty under the principles of autonomous morality. It seems to be a necessary religious duty in any religion that attributes universal benevolence to the divine being. Yet even those who believe there is no divine being acknowledge that, if there were one, perfect benevolence would be a necessary attribute of such a being. All the more are all believers committed to the thesis of infinite divine benevolence. It therefore seems that there could not be a sincere and reasonable religious objection to religious tolerance. Therefore a critical moralist who demands that the law uphold religious tolerance cannot be guilty of an attack on anybody's religion.

A corollary of this conclusion is that states should stand as far clear as possible from matters of religious controversy. An increasing secularism has in fact been a feature of modern law-states. A ban on any establishment of religion by the federal authorities was written into the 1787 Constitution of the United States of America (not that this at that time prevented different religious establishments prevailing in various of the states of the union). The French revolution insisted upon the 'laïcité', that is the secular character, of the new republic, and this characteristic of the French state has continued to be proclaimed through into the constitution of the current Fifth Republic. The Indian Republic was founded on a refusal to privilege any particular religious establishment in a sub-continent of many faiths, though at the same time Pakistan came into existence as an Islamic state in circumstances of large scale population transfers, partition, and serious bloodshed and inter-communal violence. Australia, New Zealand, and Canada emerged from colonial status into independence as federations or states with no single establishment. This was rendered inevitable by the balance among the colonizing populations of Anglicans, Dissenters, Presbyterians, Roman Catholics, and persons of no faith, to say nothing of the position (usually ignored or side-lined at the time of new constitution-drafting) of indigenous peoples and their religious traditions. The United Kingdom itself was founded on the basis that English and Scots could not accept a single form of protestant establishment. Thus the Acts of Union solemnly promised that the Episcopalian forms of the Anglican Church and its articles of faith were to prevail in all time coming within England, while in Scotland the Presbyterian forms and confession of faith of the Church of Scotland were to be secured likewise in all time coming. Roman Catholic emancipation took a long time to achieve and, especially in Ireland, the long delay has left a bitter legacy. Meanwhile, the integration of Jews, Muslims, Sikhs, Hindus, Buddhists, Baha'ists, and persons of many other faiths and of none has proceeded over several generations, and the representative character of the two national churches grows more questionable though certain legal forms remain.

Other European states exhibit similar historical compromises which in many instances give to predominant forms of Christianity various forms of constitutional recognition and state support, while in various ways trying to come to terms with 'new' religions that flourish among relatively more recent immigrant sections of their populations. What no longer characterizes any law-state is the coercion of religious belief or (with a few exceptions) the imposition of civil or political disabilities on persons who do not subscribe to an established church or religion, even where some form of establishment survives. This has been one of the implications of the human rights culture that has emerged in the way traced in chapter 11. For all the other rights that international declarations, covenants, and conventions secure to us are to be enjoyed without any discrimination on religious grounds (or racial or ethnic ones, etc). Moreover the right to freedom of conscience and belief and to the free practice of religion figures among the declared rights.

There have been two streams of constitutional thought concerning this trend toward disestablishment, or non-establishment, of religion. One strand of concern has been to prevent the state having any power to intervene in religion. Disestablishment is a hedge that protects the pursuit of true religion and/or religious truth from the interfering hands of secular politicians and other officials of state. The other strand takes the other view, that churches and church-persons are only too likely to seek to exercise an illegitimate hold over the institutions of the state, and use them to the disadvantage of other faiths and sects. On the former view, establishment of religion corrupts the church; on the latter, it distorts the proper functions of the state.[4] Even those forms of religious

---

[4] M De Wolfe Howe, *The Garden and the Wilderness: religion and government in American constitutional history* (Chicago; University of Chicago Press, 1965) 6–15, contrasting the view of Roger Williams, who wanted a secure boundary to protect church from state, with that of Thomas Jefferson, who wanted to keep priests and ministers out of government. This is a contrast familiar in more than one constitutional setting.

establishment that persist in European states (another legacy, it may be remarked, of the Peace of Westphalia) do so in a highly mitigated way that diminishes the power of secular authorities on matters of religious belief and preferment to religious offices. They also preclude the exercise of undue political influence by prelates, priests, and ministers of religion. A good example of such a minimalist 'establishment' is found in the Church of Scotland Act 1929, which frees that Church from state interference in spiritual and disciplinary matters, but also enshrines the acknowledgement by the Church of the state's proper authority in its secular domain.

In the ultimately inconclusive debates on establishing a European Constitution during the years 2002–2005, a hotly contested issue concerned how, if at all, to acknowledge the historical significance of Christianity in shaping the values and culture of Europe, including ideas of constitutionalism and human rights. Should the European Union then declare roundly that Europe has been a predominantly Christian continent, or expressly dedicate the Union to God according to a Christian conception of the godhead? Could it possibly do this in the same document as it includes a Charter of Rights that asserts equal religious liberty and respect for adherents of all faiths and none? In the end, the Preamble acknowledged the contribution of faith to the development of constitutional ideas. The Charter protected all religions and freedom of belief without discrimination, and the part of the Constitution dealing with the 'Democratic Life' of the Union granted to churches and other religious or secular associations a right to participation in the discussion and framing of policy alongside other representatives of 'civil society'. The European Union is a Union that has no single religious establishment, and has no prospect of acquiring one, which is much to be welcomed according to the argument advanced here.

Religious disestablishment, or non-establishment, or at the very most a minimalist form of historically given establishment, are requirements of a just state according to the conception of autonomous morality espoused in this book, and used to define the distinctiveness of morality from law. It may be said in a similar way that a kind of 'moral disestablishment', or minimalist 'moral establishment', is called for.[5] Law is morally loaded in all the ways we have noted, and contains an implicit aspiration to justice. That aspiration requires elements of distributive, retributive, and corrective justice, including recognition of subsidiarity as a part of justice. Yet it is no part of the law's or the state's function to rule the citizen's moral opinions or to interfere with the citizen's freedom of mind, of belief, and of conscience. The duties of justice (according to some reasonable conception of justice) can properly be exacted under sanctions of law. Beyond that, law may not go without degenerating towards tyranny.

---

[5] N MacCormick, *Legal Right and Social Democracy* (Oxford: Clarendon Press, 1982) ch 2 especially at 36–38; 'A Moralistic Case for A-Moralistic Law?' *Valparaiso University Law Review* 20 (1985) 1–41 especially at 11–18.

15.4 Law, Justice, and the Positivization of Human Rights

Because law ought to be just, there is always a risk of complacency concerning the law we actually have. If we are too inattentive to the promptings of critical morality, we may blind ourselves, or may just fail to notice, ways in which law is unjust when it does no harm to ourselves. There can indeed be unjust laws, and what is alarming about this is that they are perfectly genuine laws, upheld and enforced through the coercive power of the state. 'An unjust law is a corruption of law'[6]— yes, but it is real law that is thus corrupted. But how far can this corruption go? Are there no limits?

We might take the analogy of an urban water supply. Water supplies serve many purposes but include centrally the purpose of providing safe drinking water to the population served. All water supplies contain some impurities, but these have to be kept down to a level compatible with ordinary human health (leaving people with special sensitivities or special needs to make their own provision for these). Water supplies can however become more or less seriously contaminated. Still, contaminated water is really water—and by filtering it and boiling it one might be able to make it safe, if not actually palatable. But then is there not a point beyond which the contamination changes the character of what lies before us? So much chlorine might be spilled in at the purification plant that what we have is more properly described as hydrochloric acid than as water. Contaminated water can become so adulterated that it is no longer fit to be called water at all, even though the mixture before us still can be analysed as including water in its composition. At any rate, it is not water in the sense in which the term is used in the phrase 'water supply', because that phrase is partly defined by the (or a) purpose to which supplying water is orientated—namely, its being fit for human consumption.

If that analogy holds, it would seem that although many laws are in fact unjust or very imperfectly just, there could be contamination or corruption to a degree so extreme that it would remove a practice of governing from the description 'law' at all. We can read (with extreme horror) about the way Nazi death camps were run. We can acknowledge that a kind of order was sustained, so effectively indeed as to permit the commission of mass murder by industrial means on an until-then unbelievable scale. But are we constrained to call such a regime of governance 'law'? We can survey the conditions of chaotic dictatorship that obtained in, for example, Uganda under the rule of Idi Amin. Need we call such a mode of governance 'law' and can we possibly call that unhappy country in that period a 'law-state'? Given sufficient ruthlessness, a kind of order can be kept, but 'law and

---

[6] St Thomas Aquinas, *Summa Theologiae* (a concise translation, ed T McDermott) (London: Eyre and Spottiswoode in association with Methuen, 1989) I-II, q 95. So far, I have given the quotation in an incomplete form. We shall shortly confront the whole sentence: 'An unjust law therefore appears to be no longer legal but rather a corruption of law'. See also Finnis, *Natural Law and Natural Rights* 363–366.

order' no longer obtains—here is order of a kind surviving a breakdown of law and abandonment of any pretence at legality. Sometimes, the abandonment of legality has been triumphantly proclaimed, as by early Bolsheviks in the USSR, who considered 'law' and 'justice' to be superstructural elements of capitalism, producing the kind of false consciousness that could lead those oppressed by capitalism to suffer their oppression uncomplainingly.[7]

How then could we establish the point at which the wholesale abandonment of any pretension to justice brings already corrupted law to the point of being non-law, failed law, mere tyranny or simple anarchy? There is an obvious difficulty about answering this question. According to the idea of morality developed in the previous chapter, moral opinions and judgments have an inherently controversial and discursive character. The history of philosophy and the practice of politics reveal a considerable multiplicity of theories and conceptions of justice. All may agree that law ought to be just, and even perhaps that law could be defined as a practice of governance that ought to be just. More cautiously, one could at least hold that, given the character of institutional normative order in the context of states and associations of states, any reasonable morality has to include a demand for justice in the content and administration of law. Whichever way you put it, however, disagreement breaks out after this point. What is justice, what is injustice? How much (if any) inequality in the distribution of resources among people can be acceptable as just? What does justice require in the way of criminal procedure, with what provision for pre-trial, or pre-charge, detention, and questioning of criminal suspects? Is strict liability for certain kinds of damage to property ever just? Is it just to permit vicarious liability of an employer company for the wrongs done by its employees? Or is this a case of letting expediency defeat justice? Such questions can be multiplied almost infinitely, in the confident expectation that reasonable people can be found who will offer different reasonable answers to all of them. To find a defining point on a scale of injustice beyond which corrupt law ceases to be law at all looks like a hopeless task. At any rate, in the practical world it would not give much guidance to somebody—a judge, for example—wrestling with the question whether to class as 'law' or 'non-law' some morally questionable rule that a state prosecutor or a private individual demands that she apply in a given case.

There is, however, an important qualification to add here. There can be conflicting theories or judgments about what is just, both in general and in particular cases, even among reasonable persons deliberating reasonably. But this does not mean that all disagreements are reasonable. As was said in chapter 14, morality is discursive as well as controversial. Sound moral judgments or principles are ones that could be assented to in a context of uncoercive discussion among persons

[7] E B Pashukanis, *Law and Marxism: a general theory* (trans B Einhorn; ed, with introduction, C Arthur (London: Ink Links, 1978); cf R Cotterrell, *Law's Community* (Oxford: Clarendon Press, 1995) 121–126.

who acknowledge each other as equals and who seek to talk their way through to conclusions that ought to be acceptable to everybody involved. They ought to be so acceptable since everybody's interests and intuitions on the subject would have been taken into account in the process of working towards a conclusion. This, however, is a purely ideal picture of the emergence of moral opinions and principles from a discourse of equals. Real life never quite matches, or comes often all that close to, such a picture.

Nevertheless, it may be possible to detect kinds of approach to a problem, or kinds of solution adopted, that cannot be imagined to be capable of surviving in such a discourse.[8] These we may characterize as approaches and solutions that cannot reasonably be accepted as reasonable approaches or solutions at all. A rational person cannot accept that they could be conceived as rationally acceptable views. Whatever exactly we mean by 'race', claims for the perpetual subordination of members of one race to members of another, or for the subordination of women to men, seem to me to be examples of claims that cannot come into contention as reasonable claims at all. In some circumstances of ignorance about human genetics it is possible to conceive of people being unable to perceive their unreasonableness, but in fact they are and always have been radically unreasonable.

This makes it possible to state what in principle is the line beyond which governmental arrangements in a state cease to be properly classifiable as law, or particular rules lose the character of legality. That is, if what is done cannot be accounted for under any possible conception of justice that could reasonably be adopted or advocated by a reasonable person willing to subject his or her beliefs to discursive scrutiny, then what is thus done by way of rules and practices of governance would not properly count as law.[9]

Even if that is clear as a matter of principle, it is bound to be vague in practice. It would be pretty controversial to apply even if everybody were to accept it as a matter of principle. For sure, we cannot find in this principle a clear and uncontroversial line that sets the limits of law. This is what makes particularly significant the developments discussed in chapter 11 concerning constitutional charters of fundamental rights that exist in so many contemporary states and concerning international declarations, covenants, and conventions safeguarding fundamental human rights, or rights fundamental to particular supra- or trans- national entities such as the European Union. These are all instruments with strong commonalty though not identity of content. They contrive to 'positivize' what would otherwise be controversial and inexact moral (or 'natural') rights. They turn a morally controversial limit on law into a positive, institutional, and authoritative set of legal limits.

---

[8] R Alexy, *A Theory of Legal Argumentation* (trans R Adler and N MacCormick) (Oxford: Clarendon Press, 1988) 287–289.

[9] Cf R Alexy, *The Argument from Injustice: a reply to legal positivism* (trans B Litschewski Paulson and S Paulson) (Oxford: Clarendon Press, 2002), developing an argument by Gustav Radbruch.

As usual, there is a price to pay, a loss of autonomy by decision-makers of several kinds, a loss of absolute sovereign autonomy of states. Populist journalists and politicians can decry as essentially alien and undesirable the 'rights culture' that ties the hands of states with a war on terrorism to fight, or whatever. Yet surely deep respect is due to this development. Acknowledging that we cannot clearly establish abstract principles that settle clear limits to law, surely we do better to try to establish a positive set of limits, with tribunals of judgment that sit outside the framework of any state but are representative of many. The European Court of Human Rights is a good example of such a tribunal. No national law is legitimately binding as law if it is judged by such a tribunal to violate any one of the fundamental human rights contained in the Convention (or it might be 'Covenant', or 'Charter', or even 'Universal Declaration'). Only states willing to cut themselves loose from the Council of Europe and the European Union, and to forgo the advantages that membership brings, can evade this positivized system of natural law. To have achieved this is to have achieved both a precious advance in civilization and the basis for a fresh appreciation of the character of law as institutional normative order in the context of the sovereign—or post-sovereign—state.

15.5 Law and its Implicit Pretension to Justice

Are there further arguments whereby to bolster up the claim that there is some kind of necessary pretension to justice built into the work of legal institutions? It seems so. Such arguments draw attention to implicit pretensions or claims that appear to be necessarily bound up with performance of the interactive roles of the law-making, judicial, and executive institutions or agencies of the state. Legislatures elected or appointed in procedurally elaborate ways can deliberate in complex and sequenced steps toward enacting certain normatively intelligible sentences into being 'laws'. These laws fall to be applied—and, necessarily, interpreted—by the courts, whose decisions to this effect are normally considered to have some weight as precedents. Government organs and agencies pursue policies within the scope of the discretion available to them under the laws and subject to some kind of answerability before the legislature.

Much of what such agencies actually do, or indeed can do, consists of the issuance of various forms of linguistic utterance—what are sometimes called 'speech acts'.[10] Once they issue general norms as laws or more individualized ones as general or special orders and commands clad with legal authority, the actual physical activity of following these up rests in other hands. Less exalted officials and agencies, civil and military, are charged with ensuring their faithful observance. As agencies established under a constitution, and exercising under the constitution powers specifically in respect of the law—its enactment, application,

---

[10] J Searle, *Speech Acts* (Cambridge: Cambridge University Press, 1969).

or executive enforcement—their speech acts necessarily have a certain character, and involve certain background assumptions. The background assumptions include what J L Austin called 'felicity conditions'.[11]

A person who blows a whistle can be understood (including self-understood) as penalizing a player for being offside only if a game exists in which there is an offside rule. It must also be the case that this person is actually exercising office as a referee in a specific ongoing game played under the rules of that game, and considers a player to have intervened from an offside position. So likewise, an act of legislating, or purporting to legislate (or, respectively, judging or purporting to judge a civil or criminal case) can intelligibly be performed only in the context of a legal system by a person who credibly purports to be exercising relevant authority within this system.

These reflections indicate why certain pretensions, certain implicit claims, seem necessarily built-in to legal-institutional activities involved in the creation of legal norms.[12] Any person or assembly which expresses itself as enacting and promulgating the law enshrined in a certain text that it enacts must necessarily in so doing purport to be the holder of a constitutional position appropriate to this activity. They purport to have constitutional authority, so far as concerns preconditions of their being able to legislate. So far as concerns the legislative output, they purport to be legislating on subject matters on which they are constitutionally competent to legislate. They likewise purport to be duly observant of any binding side-constraint on the exercise of authority, such as required respect for fundamental rights in the constitution or in an international convention of some kind. Is there anything else?

In the spirit of the present book's cumulative arguments, we must surely take note that there has also to be some kind of tacit representation concerning the content of the enactment. It is after all supposed to be a law, so it ought to be readable as containing prohibitions, positive mandates, empowerments, and the like of an intelligible kind. More than that, perhaps they have to be cast in a way that is compatible with the legislators behaving in a way appropriate to the idea of lawmaking. For example, legislation often bears a title like 'Administration of Justice Act', but never 'Administration of Injustice Act'. Sometimes a body of opinion in the country regards as deeply unjust a newly introduced law—for example, a 'Countryside Alliance' may condemn as deeply unjust laws they believe to be inspired by fastidious townspeople laying down a ban on fox-hunting with packs of

---

[11] J L Austin 'Performative Utterances' in Austin, *Philosophical Papers* (ed J O Urmson and G J Warnock) (Oxford: Clarendon Press, 1961) 220–229. Cf J L Austin, *How to Do Things with Words* (Oxford: Clarendon Press, 1962).

[12] For a cautionary note, see Carsten Heidemann 'Law's Claim to Correctness' in S Coyle and G Pavlakos (eds), *Jurisprudence or Legal Science?* (Oxford: Hart Publishing, 2005) 127–146. Heidemann is perhaps unduly sceptical about the degree to which a legislator's claim to being legally correct necessarily evinces some aspiration to justice, at least a purported aspiration to justice. Cf E Melissaris, 'The Limits of Institutionalised Legal Discourse' Ratio Juris 18 (2005) 464–483.

hounds. We will look in vain, however, for Acts entitled 'Unjust Ban on Hunting with Dogs Act 2005', or 'Unfairly Repressive Law concerning Attacks on Religion', to take another current case.

This may evidence nothing more than that it would be politically self-defeating to use such titles in legislation, since one would at one and the same time enjoin obedience to a norm while suggesting that the injunction is an unjust, partial, and unfair one, thus lacking moral legitimacy. It is arguable, however, that, true as that point is, the matter cuts yet deeper. The point is not that all legislation does achieve justice by any criterion of justice, but that all legislation ought to express a coherent, even if contestable, conception of justice. One theory of justice says that needless infliction of pain on any sentient creature is unjust, and the prevention of human activity that inflicts such needless suffering is demanded by justice. Another view sets human freedom higher in the scales of justice than animal suffering, especially in cases of pest control and sustaining environmental balance. Only legislators convinced of the former view in competition with the latter can sincerely participate in enacting the law banning hunting with hounds. It would not only be politically silly to call it an unjust law in the moment of enacting it. It would also be conceptually inept and self-refuting.

This may be connected to certain essentials of law-applying activity. Courts in some legal traditions are known as 'courts of justice', or 'of justiciary', and judges may also be called 'Justices'. '*La justice*', '*die Justiz*' may be terms that denote the system and apparatus of judicial application of law, and so on. The task of judges and courts is not only to apply rules issued by the legislature but, more generally, 'to do justice according to law'. This duty of judges to act justly may sometimes sit uncomfortably with their duty under the constitution to defer to the laws enacted by the legislature, for enactments may express a conception of justice that is repugnant to the judges' own, or they may indeed express no satisfactory conception of justice at all, being in that case more or less thoroughly bad laws.

An adequate theory of legal reasoning involved in the application of law and the justification of law-applying decisions shows what kinds of reasons are sufficiently good taken individually and cumulatively to genuinely justify a decision.[13] For laws to play the part they should play in a process of reasonable decision-making, they have to have a certain character. They must be capable of interpretation as in some way oriented to the common good of the persons governed by the law, and, so far as possible, others affected by it. The pursuit of particular goods has to be within the constraint of some reasonable conception of justice.

For this reason, a certain pretension to justice, that is, a purported aspiration to be achieving justice (even if this be the mask of a more partisan or sinister intent) is necessarily evinced in the very act of law-making in the context of a law-state. For here legislative deliberation is carried on in public and open to

---

[13] For a recent account of this built on the institutional theory of law, see N MacCormick, *Rhetoric and the Rule of Law* (Oxford: Oxford University Press, 2005).

critical consideration by journalists, commentators, academics, and, not least important, all citizens and especially those who are politically active. Law-making acts are acts which implicitly purport to advance some aspect of the common good consistently with the constraints of a reasonable conception of justice, or to advance some aspect of such a conception as itself a component element of the common good.

It is instructive to consider in this light how important it may be to insist on open and public justification of legislative proposals, and of thorough debate concerning amendments to such proposals. Public deliberation creates a context in which the proponent of a measure has to state some reason why it is for the common good to enact this into law. One can just about imagine for example a public statement made around 1942 by some Nazi official about the desirability of re-settling Jews outside Germany, and some argument being offered for this. A proposal that the deportation of these persons take place, not for mere resettlement, but for systematic gassing and incineration is barely imaginable in any public forum. Even in the dreadful times in which this was actually done, albeit by the orders of a domestically unchallengeable one-party dictatorship, no public justification or even acknowledgement of the extermination programme was ever attempted. There are things which humans can do yet which it appears they cannot avow. They certainly cannot avow the doing of them in the name and forms of law.

All this further reinforces the conclusion that notwithstanding the conceptual distinction between institutional law and autonomous morality, there are moral minima that have to be satisfied by anything that one can acknowledge as law. Any exact test for this has to be a positivized one, such as has been achieved by means of entrenched and justiciable human rights. Without such a positive test, the limit is an always disputable one, but the limit-in-principle established above could still have serious practical consequences in the context of moral dilemmas faced by judges and others living in regimes of corrupted law.[14]

15.6 Some Observations on 'Positivism' and 'Natural Law'

We have already commented on the 'posited' or 'positive' character of general legal norms enacted by a legislature and of more specific or even individual decisions handed down in implementation of law by the executive and the judiciary acting within their own proper spheres. The institutional character of institutional normative order has been a running theme of this book, and the 'positive' character of law is simply another way of expressing this. It may indeed be that there are some moral codes or ways of living that have a similar positive or institutional character, and 'positive morality' might be a suitable name for such codes. Some

---

[14] Cf D Dyzenhaus, *Hard Cases in Wicked Legal Systems* (Oxford: Clarendon Press, 1991).

forms of religious observance might, for example, involve some such code, but it would be a travesty to say that religions are necessarily or in most cases properly characterized in this way. The autonomous conception of morality developed in this work stands anyway in sharp contrast with both positive morality and positive law. It is morality thus conceived that is necessarily distinct from institutional law.

But autonomous morality makes certain demands of law, and commends the withholding of the appellation 'law' from any positive enactments that absolutely violate any reasonable conception of justice. The arguments for this position have been stated in the preceding two sections of the present chapter. On this analysis, laws are not necessarily just, or good in other ways. They may be grounded in grave misconceptions about the common good, and yet fulfil the law's own internal tests for legal validity. But there is some moral minimum without which purported law becomes un-law. 'No longer legal but rather a corruption of law.' Then the duty of a decent human being is to evade, disobey, even resist to the extent that this is feasible. In this situation, 'Obey punctually, but censure freely' is then wrong on both its legs—the opportunity for free criticism ('censure') of the practices of government is unavailable, and the grounds for voluntary obedience do not exist.

The school of thought known as 'legal positivism', at any rate in its more austere and rigorous forms,[15] absolutely excludes the possibility that there is any moral minimum that is necessary to the existence of law as such. The positive character of law is all there is to it. Conversely, the question of the moral value of obedience to law is always an open one. According to that conception of legal positivism, the present version of institutional theory is non-positivist, or, if you wish, 'post-positivist'.[16] Conversely, if the universe of human thought is necessarily divided into two mutually exclusive camps, such that anyone who admits any moral minimum to be essential to the existence of law belongs outside the positivist camp and in that of its rival, this theory belongs in that rival camp. Believers in this two-way-divided universe of jurisprudence assign to the category 'natural law' any theory that fails their austere test for positivism. Such believers will therefore characterize the present work as a form of 'natural law'.

In truth, such dichotomies are rarely revealing of any important truth. Much of the analysis and argumentation of this book has emerged from its author's reflection about, and indeed intellectual inheritance from, the work of H L A Hart and Hans Kelsen, both of whom are typically taken to be paradigms for legal

---

[15] See the discussion of the 'separability thesis' in L Greene, 'General Jurisprudence: A Twenty-Fifth Anniversary Essay' Oxford Journal of Legal Studies 25 (2005) 565–580, at 570–573; and see M Kramer, *Law without Trimmings* (Oxford: Clarendon Press, 1994), W J Waluchow, *Inclusive Legal Positivism* (Oxford: Clarendon Press, 1999), and J Coleman, *The Practice of Principle* (Oxford: Clarendon Press, 1999).

[16] On 'post-positivism', see V Villa, 'A Definition of Legal Positivism' in M Pavcnik and G Zanetti (eds), *Challenges to Law at the End of the 20th Century: Legal Systems and Legal Science* (ARSP-Beiheft 70, Vol IV) (Stuttgart: Franz Steiner Verlag, 1997) 22–29; V Villa, 'Legal Theory and Value Judgments', Law and Philosophy, 16 (1997) 447–77.

positivism. In its intellectual inheritance, and in the particular contrast drawn between the positive, institutional character of state law and the autonomous character of morality, this book belongs in the same tradition as those of Hart and Kelsen, and, I hope, represents an advance upon its predecessors. On the other hand, various contemporaries have pretty convincingly established that there is a need for improvement and correction to some of the tenets of Hartian or Kelsenian positivism. Thinkers such as John Finnis,[17] David Dyzenhaus,[18] Derek Beyleveld and Roger Brownsword,[19] Robert Alexy,[20] and others could in various ways characterize themselves as belonging in one or another school of 'natural law'. Ronald Dworkin, so far as I know, would reject any such characterization but has also made enormously important points in his critique of positivism. Moreover, the great classics of Thomistic natural law and the writings of seventeenth and eighteenth century jurists concerning natural jurisprudence[21] and the law of nature yield many insights into the character both of law and of morality that no sensible person could neglect. It is better to reject the aforesaid dichotomy as based on a misleading account of the history of legal ideas than to trouble responding to the question: 'Are you a positivist or a natural lawyer?'. The question in what sense 'human nature' or 'the nature of things' can support arguments about good moral principles or sound legal foundations is one we have not had to pursue in the present work. The 'natural' character of institutional normative order is not here in issue, though it is certainly natural at least in the sense of being neither miraculous nor unusual.

It is perhaps most sensible to say that this book presents an institutional theory of law, and that this theory draws inspiration both from some strands of thought previously advanced by self-proclaimed 'legal positivists' and from others derived from 'natural law' theorizing. It is post-positivist, if not anti-positivist.

---

[17] Finnis, *Natural Law and Natural Rights* 363–366.
[18] Dyzenhaus, *Hard Cases in Wicked Legal Systems*.
[19] D Beyleveld and R Brownsword, *Law as a Moral Judgment* (London: Sweet and Maxwell, 1986).
[20] R Alexy, *The Argument from Injustice: a reply to legal positivism* (trans B Litschewski Paulson and S Paulson) (Oxford: Clarendon Press, 2002).
[21] See, eg, K Haakonssen, *Natural Law and Moral Philosophy: from Grotius to the Scottish Enlightenment* (Cambridge: Cambridge University Press, 1996).

16

Laws and Values: Reflections on Method

16.1 Introduction

The opening chapter of this book gave a short account of the ground to be covered in it, and a brief description of the way the inquiry would proceed. It concluded:

Whether an interpretative-analytical study of the present kind is of any value is a debatable question. Rather than enter into this debate here, however, it seems wiser first to present our account of law and let readers judge for themselves whether they find it illuminating for whatever purposes they bring to the reading of it.

The promise then made was to pick up in the concluding chapter a discussion of the assumptions about method—indeed about methodology—that underlie the main theses of the book. The time has come to redeem this promise.

The discussion of these assumptions has six main parts. The first deals with whether it is appropriate to start out with a definition, whether this entails a strongly conventionalist approach to legal theory and, if so, whether one necessarily falls prey to the 'semantic sting'. The second tries to show how analysis contributes to the explanatory goals of explanatory definition, and confronts the question whether the theory that emerges is in some undesirable way anti-pluralistic. The third advances an account of the validity of legal knowledge as knowledge of institutional facts. The fourth develops the thesis that institutional facts are also interpretative facts, and require an account of interpretation that draws on theories about focal meaning and constructive interpretation. The fifth returns to the issue of the gap between ideal law and social reality and the need for awareness of the findings of empirical social sciences in relation to legal institutions. The sixth rebuts a possible charge concerning eclecticism or syncretism in methods advocated in the preceding five sections. The way is then clear for a statement of final conclusions—and then for a coda about the persisting self-doubts of legal scholarship.

16.2 Definition, Conventionalism, and the 'Semantic Sting'

The starting point of the present work was an 'explanatory definition': 'law is institutional normative order'. Some might say that starting in this way is starting from a grave mistake. H L A Hart, for example, warned several times against reliance on definition as a starting or a finishing point for legal theory. His inaugural lecture 'Definition and Theory in Jurisprudence'[1] deprecated 'traditional' definition *per genus et differentiam*, that assigns the defined term to a more general class and then accounts for its specific features separating it form other members of the class. This does not work, he says, for concepts that are themselves highest-level classes (*summa genera* in Latin), nor for typical normative terms in legal usage, and yet other ways of elucidating our terms might be available, such as the Benthamite approach of defining by 'paraphrasis', explaining the way a term is used by paraphrasing it rather than defining it directly. In *The Concept of Law* he returned to the same theme in a slightly different way. He argued that one should give an account of certain very important features that are present in most cases of what we call law, or central cases, and use these to clarify rather than strictly to define the concept, allowing for the inevitable vagueness and open texture of a term like 'law' and the presence of 'borderline cases' such as international law, primitive law, or customary law.[2] With at least one notable exception,[3] this Hartian opposition to definition seems to have established a broadly accepted methodological practice among English-speaking jurists in the last fifty years. Yet it is open to challenge.

The genus 'normative order'[4] is clearly a more general category than 'law', and to define law as a particular kind of normative order is therefore an obvious possibility. If the differentiating feature of being 'institutional' is also susceptible of satisfactory explanation, it would seem that the way forward is perfectly clear. Certainly, the approach to explanation of norms, normative order, and institutionality might be obscure, or circular, or in some way confused or confusing. If so, that would be a flaw in the execution of the explanations at which a practice of explanatory definition aims, not a proof of its unsuitability as a method. Anyway, chapters 1 and 2 above do not seem to be flawed in any of those ways.

The existence of borderline cases is hardly an objection, for just as there may be what seem to be borderline cases of 'law' so too these may prove to be borderline cases of institutional normative order. Open texture is as much a feature of the explanatory terms as of the term explained. Moreover, since explanatory definition

[1] Law Quarterly Review 70 (1954) 37–58; reprinted in H L A Hart, *Essays in Jurisprudence and Philosophy* (Oxford: Clarendon Press, 1983) 21–48; 'though theory is to be welcomed, the growth of theory on the back of definition is not' (at 25).

[2] Hart, *Concept of Law*, 12–15. William Twining shares this view, and shows that Karl Llewellyn was ahead of Hart's game in this respect. See W Twining, *Globalisation and Legal Theory* (London: Butterworths, 2000) 79–80.

[3] See R N Moles, *Definition and Rule in Legal Theory: a reassessment of H L A Hart and the positivist tradition* (Oxford: Basil Blackwell, 1987). In a different tradition, Robert Alexy concludes with a (summative) definition in his *The Argument from Injustice* (trans S Paulson and B Litschewski Paulson) (New York, NY: Oxford University Press, 2002) 127–130.

[4] The concept of normative order is also used by Hans Kelsen (to whom indeed I owe it)—see, eg, his *General Theory of Norms* (trans M Hartney) (Oxford: Clarendon Press, 1991) 214–215, as one among very many instances.

is also partly stipulative[5]—choosing one particular sense of the term to be defined and offering an explanation only of that—it is easy to account for other senses of the term that relate to the stipulated sense, but fall outside it. As noted in the Introduction, and as argued in chapter 14, 'law' in the sense of 'moral law' concerns normative order, but not institutional normative order. 'Law' in the sense of scientific law concerns some discerned causal order in nature, not a normative order. A good explanatory definition may in this way help rather than hinder a sensitive understanding of related but different senses of the term one seeks to explain. It acknowledges, but is not bound by, the always fluid conventions about the meaning and use of conceptual terms like 'law' found in natural languages like English.

Order in the sense of orderliness is not particularly problematic as an element of the explanation. It is once one comes down to the norm or the concept of the normative that a bedrock is reached of that which can be understood by acquaintance, and picked out by something like ostensive definition, but not made the subject of a further level of explanatory definition. This is a point to which we shall return in 16.3, below.

Meanwhile, let it be observed how an explanatory definition relates to a 'What is?' question. 'What is law?'—'It is institutional normative order, and now I shall explain to you what these terms mean.' Of these two sentences the former is an intelligible question, and the latter an intelligible, relevant, and potentially illuminating answer. If the explanation proceeds successfully, the questioner will have acquired an insight into the elements that make up a legal system. He or she will have acquired a new or an improved capability to pick out and perceive features— law and legal system—that are common to many states, though with many local differences. They will also be able to understand that these elements are also common to many organizations that are not states, but may be in various ways statelike. This is not a very exalted capability, but if the explanation is a richly textured one, it may yield quite a lot of new insight and wisdom.[6]

---

[5] There is after all such a thing as 'virtuous stipulation', as argued for by Andrew Halpin in 'Concepts, Terms, and fields of Enquiry' Legal Theory 4 (1998) 187 at 195–8. Cf Richard Robinson, *Definition* (Oxford: Clarendon Press, 1964). Robinson draws attention to one kind of 'real definition' that he thinks is better described as 'analysis' (171–180) Later, he adds that this may lead on into synthesis and then an attempt at improvement of concepts, saying 'Like the analysis . . . of concepts, the improvement of concepts is often a very difficult and groping operation . . . Every improvement of a concept carries along with it a stipulative redefinition of the word expressing the concept' (p 187). The 'explanatory definition' advanced here is put forward in that spirit. Brian Bix's account of 'the (various) purposes of conceptual definitions' seems also compatible with or perhaps even favourable towards the present approach: see B Bix, *Jurisprudence: Theory and Context* (London: Sweet & Maxwell, 4th edn, 2006) 19–25.

[6] Is this then an 'essentialist' claim as characterized and deprecated by Brian Tamanaha, *General Jurisprudence* 135–145? It is not so in the sense of discovering a single essence in whatever is conventionally called law. But it does depend on a view about the values which it is important to realize through the institutionalization of normative order in the context of the state and other partly statelike forms of organization. It is of the essence of law, I claim, that it *should*, not that it everywhere does, realize these values. This is a matter of 'focal meaning' as discussed at 16.6 below.

We may contrast a different kind of 'What is law?' question. 'Mrs Vo has had her pregnancy terminated by wrongful negligence, and seeks a remedy asserting the right to life of her lost child—what is the law on that?'[7] Here, the questioner seeks an answer to a concrete legal problem in some postulated jurisdiction. This questioner can get a satisfactory answer only from someone who knows or can find out relevant conventions, statutes, precedents, principles, and the like, who can offer a compellingly good or at least reasonably persuasive interpretation of these in relation to the actual or hypothetical case, and put that forward as the answer to the question. Ronald Dworkin has argued that there is no sensible or interesting 'What is law?' question that is not a more or less disguised version of this second, practical, type of question.[8] Surely this is mistaken. Once I understand what institutional normative order is, I can understand how norms contained within it bear upon concrete practical questions. I can then, indeed, proceed to raising and answering such questions. But the theoretical background to the practical questions is different, and a good answer to the theoretical question neither entails nor is entailed by a good answer to any one of the more or less infinite number of practical questions a life under law can throw up.[9]

It is important to emphasize the difference between the present approach and a conventionalist one. Doing so will also enable us to avoid falling prey to the 'semantic sting'.[10] Manifestly, any definition is about semantics, about what the defined word is taken to signify. Where definitions are proposed as a matter of conventional semantics, being 'lexical definitions',[11] they have a conversation-stopping quality. 'Why do you call the sky blue?' 'That's just what blue means— there is a range of colours that it is correct to call blue in English, and a cloudless sky in daytime is one of these.' End of argument. This conversation-stopping

---

[7] Cf *Vo* v *France* ECHR no 53924/00, §§41, 62–64, 70, 84. As a matter of European human rights law, there is no available remedy in such a case, according to the Grand Chamber of the European Court of Human Rights— ch 5 above, at n 10.

[8] R Dworkin, 'Hart's Postscript and the Character of Political Philosophy' Oxford Journal of Legal Studies 24 (2004) 1–37 at 3–5, 19–22.

[9] Halpin has also argued in 'The Methodology of Jurisprudence: Thirty Years off the Point' (Canadian Journal of Law and Jurisprudence 19 (2006) 67–105 at 91–2) that legal theorists have been mistaken in separating the theoretical and the practical questions in this way, and concentrating too much effort on the former: 'What are the appropriate roles for legal theory? Primarily, to clarify the means whereby the law expresses and attains the resolution of controversy. From which follows the role of illuminating within the continuing practice of law the potential directions which that resolution might take . . .'. This latter task is certainly an urgent one, and I have contributed to it in *Rhetoric and the Rule of Law* (Oxford: Oxford University Press, 2005), but it seems to me to presuppose the kind of theory attempted in the present book, not to make it redundant.

[10] This is Dworkin's term for the kind of conversation-stopping definitional move considered in the present paragraph. See *Law's Empire* at 45: 'People are its prey [the prey of the 'semantic sting'] who hold a certain picture of what disagreement is like and when it is possible. They think we can argue sensibly with one another if, but only if, we all accept and follow the same criteria for deciding when our claims are sound.' Myself, I think it is of value to discuss such criteria and explain reasons for adopting them; not that pre-existing agreement on them is necessary, nor that conversation with those who reject them is pointless.

[11] R Robinson, *Definition* (Oxford: Clarendon Press, 1964) 35–58.

quality applies whenever one engages, or attempts to engage, in recording and accurately reporting linguistic conventions, as dictionary-makers do. If they are right about a given word, then that is just what the word means (or means in one of its senses) and there is nothing further to discuss. We might want to study the phenomena to which the term conventionally refers, and to seek a better understanding of these phenomena. But the conventional (or 'lexical') definition cannot contribute anything to that, and the reason why the phenomena can be called 'law' (or whatever) is already given—that is what the word means in English.

To repeat, explanatory definitions are not in that way conventionalist.[12] As an explanatory definition, 'law is institutional normative order' does not purport to rest upon conventional semantics or to report some finding about the language-use of the average English speaker or even the average legally well-informed English speaker. Explanatory definitions are by no means conversation-stopping. They stand or fall on the quality of explanation that is offered to back them up. To propose such a definition is to essay the best, most attractive and most illuminating account available of the subject matter in view, and to propose on that account that for the purposes of the ongoing theoretical inquiry the term be used in this way rather than some different one. An audience's ability to comprehend and evaluate the explanation depends upon its members already having some convention-based (but perhaps for any given person more or less idiosyncratic) pre-understanding of the term defined. For each such person, the issue is whether the explanatory definition and the back-up explanation do offer an enriched, and perhaps somewhat altered, understanding compared with her/his starting point, or pre-understanding. Such an enhanced understanding is not the same as an enhanced capability for insightful, skilful, and persuasive work in answering practical questions within the legal domain, though it is not likely that understanding and skill will prove to be completely independent of each other.

16.3 Analytical Explanation and Legal Pluralism

The method of explanation used in this book has been an analytical one. Since law is supposed to be a kind of 'normative order', the explanation we give of it must first explain the elements of normative order. These elements are the norms whose observance (to some extent) renders interpersonal conduct to some extent orderly. Next, it must proceed to an explanation of institutions and institutionalization, thus building up the concept 'institutional normative order'. All this would fail as an explanation if the underlying idea of the 'norm' were unintelligible, for so then would be 'normative order'. 'Norm' is here the problematic term, not 'order' as distinct from 'disorder'. We do indeed confront in this something that is used in

---

[12] Hence the present approach rejects the kind of 'conventionalism' proposed by Tamanaha in *General Jurisprudence* 166–170.

explanation but that cannot itself be explained in the same way. Chapter 1 faced that problem by inviting the reader to reflect upon a practice with which she or he is assumed to be familiar in some context or another of everyday life. The practice was that of queuing at some point of service, and waiting to be served on the 'first come, first served' basis. This is a matter of mutual co-ordination that in its own narrow compass makes interaction more orderly, less threatening or chaotic than it might otherwise be.

Human beings are through-and-through norm-users, capable of achieving a kind of voluntary order among themselves by common observance of common norms. They are also capable of understanding this and reflecting upon the way they do this. The best explanation that can be offered is to bring a sufficiently vivid example into the consciousness of one's readers or hearers, so that they can confirm from their own experience this special aspect of universal human experience. Anyone who has read this book up to the present point must at least be conscious of being able to read a book and appraise an argument. Let such a person reflect also on the norms that structure language, or the critical reading of a text, as well as on the queue.

David Hume famously introduced into philosophical discussion the distinction between 'is' and 'ought', and the difficulty of explaining just what the difference is.[13] Thomas Reid acknowledged the point, but declared roundly that any person who understands the English language stands in no need of an explanation how to use the word 'ought', or indeed the word 'is'. It is a distinction immediately obvious to us.[14] Certainly, this seems so when we consider practical examples like queuing or speaking. One can bring together an assemblage of reminders that one hopes will draw to another's attention that of which she/he is already aware, in what may not yet be an articulate way. So far as concerns norms, I offer the still-puzzled reader nothing better than a further reading of chapter 1, considered yet more attentively than before.

What then of institutionalization? This, according to the suggestion in chapter 2, occurs whenever we encounter a two- or more tier normative practice. Not merely is there a queue, but there is a system for managing the queue (for example, the numbered ticket-roll) and there are queue managers who ensure that customers get served in their proper turn according to rules adopted about the managed queue. The existence of norms authoritatively issued as rules depends on this kind of tiered practice, and in this setting we therefore find norm-givers as well as norm-users. Nevertheless, the most basic understanding of norms ought to be in

---

[13] D Hume, *A Treatise of Human Nature* (ed L A Selby-Bigge, revised P H Nidditch) (Oxford: Clarendon Press, 2nd edn, 1978) 469–470 (Book III, Part I, s 1, last three paras).

[14] T Reid, *Essays on the Active Powers of the Human Mind* (with introduction by B Brody) (Cambridge Mass and London: MIT Press, 1969) at 470–471 (Essay V, ch 7). Responding to Hume's demand that 'ought and ought not be explained', Reid says, 'To a man that understands English, there are surely no words that require explanation less. Are not all men taught from their early years, that they ought not to lie, nor steal, nor swear falsely?'

terms of the norm-user, for we can conceive of many contexts of norm-use without the presence of any norm-giving authority, but the converse is inconceivable—norm-givers without norm-users. Hans Kelsen, after tackling heroically the 'great mystery' of the ought,[15] increasingly fell away from his initial insight and in his later work sought to explain norms as species of imperatives,[16] seeking to re-open one of the great blind alleys in the history of practical philosophy generally and legal philosophy more particularly. In the work he did about the 'internal aspect' of rule-governed conduct, H L A Hart contributed immeasurably to a user-oriented understanding of norms. Perhaps his later work on 'peremptory reasons'[17] represented a turning-away from his own best insights, but never to the extent of Kelsen's apostasy on this point.

Anyway, institutionalization can be viewed on the small scale or on the grand scale, as grand, for example, as in the case of a state's constitution or the founding treaty or charter of a great international or supranational organization. There is no need to repeat the detail of chapter 3 here. What is worth stressing, however, is the central place held by the constitution as the adopted or, in some few cases such as that of the United Kingdom, evolved,[18] set of framework norms that define and empower the various institutional agencies of state, and set limits on the powers they can exercise. This is not a 'rule of recognition', though courts empowered by a constitution may each be envisaged as working according to some criteria settling what rules and principles they should apply as law. A constitution is a compendiously instituting-and-empowering set of interlocking norms, usually in the form of explicit rules backed up by always contestable ideological underpinnings of the kind that judges and jurists articulate in the form of 'constitutional principles' or 'fundamental values of the constitution'.

Why are some formally adopted constitutions actually functional ones? What makes constitutions work, when they do work? Obviously, what makes them work is the will of whichever people conceive the constitution to be their constitution, when there are enough such people, sufficiently agreed (though certainly never unanimous) about the ideological underpinnings. What they agree on, however articulately or tacitly, is a common norm that they ought to respect the constitution thus underpinned, and that anyone purporting to exercise public power must do so only in the terms permitted by the constitution. Self-aware sharing of such a norm (not necessarily made explicit at all, or in the same terms by all participants) amounts to a custom (like the inarticulate queuing norm considered in chapter 1). The custom can be formulated in some such terms as: 'everyone in state *S* ought to co-operate in ensuring the state functions in terms of

---

[15] Cf references in MacCormick, *Questioning Sovereignty* 1. See also Kelsen, *Hauptprobleme der Staatsrechtslehre* (Tübingen: J C Mohr, 1911) 441.

[16] H Kelsen, *General Theory of Norms* (trans M Hartney) (Oxford: Clarendon Press, 1991) 1–3.

[17] H L A Hart, *Essays on Bentham* (Oxford: Clarendon Press, 1982) 253–255.

[18] E Wicks, *The Evolution of a Constitution: Eight Key Moments in British Constitutional History* (Oxford: Hart Publishing, 2006).

constitution *C* according to established principles', and one can very properly call this a basic norm. Kelsen, who became bogged down in the 'act of will' approach to explaining norms, argued that custom itself can be norm-creating only if it is authorized by some norm.[19] Adoption of the norm-user's perspective as fundamental to the reality of norms and the normative purges this error. It also makes it clear that although a basic norm is indeed presupposed in the case of any working constitution, it is not a *mere* presupposition. It is the content of a living custom, a convention that can be articulated as an explicit norm.

These reflections on constitution and basic norm may give rise to a fresh criticism. The theory put forward might be characterized as anti-pluralist, being hopelessly narrowly focused on the writer's own state-law, or sub-state-law, taken in juxtaposition with closely similar forms of law from other states in the same 'western' legal tradition?[20] Is this just another version of what William Twining has justly castigated as the 'country and western' approach to jurisprudence? Should one not, at a time of acknowledged globalization of legal and economic activity, entertain a broader picture? Should one continue to treat states as the natural and necessary focus of concern for lawyers, and ignore the many other forms of normative ordering which are alive in the world today? It would be distressing if such criticisms were found to be just, for the present work belongs to a series on 'Law, State, and Practical Reason' which aims (among other things) to contribute to a recognition of the extent to which legal order has shifted 'beyond the sovereign state'. In this way it seeks to contribute to the tide of contemporary opinion in favour of legal pluralism, not to obstruct it.[21] One point which has been repeated throughout this book is that law as institutional normative order can be found in many contexts other than that of each single state. This is so, both because of the way international and transnational organizations have developed law beyond state boundaries, and because many of the organizations active in civil society have their own internal institutional ordering. States may indeed claim primacy over such organizations (eg, churches, international sporting associations), but the organizations need not in turn, and sometimes do not, acknowledge that primacy in the form in which it is asserted by one or another state. States represent one form of institutional normative order arranged around and through a typical range of institutions of the kind discussed in chapter 3. Empires ancient and modern, feudal kingdoms, absolute monarchies, and tribal societies did not have the same institutional framework, but that is not to say they had no

---

[19] Kelsen, *Pure Theory* 225–226; for a sharply different, and preferable view, see J Bjarup, 'Social Action: the Foundation of Customary Law' in P Ørebech, F Bosselman, J Bjarup et al, *The Role of Customary Law in Sustainable Development* (Cambridge: Cambridge University Press, 2005) 89–157, especially at 135–151.

[20] W Twining, 'Comparative Law and Legal Theory: the Country and Western Tradition' in I Edge (ed), *Comparative Law in Global Perspective* (Ardsley, NY: Transnational Publishers Inc, 2000) 21–76.

[21] On pluralism, cf Twining, *Globalisation and Legal Theory* 224–233; Tamanaha, *General Jurisprudence of Law and Society* 192–200.

institutional framework, and no institutional normative order. The same goes for contemporary theocratic states.

Law as institutional normative order comes with many variations of form and content. Moreover, as has been said repeatedly, no advocacy is here offered in favour of abandoning the use of the word 'law' in contexts of non-institutional ordering, or indeed (in the case of scientific laws) non-normative ordering. The author of a work of jurisprudence cannot, and should not try to, place some kind of ban on the richness and creative ambiguity of a fluid and always evolving natural language like English. There are interesting analogies as well as traceable differences between different kinds of 'law' recognized both in everyday speech and in more technical literature.

It remains the case, however, that in the world that we currently inhabit states have a very prominent role in the articulation and administration of public force. Enforceable law and thus enforceable rights tend therefore to be those that belong to, or are recognized and in some way adopted by, state tribunals and agencies. This means that state-law still matters very acutely to very many people and is naturally a central point of attention for most people who engage in professional practice of the law. That justifies the approach taken here, not of arrogating the term 'law' or the concept of law solely to the mastery of one state or all states, but of presenting a theory in which the comparative practical importance of state law can be seen for what it is.

16.4 Legal Knowledge and Institutional Facts

This book has at several points acknowledged the power of Niklas Luhmann's system-theoretical thesis that any system of communication and communicative action operates with some fundamental binary distinction that it uses in all its operations. The institutional theory advanced here proposes the distinction between right and wrong, more strictly, between wrong and not-wrong, as the fundamental one in a normative order. In developed law, of course, this further bifurcates between criminal wrongs that are punishable and the various forms of civilly wrongful conduct that can lead to the imposition of civil remedies of various sorts. Moreover, in the context of two- or more tier institutional order, there are powers as well as rights and wrongs. This introduces the valid/invalid opposition as a distinct dimension of normative judgment.

'Wrong' enables us to define 'duty', the duty to refrain from any wrongful act and to do each thing that it is wrong not to do. The concept of a duty's being in given circumstances owed to another person, equivalent to the idea that it would be a wrong to that person to breach this duty, enables us to understand 'passive rights'. Since one may do what is not wrong, the idea of an active right or liberty can be presented by simple negation of 'duty'. All this presupposes that we can identify the bearers of rights and duties, potential exercisers of powers, those whom the law clothes with personality, and endows with various capacities according to various kinds and conditions of persons. Law can also define what are 'things' for its purposes and regulate extensively rights to things, rights over them, and rights in them. From all this we construct the concepts of property and ownership, and related ideas.

But do we 'have' rights, or duties, or powers really? What is going on when we ascribe to persons duties, rights, liberties, immunities, powers, and the like? Ascriptions of such positions or relations (or relational attributes) to persons express judgments of fact—that is, of 'institutional fact' as defined at the very beginning of the book. Each 'person' is some kind of individual or collective entity which we consider to satisfy the conditions the law lays down for being a person of some relevant status. Each time we ascribe to some such being some legal position, or some legal relationship (eg, an obligation) with another person, or some more complex proprietary relationship involving both ascertained persons and ascertained 'things', we are interpreting and applying relevant norms. We are also relying on an understanding of the factual situation that is informed by our interpretation of the norms.

Thus do we answer one of the basic questions of this book, namely, the question whether legal knowledge is possible and whether law schools have a genuine right to a place in great institutions of learning and science. The answer is 'Yes' in both cases. Legal knowledge results from interpretative inquiry into law as a conceptual category and into different departments and sub-departments of law. These include public law (including European institutional law, state constitutional law, regional constitutional law, local government law, and administrative law), criminal law (both the general part and the laws relative to particular kinds of crime, and the law on criminal evidence and procedure), private law (including the law of persons, the law of succession, the law of obligations—tort, contract, and restitution—the law of property, the law of trusts, company law and commercial law, as well as civil evidence and procedure). Chapters 10 to13 have already indicated in an abstract and general-theoretical way the character of the knowledge developed in these domains.

Ronald Dworkin offered a challenge to analytical jurisprudence in his Hart lecture of 2001—'if this is descriptive, of what is it a description, and in what way?'[22] Statements about institutional law, or statements of law offered in a judicial or law-advising or legal-doctrinal context, describe the state and its institutions in some specific place—or some other non-state institutional entity according to context. A description of French law, if accurate, tells us how things currently stand in France in respect of whatever legal subject-matter we are discussing. The same goes, *mutatis mutandis*, for a description of Scots law (Scotland being a

[22] R Dworkin, 'Hart's Postscript and the Character of Political Philosophy' Oxford Journal of Legal Studies 24 (2004) 1–37, at 9–12; for a riposte, see A Halpin, 'The Methodology of Jurisprudence: Thirty Years off the Point' Canadian Journal of Law and Jurisprudence 19 (2006) 67–105 at 76–77.

sub-state polity), of EU law (the European Union being a trans-statal polity or commonwealth). Or for a description of the canon law of the Roman Catholic Church (the Church being a non-state religious organization).

This neither amounts to nor depends on a theory about language use in French or English or Church Latin or whatever. The institutional theory of law is one that shows how it is possible to describe accurately or convincingly institutional facts that belong in the context of the relevant state or other polity or organization. It is a theory that cannot be advanced without some serious assessment of the values to which institutions of this kind are oriented, and this must indeed involve consideration of the best possible representation of these values for the context that is assumed. But here 'law' is not the only interpretative concept in issue. Law is a supreme practical category for those engaged in legal decision-making or advocacy. But scholarship (or 'science' in some cultures) is the supreme practical category for those engaged in doctrinal or jurisprudential study and in advancing an account of its epistemological foundations.[23] While it is true that the values implicit in law have a necessary and proper motivating and justifying force for judges and advocates, the ideal of objectively understanding the subject-matter of a branch of scholarly or scientific study supremely guides and justifies good scholarship. A judge's vocation is to justice in concrete cases, a scholar's is to understanding.

The understanding of a practical category like law is value-laden, for reasons that have yet to be thoroughly explored. To construct or rationally reconstruct an account of some branch of law in some jurisdiction, one must of course expound the value-elements essential to that body of law, and one must indicate what are the possibilities for developing new arguments that would further develop these values. One must be candid about deficiencies and about the possibility of their amelioration or rectification. The truth about the law concerning restitution, or judicial review of administrative action, or corporate criminal liability, to take but a small random set of examples, cannot be disclosed simply by acting as an animated index to the law reports or the statute book, and by copying out relevant texts. One has to elucidate essential concepts in a manner compatible with, but far more fine-grained than, that indicated in part 3 of the present work. One has to consider statutes and preparatory materials—reports of commissions or parliamentary committees, explanatory memoranda by government ministries, even the texts of legislative debates. One has to consider judicial decisions and the dicta of judges expounding principles and values they consider to be essential in the justifications offered for their decisions. One has to, or at least one may, seek to provide a more sympathetic or comprehensive rationale for the legal materials developed so far in this domain. One may certainly draw attention to comparative materials from other legal systems that express, or perhaps better express, a convincing view of the underlying rationality for the matter in hand. Relevant lessons may also be derived from legal history. Given this rich range of materials, a

---

[23] Cf J Dickson, *Evaluation and Legal Theory* (Oxford: Hart Publishing, 2001).

rational reconstruction yields a critical account of the governing rules in the light of the principles and values which underpin them.[24] This may indicate the scope for future interpretations of law that will rectify anomalies in current understanding, including current judicial practice. This is certainly work that calls for application of creative intelligence, developing persuasive conceptions of the concepts deployed in the given branch of law. Nevertheless, it still demands a degree of detachment.

Thus the fruits of scholarly inquiries into law are knowledge of legal norms (regulations rules, principles, etc) and legal relations, and the values to which they are oriented, both in general and in particular. Such knowledge relates to some state or polity or organization. Legal norms, like norms of all kinds, are what Ota Weinberger classes as 'thought-objects',[25] not items among the physical furniture of the universe. They belong in what Karl Popper designated as 'World III'.[26] That is, they have real existence though they are not part of the material world that is apprehended through natural sciences such as physics, chemistry, physiology, and the like. They exist as elements of inter-subjective meanings available to human understanding through interpretation. They are not part of the psychic state of any particular person at any given time. Nor are they the physical substratum which is necessarily used for storage of that which is interpreted. Shakespeare's play *Hamlet* is not identical with any particular book in which it is printed, nor is Isaac Newton's *Principia* or Albert Einstein's *General Theory of Relativity*. Each of these exists (as a play, as a scientific exposition of a physical theory) in the same way whether or not anyone is at a given moment reading or thinking about it, or presenting a production of the play or doing an experiment to illustrate the theory. The same goes for the Finance Act 1953, or for the case reported at page 37 of the Law Reports, Appeal Cases for 1977. The statute and the law report are not identical with any of the books in which they are recorded, and exist whether or not anyone is thinking about them or acting as required or authorized by them, or applying the precedent in a current case. They do not occupy any segment of space, but they have a continuous existence in time, or had such an existence, in the case, say, of a now-repealed statute or an overruled precedent.

How can such figments then be considered real? One part of the answer is to reflect on changes in the physical world, events that really occur, and that are explicable only on account of episodes in which some person's acting can be

[24] Cf R Alexy, *A Theory of Constitutional Rights* (trans J Rivers) (Oxford: Oxford University Press, 2002) 6–10 on the 'analytical, empirical, and normative' elements of legal doctrine according to his conception of it.

[25] O Weinberger in N MacCormick and O Weinberger, *An Institutional Theory of Law* (Dordrecht: D Reidel & Co, 1986) at 32–38 on norms as 'thought objects'.

[26] K Popper, *Objective Knowledge* (Oxford: Clarendon Press, 1973) ch 4; cf Ota Weinberger, 'Facts and Fact-Descriptions' in MacCormick and Weinberger, *An Institutional Theory of Law* ch 4. See also P Morton, *An Institutional Theory of Law* (Oxford: Clarendon Press, 1998) 3, 12, 58.

imputed to the following of a norm, or the presenting of a play, or the carrying-out of an experiment to test a theory. Without reference to the 'World III' object, the reason for the occurrence, indeed the character of the occurrence, of the 'World I' event would be wholly unintelligible.

Implicit in all the foregoing is this important truth: institutional facts are also interpretative facts.[27] Assertions of them in individual cases and in general can be controversial, and resolution of controversy calls for judgments about the underlying values to which legal norms—rules and principles—give concrete form. Thus we come to the point at which it is necessary to attend to the kind of interpretation that is at stake when we seek to understand the legal signifi-cance of facts and events, interpreting them by reference to law as some kind of 'institutional fact'.

16.5 Law, State, Civil Society—'Focal Meaning' and 'Constructive Interpretation'

Part 3 of this book represents the moment of synthesis, following the analytical work done in parts 1 and 2. There, in discussing law, state, and civil society, I suggested that an account of law, and in particular a discussion of any branch of law such as public law, criminal law, or private law has to be cast in terms of certain underlying values. A state whose officials conduct affairs with a view to the general good rather than their private benefit is of real value. One in which there are functioning checks and balances among those who exercise public powers is able to secure the rule of law as a condition of human liberty. Public law becomes intelligible only from this perspective. Respect for institutionalized human rights is a condition of justice among persons, though it is not all that is required in order to achieve justice within one or another reasonable conception of that virtue. Constitutional or other entrenchment of fundamental rights becomes fully intelligible only from this perspective. An effective and properly functioning system of criminal law and criminal justice is essential for that relative security of mutual expectations which is a condition of the civility of civil society. Criminal law becomes fully intelligible only from this perspective. Private law both secures the bases of private and family life, and makes possible an exchange-based market economy. Private law becomes fully intelligible only from this perspective.

Public law schemes aimed at achieving distributive justice through the tax system and regulatory regimes that establish *mala prohibita* determine the extent to which a market economy can be characterized as a 'social market economy'. Much

[27] Dworkin treats 'interpretive facts' as a category opposed to that of 'institutional facts', in his 'On Gaps in the Law' in P Amselek and N MacCormick (eds), *Controversies about Law's Ontology* (Edinburgh: Edinburgh University Press, 1991) 84–90 at 85. For reasons explained in the present work, this is incorrect.

of political debate and conflict concerns the issue of social or distributive justice, and how far it is proper or wise to superimpose publicly enforced conditions on whatever obligations citizens freely contract among themselves. In a broad sense it might be right to claim, as did Lord Stair in one of the most impressive institutional essays of the early modern law, that the 'three principles of positive law [are] society, property and commerce'.[28] But we need to observe that the balance between the demands of society (social solidarity) and those of commerce (commercial liberty) is always contested, so the property regime that emerges is coloured by the balance thus struck—and the same goes for the law of obligations. All market economies are also social; but they are not all so to the same extent.

If all that is correct, a coherent account of the nature of law, and a coherent account of the character of any modern legal system, have to take seriously the very general values that are inherent in the character of the legal enterprise. This may, however, seem to call in question the pretension of the legal scholar or legal philosopher to be developing a body of objective knowledge. Objective knowledge, it may be claimed, has to be value-free, because all values are an expression of human subjectivity. Since any jurist's values are subjective, the orientation of his or her account of law to certain values must defeat any claim to objectivity in the jurist's output.

Such a challenge needs to be met head-on, for it applies to the study of any human activity or institution inside the law or outside it. Economics only makes sense on the basis of assumptions about rationality in the pursuit of value. Rationality is then a value, even if economists are content to treat the other values that rational people pursue as expressible simply in terms of the preferences they happen to have. Art is not explicable simply in terms of objects that happen to be gathered in institutions that we call art galleries, nor are artists simply those who concern themselves with producing objects of that kind. Art is an expression of aesthetic value, and only by reflecting on what is or might reasonably be presented as aesthetic value can one get the point of art. Education is not just whatever system of drilling and lesson-imparting happens to go on in 'schools' or 'universities', it is essentially about the development and transmission of knowledge and understanding of the human and natural world, such knowledge and understanding being of value to humans. Good education imparts it successfully, bad teaching falls short of achieving this. We cannot know what counts as a car, or a painting, or a geography lesson except in terms of what would be a good, well-functioning, instance of the object of our inquiry. If 'intelligent design' is an example of a reasonably tenable scientific position that offers a serious approach to understanding the life sciences, then it can properly be included in a school science syllabus. If it is a bogus science, wrapping up dogmatic theology in the appearance of a serious rival to Darwinian evolutionism, it could properly be the subject of a class in the

---

[28] James, Viscount Stair, *Institutions of the Law of Scotland* (D M Walker (ed), from the second edition of 1693) (Edinburgh: Edinburgh University Press, 1981) I.i.18 (p 91).

history of ideas but could not be properly included in a science syllabus in a respectable school or university. We cannot decide which it is without making a value judgment, and offering reasons for it.[29] Different people may disagree, even in good faith, about the weight of these reasons, but it does not follow that there is nothing to choose between them.

This representation of the character of explanation and understanding in the human social realm is vastly indebted to the work of John Finnis, who in turn acknowledged a debt to Max Weber.[30] Explanation of conceptual terms has to go forward on the basis of what Finnis calls their 'focal meaning'. Any human activity or enterprise manifests itself in many forms and instances. Some seem clearer or more central, more 'focal' examples of the activity or enterprise than others. This is because some instances better exemplify the values to which the enterprise is properly considered to be oriented. There is at least an analogy of this to be found in Ronald Dworkin's deployment of the idea of 'interpretive concepts'.[31] These are concepts that cannot be put into operation save by invoking some value or values which enable us to use them in a way that illuminates or makes intelligible some feature of our social and political world. It follows, according to Dworkin, that only the theory that can produce the most satisfactory or attractive holistic account of all that is of real value to human beings can finally achieve true know-ledge of the social world.[32] Objectivity depends on values and on giving the best and most coherent account of these. Elucidation of values is not the antithesis of objectivity, but its precondition. Indeed, objectivity itself matters only as a value in the context of some pursuit of understanding and truth.

To defend the approach to explanation taken in this book requires acceptance of the elements shared by Dworkin and Finnis, despite much that divides other parts of their theoretical approaches. The methodology of the kind of explanation offered here has to be interpretative or hermeneutic. That is, it must seek to understand the practices and institutions of human beings in terms of what makes them intelligible and worthwhile, or at least on balance worthwhile, to their human participants.[33] It does not follow that a degree of detachment should not

---

[29] See the recent decision by Judge John E Jones, III in *Kitzmiller v Dover Area School District* (2005) WL 578974 (MD Pa 2005), doubting the scientific standing of intelligent design.

[30] J Finnis, *Natural Law and Natural Rights* (Oxford: Clarendon Press, 1980) 12–18, citing M Weber, *The Methodology of the Social Sciences* (trans and ed E Shils and H A Finch) (New York, NY: Glencoe Free Press, 1964) 58, 76–82; also J Freund, *The Sociology of Max Weber* (trans M Ilford) (London: Allen Lane, Penguin Press, 1968) 51–61. B Leiter in 'The End of Empire: Dworkin and Jurisprudence in the 21st Century' Rutgers Law Journal 35 (2005) 165–81 ascribes to Finnis the 'primary intellectual force' behind debate on juristic methodology.

[31] See R Dworkin, *Law's Empire* (Cambridge, Ma: Harvard University Press, 1986) 48–68 on 'interpretive concepts'. Cf Stephen Perry, 'Interpretation and Methodology in Legal Theory', in A Marmor (ed), *Law and Interpretation: Essays in Legal Philosophy* (Oxford: Clarendon Press, 1995) 137–154.

[32] R Dworkin, 'Hart's Postscript and the Character of Political Philosophy' Oxford Journal of Legal Studies 24 (2004) 1–37 at 35.

[33] See P M S Hacker, 'Hart's Philosophy of Law', in Hacker and J Raz (eds), *Law, Morality, and Society: Essays in Honour of H L A Hart* (Oxford: Clarendon Press 1977) 1–25 at 12–18 on

296 Law, Morality, and Methodology

also be sought by the social scientist, or (in the present case) the jurist.[34] To understand law is not merely to study closely and deeply what law exists in any one country or tradition. Recognition that states, and not only states, normally have law makes different state-societies mutually intelligible. This amounts to the discovery or the simple awareness that they each realize a certain degree of normative order upheld or supervised in various ways by legal institutions that are the supreme governing institutions of the state. The states in question belong to the same genus of law-states even though they may have very different modes of institutional organization and (certainly in the details) differences in the normative content of their legal rules and principles. French law is emphatically not English law nor American law, Swedish is not German and so on and so on. French law separates public from private law in a quite distinctive way and with consequences that have historically led some commentators from other traditions to doubt whether '*droit administratif* really merits the appellation 'law' at all[35]—yet it obviously does, and can quite properly be translated as 'administrative law'. Supporters of the French or Italian conception of separation of powers find unacceptable the view that judges can through their precedents effectively make law, and cannot regard executive rule-making powers delegated by the legislature as involving 'legislation' properly so-called. Nevertheless, to say that the different countries we have mentioned do not all have law in the same sense as each other would be as misleading as to say that English, Italian, Swedish, and French are not all languages in the same sense of the term 'language' notwithstanding the differences of vocabulary, inflection, syntax, etc that differentiate them as languages.[36]

   This is one reason why we should doubt at least one of the implications Dworkin derives from his interpretation of the character of 'interpretive' concepts. In interpreting law (or in interpreting a Shakespeare play), says Dworkin, our task is to make it the best of its kind that it can possibly be.[37] But surely I do not have to be thinking how to make French law be seen in the best possible light when

---

'Hermeneutics and the Concept of Social Obligation', and compare N MacCormick, *H L A Hart* (London, Edward Arnold, 1981). Hacker's was, I think, the first use of the idea of 'hermeneutics' in English-language jurisprudence.

   [34] Compare J Dickson, *Evaluation and Legal Theory* (Oxford: Hart, 2001), suggesting that a theorist has to consider law on the basis of an evaluation of what makes it important to participants, but need not her- or himself be committed to those values that motivate participants in order to succeed in pursuing the theoretical enterprise.

   [35] A V Dicey made a famous, but in the end unsuccessful, attack on *droit administratif* in his *Introduction to the Study of the Law of the Constitution* (ed E C S Wade) (London: Macmillan, 10th edn, 1964) ch 12, 328–405.

   [36] Halpin argues in 'The Methodology of Jurisprudence: Thirty Years off the Point' (Canadian Journal of Law and Jurisprudence 19 (2006) 67–105 at 87–88) that there is a 'question-begging difficulty inherent in the effort to seek a general definition of law for all municipal legal systems'. If an explanatory definition in the present sense is to be of any value, it must help us toward understanding what it is that law-states have in common even despite their manifold differences. If not all states turn out to be law-states this may be even more illuminating, since it is a proposition confirmed by common sense.   [37] See *Law's Empire* 52–56 on constructive interpretation.

I am seeing that France really has law that is interesting and perhaps fruitfully comparable with Scots, or American, or English law. Someone might share some of the attitudes Dicey brought to bear in his critique of *droit administratif* without being even tempted to conclude that this is anything other than a kind of 'law', and an important part of the law of the French Republic. Used comparatively and as a tool for understanding common elements among different states, law can indeed only be understood in terms of the orientation of those engaged in law-work towards peace, justice, and related values, albeit often ineptly and sometimes with deeply undesirable side-effects. But there can and should be no assumption for this purpose that our duty is to depict any particular legal order in the best light possible, showing how it can best realize justice with least adverse side-effects.

That is indeed a significant element in practical law-applying activity within the system, but it is not a part of the concept of law itself. Because law implicates the kind of values it implicates, it guides in a particular direction the practical application of legal rules and their interpretation for the purposes of application. But that follows from, rather than constituting, the meaning of the term 'law'. As institutional normative order, law is an omnipresent feature of states and of sub- and super- or inter-state polities. Our understanding of it has to be in terms of its functionality towards certain values. This has, however, to be qualified with a certain grim realism about the omnipresent possibility of failure, and the high likelihood that any real system will have serious blemishes judged in the light of the very values which are the final causes of institutional normative order.[38] Some work of legal interpretation can be put forward with a view to exhibiting in a ruthlessly clear way what are the incoherences and injustices in a current body of law, hoping thereby to bring about recognition of defects and political pressure for reforms.[39]

Moreover, most people engaged with the law are mercenaries. Lawyers, judges, and police and prison officers work for payment—and so do law professors. In working with law, we work with that which has an in-built value-orientation of the kind described here. But we do not do so only for the sake of these values. It is a perversion of the vocation to law if a person so employed pursues personal gain at the cost of justice, peace, and the like, as distinct from accepting legitimate payment for faithfully playing his or her part in the administration, enforcement, or study of the law. That such perversion exists in some measure wherever law is practised, enforced, and studied we need not doubt for a moment. It is not

---

[38] For a critique of over-extensive claims about 'constructive interpretation', see W Twining, *Law in Context: Enlarging a Discipline* (Oxford: Clarendon Press, 1997) 174–177; Twining and D Miers, *How to Do Things with Rules* (London: Butterworth, 4th edn, 1999) 377–379; Twining, *The Great Juristic Bazaar* (Aldershot: Ashgate/Dartmouth, 2002) 34–37, 472–473.

[39] This can even extend over into satirical novels that highlight how the law current in some jurisdiction is going wrong. A P Herbert's satire *Holy Deadlock* (London: Methuen, 1934) expressed a critical interpretation of divorce law and practice as it operated in England in the 1930s, and was certainly influential in contributing to the development of a political climate in which divorce law reform became possible.

evinced in the case of a lawyer who, as advocate, presents her/his client's case in the best possible light, even when the advocate's private opinion is that actually the other side's case is the stronger—for it is the judge's role to decide that, not the advocate's.

16.6 'Mind the Gap!'—Again

Predictably, there will be readers of this book who will consider that the account of law as institutional normative order is built around a naïve and unduly optimistic set of values. These contrast startlingly with the state of the real world and the real social circumstances in which legal systems are to be found. Confronting the squalor and misery of prison life, the glaring inequalities of life in contemporary cities even in wealthy countries, the cynicism and callousness exhibited by many officials, the brutish indifference to civilized values exhibited by many young people high on drink or drugs, how dare one utter platitudes about criminal law securing the civility of civil society? Given huge and growing inequalities of income and wealth between the capitalist elite and the rest, alike in rich and poor countries, why go on about law as a system geared to justice, whether distributive justice via public law or corrective justice via private law? As Roger Cotterrell has argued, philosophical jurists need to get out of their armchairs occasionally and take a look at the real working of real legal institutions in actual present societies.[40] At the very least, they need to take more seriously the findings of those who have pursued empirical sociology of law in this way. Legal systems and legal practices are perhaps as often causes of real suffering and indeed real injustice as the reverse. Why privilege justice as a special virtue of law, if real law is often wanting in justice?

Yet another analogy may help towards an answer. It is clearly the case that the driving of motor cars is a major cause of death and injury in contemporary societies. Accident rates are interestingly variable from one country to another, but none is spared the frequently recurring grief and misery inflicted on people by car accidents. Many professionals, from traffic police to accident and emergency surgeons, are kept in employment trying to deal with this menace. There would, however, be something obviously perverse about developing a theory concerning cars according to which they are to be considered efficient instruments for killing and maiming people, and are accordingly to be appraised as contributing to the employment prospects of police officers and surgeons. Cars, unlike tanks, are to be valued not for their lethal potentiality, but despite it. They are for efficient, comfortable, speedy, and safe personal transportation—with no doubt an element of the 'status symbol' thrown in. Manufacturing developments which can make

---

[40] R Cotterrell, *The Politics of Jurisprudence: a Critical Introduction to Legal Philosophy* (London: Butterworth, 1989).

cars safer, at least for their occupants, are prized, and advertisements stress such features. Legislators, and ministers with delegated powers of executive rule-making, develop a battery of regulatory rules and standards, sometimes enforced under strict liability regimes, to try to ensure that dangers arising from car use are kept down to some acceptable level in balance with the other values we have noted. Cars are desirable personal transportation facilities with dangerous side-effects. They are not lethal weapons with desirable person-transporting side-effects. This is an objective fact about cars in contemporary societies. It is an objective fact mirrored in the attitudes and preferences of motorists, pedestrians, manufacturers, car dealers, law-makers, and others. It is not a fact about these attitudes, but one that depends upon them. It is a fact that is not contradicted by the occasional use of cars to inflict wilful and deadly injuries, or as getaway vehicles from robberies or the like. You do not have to be a genius to differentiate the abuse of something from its proper use, even though the possibility of abuse is built into the features that facilitate proper use.

In the same way, but with much greater complexity, we can contrast the harmful and unjust effects of many laws and much administration and enforcement of law with the aspiration to civility and justice that is intrinsic to legal institutions. The harm and injustice are undesirable (though perhaps in some degree unavoidable) side-effects of institutions whose proper end (or 'final cause') is the securing of peace and civility in circumstances of justice which enable fair and free markets to function. To put it the other way round is to say what cannot be seriously maintained—that legal systems function properly to the extent that they facilitate tyranny and exploitation, though sometimes they produce justice and civility as side-effects. In the same way, one might point out that only someone who can speak a language can deceive people by telling them lies. But if we supposed that deceit were the function of human linguistic communication as distinct from a normally undesirable side-effect, we would say what cannot be taken seriously. For, as Thomas Reid long ago pointed out, no one would then be able to learn a language, and deceit by means of spoken lies would in fact be impossible.[41]

'Mind the gap!' is the moral of the story so far. It is hardly disputable that a conceptually satisfactory understanding of law that looks to its focal meaning and acknowledges the character of an interpretative concept like law must take fully into account the values to which legal activity is essentially oriented. But this makes urgent attention to the gap between law grasped conceptually and law in its actual social implementation and impact. It is thus an important question to ask what lawyers, judges, and law-enforcement officers actually do. Systematic accounts of answers to this and like questions that are the fruits of research in the sociology of the professions or of law, or of criminological study, or of applied

---

[41] See T Reid, *Essays on the Active Powers of the Human Mind* (with introduction by B Brody) (Cambridge, Mass and London: MIT Press, 1969) at 443 (Essay V, ch 6), on the impossibly self-defeating character of deceitfulness: 'Without fidelity and trust, there can be no human society'.

economics, command the serious attention of anyone who is concerned with or about law. This applies especially to those who are engaged in juristic or philosophical study of it, or in the development of legal doctrine and scholarship. For there has to be some kind of reflective equilibrium between the conceptual understanding of a category like 'law' and methodologically respectable empirical accounts of the multifarious sorts of activities that people undertake in ways that purport to be oriented towards law.[42] Some theorists' assumptions about the character and value-orientation of law might turn out to fit badly with a substantial part of the most convincing empirical accounts. This would not amount to refutation of the conceptual account in question, but it would render more persuasive the case for an account that gave a better fit. The present theory of law as institutional normative order seems to fit better than most rivals with empirical understandings of legal activity, while also accounting for the way law is a category of human practical life, revealed in the value orientations we have been discussing. If so, this is indeed a point in favour of the theory.

For those who remain uneasy about the argument that law as a conceptual category cannot simply be equated with what lawyers do, let us review another analogy, concerning health and health professionals. 'Health' is very obviously a value, instantiated by all those organisms that are in good shape as the kind of organism they are. Mental and physical health are of great concern to human beings, and the organization of health services, whether in the public or the private sector of the economy, or in some mix between these, are matters of perennial concern and controversy. The regulation and licensing of various sorts of practitioners is a matter of concern, and all contemporary states have established public institutions and laws that deal with this, in what purports to be the public interest. We could construct a theory that might be called 'medical realism', which would say that medicine is no more than the aggregate of the practices of those who practise medicine and related health professions, being publicly certified as competent to do so. There would seem to be a certain blunt truth in this. Medicine is what doctors do in fact, and nothing more pretentious.[43]

But what if it turns out that some things doctors do actually harm patients? What about so called 'iatrogenic' diseases? When I was young, medical people advised us to stay away from swimming pools in warm weather, because polio was apparently a water-borne disease—was that medically correct, because doctors then said it was? I recall also a time when doctors still advised women that smoking cigarettes was beneficial as a way of controlling nervous disorders. It is still the case that hospitals make some people sick through MRSA infection while attempting to cure them of something else.

---

[42] Cf Cotterrell, *Law's Community* at 222–234; Tamanaha, *General Jurisprudence of Law and Society* at 77–107.

[43] Cf Oliver Wendell Holmes, Jr: 'The prophecies of what the courts will do in fact, and nothing more pretentious, are what I mean by the law' ('The Path of the Law' in *Collected Legal Papers* (London: Constable & Co, 1920) 167–202 at 173).

The moral of this story is that medicine is about the promotion of health and the prevention of disease, but that humans are capable of mistakes in pursuing these objectives. Epidemiological and other empirical studies about the way the health professions work are of enormous importance and can contribute in all sorts of ways to critique of and reform in medical practice. But they do not displace the value concepts 'health' and 'disease' from their central place in a conceptual account of medicine. The same goes for law, *mutatis mutandis*. Again, though, the fact that 'health' is an interpretative concept would not justify our concluding that the study of medicine should seek to present it always in the best light possible. We have to be candid about failure as well as success. Those who developed and those who prescribed the drug thalidomide did so with the best of intentions and motives toward the reduction of pain and the diminution of discomfort in the early months of pregnancy. But this was a disaster that blighted many lives. The well-intentioned (but also profit-oriented) pursuit of health in this case caused deformity, damaged children, and brought grief and suffering to parents. As prescribed to pregnant women, thalidomide was bad medicine, in every possible sense of that phrase. But the concept medicine applies to this case also, as well as to the brilliant achievements of those who developed penicillin, or pioneered kidney transplantation, or in vitro fertilization.

Of course, from the point of view of the practitioner, one with a true vocation to the healing arts, the idea of medicine as oriented to whatever is truly the health of human beings, physical and mental, is a motivating idea. The effort to understand some form of cancer, or schizophrenia, or depression, to find its causes and its potential cures, and meantime to alleviate as well as possible what cannot yet be cured, has the aim of bringing about the best currently achievable health for this patient or those afflicted persons. Interpretative concepts are indeed in this way intrinsic to motivation within a certain practice. This explains why in their more detached descriptive uses they remain nevertheless value-oriented in the descriptions they enable us to give.

It does not undermine the project of detached description, and indeed it is in the detached and descriptive mode that legal science and legal theory do and should proceed. The objectivity of good scholarship is different from the impartiality coupled with commitment to justice of good adjudication. That is, scholarly objectivity contrasts with, but fully takes account of, the motivating commitment that is engaged when we step over from legal science or legal theory into such roles as that of advocate, judge, law-reformer or legislator.[44] This is not

---

[44] Dickson, in *Evaluation and Legal Theory* (Oxford: Hart Publishing, 2001) makes a case for the scholar's taking a relatively detached stance, while remaining engaged with value-concerns. For a defence of a somewhat more engaged and prescriptive stance, see F Schauer, 'The Social Construction of the Concept of Law: A Reply to Julie Dickson' Oxford Journal of Legal Studies 25 (2005) 493–501. For an excellent general, but critical, survey of recent methodological debates, see A Halpin, 'The Methodology of Jurisprudence: Thirty Years off the Point' Canadian Journal of Law and Jurisprudence 19 (2006) 67–105.

a claim to have found some 'Archimedean' point outside, perhaps 'above', the practical activity from which one looks down on the activity and sees that it represents nothing real.[45] Rather, as Luhmann points out, it involves a kind of self-observation of the legal system from within it, but an observation that is not aimed directly at the solution of particular current practical problems arising within it.[46]

16.7 Facile Eclecticism?

An important part of the message of part 3 of this book concerned the interplay between law, politics, and economics as elements within the totality of contemporary social life. The civility of civil life is expressed in, and depends on, this interplay. Luhmann's system-theory affords a grand-scale sociological account of this, portraying law, politics, and economics (along with others) as major sub-systems of the whole social system. Each is distinguished by its own holistic self-conception, and each receives inputs from the others only through interpreting them in the coding appropriate to the receiving system. This is a social world of imperfect mutual understanding in which each system is constantly adjusting to inputs from others which are in turn likewise in perpetual self-adjustment.

The institutional theory of law presented in this book is not derived from sociological system-theory, nor are any of its main theses entailed by system-theory. Nevertheless, the two approaches are strikingly mutually compatible, not least (as just noted) in relation to the role system-theory assigns to internal self-observation within a system. To repeat a point made in the introductory chapter:

Law involves both front-line activities of law making, judging, advocacy, counselling, drafting, and doing, and second-line activities of observing these activities from within the practice taken as a whole. The actor of the second line, the student or scholar of law, concerned with jurisprudential or doctrinal exposition of it, has a certain detachment by contrast with front-line actors. On the other hand, this second-line actor has also a relatively high degree of engagement by contrast with purely external observers. These latter (for example) take the whole corpus of legal activity, including the output of legal scholars and legal theorists, as a subject matter for study from the standpoint of sociological or anthropological inquiry or of economics or political science.[47]

It follows that there is a difference between law and politics (or law and economics) as well as an important measure of overlap between them. No important legal

---

[45] Dworkin has criticised the 'Archimedean' methodology of Hart and others in their claim to be pursuing a theory of knowledge extraneous to the knowledge it purports to explain. See 'Hart's Postscript' Oxford Journal of Legal Studies 24 (2004) 1–37.

[46] The methodology here defended does not purport to be Archimedean in this sense, on the grounds explained by Luhmann, *Law as a Social System* (Oxford: Oxford University Press, 2004) 58–59, 305–307.   [47] See pp 5–6 above.

question lacks political implications, and vice versa. Nobody could have a well-considered philosophy of law which did not mesh with an equally well-considered position in political philosophy. But this would not mean that either collapses into the other. To accept Luhmann's line on this is necessarily to reject that of Dworkin, who presents an essentially unitary view of legal and political philosophy.

Equally, however, one need not go the whole way with Luhmann, for whom individual human beings enter sociology as 'psychic systems', interacting with the other surrounding systems. Such a view is totally contradictory of the insistence on moral autonomy around which the account of the distinctiveness of morality and law was built in chapters 14 and 15. The debts owed in these chapters are to the 'discourse theory' of Robert Alexy, and in turn to Jürgen Habermas, and beyond them, to Kant. It is a notorious fact that Luhmann and Habermas were mutual adversaries in the intellectual realm.

It is easy therefore to foresee at this point critics levelling at the present work accusations of facile eclecticism, or methodological syncretism. They may well say this is just an instance of a jurist flitting in a light-minded way from incompatible theory to incompatible theory, selecting attractive-seeming portions and lumping them together in blithe disregard of their deep incompatibility. Such criticism would, however, be ill-founded. To be over-impressed with such accusations would involve retreating into the kind of theoretical isolationism castigated by Roger Cotterrell. The fundamental premises of the argument from moral auton-omy come first, as far as I am concerned. Human societies are societies of persons with a capacity to realize moral autonomy in their lives. This can occur in conditions of civil society (perhaps in others as well, but certainly in civil society), where civil interaction of persons is possible. Civil society requires some form of law, and the legal order of a constitutional state, or law-state, is certainly a key element in securing civility. But other key elements are economic relations and politics. To accept system-theory for the light it sheds on these interacting elements does not require one to abandon critical judgment in respect of some less convincing parts of the theory. The same goes for other bodies of thought on which I have drawn in this book and its companion volumes.

16.8 Final Conclusions

What this book has established about law and legal knowledge can be summarized as follows:

1 Normative order is possible, because humans are norm-users. They can and everywhere do co-ordinate their activities by reference to shared or common standards, even without making these explicit and without formalizing them in any way. This very capability for co-ordination in turn makes possible formal-ization, or institutionalization, of norm-establishing, norm-applying, and

norm-enforcing agencies. Constitutional states are a very spectacular example of this. But always in the final analysis the formal rests on informal, customary foundations.

2 Institutional normative order makes possible the explicit enactment of legislated rules and the articulate development of background principles through adjudication and through development of legal science. Law as institutional normative order thus comes to be a complex and systematic whole. Within it, persons are defined and can occupy a variety of ever-changing legal positions and relations. To know of these is to have knowledge of institutional facts. This depends on interpreting facts and events that exist or have occurred, or that will or may occur, in the light of institutional or non-institutional norms and their background values. Such knowledge is potentially motivating, though in many cases where such an interpretation could be advanced no one actually advances or takes account of it.

3 The institutional character of law is intelligible only on an assumption concerning the intrinsic ends of the enterprise of governance under law: these are the realization of justice and the common good, according to some reasonable conception of these.

4 The systematicity of law is best observed by considering the subdivision of the whole body of legal material into such categories as public law (with the contemporary satellite of human rights law), criminal law, and private law, or further subdivisions of these. To make these fully comprehensible, one has to consider the differing but complementary values implicit in these legal domains: orderly government and distributive justice; civil peace and retributive justice; private life and market economy, underpinned by remedial measures of corrective justice.

5 Institutionalization of law entails that state law has a positive ('posited') character. Accordingly, law stands in fundamental contrast with autonomous morality, though the human capacity for conceiving and pursuing the imperatives of an autonomous moral code may well require the context of civility that state law can bring about. The distinctiveness of law from morality by no means entails that the law itself or its intelligent study can be value-free. Indeed, a sound theory of law can and should affirm that essential to existence of any institutional norm as a law must be some minimal satisfaction of basic requirements of justice. This itself is in the contemporary world institutionalized through Human Rights Conventions, Charters, and the like.

16.9 Coda

At the very end, it is necessary yet again to confront a fear that has been perennial among legal thinkers. This may be provoked afresh by the admission that reference to value must enter into any exposition either of the general character of law or of some body of law actually in force somewhere—for example, contract law in France, or administrative law in Norway, or European Community law about competition.

The fear is that such reference to value deprives legal theory and legal scholarship (legal doctrine, legal dogmatics, legal science, academic law) of any pretension to scientific character. Were this true, law schools, so far as they are anything more than trade schools teaching the skills and tricks of a sometimes questionable kind of job, would be purveyors of ideology, not disseminators of knowledge and learning. Were it true, jurisprudence would become, or be seen as what it has been all along, an exercise in legitimation of the actual state and its mode of government. Were it true, law professors would be mere apologists for the established order of things, interpreting that in the most attractive possible light. Those who could not in conscience take on this role could have no role other than to be iconoclasts within the academy, trashing received doctrines and presenting alternative versions that systematically turn on their heads the values and value-laden accounts laid forth by the orthodox. Such work would admittedly not be scientific, but it would be no more unscientific than the orthodox accounts of law that otherwise prevail. Sure, it may be ideology—but it is honest and open ideology, not a legitimating ideology masquerading as some kind of objective legal science.[48]

The answer to this reiterates the point that human artefacts and contrivances, including any rules by which people try to live, or get others to live, have to be understood functionally. What is their point, what is the final cause to which they are oriented? They perform well or ill, are in good shape or bad, to the extent that they can be seen to work towards these essential ends with a minimum of regrettable side-effects. It is undoubtedly controversial what functions should be ascribed to law in general or to particular laws or any other human production. Failure to confront and account openly for values involved, and to defend one's own proposals as to what the relevant values are, may confer on work about law an apparently greater objectivity than if a proper open-ness were practised. But it is this concealment of value-orientation, not its open avowal, that is ideological in a sinister sense. Honest interpretation that is open about the values it presupposes and that is as alert to system-failures as system-successes judged against those values is the best objectivity that is available to the human sciences, jurisprudence included.

---

[48] J Balkin, *Cultural Software: A Theory of Ideology* (New Haven, Conn: Yale University Press, 2003); cf W Lucy 'What is Wrong with Ideology?' Oxford Journal of Legal Studies 20 (2000) 283–300, reviewing D Kennedy, *A Critique of Adjudication: fin de siècle* (Cambridge, Ma and London: Harvard University Press, 1997).

Index of Names

Subject Index

abortion 79–82, 247–8, 252
accession 140
acquisition 140
act, juristic (act-in-law) 88
action 5, 77–8, 89, 219, 220, 234
Acts of Union 1707 (UK) 269
adjudication 42, 55–7, 178, 196, 201–5
administration 42, 172–4 .
adulthood 97–9
aesthetic value 294
Afghanistan 188
agency 84
alluvion 140
analysis 5, 7, 75
anarchy 257, 292
animals, cruelty to 86–7, 275–6
anthropology 68
argumentation 258–60; *see also* reasoning
aristocracy 203
art 294
artificiality 83,84, 235–6
attribute, positional 75–6, 304
attribute, relational 75–6, 111, 183, 290, 304
Australia 208
authority 22–4, 26, 39, 94
autonomy 4, 59, 106, 203, 241, 249–52,
    255, 266, 303–4
    of public law 176
autopoiesis 177, 229–30

bankruptcy 97, 231
base/superstructure 229
basic norm 25–6, 49, 52, 57, 59–60, 68,
    161–2, 287–8
benevolence 267–8
Bill of Rights (USA) 193, 200
binary distinction 101, 177, 209, 226
bindingness 161–2
blasphemy 217, 267
'born alive' rule 79
brand name 148
buildings, historic 86
burden 143, 145

Canada 201, 248, 268
cannabis 246–7, 253
capacity 77
    active 83, 88, 89–95, 226
    passive 83, 86–7; (transactional) 87–8, 95,
    122, 226

    for responsibility 89, 91–3, 125
    transactional 89, 93–5, 139, 157, 231
capitalism 219, 228
car 61–2, 66, 72, 214, 298–9
certainty, legal 259
charisma 155, 244
Charter of Fundamental Rights 132–3, 198–9,
    200, 203
checks and balances 43, 46, 190, 293
childhood 97–9
Church of Scotland Act 1929 (UK) 269
citizenship 199, 201
civil law, civilian tradition 99, 295
civil liberty 106, 166–7, 178–80, 189, 264–7
civility, civil society 3, 4, 15, 53, 58–9, 72–3,
    111, 169, 175, 207–18, 223–6, 238–9,
    266, 293, 304
claim
    to correctness 260, 264
    implicit 275
    –right, *see* right
clan 207, 208
class 177, 253
coercion, coerciveness 54–5, 107, 128, 187,
    208–9, 227–8, 271, 288
cognitive science 65–8
commerce 145, 225–6, 294
commixtion 140
common law tradition 41–2, 56, 99, 109, 111,
    149–51, 195, 297
competence 94–6, 157
compulsory purchase 141
concretization 254; *see also determinatio*
confederation 48–9, 169
confiscation 141
confusion 140
Conseil Constitutionnel 193, 196, 203
conservatism 64
constitution 35, 42, 59–60, 64, 68, 126,
    181–2, 256, 258, 287
    formal/written 45–7, 49
    EU, of 48–9
    France, of 47
    functional 46–7, 49, 52, 161
    UK, of 47, 56
    USA, of 47
constitutional state, *see* law–state
constraint 33, 103
continuity, institutional 78, 82–3, 162
contract as institution; *see* law of contract